WATER AND LAND USE

WATER AND LAND USE

PLANNING WISELY FOR CALIFORNIA'S FUTURE

Karen E. Johnson and Jeff Loux

WATER AND LAND USE
PLANNING WISELY FOR CALIFORNIA'S FUTURE

Karen E. Johnson and Jeff Loux

September 2004

Cover painting courtesy
  © Wayne Thiebaud / Licensed
  by VAGA, New York, N.Y.
"Waterland" by Wayne Thiebaud
  1996, oil on canvas, 48″ x 60″
Cover and book design
  by Solano Press Books
Index by Paul Kish,
  Rohnert Park, California

ISBN-923956-78-6

Solano Press Books
Post Office Box 773
Point Arena, California 95468

tel   (800) 9310-9373
fax   (707) 884-4109
email   spbooks@solano.com
internet www.solano.com

Notice

Before you rely on the information in this book, be sure
you are aware that some changes in the statutes or case
law may have gone into effect since the date of publication.
The book, moreover, provides general information about
the law. Readers should consult their own attorneys before
relying on the representations found herein.

*To Sydney and Kyle, whose births allowed
me the time to work on this book, to my
parents Bob and Lois for their inspiration,
and most of all to Bert for his endless
support in every venture I undertake*
– Karen

*For the girls who keep me afloat:
Kerry, Kati, Becca, Allie, and my mom*
– Jeff

Chapters at a glance...

Contents

Contents

Contents

Contents

Contents

Contents

Contents

Preface

We believe this book is long overdue. It links water resources and land use planning, two subjects that historically have been addressed separately and dealt with by separate agencies, departments, and professionals. This book bridges the gap between those who plan for California's water future and those who plan for the state's land use future.

What This Book Is About

The book is both a basic information source and a "how to" handbook for anyone interested in water resources planning and management.

Chapter 1 offers a glimpse of California's water history as it applies to land use and urban development, and provides background on why linkages between water and land use are so critical. The chapter also describes why connections between growth and water supply have not occurred in the past, and offers a set of themes that define today's complex environment.

Chapters 2 and 3 summarize the vast array of statutes, requirements, policies, and practices that water planners and land use planners need to know. Chapter 2 identifies statutes, regulations, and practices that apply to long-range water planning, including recent legislation linking supply and growth, and chapter 3 describes California's various land use planning and zoning laws, requirements, and practices that relate to resources. Together, the two chapters provide a framework for integrating land use plans and decisions with water resources.

Chapters 4, 5, and 6 serve as a technical handbook that shows how to integrate water planning and land use planning comprehensively and analytically. Chapter 4 explains how to conduct detailed water demand analyses that can be used to meet a variety of planning and regulatory requirements. The methodology used for these studies reflects the state-of-the-art in demand projection that is likely to become the standard approach for all water purveyors in the future.

Chapter 5 defines the available water sources in California, and describes how to assess the reliability of supply for various types of water years. The chapter also shows how to integrate new and emerging supply choices into future water scenarios.

Chapter 6, which explains the principles and process of Integrated Resource Planning, brings demand and supply together. It also demonstrates how to package a set of programs, projects, and actions into resource alternatives that can be communicated to and evaluated by the public and other agencies and reviewers.

Chapter 7 discusses the water quality considerations that must be integrated into land use and water planning, and identifies the key features and variables of a watershed approach to source protection. In addition, the chapter offers suggestions for practical urban design that can integrate resource protection strategies into the built environment.

Chapter 8 recognizes today's reality that working collaboratively with a variety of interests, agencies, and stakeholders is both necessary and valuable. The chapter offers a framework for understanding and participating in collaborative decision-making processes in water policy and land use that facilitators, watershed coordinators, planners, analysts, and anyone else involved in multi-party, multi-agency programs or projects will find useful.

Who Might Benefit from This Book?

This book is meant to meet the needs of many different professionals working in California in the water or land use arena.

For the land use planner "in the trenches" at a city, county, or regional agency, the book provides a snapshot of California's water supply and water quality issues, and describes the laws, tools, and approaches planners use or should use as they plan for water. In particular, chapters 1 and 2 offer background on California water and the many laws and environmental requirements which planners need to know. Chapters 4 through ;6 are useful in providing a detailed, step-by-step methodology to meet recent legislative requirements for linking water supply and land use decisions. Chapter 7 illustrates innovative design features for capturing and cleaning up urban runoff, which is becoming particularly critical as stormwater permitting requirements expand.

For the water resources planner, consultant, or engineer, the book offers a glimpse into the world of land use planning and describes how water resources fit into the structure necessary for creating California's future communities. It serves as a step-by-step guide for data collection, analysis, and planning techniques, and suggests an approach for preparing an integrated resources plan. Those already familiar with water issues in California will benefit from chapter 3's description of the land use process and planning requirements and, in particular, from suggestions for integrating resource planning into both long-term and day-to-day development. In addition, chapter 4 presents a detailed methodology for linking land use planning with water demand projection that can identify the need for new water supply or infrastructure improvement, at the same time minimizing the perception of growth inducement. Information about and approaches to managing and analyzing water supplies, described in chapter 5, will support the efforts of planners to craft an integrated approach, described in chapter 6, that can guide decisionmaking.

For the water conservation specialist, environmental professional, water supply engineer, and resource manager, the book identifies ways to stretch California's existing water supply, develop new sources that have a minimal effect on the environment, and link resource decisions with the California Environmental Quality Act and other similar laws. Chapters 2 and 3 present the legislative basis for these considerations, while chapters 4, 5, and 6 describe efficiency measures that can be implemented in a water planning process along with other related environmental standards.

Watershed planners and drinking water source protection engineers will find chapters 7 and 8 particularly relevant. Chapter 7 examines the linkage between various land uses and their effect on water quality, with an overview of suggested management practice. Chapter 8 discusses how to establish and work within collaborative groups and multi-agency/multi-stakeholder situations.

For the attorney, policy specialist, decisionmaker, or state or federal government official, the book is a "one-stop shop" for laws, policies, regulations, and best practices that influence water resource planning as it relates to land use and urban growth. In particular, chapters 2 and 3 illustrates the types of water planning and land use planning, respectively, that is done at the local government level. Chapters 5 and 6 shows how to integrate supply opportunities into a comprehensive long-range plan, given the uncertainties and risks with water planning in California.

For all readers, this book suggests hundreds of information sources and references (including many that are Internet-based), along with numerous case studies that have shaped water issues. These seminal studies offer a starting point for thinking about the water resources and land use challenges we face as a society.

The Authors' Goals

This book does not present a particular political philosophy or agenda. It is intended as a building block to protect and enhance the quality of California's future environment and, for that matter, of any state wishing to optimize its water supplies. The authors are committed to protecting and restoring the streams, rivers, wetlands, and other aquatic resources that contribute enormously to the habitat and quality of our state. At the same time, we are equally committed to sustaining California's communities and economic well being with thoughtful future water and land use planning. And finally, we are unabashedly interested in community equity. Water solutions should be cost-effective. This is not to say that we should avoid paying the environmental and social costs of water production, but we should be ever mindful of the costs to urban and farm users alike. For those versed in the tenets of sustainability, this prescription will look familiar: environment, economy, and equity–referred to as the three "e's" of sustainability–addressed as a package.

For many in the no-growth or environmental community, this book may read like a prescription for building more water projects and freeing up resources for more population growth and, ultimately, the demise of the state's natural resources. We think differently. The population is here and growing. Many of us may personally lament that fact, but to avoid thoughtful water planning in the hope that the population will not come to the state or to our community is to ensure the demise of our natural heritage. Water *is* the California crisis of the next fifty years. We can either continue with outmoded solutions that have resulted in environmental and economic problems and endless legal stalemates, or we can move toward more analytical, creative, and inclusive management of resources.

For many in the economic development community, the book may read like a treatise on how to entangle plans and projects in lengthy regulatory reviews and processes of public involvement, and how to avoid the real choices of new reservoirs, dams, and pipelines. We think differently. We seek to stretch what we have through conservation, reuse, and recycling, transfers, and conjunctive use of ground and surface water. But we understand that management of existing sources alone cannot meet future need. We support the development of new water sources or storage of winter flows where they are cost-effective and result in the fewest negative environmental and community effects. We do not believe, for example, that the robust agricultural industry should simply step aside and sell its water to satisfy insatiable urban thirst. Yet, where appropriate, water transfers can be part of our future. Developing the *right* source when and where it is needed can accomplish the three "e's" of sustainability. A groundwater basin, for example, can serve as storage, avoiding the impact a new on-stream reservoir has on habitat. Recycling can provide water for specific uses, saving precious potable water for drinking.

There is plenty of room for pessimism. With 12 million new Californians in the next 20 years, with water shortages predicted as high as 2 to 4 million acre feet annually (in a normal year!), and with potentially less favorable hydrologic conditions, one could easily paint a doomsday picture. But we are decidedly optimistic. Working together, stakeholders from the environmental, business, water, and public communities can craft solutions that offer a sustained water future for the state.

We can accept no less.

Karen E. Johnson
Jeff Loux
August 2004

About the Authors

Karen Johnson is a Water Resources Planner with 20 years of experience in water supply and infrastructure planning. As a consultant for public agencies and private water companies, she manages all aspects of water system planning projects, including water demand analyses, sizing and siting of facilities, alternatives analyses, and drinking water watershed protection strategies. She teaches one-day professional development classes for U.C. Extension at Davis and Berkeley on water resources planning. She has a B.A. in Environmental Studies and Planning from Sonoma State University.

Jeff Loux is the Director of the Land Use and Natural Resources Program at the University of California, Davis Extension and an Adjunct Faculty member in the Landscape Architectural Program in the College of Environmental Design at U.C. Davis. His program is responsible for more than 100 classes, conferences, and training sessions each year to nearly 3,500 professionals in land use planning, resource policy and management, water policy, and environmental law. Dr. Loux has consulted for local, state, and federal governments and various nonprofit organizations on water policy, land use, and environmental issues, served as Planning Director of the City of Davis, and continues to serve as a mediator for the Water Forum in Sacramento. Dr. Loux holds a doctorate from U.C. Berkeley in Environmental Planning with a specialty in groundwater management.

Acknowledgments

The authors gratefully acknowledge Kerry Daane Loux, Landscape Architect, for the urban design/water quality graphics in chapter 7 and Bert Verrips for his meticulous review and contributions to chapters 4 through 7. We acknowledge Roger Putty and Erick Heath, as well as John Hurlburt of East Bay Municipal Utility District and Fran Garland of Contra Costa Water District for their technical review and insights on specific chapters. Thanks to Erica Jago Thear for her graphic skills used throughout this book. We acknowledge Jeff Loux's colleagues at the University of California, Davis Extension: Dennis Pendleton, Jim Lapsley, Monica Jackson, Nancy Barker, Sandy Cooper, Patricia McCarty, Rose Cook, and Susan Starr for allowing Jeff the time and opportunity to work on this book, and to students Jon Quok and Lauren Fabrizio for assistance in graphics and tables. Karen Johnson acknowledges Art Jensen for being generous with his time and ideas on supply planning, and Harry Blohm for sending her to work in Egypt, thus offering her a broader perspective on water resource issues and resolutions.

We would also like to acknowledge the staff members of the Water Education Foundation and the Water Forum, and Tom Gohring of the California Bay Delta Authority staff for invaluable ideas, sources, and contacts in the water resources arena. We both wish to thank our publishers, Warren Jones and Natalie Macris, for keeping us on task and giving us this opportunity, and to Julie and Pat Shell for their editorial and layout expertise.

CHAPTER 1

Water and Land Use Are Inextricably Linked

Water, it has been said, follows the plow, flows uphill towards money, and is more worthy of a good fight than whiskey. At the risk of creating yet another hydrologic homily, water meanders inexorably toward urban development.

The settlement history of the American West, and more specifically that of California, is tied directly to the ability to secure reliable drinking and irrigation water, use waterways as travel corridors, and protect structures, however temporarily, from rising floodwaters. Water and growth have always been linked. And in today's complex environment, comprehensive and sophisticated planning solutions are essential to a sustainable future.

In this book, we explore the relationships between urban development and water resources law, policy, and planning. We try to identify future trends and highlight various analytical approaches and technical and policy tools to cope with a challenging future. We also highlight case studies that demonstrate how these techniques can be applied in complex political and institutional settings. In the following introductory section, we sketch the parallel development of water resources and urban growth in California, and consider where we are today, and where we may be heading.

The settlement history of the American West is tied directly to the ability to secure reliable drinking and irrigation water, use waterways as travel corridors, and protect structures, however temporarily, from rising floodwaters.

A Brief History of California's Urban Growth and Water Development

A Snapshot of Today

At the turn of this century, California's population was estimated at approximately 34 million people, with nearly 9 million acres of irrigated agriculture. Table 1-1 shows in simplified terms how the population is served with water. The chart also indicates the major water sources available today. The major surface water importation projects are the Central Valley Project (primarily agricultural water), State Water Project (primarily urban water use), Colorado

Table 1-1. California Net Water Supplies in million acre-feet	
SUPPLY	2000 "AVERAGE" YEAR
Surface	
CVP	6.7
SWP	3.7
Other Federal Projects	0.7
Colorado River	5.3
Local	11.5
Required Environmental Flow	22.7
Net Groundwater*	7.7
Recycled and Desalted	0.3
TOTAL (rounded)	**58.6**

* Net groundwater excludes amount recharged and reused from natural flows.   Source: DWR State Water Plan 2003

River water (both urban and agricultural), and local importation projects such as San Francisco's Hetch Hetchy system. Environmental water use makes up a significant amount of supply in an average year, accounting for nearly 23 million acre feet for required instream flows, wildlife refuges and wetlands, and wild and scenic river flows.

In California, today's population and agricultural base are sustained by more than 1.5 million acre-feet of groundwater pumped in excess of recharge on an average annual basis.

Several points are worth noting. First, just about everyone's water in California seems to come from somewhere else. Figure 1-1 illustrates the magnitude of water that moves around the state to satisfy today's needs. In addition, today's population (and agricultural base) is sustained by more than 1.5 million acre-feet of groundwater pumped in excess of recharge on an average annual basis.[1]

During a dry year or an extended drought, the levels of groundwater withdrawal are much higher as groundwater makes up the difference when rainfall, runoff, and surface water storage become scarce. While this level of overdraft may not result in immediate impacts, over the long term it may have serious consequences in terms of seawater or contaminated water intrusion into the

1. There are many definitions of groundwater "overdraft," and various definitions of groundwater yield such as "sustainable, perennial, operational and safe." Chapter 5 and the glossary provide more detail on these definitions. In simple terms, overdraft has historically meant that more groundwater is extracted than is replenished to an aquifer on an average or ongoing basis. Sustained, perennial, or safe yield has historically meant the amount of extraction that can be accommodated in a basin without incurring any serious impacts. In any given year or several year period, groundwater extraction in excess of recharge may be a valuable management technique to fully utilize the value of the basin. The problem occurs when one or several impacts result from the overdraft, such as land subsidence, water quality degradation, or a drastic lowering of water levels (*see* the glossary and chapter 2 for more information). Because of the confusion in terms, many analysts now prefer the term "operational or management yield." This means the amount and timing of groundwater extraction that can be accommodated over a long period of time to meet certain management objectives in the basin and avoid the impacts noted earlier.

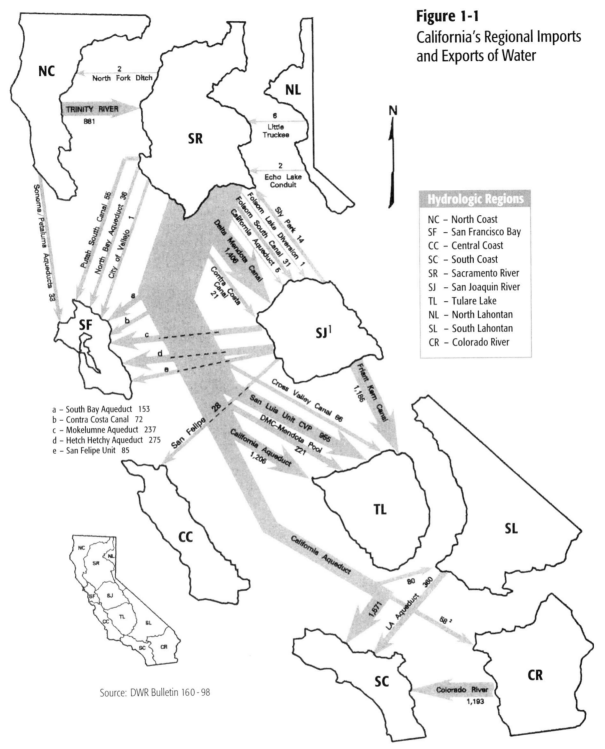

Figure 1-1
California's Regional Imports and Exports of Water

Hydrologic Regions

NC – North Coast
SF – San Francisco Bay
CC – Central Coast
SC – South Coast
SR – Sacramento River
SJ – San Joaquin River
TL – Tulare Lake
NL – North Lahontan
SL – South Lahontan
CR – Colorado River

a – South Bay Aqueduct 153
b – Contra Costa Canal 72
c – Mokelumne Aqueduct 237
d – Hetch Hetchy Aqueduct 275
e – San Felipe Unit 85

Source: DWR Bulletin 160 - 98

aquifers, land subsidence, expensive pumping costs, or dislocations of land use. Also, during dry years, water for urban use becomes limited and can require cutbacks, and environmental uses become stressed. Of the total amount of water applied each year, approximately 80 percent is applied in the agricultural sector and 20 percent is applied in the urban sector.

1. Exports from the Sacramento-San Joaquin Delta are taken from commingled waters originating in both the Sacramento and San Joaquin River Regions.

2. Exchange

Shasta Lake in time of drought

Owens Valley in time of flood

**California's hydrologic patterns—
The two extremes**

Fundamentally, it is the geographic and temporal distribution of rainfall and runoff that drives California's complex water enterprise and leads to so many controversies. Over two-thirds of the state's available water falls on the northern part of the state, while over two-thirds of the state's population and vast acreage of irrigated agricultural land are in the southern part of the state. Standing between the two is the labyrinth of wetlands, sloughs, channels, marshes, and islands that comprise the Sacramento River-San Joaquin River Delta. The Delta, home to countless special status wildlife species and habitats, and critical as a water source for many surrounding communities, has become the locus of vast amounts of time, money, and effort in trying to resolve the state's long-term water issues. This has led water planners to seek transfers, imports, diversions, and movements of water unprecedented in the nation.

Equally challenging is the timing of rainfall and runoff. Much of the state experiences a Mediterranean climate with a warm and dry spring through early fall (May–October) and, depending where you are, a comparatively wet late fall, winter, and early spring (November–April). This leads water planners to focus on peak summer use and irrigation scheduling. Seasonal variation is more predictable than the variation from one year or a set of years to the next. Short- and long-term droughts are simply the norm in California's hydrologic make-up, leading water planners to analyze drought contingency options and seek numerous sources of reliable supply. It also requires that planners study many types of years to determine how to manage water: wet years, average years, dry years, multiple dry years. With these uncertainties as a backdrop, water service reliability has become one of the major issues facing California's future.

A Bit of History

The history of California water use has generally involved a conflict between competing users, inadequate, uncertain, or variable water supplies, and the vagaries of climate. For significant water-related events that have shaped this history, *see* pages 5 and 6.[2]

The Early Years (1769–1900). The period from initial European settlement through the Gold Rush and toward the turn of the

2. This section provides only a thumbnail sketch of water events, focusing on the last 50 years. For a comprehensive, detailed account of California's water history, *see* Norris Hundley, "The Great Thirst; Californians and Water: A History," University of California Press 2001.

Important Water Events in California

1850 California becomes the thirty-first state. Newly established Office of Surveyor General assigned to water projects.

1860 Legislature authorizes the formation of levee and reclamation districts.

1884 Court ruling in *Woodruff v. North Bloomfield, et al.,* stops release of hydraulic mining debris into California rivers.

1884 In *Lux v. Haggin,* California Supreme Court reaffirms legal preeminence of riparian water rights.

1901 First California deliveries from the Colorado River are made to the Imperial Valley.

1901 U.S. Bureau of Reclamation is established.

1905 The first bond is issued for the Owens Valley project. Flooding diverts the Colorado River into the Imperial Valley, forming Salton Sea.

1907 Second bond issue for the construction of Owens Valley project approved to move water to Los Angeles.

1907 San Francisco's Hetch Hetchy project approved.

1913 Los Angeles Aqueduct opens for service; exporting Owens Valley water to Los Angeles.

1922 Colorado River Compact gives 7.5 million acre-feet per year to each of the river's two basins—Arizona and California.

1922 Hetch Hetchy Valley is flooded to provide water supply for San Francisco.

1928 Boulder Canyon act is passed by Congress, allowing construction of Hoover Dam and other facilities on the Colorado River.

       Federal government assumes most of the expenses for the Sacramento Valley Flood Control System due to the passing of the Rivers and Harbors Act.

       California's constitution is amended to include Article X, Section 2, which makes all water use required to be "reasonable and beneficial."

       Beginning of California's worst drought of the 20th century, which lasts until 1934; drought period is used to measure the storage and transfer capacity of all water projects.

1931 State Water Plan is published, outlining statewide use of water resources.

       County of Origin Law is passed, guaranteeing counties the right to reclaim their water from an exporter if needed in originating area.

1933 Central Valley Project (CVP) is passed; design and later construction begins.

1933 Construction begins on the All-American Canal in the Imperial Valley and on Parker Dam on the Colorado River.

1940 Metropolitan Water District of Southern California's Colorado River Aqueduct is completed and makes its first delivery in 1941.

1944 Mexican-American Treaty guarantees Mexico 1.5 million acre-feet annually from the Colorado River.

1951 Feather River Project is authorized by the State and later becomes part of the State Water Project.

       Shasta Dam makes first deliveries to San Joaquin Valley.

1957 State Water Plan is published.

1959 Delta Protection Act passed to resolve issues of legal boundaries, salinity control, and water exports.

1959 Burns Porter Act ratified by voters: $1.75 billion bond measure to build State Water Project.

1963 In *Arizona v. California,* the U.S. Supreme Court decides in Arizona's favor, allocating 2.8 million acre-feet of Colorado River water a year to Arizona.

1966 Construction of New Melones Dam on the Stanislaus River begins after 20 years of argument over its size and environmental effects; it is completed in 1978.

1968 Congress authorizes the Central Arizona Project (CAP) to deliver 1.5 million acre-feet of Colorado River water a year to central and southern Arizona.

       Congress passes the Wild and Scenic Rivers Act.

1970 The National Environmental Policy Act (NEPA), California Environmental Quality Act (CEQA), and California Endangered Species Act are all passed.

1972 California Legislature passes its own Wild and Scenic Rivers Act in order to preserve North Coast's remaining free-flowing rivers.

       Federal Clean Water Act passed to clean up the nation's polluted waters.

1972 First State Water Project deliveries to southern California.

       Congress passes the Federal Endangered Species Act (ESA).

Important Water Events in California *continued*

1972	Congress passes the Safe Drinking Water Act.
1976	Severe drought lasts for two years; rationing and cutbacks of water use occur in many areas.
1978	State Water Resources Control Board issues Water Rights Decision 1485 establishing water quality standards for the Delta.
1982	Proposition 9 (SB 200), the Peripheral Canal package is defeated soundly in a Statewide vote.
	Reclamation Reform Act raises from 160 acres to 960 acres the amount of land a farmer can own and receive low-cost federal water, as well as other policy changes.
1982	California Supreme Court in *National Audubon Society v. Superior Court* rules that the public trust doctrine applies to Los Angeles' diversion from tributary streams of Mono Lake.
	Dead and deformed waterfowl discovered at Kesterson Reservoir, alerting people to problem of selenium-tainted agricultural drainage water.
1984	Legislation passed requiring urban water management plans.
1986	California Court of Appeals ruling (*Racanelli Decision*) instructs the State Board to consider all beneficial uses, including instream needs, of Delta water when setting water quality standards.
	Safe Drinking Water Act changes and Toxic Enforcement Act passes, prohibiting the discharge of toxic chemicals into State waters.
1986	State Board's Bay-Delta Proceedings start to consider revisions of D-1485 water quality standards.
1987	Drought begins; ends in 1992.
1989	Appellate court holds that fish are a public trust resource in *California Trout v. State Water Resources Control Board,* a challenge to Los Angeles' Mono Basin rights.
	MWD and Imperial Water District come to the agreement that MWD will pay the costs for agricultural water conservation projects and receive the water conserved.
1990	Landscape Water Conservation Act is passed.
1990	Memorandum of Understanding is signed, beginning the implementation of urban water conservation programs.

1990	After 19 years of litigation, Inyo County and the city of Los Angeles agree that they will jointly manage Owens Valley water.
	The first municipal seawater desalination plant on the west coast opens on Catalina Island; Santa Barbara working on one also.
1992	Low-flow plumbing required in new development.
	Congress approves CVP Improvement Act; raising environmental uses as an equal purpose of the CVP to water supply.
	Unusually wet years begin in California and last until 1998.
1994	State Board amends Los Angeles' water rights to Mono Lake, restricting water diversion until the lake rises 20 feet.
	Bay-Delta Accord sets interim water quality standards to protect Delta estuary.
1995	New water quality plan for the Delta is adopted by the State Board and begin hearings on water rights.
	Water transfer agreement between Imperial Irrigation District and San Diego County Water Authority is proposed amid much controversy.
1997	Second most devastating flood of the century occurs, caused by the New Year's storms.
	SWP's San Luis Obispo/Santa Barbara Aqueduct is completed.
1998	CalFed Bay-Delta Program continues to work on a long-term plan to "fix" the Delta.
	California Colorado River users attempt to develop a plan to reduce the state's use of river water due to the insistence of the Interior Department and six other Colorado River states.
2000	$2 billion bond is approved to finance water quality, flood protection, and environmental restoration measures.
	CalFed releases long-term Delta plan, published record of decision and begins to implement plan.
	Sacramento Water Forum signs agreement.
2001	Senate Bills 610 and 221 pass, linking water supply and land use planning for large-scale projects.

Source: Based on "Layperson's Guide to California Water," Water Education Foundation, 2000; used with permission

nineteenth century might be termed "local development." Prior to the 1840s, there were many examples of local irrigation and storage systems, stream diversions, and modest use of springs and groundwater. Even in the early Spanish missions, pueblos, and presidios, land and water were linked, although not always well. For example, half a dozen fledgling mission or pueblo sites had to be relocated when water that was presumed to be plentiful grew scarce. Spanish, and later Mexican land grants, had specific provisions for water rights that may or may not have accompanied land ownership. Water quality and land use were connected. There were numerous local ordinances, rules, and physical solutions to keep water-polluting activities (such as livestock washing and care, laundry, etc.) from domestic drinking sources (*see* Hundley 2001, pp. 27–65).

Still, it was not until the United States took over the territories (in 1846) and the subsequent Gold Rush period that water development began in earnest. By 1854, more than 4,000 miles of sluices, flumes, weirs, and ditches were built to conduct the massive hydraulic mining projects in the Sierra gold-mining regions. These same facilities served the camps and towns with water. Remnants of these systems still operate today, laced across the foothills' landscape.

By 1854, more than 4,000 miles of sluices, flumes, weirs, and ditches were built to conduct the massive hydraulic mining projects in the Sierra gold-mining regions.

From early European settlement through the turn of the century, water development expanded steadily, primarily from local stream diversions, groundwater and spring use, and agricultural irrigation canals, ditches, and local storage projects. Private water companies were formed, especially in the farming valleys. Water rights that would come to dominate much of the next century of water development were perfected during this era. The battle between sole reliance on riparian rights and a move toward a more complex system of riparian and appropriative water rights emerged in the latter part of the century.[3]

From an urban growth point of view, water development and use were still largely local matters, although the population was beginning to increase based in part on the availability of water. In 1846, for example, the non-aboriginal population of California was approximately 10,000 people.[4] By 1851, after the Gold Rush, that population had risen to nearly 100,000. And, by

3. *Lux v. Haggin* (1886) was a seminal decision over water rights by the California Supreme Court. In essence, the court concluded that riparian water rights (based on owning land adjacent to a water course) and appropriative water rights (based on obtaining water and diverting it to other lands for use) were both valid and could exist simultaneously in California. Riparian rights occur on all private and public lands adjacent to water courses. Appropriative rights could supersede riparian rights if they were perfected prior to the riparian rights. Subsequent case law and legislation has created a complex hybrid system in California of water rights permits, assessment of harm or impact of one right over another, and various layers of superiority of water rights. *See* Littleworth and Garner 1995, for a detailed explanation.

4. The "pre-contact" native population has been estimated at between 150,000–300,000 people. These numbers declined rapidly to about 20,000 native Americans in California by 1900. *See* Hundley 2001, p. 66.

The Hetch Hetchy reservoir system, managed by the SFPUC, supplies water to 2.4 million people in the San Francisco Bay Area.

SFPUC = San Francisco Public Utilities Commission

1900, with growing urban centers and agricultural uses, the population was approaching one million (Hundley 2001, p. 66).

Still, the booming city of San Francisco had only tapped its local resources, and was just beginning its quest for supplemental water. Los Angeles was still a modest agricultural town, but was about to boom and make its statement in the world of water development. Population growth began to rise in lockstep with the new water enterprises.

First Big Projects to Serve Urban Use (1900–1930). The next era in California water development might be termed "the era of the first importation projects" or as Hundley (2001) has called it "urban imperialism." From the turn of the century through the early 1930s, fueled by rapid agricultural and urban growth, communities turned to major water importation projects. They did so, however, without significant influence from the state or federal governments, and often, as history has shown us, with extraordinary conflict between regions and unprecedented environmental damage.

Los Angeles turned to the Owens Valley, obtaining water rights in 1905, completing the first aqueduct in 1913, and beginning to withdraw water soon after. The battle over Owens Valley water is well documented.[5]

From an urban growth point of view, the new water supplies fueled rapid expansion. They enabled the growth and development of the City of Los Angeles and the rise of many parts of Los Angeles County such as the San Fernando Valley, initially as an agricultural area and later as one of the most rapid urban expansions in history. The city's population increased from about 100,000 people at the turn of the century to over 300,000 in 1910 and over 500,000 by 1920. The City of Los Angeles expanded in size through various annexations from 100 square miles in 1910 to more than 360 square miles in 1920 (Hundley 2001, pp. 138–140).

Water and Growth—Inextricably Linked. During the same time period, San Francisco was pursuing the Hetch Hetchy project to divert the flows of the Tuolumne River through a series of reservoirs, canals, and pipelines toward San Francisco and the communities to the south ("the Peninsula"). This project raised significant conflict in the conservation community, symbolized by the very vocal and very public opposition of John Muir and his colleagues and supporters over damming the Tuolumne and creating Hetch Hetchy reservoir.

During the time of these first major projects, the state's agricultural value and population rose rapidly. While much of this population growth occurred in agricultural areas and small resource-based communities,

5. *See* Hundley 2001, pp. 141–171; Water and Power by William Kahrl 1982; and Cadillac Desert by Marc Reisner 1993, pp. 52–103.

well over half occurred in the two emerging metropolitan centers on the shoulders of the new imported water.

Era of the Great Projects. The 1930s saw a shift in water development as the federal (and somewhat later, the state) government entered the fray, while local water districts and private water companies continued to grow in magnitude and importance. This might be termed the era of the "great projects," looked on with a certain nostalgia by the water engineering establishment, and as the death of significant parts of the natural landscape by the environmental community.

The Central Valley Project (CVP), began as a state project in 1933 and was taken over by the federal Bureau of Reclamation in 1937. Its first major facilities were completed in 1951. The CVP now incorporates 20 reservoirs with a combined storage of 11 million acre-feet of water, 11 power plants, 3 major fish hatcheries, and hundreds of canals, pumping stations, and related facilities. The CVP provides an average of 7 million acre-feet of water annually to nearly 250 contractors, primarily for agricultural use. In fact, the CVP serves nearly 3 million acres of farmland. Urban users make up less than 10 percent of the total project supplies, yet still account for over one million households and an average of 600,000 acre-feet per year.

Just prior to the CVP, the Colorado River projects were being developed to feed the insatiable urban demands in the southern part of the state. Hoover Dam (originally called Boulder Dam) was completed by the Bureau of Reclamation in 1928. The Colorado River Aqueduct was completed in 1941. Institutions were also gearing up to manage and finance the expanding water enterprises. The Metropolitan Water District of Southern California (MWD) was formed in 1928 to serve the many merging communities in the Los Angeles basin and eventually in much of the region. Other districts and agencies followed suit.

From 1930 through 1940, population in the City of Los Angeles alone grew by over 300,000 people to exceed 1.5 million. Without the ever-expanding and diversifying water supply base, such growth would have been difficult to sustain.

Not to be outdone, the state entered the water development arena with the State Water Project (SWP), first unveiled as part of the 1957 California Water Plan. The first of its major facilities was completed by the mid-1970s. It is important to note that the California Water Project continues to be in transition. The coastal branch of the project was completed in 1997, and many of the facilities originally envisioned as part of the project have not been and may not be built.

Shasta Dam on the Sacramento River

SWP's Banks pumping plant lifts water from the Delta to the California Aqueduct and Bethany Reservoir.

CVP = Central Valley Project
MWD = Metropolitan Water District
SWP = State Water Project

The All-American Canal demonstrates the lengths to which the State has gone to transport water.

EBMUD = East Bay Municipal
           Utility District

Environmentally-Related Legislation Influencing Water Development

1964	Federal Wilderness Act
1968	Federal Wild and Scenic Rivers Act
1969	National Environmental Policy Act
1970	California Environmental Quality Act
1972	Clean Water Act
1973	Federal Endangered Species Act
1974	Federal Safe Drinking Water Act
1989	Expansion of the Public Trust Doctrine

Today, the SWP incorporates 22 dams and reservoirs and 444 miles of canals, and serves between 2–3 million acre-feet of water annually.[6] SWP water service is roughly divided between 70 percent urban and 30 percent agricultural. Twenty-nine local or regional water districts or agencies contract for SWP water. Some of the largest are the Metropolitan Water District, Kern County Water Agency, and the Santa Clara Valley Water District.

In the central and northern parts of the state, similar, if slightly less ambitious, water works were being developed. The East Bay Municipal Utility District (EBMUD), formed in 1923, developed Pardee Dam on the Mokelumne River, the Camanche Reservoir, and the accompanying canal and local reservoir system. The Mokelumne Aqueduct was completed in 1929, five years before San Francisco's embattled Hetch Hetchy project. These projects enabled the growth and development of the "East Bay" stretching from Oakland and Berkeley throughout parts of Alameda and Contra Costa counties.

Similarly, in the southern San Francisco Bay Area, the Santa Clara Valley Water District formed in 1929 (later modifying and expanding its enabling legislation in 1951), and began to develop local reservoirs, tap groundwater resources, seek imported sources, and manage and conserve waters for future growth. Today, EBMUD and Santa Clara each serve over 1.5 million urban customers. Both districts also have become pioneers in the modern movement of integrated water management, relying on multiple local and imported sources, conservation, recycled water, groundwater recharge, and other sources and measures.

The result of this aggressive water development era was the ability of the state to grow from fewer than 5 million people at the start of the Great Depression in 1929 to more than 20 million by the mid-1960s. All told, some 1,300 dams and reservoirs were built in California during this period, resulting in the complex and controlled water landscape we have today. It has also resulted in dramatic changes to the natural landscape, the natural flow of rivers, and the fisheries, riparian corridors, and adjacent habitats that rely on the rivers.

Environmental Transition (1970–1990). The next era of water development might be termed the "Environmental Transition." Beginning in the 1960s and taking root in the 1970s, a series of factors led to a grinding halt of the major water development/importation projects and a growing stalemate between environmental interests and water supply interests. An increase in environmental and ecological awareness certainly played a role, as the

---

6. The SWP has contract entitlements to 4.23 million acre-feet per year with the 29 contracting agencies. However, because of various factors, part of the system has not been completed, and the system delivers substantially less water than initially contracted.

society's changed values found legislative and legal footholds in a myriad of new laws. These laws began to influence whether water projects could be approved or constructed and how water sources might be developed. At the same time, traditional water projects were becoming increasingly expensive at a time when federal and state funds were less available, and sites were becoming more marginal, more costly, and less desirable than previous opportunities. As a result, the last major dam built directly on a river was constructed in 1978 with the completion of the New Melones Reservoir on the Stanislaus River. Instead, water districts and water developers had to begin looking for new and creative ways to develop water with less environmental impact–to conserve, reuse, trade and transfer supplies, and to expand existing facilities to meet ever-increasing demands.

From a water development perspective, this era continued through the 1980s, as more court decisions and more environmental safeguards were enacted and few major projects occurred. Three hydrologic events influenced this period. The severe drought of 1976–77 resulted in water rationing in many areas of the state. It highlighted how vulnerable the state was, but also stimulated a growing movement to conserve and reuse water for all uses and at all levels. Soon after, and well into the 1980s, particularly wet years buffered the state against having to face water shortages, as growth continued unabated. For many, these wet years also erased memories of the drought and caused us to lose ground on developing innovative solutions. From 1987 through 1992, a less dramatic but more prolonged drought period stressed many water providers. It was at this time that long-term water system reliability came into sharp focus.

With the rise of environmental awareness and the legal footholds established, there were many heated conflicts over water projects, water use, and environmental impact. The result was often frustration on all sides of the issue. Water development interests were not able to move forward with projects they believed were needed for water service reliability. When they were able to move forward, project yields were reduced or heavily mitigated. Environmentalists believed that conservation and wise water management options were not being fully explored, and that continued water development was ecologically unacceptable and unsustainable. And many professionals from a variety of disciplines and viewpoints were coming to grips with the understanding that past damage to natural systems required a massive restoration effort throughout the state. From this stalemate of interests a more sophisticated approach has begun to emerge.

A wetland in Arcata, California, sustained in part by partially treated wastewater

There are many signs that a new approach to water management and water policy may be emerging.

Towards Collaboration and Water Management (1990–present). To suggest that the modern era is without intense conflict, competition, and continued frustration by various interests is both naïve and inaccurate. However, there are many signs that a new approach to water management and water policy may be emerging. The current era, beginning in the late 1980s and gathering momentum through the 1990s and into this decade, might be termed (at least by an optimist) "the Water Management and Collaborative Policy Era."

Dozens of efforts have begun that acknowledge water problems in a more comprehensive way, recognizing that numerous interests must be given a voice to reach a meaningful, lasting solution. This is not to say the battles do not continue. They do, and are perhaps more difficult than ever before as purveyors stretch supplies and increase competition for a scarce resource. However, the dramatic expansion of efforts to reach long-term collaborative solutions is evident.

In 1991, having spent nearly 30 years in conflict and litigation, Inyo County and the City of Los Angeles agreed on a plan to protect Mono Lake, while still allowing some water to be exported to Los Angeles. In 1992, the Central Valley Project Improvement Act was passed, which required major changes in how the CVP would operate, and increased the opportunities for cooperation between state and federal projects. In 1994, more than 40 separate water purveyors, environmental groups, business interests, and public interests joined together to address water supply issues and concerns over the ecological health of the lower American River in the Sacramento region. This process, known as the Sacramento Water Forum (*see* chapter 8) reached an historic agreement (2000) to manage water resources in a regional, coordinated fashion. The Agreement ensures adequate local water supplies for planned growth, while also protecting and restoring the ecological fabric of the lower American River.

Perhaps the most ambitious and far-reaching of these collaborative efforts is the CALFED/Bay Delta process (*see* chapter 8 for additional information on this program). While its precursors and roots go back many years, the formal process began with the signing of the Bay Delta Accord in 1994.[7] This began an unprecedented planning, research, funding, and implementation effort that includes 21 state and federal resources and regulatory agencies and a vast array of local, regional, and statewide interests to develop solutions to the ecological problems of the San Francisco Bay-Sacramento and San Joaquin rivers

---

> ## CALFED
>
> An extensive multi-agency effort to address multiple water resources problems in the Delta area (and its watersheds), including water supply, water quality, flood protection, water efficiency, and ecosystem restoration. CALFED is administered by the California Bay-Delta Authority.

---

7. The 1994 Bay-Delta accord was an agreement between state and federal officials to initiate a large-scale collaborative process to improve water quality, restore habitat, improve water reliability, and related actions over the long term in the Sacramento-San Joaquin Delta. In 1995, a framework for Delta management was created. In August 2000 the CALFED agencies formally approved the long-term plan for restoring ecological health and improving water management in the Bay-Delta system. Since that time, CALFED has been implementing various phases and action strategies of the program. In 2003, the process was further formalized when the newly-created California Bay Delta Authority took over administration of the CALFED program.

Delta, while ensuring adequate water supplies, levee integrity, and water quality protection.

Many of the recent collaborative processes (such as CALFED and the Water Forum) are just beginning to be implemented. While their lasting effects are not well known or assured, these examples suggest a new and positive direction in California water policy. The recent era seems to exhibit three broad tendencies:

- A change from *developing* new water sources to *managing* water in a series of complex arrangements that might include conservation, recycling, off-stream reservoir storage, conjunctive use of surface and groundwater, water transfers, and shared sources

- A change from single-purpose entities such as water purveyors seeking solutions on their own to multi-agency, multi-level (local, regional, state, federal), and multi-stakeholder efforts that expand the interests greatly

- Recognition (and legal backing) that water for environmental purposes is integral to the system and ecological interests must be represented in the process for any project or plan to succeed

While this trend toward collaborative management has been emerging, urban growth and its accompanying demands for water continue. Population projections indicate that by the year 2020 California will house over 46 million people. Even as water conservation programs are being implemented throughout the state in both urban and agricultural sectors, aggregate demand projections soar. In 1998, DWR estimated that by 2020, even if planned supply augmentation and improved conservation are implemented, California will face shortages of 2.4 million acre-feet *in a normal water year.* In a drought year, that figure could climb to 6.2 million acre-feet, affecting as many as 5–10 million households. More recently, the updated State Water Plan (DWR 2003), has developed scenarios or "water futures" that vary depending on levels of effective conservation, agricultural demands, and potential new sources of supply. In all of these recent projections, however, potential for serious shortages during drought are evident. No matter which assumptions you prefer, the future suggests ever more juggling of water sources, potential cutbacks and rationing, and a continued aggressive push for new supplies and hence more conflicts.

These statistics are daunting, and they highlight the importance of water resources planning, as well as the need to manage urban and agricultural water demand to buffer future shortages.

The 100,000 acre-foot Los Vaqueros Reservoir is an off-stream facility that stores Delta water during times of high water quality.

Even as water conservation programs are being implemented throughout the state in both urban and agricultural sectors, aggregate demand projections soar.

In California cities like Modesto, water is a key ingredient to success.

Linking Water Resources and Land Use

It seems both an obvious and perfectly rational proposition that water resource decisions and urban growth decisions should be closely linked. If reliable water is not available during wet, normal, and dry years, then growth should not occur in that area until the water can be assured. But what do we mean by "linkage?" In other words, if communities were integrating water and land use, what would that look like?

First and certainly most prominently for this book, would be to link the decision to plan and build with an available and reliable water supply. As we describe in later chapters, this is not simply a matter of obtaining water entitlements that match future growth projections. It involves addressing the variations in water deliveries and possible impacts to existing water users and customers, and adapting to the ever-changing land use visions of a community.

Linkage also means understanding other water resources issues within a community as it grows and develops.

But linkage also means understanding other water resources issues within a community as it grows and develops. Where are the critical water features—streams, wetlands, ponds, and recharge areas—and how can we ensure their long-term protection and ecological health? Where is there existing water supply and drainage infrastructure and how can we take advantage of it with infill development? Where do we have to expand and improve water infrastructure to accommodate growth? And finally, linkage suggests that, once we design and build a new area or redevelop an existing area, how can water be integrated into the community in an effective and sustainable way? Are there unique water conservation or water reuse potentials? Can we develop innovative drainage or flood management projects that can provide water quality, recreational, aesthetic, or ecological benefits? Are there ways to use the development process to restore natural systems or ensure acceptable water quality? Although this book focuses on the fundamental linkage between growth and water supply, each of these issues becomes a part of the planning fabric.

Why Water Resources and Land Use Decisions Are Not Always Linked

It is instructive to consider why water resources planning is not better linked to land use planning and decisionmaking. The answers lie in the political process of land use planning, divergent institutional mandates and culture, and the professional practices and approaches traditionally practiced by land use planners and water planners and engineers.

Dedication to Mandates. Water purveyors are required to provide water supply for reasonable and beneficial uses. Other water-related institutions are similarly mandated to provide drainage or flood control services, wastewater treatment, or other related activities. These mandates do not speak to land use and population growth., and do not indicate the need to balance water resource responsibilities with environmental issues or urban growth concerns. They simply indicate that it is the job of the district or agency to provide water services or flood protection or wastewater treatment services in a reliable manner.

Managers and decisionmakers of the water agencies take these mandates very seriously and historically have had less tolerance or interest in what they may consider the distraction of having to debate land use or environmental issues. Many board members of water agencies in areas where growth management issues are at the forefront (*e.g.,* Santa Barbara, Goleta, Santa Cruz, Monterey) bemoan the burden of being a *de facto* land use planning agency as they make decisions on water resources. This is not to say that the composition of water boards has not begun to change to reflect a greater emphasis on multiple policy issues such as land use and environmental concerns. Indeed, water boards that were once insulated from the complex and controversial policy debates over growth, now find themselves in the center of the storm.

Other water purveyors, small and large, have moved beyond their traditional mission to address a wide array of issues such as environmental protection and restoration, public outreach and communication (particularly related to water conservation and watershed management), and urban growth.

Despite this trend, decisionmakers and managers of water agencies fundamentally see their role as a mandate to provide water infrastructure, not as a broker for community growth. Yet, increasingly, water agencies are drawn into these discussions and are asked to play a role.

Institutional Confusion. California has what many observers call a labyrinth of water resources institutions. Over 85 percent of the state's population receives its water from 380 separate retail water providers. These agencies rely on multiple sources of water, often with many layers of water rights and contracts. Serving the retail agencies are numerous regional and county-wide water agencies, authorities, and districts. Serving the large water wholesalers are the major state and federal projects (such as the CVP and SWP) and the many locally-based importation and water supply facilities. Nearly 40 *separate* general purpose statutes enable public water resource entities in the state, and nearly half of them can and do provide water service (others provide drainage, flood control, sanitation, water replenishment, and related services). In addition, nearly 100 *special* purpose statutes create water resources districts or agencies throughout the state. Add to this scores of private water companies, and the institutional stew is indeed thick. For every one of these entities, there is a decision-making board or

EBMUD at the Center of the Storm

The East Bay Municipal Utility District is an example of a water board grappling with land use and environmental issues. EBMUD has responsibility for more than 1.3 million urban customers and over 200 million gallons per day of water service in Alameda and Contra Costa counties. EBMUD receives most of its water from the Mokelumne River in the Sierra Nevada, stored in foothill reservoirs in Pardee and Camanche and transported to five local terminal reservoirs.

In the past three decades the board of EBMUD has been very active in urban growth issues. EBMUD is viewed by many as a pioneer in establishing comprehensive approaches to water conservation. In addition, many of EBMUD's board members have been elected on environmentally-oriented platforms.

In the late 1980s and early 1990s, EBMUD faced a dilemma: whether to serve a large proposed urban development (Dougherty Valley) outside its established service boundaries and potentially put existing customers at risk. In short, EBMUD chose not to serve the new proposal and found itself in multi-year litigation. Ultimately EBMUD prevailed, but as a result of the experience it spent the decade working on state legislation to better link water and growth decisions. For more information on the results of these legislative efforts, *see* chapter 2. ∎

council with historical relationships in its community and very specific interests and ways of planning and managing water supplies.

As an example, in the Sacramento Water Forum, a collaborative-policy process to resolve long-term water supply issues in the Sacramento area (*see* chapter 8), there are more than 40 separate signatories to the regional water agreement, including large and small water districts, companies and agencies, cities with water supply responsibility, and other interests such as business and environmental interests.

The result is a complex system of supplying water, largely obscure to the general public. As much as anything else, this explains why there is not one comprehensive, statewide set of requirements for addressing the linkages between water and growth.

Professional Differences. While barriers may be breaking down, and there are certainly many exceptional individuals who counter the following generalizations, a fundamental separation remains between those who provide professional water policy and planning services and those who provide land use planning services. Land use planners are likely to have limited background in hydrology, water policy, or public facilities engineering. Land use planners have multiple priorities on any given project or plan and limited time to explore the details of individual resource issues such as water. Likewise, water planners may appreciate the need for long-term land planning, but are not likely to have the background in land use law, site planning, permitting, and processing necessary to link their well-crafted engineering solutions to the messy world of land use policy and public deliberation. To each profession, the other's is a black box within which most would prefer not to dabble.

Land use issues swirl within a dynamic and complex matrix of tax revenue and fiscal realities, environmental concerns, growth-related impacts, and social and community issues.

This is particularly true of the complicated and often controversial public policy debates in which land use planners often find themselves. The issues are rarely clear, quantifiable, or focused on technical considerations. On the contrary, land use issues swirl within a dynamic and complex matrix of tax revenue and fiscal realities, environmental concerns, growth-related impacts such as traffic and air quality, and social and community issues such as visual impact and neighborhood compatibility. Engineering professionals may have great appreciation for these issues, but not necessarily the professional tools and techniques to consider them in their analyses.

Land use planners often lack the technical and quantitative background to integrate water resource information into their plans and projects. The technical nuances of water supply modeling or examination of drought probability may not translate well into a project development decision. Just as likely, the entrenched and historical political nuances of many water purveyors may not be well understood or appreciated by the political decision-makers in the land use world.

The solution to this separation is as obvious as it is difficult. Both planning and water resources professionals need to appreciate the critical role the other plays and learn enough about what is required and the conceptual approaches used to readily integrate each other's data and analysis. A collaborative relationship takes more time and patience than simply accepting or rejecting the solutions the other offers. This is especially true when those answers do not solve the technical problem at hand or conform to all the elements of the policy debate. It requires working together on real-world problems and solutions. This in turn requires support and direction from decisionmakers and managers to make sure that these collaborative efforts are encouraged.

Time Horizon, Scale, and Complexity. Making matters more difficult are the fundamental differences in time horizon and scale that water professionals must address versus those of land use planners. In California, the general plan is the comprehensive blueprint for the long-term land use growth and development of each community (*see* chapter 2). General plan law does not specify a required time horizon that communities must look toward, although typical plans set a 20-year time horizon for build-out assessments. Other land use planning documents in California, such as specific plans or the long-range development plans used by university and college campuses, may use time horizons varying from 5 to 25 years, but no consistent standard is required.

Water supply planners must look well beyond a 10- or 20-year horizon. The cycle for conceiving, planning, permitting, and constructing a water supply project has lengthened dramatically. A major water project in previous decades may have required an average of 10 to 15 years to complete. Today, a major water project can take as many as 20 to 25 years from concept to construction. More complex and stringent environmental requirements and permit processes, considerably more public concern over water projects and their impacts, scarce funding, and more competing interests have all contributed to these timelines. As a result, water supply planners are required to look out 30 to 40 years or more as they consider future scenarios.

In previous decades a major water project may have required an average of 10 to 15 years to complete. Today, a major water project can take as many as 20 to 25 years from concept to construction.

The difficulty is both technical and political. At the technical level, water supply planners often do not have land use projections beyond the 10 to 20 years that the community has accepted (through the land use planning process) on which to base projected water demands. At the political level, cities and counties are asked to speculate on possible growth that may exceed what they have mapped and may go well beyond the community's comfort levels.

Finally, the complexity and uncertainty of projections and analyses work against a collaborative relationship between water and land use. Water supplies are highly variable. They are influenced by rainfall and runoff, priorities of water rights, shortage or rationing requirements, entitlement contracts, environmental regulations, and other factors. Land use planners have no less uncertainty as they try to envision the future direction and rate of growth of a community. General plans are modified. City councils and boards of supervisors change from pro-growth to slow-growth to no-growth. Land use development markets heat up and drive planning applications or they slow down and approvals languish. The net result is a belief, not unwarranted, that planning for the future is futile. We can only react and then adapt as circumstances change. This is why one of the major themes of this book and of many resource management strategies today involves a commitment to adaptive management; that is, a planning and implementation framework that allows ongoing monitoring data to be used to change course, modify policies and direction, and adaptively manage to optimize the value of the resource.

The Political Variable. One cannot consider the issue of water supply and growth without acknowledging the political realities and dynamics of land development. In many cases, it is simply not in the best interest of land developers to be overly concerned about the potential constraints that the water cycle may place on their development project.

In communities where urban growth is hotly debated, the issue of growth inducement moves to the forefront. If water supply is planned for and secured beyond the community's planned and adopted growth projections, it is viewed as inducing more urbanization than the community has contemplated.

Also of great concern is the fear that water purveyors will become another layer of land use regulation in an already regulated environment. During the decade-long debates (1990–2001) over legislation to formally link water supply and land use decisions, the issue of who should be responsible for growth decisions came up frequently and intensely. The development and building community did not want to see water purveyors given authority or responsibility for land use (nor did the water purveyors). The municipal lobby did not want to lose any local control or autonomy over land use decisionmaking.

Does water supply induce growth or does water supply respond to growth demands that would exist in the absence of resource availability?

The Growth Debate. Does water supply induce growth or does water supply respond to growth demands that would exist in the absence of resource availability? Perhaps the most objective position is to acknowledge that the factors are inextricably linked. Employment opportunities, perceived quality of life, natural increase, and the possibility of owning land certainly contributes to the various waves of California's growth. However, without sustained and reliable water supplies, none of this growth could have been accommodated. Real estate interests develop land; they do not project population. But in the end, all of these inputs result in the quest for reliable, high quality water supplies; and these supplies then accommodate the urban and agricultural expansion that has become a constant force in this state.

0
194
North Coast

10
28
North Lahontan

85
989
Sacramento River

0
287
San Francisco Bay

63
711
San Joaquin River

720
851
Tulare Lake

270
308
South Lahontan

172
270
Central Coast

944
1,317
South Coast

147
158
Colorado River

Legend	
172	Average Year (taf)
270	Drought Year (taf)
Central Coast	Region

Adapted from DWR Bulletin 160-98, the 1998 California Water Plan. The 2003 California Water Plan does not provide such clear projected shortfalls, but instead gives scenarios that show varying water futures.

Today's Complex Water Planning Environment

What might the near-term future hold? Put simply, there will be more population, more competing demands for water, and a more uncertain and complex regulatory and stakeholder environment within which to develop new sources of water. Figure 1-2 illustrates projected future water demands for the state, and one potential scenario for shortfalls by region. It is clear that under any future scenario, the need for thoughtful and informed management of the resource is essential, and that planning for a better and more strategic linkage between growth and water availability is needed.

As communities harden their demand for water by increasing water use efficiency, the ability to respond easily to prolonged droughts and shortages diminishes. This puts more pressure on accurate forecasting, sound risk assessment, and multiple options for water supply. Prolonged drought and critical shortages will continue on a statewide and regional basis. We will continue to have a plethora of independent water districts and agencies responsible for providing water. And most analysts agree that we cannot easily build our way out of this water supply problem since water projects now take many decades and result in lower water yields than in previous years.

The overall result is a serious challenge facing the water planners and land use planners of this and the next generation.

Towards Integrated Water and Land Use Planning

This book describes an approach designed to integrate community development and water resources planning. For the land use planner, the approach may be best thought of as a telephoto lens through which one views community planning, particularly as it relates to water infrastructure. Focus on water issues from the outset; use the water cycle as an organizing principle and a critical variable in land use planning. For the water planner, the approach is more a panoramic lens that provides a broader perspective on the water enterprise than simply engineering a system. Growth and development pressure, both urban and agricultural, are fueling water decisions (and always have). This process is political and complex and does not isolate water resources from all the other issues. Perhaps both disciplines can learn to appreciate, understand, and embrace the others' constraints, analytical models, and context.

Several major themes are highlighted throughout this book. These themes are further defined and explained with examples, techniques, and case studies in subsequent chapters.

- **It is the era of partnerships and collaboration.** Water planning involves managing the resource with creativity and an understanding of complex laws and institutions, multiple stakeholders, and frequent collaborative opportunities. Purveyors can no longer act as individual agencies, organizations, or individuals in seeking water solutions.

Most analysts agree that we cannot build our way out of this water supply problem since water projects now take many decades and result in lower water yields than in previous years.

Water continues to be a significant political issue in urban and agricultural settings.

- **Water quality and quantity are always linked.** Planning and investment for water quality is becoming as critical as investments in water quantity as purveyors seek future water supplies. Impacts to water quality, especially groundwater, can have dramatic implications on water supply availability and related environmental issues.

- **The need to address uncertainty will increase.** Uncertainty goes beyond the obvious variations in hydrologic year, season, and timing of rainfall and runoff. Uncertainties in water contracts and entitlements, environmental requirements, and legal constraints will mean an expanded role for thoughtful planning, risk assessment, and contingency strategies.

- **It is the era of water management, not just water development.** Few in the water business today use the term "water development." Instead, "water management" is the dominant phrase. Conjunctive use of surface and groundwater, water transfers, off-stream storage, recycling and desalination, shared sources and facilities, environmental water use, water conservation, and other creative and relatively new approaches to stretch and manage our supplies are no longer exotic sources; they *are* the new sources. Multiple sources of water are necessary to serve future populations.

- **Groundwater and surface water are linked.** While water rights and institutional arrangements may not have caught up with the trend, all sources of water need to be looked at as an integrated system to resolve future water issues.

- **It's going to get tougher.** As population growth increases, and environmental needs increase, we will be faced with chronic shortages and even higher levels of competition for the resource. Water conservation efforts and creative ways to stretch existing supplies may have reduced our flexibility in the future to respond to drought and related changes.

  As population growth increases, and environmental needs increase, we will be faced with chronic shortages and even higher levels of competition for the resource.

- **The public will be involved.** Unlike in past eras, many varied and sophisticated interests now scrutinize water decisions. Interested stakeholders have come to expect opportunities to interact and resolve problems collaboratively.

- **Tools and techniques can help.** Relatively straightforward tools and techniques are available to link water resources and future growth in a rational and effective manner. This book illustrates how they have been applied in a variety of case studies and how to apply them in other situations.

  Relatively straightforward tools and techniques are available to link water resources and future growth in a rational and effective manner.

Chapters 2 and 3 of this book are devoted to an overview of the legislative, policy, and regulatory context within which water planning and land use planning operate today. They establish the framework for an integrated approach to water and land planning. Chapter 4 looks in detail at how to address water demands and why this analysis lies at the heart of an integrated planning approach. Chapter 5 looks at analyzing water supply options and how to make the most of the creative approaches being examined today.

Chapter 6 shows how to integrate the supply, demand, and alternatives evaluation process to prepare integrated resource plans, and how this approach can meet current requirements for linking water and growth. Chapter 7 examines the critical linkage between water quality and water quantity, and explores the multiple goals of watershed management as it relates to protecting urban water supplies. This chapter includes a discussion of how to plan and design communities to maximize water efficiency and water quality protection. The eighth and final chapter provides a brief glimpse into how collaborative policy processes can transform the way water is planned in the future in California.

CHAPTER 2

Legislative, Regulatory, and Policy Framework for Water Planning

The laws, policies, and regulations governing California's water resources are varied, often overlapping, promulgated by a variety of institutions, and complex. Many seemingly unrelated laws influence water use in a profound way. The federal and state endangered species acts, for example, have a dramatic effect on the availability of water supply and the use of water for environmental purposes.

This chapter describes existing laws, regulations, and requirements that provide the framework within which water purveyors plan for water resources. It focuses on those elements of federal, state, and local laws and regulations that influence water supply planning and management for existing and future urban uses. Water resources professionals and land use planners need to have an appreciation of this framework to understand how to plan for future water supplies and how to link land use and growth decisions with water availability, reliability, and quality.[1] Table 2-1 summarizes the key federal and state laws and legal decisions affecting water allocation, management, and planning in California today. These laws are further defined in appendix A.

Planning for future water supplies requires an understanding of prevailing water rights and permits, and the ability of the water purveyor to secure long-term supplies. Equally fundamental is an understanding of the major sources available, whether it is the federal Central Valley Project, the State Water Project, a local water development effort, or alternative sources. In each case, water contracts and the conditions, requirements, and reliability of the deliveries must be understood. This is all heavily influenced by the spectrum of statutes

Planning for future water supplies requires an understanding of prevailing water rights and permits, and the ability of the purveyor to secure long-term supplies.

---

1. Other publications such as *California Water* by Arthur L. Littleworth and Eric L. Garner, Solano Press 1995 and *California Water Law and Policy: Volumes 1 and 2,* by Scott Slater, Lexis Publishing 2002, provide comprehensive detail and legal perspectives on water rights, statutes affecting water supply, and water quality.

Using the California Water Plan

The State Water Plan is a first source for any water master plan, urban water management plan, or Integrated resources plan. It provides regional and statewide data and projections, potential new water supply and management opportunities, and a comprehensive delineation of laws, regulations, and statutes that water managers and planners need to be aware of as they plan for future water resources.

The Water Plan provides extensive data on water demand analysis, water use efficiency for urban and agricultural water, and related topics of interest to water planners. The Plan also provides an assessment by hydrologic area of current water use, future demand projections, various projected scenarios, and a comprehensive list of major proposed projects to augment local and regional water supplies. ■

CEQA = California Environmental Quality Act
CVP   = Central Valley Project
CVPIA = Central Valley Project Improvement Act
CWA   = Clean Water Act
DFG   = Department of Fish and Game
DWR   = Department of Water Resources
EPA   = Environmental Protection Agency
ESA   = Endangered Species Act
FERC   = Federal Energy Regulatory Commission
NEPA   = National Environmental Policy Act
NOAA   = National Oceanic & Atmospheric Administration
NPDES = National Pollutant Discharge Elimination System
OPR   = Governor's Office of Planning and Research
SWP   = State Water Project
SWRCB = State Water Resources Control Board
TMDL = Total maximum daily load
USFWS = U.S. Fish and Wildlife Service

listed in Table 2-1, particularly those that address environmental protection. Water for environmental purposes has become a major emphasis in California's water policy, and will continue to be a significant factor in all future water solutions. Over 45 percent of California's overall water use is dedicated for environmental purposes such as in-stream flows, fisheries releases, and wetlands maintenance.

State Water Planning

The California Department of Water Resources (DWR) is mandated to publish the *California Water Plan* and update its status every five years. Since 1957, DWR has developed seven updates to the Water Plan, known as the Bulletin 160 series. The most recent version of the Water Plan was published in 2003; with several sections and additions still in progress. The Water Plan is a comprehensive assessment of California's agricultural, environmental, and urban water needs, and an evaluation of water supplies, water management activities, and related issues to assist federal, state, regional, and local entities in making future water resources decisions. The Water Plan does not formally dictate any planning or facilities decisions on the part of local or regional water agencies or even DWR itself.

The Water Plan update process encompasses considerable public, technical, and agency involvement to reflect current needs and issues. In the 1998 update, water supply reliability and environmental water uses and restoration programs were a primary focus of the plan. The 2003 Water Plan update is still in process, but is grappling with similar issues. In addition, based on recent state legislation, the Water Plan must include details on how each hydrologic region of the state can supply its present and future water needs with existing supplies, conservation, desalination, recycled water, or other "local/regional" sources before considering importation projects.[2]

Another useful statewide water resources document is Bulletin 118, published periodically to describe conditions in California's groundwater basins. The most recent Bulletin 118 (DWR 2003) also describes required and recommended components of local ground water management plans and various management activities occurring in basins. Bulletin 118 sets forth water balances for each of the state's basins, and is an excellent "first source" for data on groundwater.

2. Assembly Bill 672, passed in 2001, requires the State Water Plan to look more closely at developing local and regional sources of water within each of the hydrologic regions in California, before considering importation or inter-basin movement of water. The legislation does not specify how the Water Plan is to accomplish this task, but sets a general direction for the Department to follow.

Table 2-1. Statutes and Institutions Allocating, Managing, and Planning California's Water Resources

Statute, Case Law, Code, or Legal Interpretation	Primary Implementing Entity(ies)	General Purpose Related to Water Resources Planning
ALLOCATION OF WATER		
California Constitution Article X, Section 2	All entities in the State	Use the State's water in a reasonable and beneficial manner. Prohibits water waste and unreasonable use or diversion.
Riparian Water Rights	Courts and State Water Resources Control Board, Water Rights Division	Owners of land on a stream can divert and use (but not store) a portion of the flow on the adjacent land for reasonable and beneficial uses.
Appropriative Water Rights	Courts and State Water Resources Control Board, Water Rights Division	A person can acquire a right to divert, store, and use water on any land, provided the use is reasonable and beneficial and is surplus to that used by earlier appropriators. "First in time, first in right" rule of priority applies between appropriators.
Water Commission Act	State Water Resources Control Board	The Act established a system of State-issued permits and licenses to appropriate water and procedures for adjudication of water rights.
Groundwater Management	Courts, Groundwater Management Districts, Certain Water Districts and Agencies	Groundwater management in California may be accomplished either by a judicial or state board adjudication of the respective rights of overlying users and exporters, or by local management of rights to extract and use groundwater as authorized by statute or agreement. Statutory management may be granted to a public agency or to a management agency created expressly for that purpose by a special district act.
Public Trust Doctrine	All entities in the State	Doctrine states that public rights to the use of tidelands and navigable waters are inalienable. The doctrine also includes protection of fish and wildlife, preserving trust lands in their natural state, and related open-space uses. SWRCB in coordination with Fish and Game routinely implements the public trust doctrine through terms and conditions in water rights permits and licenses.
Federal Power Act	Federal Energy Regulatory Commission (FERC)	The Act created a federal licensing system administered by FERC, requiring that a license be obtained for hydroelectric projects using navigable waters or federal land.
Area of Origin Protections	State Water Resources Control Board	While the Central Valley Project and State Water Project were being developed, the area of origin provisions were added to the water code to protect Northern California water supplies from being depleted as a result of the projects. In 1984, additional area of origin statutes were enacted, including protection of groundwater export from the Sacramento River-Delta basins.
ENVIRONMENTAL REGULATIONS		
Federal Endangered Species Act	U.S. Fish and Wildlife Service and NOAA Fisheries	The ESA is designed to protect endangered and threatened species and promote their recovery. Species are listed through a process; recovery plans and critical habitat designations are developed. Listed species can not be "taken" without an incidental take permit. ESA allows "incidental take" as part of habitat conservation planning (and for specified scientific purposes). ESA requires that federal agencies consult the USFWS or the NOAA Fisheries to ensure that their actions do not jeopardize the species or its habitat.

Source: DWR

Statute, Case Law, Code, or Legal Interpretation	Primary Implementing Entity(ies)	General Purpose Related to Water Resources Planning
ENVIRONMENTAL REGULATIONS (continued)		
California Endangered Species Act	Department of Fish and Game	The Act is similar to the federal ESA, only the California Department of Fish and Game makes listing recommendations and offers project opinions.
Natural Communities Conservation Planning Act	Department of Fish and Game	A program to identify habitat needs of species before they become threatened or endangered, and to develop regional conservation plans to protect species and habitats compatible with local development and growth.
Dredge and Fill Permits (Sec. 404 of the Clean Water Act)	U.S. Army Corp of Engineers and Environmental Protection Agency	Section 404 of the federal Clean Water Act regulates the discharge of dredge and fill material into U.S. waters and wetlands. Discharge can only occur if a permit is granted by the Army Corp of Engineers.
Public Interest Terms and Conditions	State Water Resources Control Board	The Water Code authorizes the SWRCB to impose public interest terms and conditions to conserve the public interest when it issues permits to appropriate water and grants water rights.
Releases of Water for Fish	Dept. of Fish and Game, State Water Resources Control Board	Fish and Game Code sections provide protection to fisheries by requiring water diversion and dam projects to allow enough water to pass through or appropriate water to support affected area fisheries.
Streambed Alteration Agreements	Department of Fish and Game	Fish and Game Code sections 1601 and 1603 require that any governmental agency or private party altering a river, stream, lakebed, or channel enter into an agreement with DFG. The agreement may include provisions designed to protect habitat.
Migratory Bird Treaty Act	U.S. Fish and Wildlife Service	This Act implements various treaties for the protection of migratory birds and prohibits the "taking" of protected birds on the migratory list.
National Environmental Policy Act	All federal agencies	NEPA directs federal agencies to conduct an environmental review for all federal actions that may affect the environment. Includes analysis of plan or project alternatives, and consultation with other agencies and tribal interests.
California Environmental Quality Act	All State and local agencies	Modeled after NEPA, CEQA requires California public agency decision-makers to document and consider the environmental effects of their actions, as well as identify and implement ways to reduce environmental effects.
Fish and Wildlife Coordination Act	U.S. Fish and Wildlife Service	Any federal agency that proposes to modify or control any body of water, or issue a permit to do so, must consult with the USFWS and state wildlife officials.

Statute, Case Law, Code, or Legal Interpretation	Primary Implementing Entity(ies)	General Purpose Related to Water Resources Planning
PROTECTION OF NATURAL AREAS		
Federal Wild and Scenic Rivers Act	Federal land management agencies with designated rivers	The Act designates and protects rivers that possess extraordinary scenic, historical, wildlife, geological, or other similar values. It requires management plans for these rivers and prohibits impacts to free-flowing conditions. The Act prohibits federal agencies from having any involvement in projects that adversely affect rivers (or segments) designated under the Act.
California Wild and Scenic Rivers Act	State land management agencies with designated rivers	California's Wild and Scenic River System is similar to the federal system, except FERC can still issue a license to build a dam on a protected river, overriding the State system.
National Wilderness Act	Federal land management agencies	The Wilderness Act establishes a system to protect and preserve federal land designated as a "wilderness area" by Congress. Construction, motor vehicle roads, and similar things are prohibited; the areas are to remain "untrammeled" to be used for low impact recreation and habitat only.
California Wilderness Act	State land management agencies	Modeled after the federal Wilderness Act, California established a system to protect and preserve state land designated as "wilderness areas" in 1984.
WATER QUALITY PROTECTION		
Porter-Cologne Water Quality Control Act	State Water Resources Control Board and federal Environmental Protection Agency	This Act is California's comprehensive water quality control law and is a complete regulatory program designed to protect water quality and beneficial uses of the State's water. The primary method of implementing the plans is to require each discharger of waste to meet formal waste discharge requirements. Also implements various Clean Water Act provisions such as section 401 or 402.
Clean Water Act–National Pollutant Discharge Elimination System	Environ. Protection Agency, Regional Water Quality Control Boards	Officially Section 402 of the Clean Water Act, the NPDES regulates point sources of discharges in navigable waters of the US.
Clean Water Act– Impaired water bodies	State Water Resources Control Board, Regional Water Quality Control Board, Environmental Protection Agency	Section 303 of the Clean Water Act allows the EPA to designate "impaired water bodies" that require comprehensive clean-up strategies including both point and non-point pollution sources. These "plans" are called TMDL–Total Maximum Daily Load– referring to total pollutant loads a water body can accommodate.
Federal Safe Drinking Water Act	Environmental Protection Agency in partnership with State Dept. of Health Services and Regional Water Quality Control Boards	Directs the EPA to set national standards for drinking water quality. Maximum contaminant levels set by the EPA were not to be exceeded by local suppliers. 1986 amendment required contaminant-specific standards and a series of grant and protection programs. 1996 amendment required that states create revolving funds to be eligible for federal funds.
California's Safe Drinking Water Act	Dept. of Health Services and State Water Resources Control Board	Under this Act, the Department of Health Services is required to regulate the State's drinking water which includes: setting and enforcing federal and state standards, administering water quality testing programs and issuing permits for public water system operations. SWRCB needs to consider the effects of all Delta and upstream water users in setting and implementing Delta water quality standards.

Statute, Case Law, Code, or Legal Interpretation	Primary Implementing Entity(ies)	General Purpose Related to Water Resources Planning
SAN FRANCISCO BAY-DELTA PROTECTION		
Water Rights Decision 1485	Courts and State Water Resources Control Board	The decision set forth many conditions, including water quality standards, export limitations, and minimum flow rates for the SWP and CVP operations in the Delta. The SWRCB asserted that the SWP and CVP were to be operated in such a way that Delta water could meet standards and conditions it would be able to if the SWP and CVP had not been constructed.
Racanelli Decision	Courts and State Water Resource Control Board	The court ruled that SWRCB needed to separate its water quality planning and water rights functions. SWRCB was also instructed to identify and consider all beneficial uses to be protected (instead of focusing on water rights), and in allocating responsibility for implementing water quality objectives.
SWRCB Bay-Delta Proceedings	California Bay-Delta Authority, State Water Resources Control Board, California Dept. of Fish and Game, U. S. Forest Service and Fish and and Wildlife Service, NOAA Fisheries and others	Purpose of hearings was to adopt a water quality control plan and a water rights decision for the Bay-Delta estuary. Various phases have been completed, such as identifying reasonable and beneficial uses, and establishing a water quality control plan. Mitigation and fishery enhancement programs have begun to be implemented. Additional phases are not yet complete: upstream uses and operations are ongoing. Debate over these proceedings led in part to the 1994 Bay-Delta accord and the founding of the CALFED-Bay Delta Program and the California Bay-Delta Authority.
SURFACE WATER MANAGEMENT		
Central Valley Project Improvement Act (CVPIA)	U.S. Bureau of Reclamation	Significant changes to CVP's legislative authorization, placing fish and wildlife mitigation and restoration on par with water supply and power generation as a project purpose. Allows water transfers outside CVP service areas. Requires water conservation criteria for contractors. Calls for specific fish restoration projects. Calls for a land retirement program in the drainage impaired areas in the San Joaquin Valley. The California Central Valley Project Act of 1933 originally authorized the development of the project facilities.
Burns-Porter Act	State Department of Water Resources	Adopted in 1959 and approved by the voters in 1960, this Act authorized bonds for the construction of the State Water Project and sets forth various requirements for operations of the project.
Regional and Local Water Agency Formation enabling acts (*see* 1994, General Comparison of Water District Acts, DWR Bulletin 155-94)	All water purveyors	Two methods are used to form local or regional public districts for developing, controlling, conserving, managing, or distributing water in California: the enactment of either a general or special act district (although types of districts and enabling statutes vary). Private corporations and investor-owned utilities may also provide water supply.

Statute, Case Law, Code, or Legal Interpretation	Primary Implementing Entity(ies)	General Purpose Related to Water Resources Planning
WATER USE EFFICIENCY		
Urban Water Management Planning Act	All water purveyors of a certain size	This Act requires that urban water suppliers with more than 3000 customers or 3000 af/yr plan and adopt water management and conservation plans for five-year increments over the next 20 years. In response to the drought in 1991, the Act was amended to require suppliers to estimate water supplies at the end of one-, two-, and three-year droughts, and to develop contingency plans for severe shortages. The Act has subsequently been amended periodically to include additional groundwater information, recycled water, and water transfers.
Water Conservation in Landscaping Act	Cities and counties, Dept. of Water Resources for technical support	A statewide model water-efficient landscape ordinance was drafted as a result of this Act, which would become effective in cities and counties that had not drafted their own ordinance based on the model.
Agricultural Water Suppliers Efficient Management Practices Act	Department of Water Resources provides technical support	The Act formed an advisory committee to review efficient agricultural water management practices. The committee eventually drafted a Memorandum of Understanding to implement practices and establish an Agricultural Water Management Council.
Agricultural Water Conservation and Management Act of 1992	Department of Water Resources provides technical support	This Act gives any public agency that supplies water for agricultural use authority to institute water conservation programs or efficient management programs.
Water Recycling Act of 1991	Department of Water Resources provides technical support	The Act describes the environmental benefits and public safety of using recycled water as a reliable and cost-effective method for helping to meet California's water supply needs. A statewide goal to recycle 700 taf/yr by 2000 and one maf/yr by 2010.
WATER SUPPLY/LAND USE LINKAGES		
Senate Bill 221 of 2001; Subdivision Requirements; generally in Cal. Gov't Code section 66473	Cities and counties implement directly with local water purveyors assistance, DWR/OPR technical support	For large residential subdivisions (more than 500 units or 10 percent of total water purveyor connections), a city/county must find that a reliable water supply exists, taking into account future planned growth and water sources. Future sources must demonstrate their viability.
Senate Bill 610 of 2001; Water Supply Assessment Requirements; generally in California Water Code sections 10631, 10656, 10910, 10912, 10915, and 10657	Cities and counties implement directly with assistance from local water purveyors; DWR/OPR technical support	For large development projects or plans (residential, commercial, industrial, or mixed use generally equivalent to 500 or more residential units), a water supply assessment must be completed as part of the CEQA (environmental) review process and be included in the decision process.

Water Quality Protection

Four major laws regulate water quality protection in California: the Porter-Cologne Water Quality Control Act, the federal Clean Water Act (CWA), the federal Safe Drinking Water Act, and the California Safe Drinking Water Act (SDWA).[3]

The Porter-Cologne Water Quality Control Act, adopted in 1969, is California's comprehensive water quality law, establishing an extensive regulatory program and planning and management functions to protect water quality and beneficial uses of the state's water. The Act establishes the State Water Resources Control Board (SWRCB) authority to preserve and enhance the quality of California's water resources, and to ensure proper allocation and efficient use of water for present and future generations. The State Board's duties are generally divided into the divisions of Water Rights, responsible for water allocation decisions, and Water Quality, responsible for overseeing a variety of regulatory and funding programs including watershed management, water quality permitting, and planning activities of the nine Regional Water Quality Control Boards (RWQCBs) located around the state. The Regional Boards and their staff members develop basin plans, issue waste discharge permits, seek enforcement actions against violators, and monitor water quality under the guidance of the State Board and the Environmental Protection Agency (EPA).

A Water Quality Control Plan has three primary components: (1) identifying beneficial uses of water to be protected; (2) establishing water quality objectives; and (3) implementation programs to meet those objectives.

One of the primary activities of the Regional Boards is to develop Basin Plans (or Water Quality Control Plans) for each major hydrologic region or watershed system in the state. These plans have three primary components: (1) identifying beneficial uses (of water) to be protected; (2) establishing water quality objectives; and (3) implementation programs to meet the water quality objectives. Beneficial uses include uses such as domestic, agricultural and industrial supply, power generation, recreation and aesthetic use, navigation and preservation, and enhancement of fish, aquatic, and wildlife resources. Water quality objectives or standards are the levels of water quality constituents established to protect beneficial uses. Implementation plans include a description of actions to be taken to achieve the objectives and a monitoring, management, and enforcement program. These plans often have a far-ranging effect on water management and land use decisions within a particular region. For example, the Water Quality Control Plan for the San Francisco Bay/Sacramento-San Joaquin Delta, completed in 1995, is a major factor in the vast network of

---

3. Other statutes and requirements also affect water quality such as hazardous waste legislation, toxic pits clean-up requirements, and underground storage tank requirements (*see* California Health and Safety Code §§ 252000–253000 as a general reference). Also, many specific court decisions or RWQCB or SWRCB orders and plans for water quality standards, and other related regulations, affect water quality in particular areas and water sources. This section of the book is meant as an overview only.

water planning and management, facilities operations, and water rights proceedings of the many entities involved in the Delta region.

The **Federal Clean Water Act** must also be considered in order to understand how the State and Regional Boards implement water quality plans. Originally passed in 1972, the Clean Water Act establishes many programs and requirements to meet surface water quality standards throughout the country. Although the EPA administers the Act, the primary responsibility for its implementation falls to the states, and for California, the State Board and Regional Boards. Among the many provisions of the Clean Water Act, the following are briefly discussed because they are essential for an understanding of how water resources are managed:[4]

- National Pollutant Discharge Elimination System (NPDES) (Section 402 generally), establishing pollution discharge permits
- Section 401, requiring water quality certification for dredge and fill permits and hydroelectric power projects
- Section 303(d), establishing impaired water bodies and establishing total maximum daily load (TMDL) programs

NPDES = National Pollutant Discharge Elimination System
WDR = Waste discharge requirement

The **National Pollutant Discharge Elimination System** is a permit system originally designed to regulate point sources of dischargers into surface waters of the United States. In 1987, the NPDES system was amended to include nonpoint sources of pollutants and regulation of certain types of stormwater runoff. Under the Porter-Cologne Act, the State Water Resources Control Board and Regional Boards have the primary responsibility to issue discharge permits pursuant to the Basin Plans and their water quality objectives. State law (not the Clean Water Act) also authorizes the State Board and Regional Boards to issue permits for discharges onto land and potentially into groundwater. These permits, generally known as Waste Discharge Requirements (or WDRs), address some agricultural discharges, industrial or food processing discharges, and similar activities that do not discharge into a water body.

Point source dischargers include wastewater treatment plants, industrial facilities, and any other identifiable discharger of waste that could have an impact on state waters. These users must obtain NPDES

Old mines can continue contaminating water supplies and fisheries long after abandonment.

4. The Porter-Cologne Act and Clean Water Act contain an array of additional provisions and requirements designed to influence water quality throughout the state. The State Board and Regional Boards have developed numerous classifications of permitted activities and types of permits. Landfills, for example, are regulated under a separate permit. Some permits are individual to the discharge source; others are regional or general in nature (*i.e.*, a set of prescribed best management practices are followed when conducting the activity, and an applicant need only file a notice of intent or a simple application to ensure compliance). *See* the State Water Resources Control Board website for a list of their activities in managing the state's water quality (www.swrcb.ca.gov).

permits that meet formal waste discharge requirements, monitor water quality, and file reports to ensure compliance and consistency with the Basin Plan and water quality objectives. Often the process of obtaining a major NPDES permit can result in a watershed-level planning effort. The Watershed Management Initiative (WMI) in the Santa Clara Valley is such an example. Various permit needs, including regional wastewater treatment requirements, have led to a multi-year, multi-agency, and stakeholder effort to ensure improved water quality in the southern part of the San Francisco Bay.

Since 1987, various nonpoint sources of pollution have been subject to regulation. Section 402(p) of the Clean Water Act establishes five categories of nonpoint source dischargers:

- Facilities already covered by NPDES permits before 1987
- Industrial facilities, including large construction sites
- Large municipal separate stormwater systems (population exceeding 250,000)
- Medium-size stormwater systems (population of 100,000–250,000)
- Facilities that EPA determines to have stormwater discharges in violation of water quality standards

At this time, municipalities with more than 250,000 people (or areas with contiguous cities whose total population exceeds 250,000), cities of 100,000–250,000 people with separate stormwater systems, major industries, and construction projects that disturb more than five acres must obtain an NPDES permit to discharge stormwater runoff. Smaller cities (population of 100,000 or less) and construction sites of one to five acres are being included in these regulatory requirements as of 2003. The stormwater permits require that cities:

[D]evelop, implement, and enforce controls to reduce the discharge of pollutants from municipal separate storm sewers which receive discharges from areas of new development and significant redevelopment....

Implementation of these nonpoint source permit requirements can result in area-wide erosion control and sediment reduction strategies, programs that reduce pollutants entering the system, and in some cases some level of treatment or clean-up facilities. It is worth noting that there are often local grading ordinances and other municipal or county-based requirements that address erosion control, sedimentation, and related nonpoint source discharges in any given jurisdiction. Chapter 7 illustrates various methods to address nonpoint source pollutants in stormwater runoff, particularly those that apply to urban development situations.

Section 401 of the Clean Water Act creates a process to review certain federal activities to ensure that they do not violate state water quality standards. This section requires "water quality certifications" issued by the Regional Boards for federal permits such as dredge and fill permits issued by the Army Corps of Engineers (under Section 404 of the Clean Water Act).[5] Under Section 401, the State Board also has a role in assessing the water quality implications for the licensing of hydro-electric facilities by the Federal Energy Regulatory Commission (FERC).

In California, the responsibility for issuing Water Quality Certifications falls to each of the nine Regional Boards. The type of process each Board uses for 401 Water Quality Certification varies, but typically it includes erosion control and sediment reduction plans and programs, as well as conditions, mitigation measures, and monitoring.[6]

Under **Section 303(d) of the Clean Water Act**, each state must identify water bodies (lakes, rivers, and streams) that fail to meet water quality standards and submit a list of "impaired waters" to the EPA. States are also required to determine the amount of a pollutant an impaired water body can assimilate daily without exceeding water quality standards—or the total maximum daily load for each pollutant. The goal is to develop an integrated, comprehensive watershed approach to allow the water body to recover. A TMDL program contains a number of features, including identifying the pollutant of concern, determining its primary sources, establishing acceptable loads (recognizing a margin of safety, seasonal and water year variations, and related factors), and preparing and administering an implementation plan.

Section 303(d) was not actively implemented until the mid-1980s when a series of citizen-based lawsuits brought the issue to the forefront. At this time, TMDLs might be thought of as the "technical backbone" of a watershed approach for point and nonpoint source pollution management. Nationwide, EPA estimates that over 21,000 water bodies are impaired, of which more than 500 are in California. A growing number of TMDL plans and studies are emerging in the state that are increasingly likely to influence water resources decisions and land use practices and management.

In addition to regulatory responsibilities, the State Board, Regional Boards, and EPA provide technical and financial assistance to local agencies to improve water quality through low-interest loans and grants for

The MTBE Saga

Water quality can dramatically affect the availability and reliability of water supply. For example, methyl tertiary butyl ether (MTBE), a known carcinogen that is highly soluble in water, was discovered in Southern California groundwater supplies in 1996. This was followed by similar discoveries throughout the state.

MTBE is a gasoline additive introduced some 17 years earlier, in 1979, to reduce air pollution emissions. It has a long half-life and is not easily removed by water treatment plants.

The City of Santa Monica, the first community to begin shutting down wells affected by MTBE, has had to augment its remaining uncontaminated wells with a new potable water supply financed by the chemical companies. And many other communities have followed suit.

Underground fuel tanks and inefficient two-stroke boat engines allowed on drinking water reservoirs turned out to be primary sources of transmission to water supplies. Although now phased out, MTBE will still require a massive clean-up effort to remove it from California's groundwater supplies. In this case, a contaminant designed to improve air quality wound up undermining water quality. And this in turn led to loss of water supply and the need for supplemental water to replace lost potable supplies. ■

MTBE = Methyl tertiary butyl ether

---

5. Section 404 of the Clean Water Act authorizes the U.S. Army Corps of Engineers to issue permits for the discharge of dredged or fill materials into waters of the United States, including various wetlands. So-called "404 permits" are only addressed here insofar as they influence water quality regulations. For a complete discussion of wetlands regulation, *see* Paul D. Cylinder *et al., Wetlands, Streams, and Other Waters,* Solano Press 2003.

6. The 401 Certification process is subject to the California Environmental Quality Act. CEQA compliance is required before a certification can be issued.

wastewater treatment, water recycling, storm drainage improvements, controlling seawater intrusion in aquifers, and underground storage tank clean-up.[7]

The federal Safe Drinking Water Act, administered by the EPA in coordination with the states, is the primary regulatory statute directly addressing drinking water quality. Originally passed in 1974, the Act was amended substantially in 1986 and again in 1996.

DHS = Department of Health Services

The 1996 reauthorization of the SDWA included an amendment requiring each state to develop a program to assess sources of drinking water and encourage the establishment of protection programs. In California, the Department of Health Services (DHS) is the primary agency responsible for implementing the SDWA through the Drinking Water Source Assessment and Protection Program. A drinking water source assessment is the first step in the development of a complete drinking water source protection program. The assessment includes a delineation of the area around a drinking water source (surface water or groundwater) through which contaminants might move and reach that drinking water supply. It includes an inventory of activities that might lead to the release of contaminants within the delineated area. This enables a determination to be made as to whether the drinking water source might be vulnerable to contamination. *California Drinking Water Source Assessment and Protection Program*, DHS, January 1999; www.dhs.ca.gov/ps/ddwem/dwsap/overview.

Watershed Sanitary Survey Contents

- Introduction
- Watershed and water supply system
- Potential contaminant sources in the watersheds
- Watershed control and management practices
- Water quality
- Conclusions and recommendations

For surface water sources, the DHS-required Watershed Sanitary Survey can be used to develop the majority of the surface water components of the Source Assessment and Protection Program. Title 22 of the California Code of Regulations requires that a Watershed Sanitary Survey be prepared every five years for surface water supplies (California Surface Water Treatment Regulations). A guidance manual was developed by the American Water Works Association to provide supplemental procedures to assist water suppliers in defining the scope of their survey. The survey includes a discussion of the below-listed conditions; the level of detail necessary is dependent upon the water quality concerns associated with the specific watershed and water supply.

Urban Water Management Plans

Definition and History

UWMP = Urban Water Management Plan

Since 1985, Urban Water Management Plans (UWMPs) have been required of all urban water purveyors of a certain size across the state. Once viewed as relatively narrow documents focused on water conservation, these plans are becoming a more valuable tool for both water planners and land use agencies.

7. *See California Water* by Arthur L. Littleworth and Eric L. Garner, Solano Press 1995 (new edition scheduled for 2003), for a thorough description of the federal and state governments' responsibility for the establishment and enforcement of water quality standards.

In 1983, the California legislature passed the Urban Water Management Planning Act (Water Code § 10610 *et seq.*). The Act calls for the preparation of an urban water management plan that evaluates water supplies and demands for a 20-year period for the state's major water purveyors. The Act applies to any publicly- or privately-owned water supplier providing more than 3,000 acre-feet of water annually or supplying more than 3,000 customers. DWR estimates that more than 440 agencies and districts throughout the state are subject to its provisions.

The Urban Water Management Planning Act applies to any publicly- or privately-owned water supplier providing more than 3,000 acre-feet of water annually or supplying more than 3,000 customers.

In addition to addressing water supply and demand, UWMPs must specify programs for conserving water, recycling water, transferring and selling water, groundwater use and reliability, and procedures during drought conditions. Early plans were not widely distributed to the public and were known to few outside the water purveyor's realm. With the advent of recent state legislation, these plans are becoming an essential element in the water and land use planning process. DWR has increased its interest in the plans, and offers guidance and direction to those preparing them.[8]

Process and Contents of an Urban Water Management Plan

The process for developing and adopting a UWMP is relatively straightforward. Plans must be developed by the water purveyor in consultation with local wastewater providers, local land use agencies, and with the participation of the community. Plan preparation requires a public hearing, but the plan is exempt from review under the California Environmental Quality Act.

Every five years plans must be submitted to DWR for review. Although the law gives the department authority to reject or request changes in plans, to date DWR has had a somewhat limited role in modifying local plans. Urban water purveyors must file their plans with any local land use planning agencies that may be affected, and must notify and consult with the land use jurisdictions regarding any changes or revisions to the plan (*see* Calif. Water Code § 10621). The law envisions an increased level of public scrutiny and involvement in water planning:

> Each urban water supplier shall encourage the active involvement of diverse social, cultural and economic elements of the population within the service area prior to and during the preparation of the plan. Prior to adopting a plan, the urban water supplier shall hold a public hearing for public inspection....

8. As detailed later in this chapter, Urban Water Management Plans have taken on a renewed role and significance under legislation adopted in 2001. Senate Bills 221 and 610 require findings that adequate water supplies are available for urban growth to proceed (for large development projects). Cities and counties are responsible for making these findings. UWMPs can be used as a primary information and planning tool in assessing water supply adequacy.

Recommended Contents for an Urban Water Management Plan

Although no explicit methodology is mandated, the California Department of Water Resources recommends that a comprehensive Urban Water Management Plan contain the following:

SECTION 1
Plan Adoption Process, Public Participation, and Planning Coordination

SECTION 2
History of Local Growth and Water Service and a Description of Existing Water Supply Facilities

SECTION 3
Past, Current, and Projected Water Supply
For twenty years in five-year increments including three-year worst-case water supply projections

- Groundwater
- Local and imported surface water
- Recycled water
- Frequency and magnitude of supply deficiencies (assessment of system reliability)
- Three-year worst case projection
- Supplemental water supplies
- Desalination potentials
- Water transfer potentials
- Long-term water supply options
- Description of all water supply projects and programs that may be undertaken by the supplier to meet projected needs, including a detailed description of the estimated water amount, and a timeline for implementation

SECTION 4
Past, Current, and Projected Water Use

- Current total water demand
- Residential sector, both single- and multi-family
- Commercial and industrial sectors
- Institutional/government sectors
- Landscape/recreational sector
- Agricultural sector
- Saline water intrusion barriers, groundwater recharge, conjunctive use programs
- Sales to other agencies
- Supply and demand comparisons

SECTION 5
Water Conservation Program
Response to each of the Urban and, if applicable, Agricultural Best Management Practices

- Water survey programs for residential customers
- Residential plumbing retrofit
- Metering with commodity rates for all new connections and retrofit of existing connections
- Large landscape conservation programs and incentives
- High-efficiency washing machine rebate programs
- Public information programs
- School education programs
- Conservation programs for commercial, industrial, and institutional accounts
- Wholesale agency programs
- Water conservation pricing
- Water waste prohibition
- Residential ultra-low flow toilet replacement programs
- Description of how the supplier will evaluate the effectiveness of the conservation programs and estimate the total savings anticipated
- Analysis of the cost-benefit of the conservation measures and any funding that may be available

SECTION 6
Water Shortage Contingency Analysis
Including stages of action for water shortage situations, impacts on water revenues and expenditures, and methods for measuring water use reductions

SECTION 7
Recycled Water Use
Including a description of all local wastewater collection and treatment systems, and a plan for use of recycled water

NOTE
A model plan and worksheets for calculating the required water data are available on the DWR web site:

www.dpla.water.gov/urban/water_ management/waterman.html

The required substantive elements of an urban water management plan are shown in the sidebar. In general, a UWMP describes the water purveyor's current supplies, demands, and programs, and then projects future demands and how the purveyor intends to meet them. The plan also discusses water conservation (or water use efficiency), reuse, recycling, water transfer, and related programs the purveyor has undertaken. It must also take a hard look at the reliability of the water system in average, dry, and critically dry conditions, including the condition of groundwater resources. The dry-year analyses may be a significant source of controversy, since the projections are used to accommodate future development. A UWMP must also have a planned program of cutbacks or rationing in the event of shortage and drought and must address the manner in which water quality affects water management strategies and water supplies over the long term.[9]

In 2001, the state legislature added a series of requirements for water purveyors that rely on groundwater for all or part of their water supply (see sidebar). Water purveyors are required to describe local groundwater conditions and management plans, as well as the reliability of groundwater as a future source given projected demands and extraction levels. This information may be readily available for groundwater basins that are well used and have been studied, managed, and modeled. But for many of California's basins, lack of consistent data on private pumping, total extractions, and basin yields, and the absence of groundwater modeling, will present a considerable challenge. DWR evaluates each basin across the state in its Bulletin 118-03 (DWR 2003). DWR estimates that inventory data are "fairly good" for 70 basins, or 14 percent of California's identified groundwater basins; extraction data only are available for 138 additional basins, or 27 percent; and "we know very little" for 303 basins, or 59 percent.

State of the Art in Urban Water Management Plans

The first round of UWMPs were submitted to DWR in 1985. At that time, nearly 95 percent of the agencies affected submitted plans, although their quality, level of detail, and usefulness varied. DWR reviewed the agencies' plans, but provided no comments, guidelines, or consistent methodology.

9. Assembly Bill 901 was passed in 2001 and codified in Water Code section 10631. The bill requires that Urban Water Management Plans address water quality issues as they relate to the continued ability of each purveyor to supply reliable water to existing and future customers. The requirements carry no sanction or implementation mechanisms, but presumably are to become part of DWR's review of UWMPs.

Required Groundwater Information in an Urban Water Management Plan

- A copy of any groundwater management plan adopted by the urban water supplier

- Description of any groundwater basin from which the supplier extracts water

  - Where a court has adjudicated the basin, a copy of the court order and a description of the amount of water the supplier is allowed to pump

  - For basins not adjudicated, information indicating whether DWR has identified the basin as overdrafted or has projected that the basin will become overdrafted under current management conditions, describing in detail the efforts being undertaken by the supplier to eliminate the long-term overdraft

- A detailed description and analysis of the location of groundwater pumped by the supplier for the past five years based on best available records

- A detailed description and analysis of the location, amount, and sufficiency of groundwater projected to be pumped by the supplier

- Description of the reliability of the water supply and its vulnerability during average, dry, and multiple dry years

- Description of planned replacement or alternative sources of water if groundwater is not deemed sufficient

The second and third rounds of UWMPs were submitted to DWR in 1990 and 1995, respectively. At that time, some water agencies believed the plans were designed only to address water conservation activities and not to serve as a comprehensive planning tool. Very few land use planners and local agencies used the plans or were aware of their existence. The plans often lacked clear direction for water shortages and credible analyses of future water supply options.

In 2000, UWMPs were revised once again. In this round, DWR began a concerted effort to streamline the process, increase the consistency between agencies, and improve the substance of the plans. As early as 1997, DWR contacted water agencies to clarify the content and analytical elements required, and also posted a set of checklists and worksheets on the Internet (www.dpla.water.gov/urban/water_management) so that data and analysis in the plans would be more consistent and comparable. *See* appendix B for a sample Urban Water Management Plan and an information checklist for preparing a plan from DWR.

The best UWMPs are those that are integrated with city and county general plans and the plans of local wastewater districts and other service providers.

The plans still have considerable variability. The best plans are those that are integrated with city and county general plans and the plans of local wastewater districts and other service providers. Many of the plans (notably those from Santa Monica, Long Beach, Santa Cruz, and the East Bay Municipal Utilities District) contain significant detail about water supply and demand, water shortage contingency programs, and water conservation efforts. Many plans remain deficient on detail regarding future water sources, and most do not contain risk assessment for water sources.

How to Use Urban Water Management Plans

When followed comprehensively and coordinated with neighboring water purveyors and local land use agencies, Urban Water Management Plans can be a valuable tool for future planning. Land use planners can use them to determine capacities for general plans and specific plans, and to confirm that adequate water supplies are available during project reviews and CEQA analyses. In particular, when determining the adequacy of water supplies for future development of residential subdivisions or large-scale development projects, the UWMP is a cost-effective, reliable method for ensuring compliance. However, an unclear or incomplete water demand assessment may not precisely address whether a particular development area has been accounted for in the water balance.

Water planners can also take better advantage of Urban Water Management Plans. When developing an integrated resource plan or detailed water master plan, the UWMP should form the policy basis for the water supply system. Much as a community general plan forms the basis for subsequent specific plans and actual development proposals, the UWMP can bridge the gap between the broad growth and development policies of a community and its long-term capability to deliver adequate water supplies.

Water Use Efficiency Legislation

Article X of the California Constitution prohibits the waste, unreasonable use, unreasonable method of use, or unreasonable diversion of water. It also declares that conservation of water "shall be exercised with a view to the reasonable and beneficial use thereof in the public interest." This sets the tone for encouraging efficient water use at all levels. Given the hydrologic variability of the state and the enormous costs, both economic and ecological, of major water projects, water conservation (or water use efficiency) has come to be seen as a necessary, viable, and often preferred "source" of augmented water supply.

Article X of the California Constitution prohibits the waste, unreasonable use, unreasonable method of use, or unreasonable diversion of water.

Since the most recent droughts of 1976–77 and 1987–92, California has made significant progress in pursuing water conservation strategies, most notably in the urban sector along the Central Coast and in Southern California. In the past several years, water agencies have spent more than $70 million annually on urban water conservation programs of various types throughout the state. In Southern California's Metropolitan Water District (MWD) service area, total water consumed has not increased appreciably since 1984; yet three million more southern Californians rely on that water service. The full value of conservation programs may not be felt for many years, but forecasts suggest substantial reductions in per capita water use (and per acre water use for agricultural efficiency) over the next two decades. Several legislative and policy efforts have facilitated this progress:

BMP = Best Management Practice
MWD = Metropolitan Water District of Southern California

- Statutes requiring low-flow fixtures in all new building construction. In addition, many local jurisdictions have created incentive programs or required ordinances to retrofit existing structures with water-efficient fixtures.

- Agreement by the state's major urban water purveyors to develop a consistent set of best management practices (BMPs) for water conservation statewide, and to ensure implementation by the early part of this century. Undertaken as a voluntary and collaborative process, this effort continues to evolve and adds significant momentum and clarity to the implementation of conservation.

- The Water Conservation in Landscaping Act of 1992, mandating better approaches for landscape water conservation in new development. Although this program has not been implemented consistently, in certain locations, improvements are evident.

- Several statutes related to agricultural water use efficiency, including the Agricultural Water Suppliers Efficient Management Practices Act of 1990.

This bill has led to the development of best management practices for agricultural water use efficiency. While still voluntary for most water purveyors and users, the agricultural BMPs show promise for conserving farm water.

- The Central Valley Project Improvement Act (CVPIA) of 1992, which has aided agricultural (and urban) water use efficiency by requiring contractors to implement conservation measures as part of federal water project contract renewals

- The Water Recycling Act of 1991 that sets statewide goals to develop cost-effective water recycling programs in appropriate areas throughout the state, and provides a policy basis for additional funding for these projects.

- And, finally, as part of many local and regional collaborative water policy efforts in their search to meet future demands, water conservation has moved to a prominent position.[10]

Water-Efficient Plumbing

Ultra Low-Flow Fixtures

Ultra low-flow fixtures include toilets that require 1.6 gallons of water per flush, 2.5 gallons per minute faucets, and 2.5 gallons per minute showerheads.

Both federal and state legislation have increased the use of water-efficient plumbing fixtures by requiring that the manufacture, sales, and installation of new fixtures meet certain minimum standards. The Federal Energy Policy Act of 1992 requires manufacture of low- or ultra low-flow fixtures.

California passed legislation in 1992 that requires all new and retrofitted water fixtures to be water efficient by certain dates (some were required by 1992, others in 1994 or 1997). Today, all new and redeveloped or remodeled construction projects in the state must employ low-flow or ultra low-flow plumbing fixtures. These requirements suggest more efficient use of future water, but they do not address the issue of existing water use.

A number of jurisdictions have developed and implemented retrofit ordinances or programs to improve existing urban water use efficiency. One approach is to require that when a property is sold, or in some cases, substantially remodeled, the buyer (typically) or seller must bring the older fixtures into compliance with current standards. This is generally accomplished by city, county, or water district ordinance. Specific requirements vary, but the cities of Santa Monica, San Diego, Los Angeles, and San Francisco, the North Marin Water District, and the Monterey Peninsula Water

---

10. In addition, in 1992, the state legislature also amended the California Water Code to allow graywater systems in single-family residential homes, subject to appropriate construction and operations standards and the approval of the health departments of local jurisdictions. Graywater is the wastewater from sinks, tubs, and showers, washers, and related household sources. Graywater can be used for subsurface irrigation of lawns and some landscaping, provided the system is carefully constructed and installed. Generally, the system has to be designed so that people do not come into direct contact with graywater sources. As a practical matter, graywater has not been used extensively and is not likely to be a major source of water use efficiency in the near future. Several communities have allowed graywater systems with appropriate standards.

Management District each use some form of plumbing retrofit. Another approach is to provide incentives to retrofit such as free replacement fixtures, installation support, or low interest loans for major project retrofit. Many urban water purveyors have been actively pursuing an incentive-based approach. The Goleta Water District in Santa Barbara County was a pioneer in this approach, offering toilet, showerhead, and faucet rebate and replacement programs for nearly three decades.

Memorandum of Understanding Regarding Urban Water Conservation

In 1991, the California Urban Water Conservation Council (CUWCC) developed a memorandum of understanding (MOU) defining best management practices for urban water conservation and ways to implement these procedures. More than 250 water agencies (both public and private) and public interest groups have signed the MOU and agreed to the process of implementing the list of BMPs. Other water purveyors are using the BMPs as an industry standard for developing and assessing water conservation potential. The BMPs range from water audits for residential and commercial users to conservation pricing structures for customers. The CUWCC approach provides that any sanctioned water use efficiency measure must meet the test of economic feasibility. Water agencies are encouraged to exceed the agreed-upon BMPs, but in the face of potential customer reaction having demonstrable economic value is a key ingredient.

In 1996, the CUWCC initiated a systematic process to review BMPs and their definitions, and to provide an annual update on progress toward implementation of the measures. In 1997, the BMPs were revised, consolidating the total number to 13 based on recent research and discussions about cost-effectiveness (*see* Appendix C for a complete list of the BMPs). While it is difficult to quantify the future value of these BMPs, DWR estimates that full BMP implementation could result in a net demand reduction over 2 million acre-feet of water statewide by 2030. This represents a substantial portion of the average yield of the State Water Project or over 2 percent of California's total water supply.

As part of the CALFED-Bay Delta program, a process is underway to develop a formal water use efficiency certification for urban water purveyors implementing the BMPs and meeting the objectives of the original MOU. For more information, *see* chapter 4 or the CALFED website (www.calfed.water.gov/programs/wue/WUE_UrbanWaterConservation).

CUWCC = California Urban Water Conservation Council

MOU = Memorandum of understanding

A traditional golf course with high water demands

A newer golf course with narrow fairways, extensive natural areas and lower water demands

Use of drought-tolerant native grasses

A drought-tolerant garden on California's central coast

Landscape Water Conservation

In decades past, landscape water conservation may have meant a demonstration garden in front of a local water district. And while many landscape architects and contractors, land use planners, academics, and water professionals have developed exceptional models of water-conserving landscapes, the practice of water-efficient landscaping has been neither widespread nor consistently applied. Jurisdictions historically impacted by rationing during a drought or areas with aggressive water conservation programs were leading the way. However, landscape water was not of great concern in many jurisdictions.

Today, water-efficient landscaping is viewed as an important element in the overall urban water use efficiency approach, in part because of irrigation's disproportionate contribution to peak seasonal demand and in part because landscape water makes up the majority of urban applied water for residential use.

Model Water-Efficient Landscape Ordinance. In 1990, California passed the Water Conservation in Landscaping Act. This law was intended to promote the design, installation, and maintenance of water-efficient landscapes in urban areas. The law did not prescribe a set method for achieving water savings for the state, nor did it require measurable levels of compliance and enforcement for local governments. It also did not expressly address water-pricing issues (*see* Western Policy Research 2001).

The law did mandate that the state develop a Model Water-Efficient Landscape Ordinance and required all local jurisdictions (cities and counties) to adopt the model ordinance or a functionally equivalent ordinance by 1993. The model ordinance was established in 1992 with substantial public involvement, including the landscape industry, environmental groups, water purveyors, and local officials. The model ordinance relies on the concept of establishing a water budget for a development project, park, or other landscape use. In essence, the model ordinance is designed to provide for adequate plant growth with minimal water supplied.[11]

Local jurisdictions were given the option of either adopting the model ordinance approach, demonstrating that their existing landscape conservation program was adequate, or adopting a different style of ordinance that would accomplish the conservation objectives.

11. The model landscape water use ordinance allows water use to equal 80 percent of a site's typical evapotranspiration. Restricting the total water budget presents the design challenge of careful plant selection, grouping plants in hydrozones, designing quality irrigation systems, and having a long-term landscape management plan.

Several years ago, DWR conducted a survey to determine compliance with the new law and assess what elements were most effective (*see* sidebar). Of the 58 California counties and 454 incorporated cities at the time, 60 jurisdictions issued findings that no additional ordinance was necessary, 257 jurisdictions adopted the model ordinance or a comparable ordinance, and 195 adopted limitations on irrigated turf or a similar simple standard. A variety of provisions have been incorporated into the ordinances of various jurisdictions. The most common provisions involve hydrozone groupings of plants,[12] drought-tolerant plant selection, dedicated meters for landscape use in large areas, improved irrigation technology (especially controllers and rain sensors), irrigation audits and schedules, and required soil amendments and mulch.

Many of the landscape improvements are most effective when concentrated on large-scale public and industrial areas such as schools, parks, business parks, golf courses, and government centers. This is due in part to the magnitude of water use and in part to the ability of an agency or institution to consistently implement and enforce improved practices.

Landscape Retrofit Ordinances. Several agencies are engaged in retrofitting older landscapes. North Marin County Water District, for example, has a program to pay customers who replace turf with water-efficient landscaping; the so-called cash for grass program. EBMUD provides financial assistance and rebate programs to help large sites install more water-efficient landscapes. The Municipal Water District of Orange County has been conducting pilot programs using sophisticated irrigation controllers that determine irrigation requirements based on soil moisture.

Some of the emerging growth trends in California could have interesting implications for water-efficient landscape use. The "smart growth" movement–with its emphasis on mixed use, higher density development, and reuse or intensification of existing urban centers–suggests less landscaping per housing unit and presumably less water use per capita. Conversely, trends toward larger rural homes on estate lots, "hobby" vineyards, and related rural residential development suggest greater landscape water use. The effects of these trends will

12. Hydrozone grouping means designing a landscape so that plants with relatively similar water needs are kept together. Plants requiring more water are grouped in one part of the landscape, drought-tolerant plants in another.

1990 Water Conservation in Landscaping Act

Several surveys have been undertaken to assess the effectiveness of the 1990 landscape water conservation law. A DWR survey in 1995 catalogued the manner in which some 500 local jurisdictions have complied with the law. The majority of survey respondents (86 percent) indicated that the ordinance was improving landscape water efficiency for new developments in their jurisdiction. Constraints included reduced budgets and funds for implementation and enforcement, lack of penalties for noncompliance, and inability to reduce turf areas. Many respondents indicated the need for additional training.

The Western Policy Research Institute (WPRI) conducted a study (2001) of landscape water conservation for the California Urban Water Association. Of 529 total jurisdictions, WPRI randomly surveyed 151 land use agencies and examined various aspects of the effectiveness of the ordinance. Approximately 35 percent of those sampled had adopted a model ordinance that was rated either "exemplary" or "good." Another 35 percent adopted an ordinance that was rated "fair or "poor," and 24 percent had not adopted an ordinance.

Of those jurisdictions examined in more detail, few had quantitative data to demonstrate whether the ordinance was achieving its objectives. About a third of the respondents in this survey believed the landscape ordinance was influencing water use efficiency, a third felt otherwise, and a third did not know. Lack of enforcement was cited as the most pressing problem. Respondents indicated the need for more training for landscape architects, contractors, and developers; landscape demonstration projects; promoting use of drought-tolerant plant materials, assuring compliance between the approved and installed landscapes; and promotion of conservation-oriented water rate structures. ■

CIMIS weather station system designed to assist with irrigation efficiency

Irrigated vineyard acreage near Livermore, California

CIMIS = California Irrigation Management Information System

EWMP = Efficient water management practice

Irrigation of a Central Valley orchard using a low efficiency method

play themselves out as water demands are calculated over the coming years. State legislation and local initiatives appear to have made a difference, but with uncertain results. It is often difficult to quantify landscape water use reductions. Housing densities change, base case assumptions are lacking, and ratios of single- to multi-family housing changes add to the uncertainty.

Agricultural Water Use Efficiency

Several laws and programs address water conservation in the agricultural sector. Although the primary focus of this book is urban water use, it is worth noting the contributions that agricultural water use efficiency can make.

The Agricultural Water Supplies Efficiency Management Practices Act, adopted by the state legislature in 1990, required that DWR establish an advisory committee to review agricultural water management practices. The committee developed a memorandum of understanding to implement these practices and to establish an Agricultural Management Council. The advisory committee, made up various interests in the agricultural, business, and environmental sectors, passed the MOU in 1996, having developed a list of "Efficient Water Management Practices" (EWMPs are essentially a corollary to BMPs). A number of large agricultural purveyors, responsible for more than two million irrigated acres, have signed the MOU and have agreed to its terms.

It is difficult to quantify how effective these EWMPs will be. They rely on cooperation between the individual farm owner and the water district or company supplying the water. To date, most of the large-scale progress has been in developing plans, but not on-the-ground changes. Actual on-the-ground programs occur on individual farms, but have not been developed as regional or area-wide efforts. In its Bulletin 160-98, DWR (1998) estimated that agricultural water use efficiency could result in as much as 800,000 acre-feet per year reductions in applied water by 2020. However, many variables will make the data difficult to assess, such as changing crop types, retirement or conversion of agricultural lands, and changing agricultural markets.

The CALFED-Bay Delta program (discussed further in chapter 8) has developed an ongoing program related to agricultural water use efficiency. It is an incentive-based program designed to use CALFED's funding capabilities and opportunities for joint water management programs to increase the use of water-efficient principles.

Bureau of Reclamation Contracts and the Central Valley Project Improvement Act

Based on requirements in the Central Valley Project Improvement Act of 1992, the Bureau of Reclamation has been requiring water agencies that contract for water from the Central Valley Project to develop water use efficiency standards and measures as part of renewed contracts for federal water. The CVPIA and subsequent guidelines and policies have resulted in new water pricing schedules, water meters, and other measures for conserving supplies. Additionally, agricultural water purveyors are exploring ways to meet water use efficiency standards. The CVPIA also authorizes the Department of Interior/Bureau of Reclamation to acquire certain agricultural lands in the San Joaquin Valley where drainage issues have become a serious problem, and retire them from agricultural use, thereby reducing water consumption. For additional information, *see* the CVPIA web site (www.watershare.usbr.gov).

Water Recycling

In 1991, the California legislature passed the Water Recycling Act. Citing the benefits of recycled water and its reliability and public safety aspects. The Act set a statewide goal to recycle up to 700,000 acre-feet of water per year by the year 2000 and one million acre-feet per year by the year 2010.

The Water Recycling Act set a statewide goal to recycle up to 700,000 acre-feet of water per year by the year 2000 and one million acre-feet per year by the year 2010.

As of 2000, approximately 400,000–500,000 acre-feet of recycled or desalted water service was in active operation, mostly on the Southern California coast or desert. Although this constitutes a fraction of the state's needs, DWR (1998) notes that water agencies have plans and projects for over one million acre-feet of additional water from recylcing in the next decade or more. Various local and regional efforts at increasing recycled water use are described in chapter 5. However, negative public perceptions of recycled water may continue to hinder progress toward meeting recycled water goals.

Regional Collaborative Solutions

Absent a state or federal legislative push, many local and regional efforts have made inroads in water use efficiency. An example of this is the Sacramento Water Forum, a stakeholder-based collaborative comprised of more than 40 water agencies, business groups, environmental groups, and cities and counties that have signed an agreement regarding regional water use and environmental protection of the lower American River. The water purveyors have agreed, as part of the overall package of agreements, to accelerate their implementation of best management practices and become part of a regional water conservation, monitoring, and incentive program. The Sacramento region has long been viewed as lagging behind much of the rest of the state in water conservation because of its wealth of water sources and a history of not metering water use. The Water Forum will ensure a more consistent and concerted water efficiency effort in the next 20 to 30 years. The Water Forum has established a goal of achieving a 25 percent reduction in per unit water demands over current levels. *See* chapter 8 for more information on this program. Other local and regional programs are being launched and implemented throughout the state.

Groundwater Management
Varied Forms of Local and Regional Management

In every western state except Texas and California, the use of groundwater is managed or regulated at a statewide level. In California, surface water rights and diversions are directly regulated by the state (State Water Resources Control Board, Division of Water Rights), while groundwater is managed by a variety of local and regional entities with a wide array of regulatory and management authority and institutional arrangements.

Table 2-2 and Figure 2-1 provide an overview of the variety of formal groundwater management entities in California. This is only a partial list because it does not account for individual programs that may be undertaken by water districts and agencies either on their own or in cooperation with state, federal, or local water managers (such as conjunctive use programs).

Nineteen groundwater basins have been adjudicated in some manner. In these basins, groundwater extraction limits have been set by a court (or in some cases, the State Water Board) and are carefully regulated and monitored, typically by a court-appointed water master who may come from DWR or a local water agency. Various fees and charges are levied on groundwater users to conduct management activities such as replenishment of the basin.

Thirteen groundwater management agencies have been directly authorized by special state legislation. These entities vary significantly in why they were created, how they are managed, and what authorities are granted in each case. Many agencies or districts are authorized to influence or regulate groundwater extraction directly. Most agencies can establish zones of benefit and levy fees on groundwater extraction (a water replenishment assessment or a so-called "pump tax"). Still others are primarily focused on groundwater monitoring or water quality management. Several of these agencies have been formed, but have not yet begun any active management or regulation of groundwater. For example, as of this writing, the Honey Lake Groundwater Management District has not yet appointed its first board of directors.

Several other established water districts have special legislative authority to manage groundwater actively and, in certain instances, to levy an extraction charge on groundwater use. For example, for many years the Orange County

---

Adjudication

Adjudication is a legal proceeding designed to establish rights to either a surface water or groundwater source. Typically handled through the courts, groundwater adjudication results in quantified pumping limits for all basin users.

Water Master

A water master for a groundwater basin, typically with a strong technical background in water management, keeps track of basin groundwater use, maintains monitoring records, assesses compliance with adjudication, and develops periodic reports on pumping limits and other conditions required by the basin.

Map No.	Basin	Year Initiated	Institutional Mgmt.	Map No.	Basin	Year Initiated	Institutional Mgmt.
1*	Brite Basin	1970	Watermaster–Tehachapi-Cummings County Water District	16*	Upper Los Angeles River Area	1979	Watermaster–Superior Court Appointee
				17*	Warren Valley	1977	Hi-Desert Water District
2*	Central Basin	1965	Watermaster–DWR-Southern District	18*	West Coast Basin	1961	Watermaster–DWR Southern District
3*	Chino Basin	1978	Court-appointed Watermaster–nine members	19	Honey Lake Valley Ground Water Mgmt. District	1989	Created by state legislation–board members not yet appointed
4*	Cucamonga Basin	Pending	Not yet appointed	20	Long Valley Ground Water Mgmt. District	1980	Board–elected in 1980
5*	Cummings Basin	1972	Tehachapi-Cummings County Water District	21	Mono County Tri-Valley Ground Water Mgmt. Agency	1989	Board–appointed in 1990
6*	Main San Gabriel Basin	1973	Watermaster–nine members elected from purveyor and district boards	22	Pajaro Valley Water Mgmt. Agency	1984	Board–elected as of 1984
7*	Mojave River Basin	1996	Watermaster–Mojave Water District, seven-member board	23	Sierra Valley Ground Water Mgmt. District	1980	Board–elected in 1981
8*	Puente Basin	1985	Three technical consultants	24	Willow Creek Valley Ground Water Mgmt. Dist.	1993	Board of Directors–elected in 1994
9*	Raymond Basin	1944	Watermaster–Raymond Basin Mgmt. Board	25	Mendocino City Community Services District	1987	Board first formed in 1991; later added groundwater authority
10*	San Bernardino Basin Area	1969	Watermaster–One representative from three court-appointed water districts	26	Monterey Peninsula Water Mgmt. District	1947	Recently added groundwater management
11*	Santa Margarita River Watershed	1966	Watermaster–U.S. District Court Appointee	27	Orange County Water District	1933	Added groundwater management
12*	Santa Paula Basin	1996	Three-person advisory committee	28	Santa Clara Valley Water District	1951	Added groundwater management
13*	Scott River Stream System	1980	Watermaster–two court-appointed local irrigation districts	29	Ojai Groundwater Mgmt. Agency	1991	Board–appointed in 1993
14*	Six Basins in Santa Ana Watershed	1998	Watermaster–nine-member board made up of parties to the judgment	30	Fox Canyon	1982	Board–appointed in 1983
15*	Tehachapi Basin	1973	Tehachapi-Cummings County Water District	31*	Goleta	1989	No watermaster, court has jurisdiction
				32	Desert Water Agency	1961	Limited management authority

Does not include AB 3030 plans or groundwater plans of other district activities   * Indicates adjudicated basins   Sources: DWR, Bulletin 118, 2003

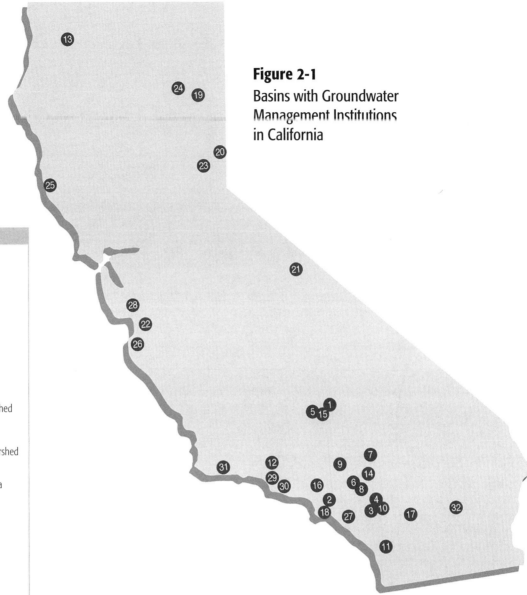

Figure 2-1
Basins with Groundwater
Management Institutions
in California

NO.	NAME OF BASIN
1	Brite Basin
2	Central Basin
3	Chino Basin
4	Cucamonga Basin
5	Cummings Basin
6	Main San Gabriel Basin
7	Mojave River Basin
8	Puente Basin
9	Raymond Basin
10	San Bernardino Basin Area
11	Santa Margarita River Watershed
12	Santa Paula Basin
13	Scott River Stream System
14	Six Basins in Santa Ana Watershed
15	Tehachapi Basin
16	Upper Los Angeles River Area
17	Warren Valley
18	West Coast Basin
19	Honey Lake Valley Groundwater Mgmt. District
20	Long Valley Groundwater Mgmt. Agency
21	Mono County Tri-Valley Groundwater Mgmt. Agency
22	Pajaro Valley Water Mgmt. Agency
23	Sierra Valley Ground Water Mgmt. District
24	Willow Creek Valley Groundwater Mgmt. District
25	Mendocino City Community Services District
26	Monterey Peninsula Water Mgmt. District
27	Orange County Water District
28	Santa Clara Valley Water District
29	Ojai Groundwater Mgmt. Agency
30	Fox Canyon Groundwater Mgmt. Agency
31	Goleta Water District
32	Desert Water Agency

Water District and the Santa Clara Valley Water District have each run highly successful programs of recharging their groundwater aquifers using fees generated from area extractors. These two districts were originally formed for a variety of water management activities; groundwater management was expressly added by the state legislature as local needs dictated. Similarly, the Mendocino Community Services District and the Monterey Peninsula Water Management District have expanded their authority over groundwater to reflect local concerns. Many other flood control, water conservation, water storage, water replenishment, and community services districts, as well as other water agencies, become involved in some form of management, although they typically shy away from any direct limitations on groundwater pumping by private users.

In addition to these formal agency management arrangements, 27 counties (or portions of counties) have adopted some form of local groundwater ordinance, including Butte, Imperial, Kern (east of the Sierra Nevada), San Diego, San Joaquin, Yolo, Shasta, Tehama, Glenn, and Inyo counties. The objectives of these ordinances vary, but many are intended to prevent groundwater from being exported outside the boundaries of the county of origin. Some counties link a prohibition on exports to overdraft conditions. There is currently no widely agreed-upon legal definition of the extent, limit, and nature of the police power for local governments in the groundwater arena.

Other areas in California have been collaborating regionally to address groundwater issues. In northern Sacramento County, for example, 18 local water suppliers have formed the Sacramento Groundwater Authority (SGA) to manage an extensive conjunctive use program for ground and surface water. In its simplest form, the program will use surface water from the American River, and potentially the Sacramento River, to replenish the depleted groundwater aquifer during periods of high surface flow and more intensive groundwater pumping during dry years to keep water in the lower American River for fisheries and related habitat. The SGA will also engage in a host of other water management activities, including technical support for water use efficiency, facilitation of water infrastructure, and coordination with local, regional, state, and federal water managers.

Groundwater Management Plans

Although the management of California's groundwater continues to be predominantly local, the state legislature did enter the arena in 1992 with the passage of Assembly Bill 3030 (Water Code § 10750 *et seq.*). This statute provides general authority for local water agencies (or collaborations among numerous agencies) to adopt groundwater management plans pursuant to specified procedures (*see* the adjacent sidebar for an illustration of the process).

AB 3030 imposes several limitations on groundwater management plans. The local agency cannot determine water rights or directly limit extraction unless all other means to manage the resource are infeasible. Nor can it impose groundwater extraction fees or replenishment charges unless a successful majority election has been held. In addition, a 3030 plan can only be enacted by a local water service agency that includes a groundwater basin not subject to existing management.

AB 3030 Groundwater Management Plan Procedure

- Hold a noticed public hearing on a Resolution of Intent to draft a groundwater management plan
- Write and publish a Resolution of Intent
- Prepare a draft groundwater management plan within two years of the intent or restart the process including appropriate environmental review
- Hold a second public hearing after the draft plan is completed
- Allow for landowners to file a formal protest to the plan
  - If a majority protest occurs (50 percent or more of the assessed valuation of the land in the district), then the plan cannot be adopted
  - If no majority protest occurs, the plan may be adopted
- A local agency may then implement the plan with any or all of the following substantive elements:
  - Control of salt or seawater intrusion
  - Management of wellhead protection areas
  - Management of recharge areas
  - Regulation of the migration of contaminated groundwater
  - Well abandonment program
  - Mitigation of overdraft
  - Replenishment of groundwater
  - Conjunctive use operations
  - Monitoring of groundwater levels and storage
  - Well construction polices or standards
  - Construction and operation of recharge, recycling, storage, clean-up, conservation, and extraction projects
  - Review of land use plans for water quality issues

Offsetting groundwater use with recycled water has reduced seawater intrusion along the Monterey Bay.

Originally AB 3030 was envisioned as a significant step forward in managing the state's groundwater. While flexible enough to account for local resource and institutional conditions, the plan also provides a consistent procedure and comprehensive range of management options and tools. Control remains local, a critical element for achieving political success, yet regional cooperation is encouraged. The statute applies to the entire state, including those places where little if any management has been considered. In 2002, the state legislature passed a second statute (Senate Bill 1938) revising the contents and requirements for groundwater management plans (*see* sidebar).

Groundwater management plans pursuant to AB 3030 and SB 1938 have several limitations. With limited authority to restrict pumping, the plan relies largely on imported surface water that is often in short supply, making the problems of overdraft and seawater intrusion more difficult to solve. The plans are voluntary and subject to protest, so an area with severe problems may not wish to initiate a plan that could become politically controversial. Moreover, the water agencies may lack the enforcement capacity to resolve long-standing problems.

To date, more than 100 local water agencies or related resource districts, cities, counties, and private purveyors have adopted various forms of groundwater management plans. And many jurisdictions have joined together to complete regional plans. Thirteen such plans have been adopted throughout the Central Valley (San Joaquin River, King's River, Merced, Sacramento County, Tulare Lake, and Turlock, to name a few), the Central Coast (Santa Ynez River), the South Coast (Orange County), and elsewhere. While predominantly in agricultural areas, the plans can affect urban water supplies as well, and many require significant regional coordination. For example, 14 entities have agreed to a groundwater management plan for the Turlock area, including three cities, two counties (Stanislaus and Merced), numerous irrigation districts, and several community services and water districts.

Past attempts to manage groundwater have often resulted in conflict and limited progress. Collaborative regional efforts provide a modicum of hope that the state's severe

SGA = Sacramento Groundwater Authority

overdraft may now have a solution. However, whether the plans will take root and afford long-term relief to California's groundwater woes remains to be seen.

CALFED Bay-Delta Program

The CALFED Bay-Delta Program is an unprecedented effort to create a framework for managing California's water resources and address a wide range of issues related to the San Francisco Bay/Sacramento River-San Joaquin River-Delta. The Delta is the largest estuary system on the West Coast, home to more than 750 species (several of them listed under the Endangered Species Act), and the hub of water systems that serve two-thirds of the state's population with potable water and more than seven million acres of irrigated farmland.

CALFED was formally managed as a co-operative venture of more than 20 state and federal agencies with management, regulatory, or water supply responsibility in or affecting the Delta (an interagency Memorandum of Understanding formally links the agencies). In 2002, state legislation created the California Bay-Delta Authority as a formal institution to manage the process. The Authority (and the CALFED program) do not have direct regulatory functions or even actual project implementation functions. CALFED relies on the cooperation of the CALFED agencies and the stakeholders and public involved in the program to accomplish its objectives. Yet no single program in the state has more influence on water management actions today than CALFED. This is due in part to its substantial capacity to fund projects and solutions that match CALFED's objectives, and in part to the agencies involved. The SWP and CVP projects operate through CALFED-related principles, and many of the key regulatory agencies rely on the CALFED

Recent Changes to Groundwater Management Legislation

With the passage of Senate Bill 1938 in late 2002, the California legislature amended Water Code section 10750 *et seq*. related to the contents of groundwater management plans authorized under AB 3030. To be eligible to receive certain funds administered by DWR for groundwater projects, a local and regional groundwater management plan must now include the following components:

REQUIRED

- Documentation outlining how the public can be involved in the plans
- Basin management objectives
- Monitoring and management of groundwater levels and quality, land subsidence, and changes in surface or groundwater quality affecting groundwater use
- A plan to involve other agencies whose service areas overlie the basin
- A monitoring program capable of tracking conditions in the basin for management purposes
- Map showing the basin boundaries (as defined in DWR's Bulletin 118), as well as other local agencies in the basin

RECOMMENDED

- A stakeholder advisory committee to guide plan development and implementation
- A description of the aquifer's characteristics, summarizing historical groundwater data such as water levels, quality, and subsidence; a discussion of key issues; and a general discussion about historical and projected water demands and supplies
- For each management objective, a description of how meeting the objective contributes to long-term reliable water supply and a list of actions to meet the objective
- Map showing monitoring sites and a summary of the type of monitoring at each location, frequency of data collection, etc.
- A description of current and planned actions by the management entity to coordinate with other land use, zoning, or water management activities
- Periodic reports on the groundwater basin status and management actions
- Periodic re-evaluation of the plan (*e.g.,* adaptive management)

For more information, *see* the Department of Water Resources *Bulletin 118-03.*

The Delta-Mendota Canal (federal) and the California Aqueduct (state) winding through the northwestern San Joaquin Valley

ISI = Integrated Storage Investigation

process for primary direction when issues of the Delta or its watersheds arise. CALFED's first phase is estimated to cost nearly $8.5 billion.

CALFED's primary substantive objectives are to:

- Provide good water quality for all beneficial uses
- Improve and increase aquatic and terrestrial habitats and improve ecological functions in the Bay-Delta to support sustainable populations of diverse and valuable plant and animal species
- Reduce the mismatch between Bay-Delta water supplies and current and projected beneficial uses dependent on the system
- Reduce the risk to land use and associated economic activities, water supply, infrastructure, and the ecosystem from catastrophic breaching of Delta levees

CALFED is now implementing the various components laid out in the program's Record of Decision in the year 2000. The program is organized around strategies to resolve four interrelated problem areas: ecosystem restoration, water quality improvement, levee system improvement, and water management.

Each of the strategies contains goals and measurable objectives, specific programs, hundreds of actions by many different organizations or agencies, and a plan for monitoring, assessing progress, and adaptively managing. Each strategy contains a timeline and funding priorities. As an example, the Integrated Storage Investigation (ISI) is part of the program to enhance reliable water supplies in the state. The ISI is a comprehensive investigation examining off-stream surface water storage options, expansion of existing surface storage opportunities, groundwater storage and conjunctive use, and related solutions to increase available storage for future use.

As another example, the Watershed Program provides financial and technical support to local watershed efforts throughout the vast drainages of the Delta to improve water supply reliability, maintain levees, and improve water quality. To understand the many elements, *see* the CALFED Bay-Delta Program, Record of Decision 2000 (www.calfed.water.ca.gov). Chapter 8 contains additional information about the collaborative process that helped shape CALFED and continues to be its mode of operation.

CHAPTER 3

Land Use Planning and Its Relationships to Water Resources

This chapter describes California's land use planning statutes, requirements, and practices and their relationships to water resources. It examines how land use planning can be informed and improved by paying close attention to water resources, and explains the required linkages between land use and development decisions and water supply availability and reliability. This chapter also looks at several examples of local jurisdictions that have highlighted water as part of their land use process.[1]

Land use planners encounter water throughout the planning process. As planners work with the community to develop a general plan or specific plan, the availability of water supplies, water resource features such as streams, wetlands and recharge areas, and policies and regulations about water quality, drainage, and flooding all play a role in envisioning the future community. When planners review development projects and master plans to determine if they comply with the established policy framework, an understanding of water availability and how to address water-related features is key. And during the course of designing the details of the built urban landscape, water has the potential to be either ignored as "hidden" infrastructure, or used efficiently and creatively as part of the project and neighborhood.[2]

During the course of designing the details of the built urban landscape, water can be ignored as hidden infrastructure, or used efficiently and creatively as part of the project and neighborhood.

1. Publications such as *Curtin's California Land Use and Planning Law* by Daniel J. Curtin, Jr. and Cecily T. Talbert, Solano Press (23rd edition) 2003 ; *The NEPA Book* by Ronald E. Bass, Albert I. Herson, and Kenneth M. Bogdan, Solano Press 2001; *CEQA Deskbook* by Ronald E. Bass, Albert I. Herson, and Kenneth M. Bogdan, Solano Press (2nd edition) 1999–2000; and *Guide to California Planning* by William Fulton, Solano Press (2nd edition) 1999, go into extensive detail on land use and environmental laws and practices.

2. This chapter spends comparatively little time addressing issues of landscape analysis to account for water features and water movement. The location of streams, creeks, and wetlands, areas of groundwater recharge, and other water-related landscape features are all critical elements to incorporate into land plans. Similarly, flooding patterns and seasonal water levels affect where certain land uses can be located and appropriate mitigation measures or special

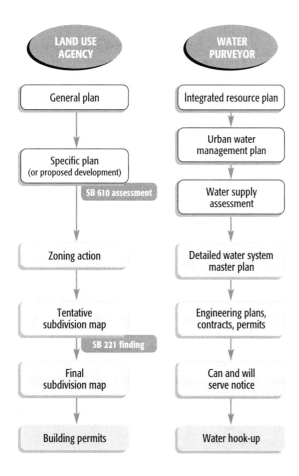

Figure 3-1
General Comparison of Land Use Planning
and Water Use Planning in California

OPR = Governor's Office of
Planning and Research

The General Plan, Specific Plan, and Local Ordinances

Water supply issues need to be addressed at all levels of planning. In California, where land use policy is generally established and implemented at the local level, this means incorporating water policies into the general plan (or comprehensive plan), specific plans (or area plans), and ordinances that guide developers and community planners. Figure 3-1 shows how the various levels of water planning generally correspond with the various levels of land use planning.

General Plan

In California, all cities and counties must have a comprehensive plan called a general plan. Sometimes referred to as a community's "constitution" or "blueprint," the general plan contains seven required elements (land use, housing, open space, conservation, noise, community safety, and transportation) and any optional elements the locality considers important (economic development, public facilities, recreation, etc.). A general plan's contents, use, and procedural and legal requirements are discussed in several publications (*see,* for example, the Governor's Office of Planning and Research (OPR) *General Plan Guidelines* 2003).

One requirement is critical for water supply issues: General plans must be internally consistent. The transportation element, for example, cannot lead to a completely different future than the land use element. In the case of water, this means that water supply and demand figures used in the general plan should be reflected in the land uses and policies in all the other elements. Besides internal consistency, general plans derive their regulatory authority from the requirement that local government decisions be consistent with each element of the general plan. Typically the emphasis has been on land development, but any decision related to infrastructure and facilities, such as a water supply project, must be consistent with the community's general plan.

design features. These land planning issues are thoroughly covered in other publications. *See,* for example, *Landscape Planning: Environmental Applications* by W.M. Marsh, John Wiley and Sons 1997; or Save San Francisco Bay Association, *Protecting Local Wetlands,* 2000. The issues are addressed here only as they relate directly to water supply planning.

Procedural Requirements for Water Resources in the General Plan. California's general plan statute[3] has several references to water resources, and numerous references are in the General Plan Guidelines published by OPR. However, the primary requirements for addressing water issues are procedural, not substantive. Individual communities are left with the task of deciding the type and level of detail of water information and policies that should be reflected in their general plans.

Prior to adopting or substantially amending a general plan, the city or county must refer the proposed action to any public water agency with 3,000 or more service connections in the area the general plan covers. The water agency then has 45 days to review the action and comment. In turn, the water agency must give the planning agency a copy of its Urban Water Management Plan, capital improvement program, current and anticipated water supplies and demands, projected conservation savings by land use type, and other related water service information. Gov't Code §§ 65352(a)(6) and 65352.5.

When developing a new or amended general plan, the statute also establishes a required link to applicable urban water management plans. General plan law states:

> Upon adoption, or revision, of a city or county's general plan, on or after January 1, 1996, the city or county shall utilize as a source document any urban water management plan submitted to the city or county by a water agency.

Gov't Code § 65302.2

Some have argued that an update or amendment to the community's general plan that exceeds a certain threshold may also be subject to the water supply availability provisions of Senate Bill 610 (2001).[4] For a comprehensive discussion of Senate Bill 610, *see* page 65.

Substantive Requirements for Water Resources in the General Plan. It is noteworthy that the general plan is not *required* to have a water resources element. Most jurisdictions use the conservation element or some combination of elements to address water issues; others use a public facilities element. By law, water, wastewater, and storm drainage services may also be addressed by the circulation element, although few jurisdictions have chosen this approach.

---

3. *See* California Government code sections 65302, 65303.2, 65303.4, 65352, and 65352.5.

4. Senate Bill 610 of 2001 states that: any "development" project exceeding 500 units of residential use (or the equivalent in non-residential use–500 hotel rooms, 500,000 square feet of retail, office uses over 250,000 square feet, industrial use over 650,000 square feet, or a mix of uses exceeding these totals) must have a "Water Supply Assessment" as part of any environmental review. While few would argue that a general plan change is a "development project," it is clear that modifying a general plan facilitates developed land use. Several lawmakers in the state have suggested that SB 610 be amended to include general plan updates and amendments.

Why Have a Water Element as Part of the General Plan?

In its most recent edition of the *General Plan Guidelines,* (2002; pages 101–108), the Governor's Office of Planning and Research recommended the idea of a Water Element as an optional component of a community's general plan. The recommended element could include data, analysis, goals, objectives, and policies for various aspects of the hydrologic cycle including water supply availability, water quality, wastewater treatment, watershed management, flood management, and possibly even protection of natural water features such as wetlands, streams, riparian corridors, and recharge areas.

There are several reasons why such an element would benefit a community. General plans are read and understood by the public in a way that water planning documents and analyses are not. Likewise, community members typically interact with the city or county far more than water districts or other special-purpose service districts. By placing many of the water-related issues and policies of the community in one document, they are accessible to the public and may be used more in community discussions. By directly linking each aspect of the water system (water supply, wastewater, and drainage), projections and forecasts used by the city, county, or special district can be more consistent and transparent to the public. For example, future water supply demands, wastewater demands, and drainage needs could all rely on the same land use-based analysis stemming from the general plan build-out projections. This can help with general plan consistency, coordinated infrastructure, and capital projects plans.

An integrated Water Element may also lead to reduced costs and increased efficiencies for needed infrastructure. For example, placement and siting of wastewater treatment and conveyance facilities can be better linked to potential land uses that might accommodate recycled water such as golf courses or industrial areas. Watershed protection policies might be better linked to groundwater recharge needs or stream/riparian protection policies. And, finally, an integrated Water Element can help with other regulatory compliance and planning requirements such as water quality discharge permits, wetland protection requirements, and water supply assessments (as required under Senate Bills 221 and 610; *see* chapter 3). ■

The conservation element of the general plan must include the following:

> [C]onservation, development and utilization of natural resources including water and its hydraulic force, forests, soils, rivers and other waters, harbors, fisheries, wildlife, minerals, and other natural resources. Gov't Code § 65302(d)

A relatively recent addition to conservation element requirements relates directly to water resources:

> That portion of the conservation element addressing waters shall be developed in coordination with any countywide water agency and with all district and city agencies which have developed, served, controlled or conserved water for any purpose for the county or city for which the plan is prepared. Coordination shall include the discussion and evaluation of water supply and demand information described in Section 65352.5, if that information has been submitted by the water agency to the City or County. The conservation element may also cover:
>
> (1) The reclamation of land and waters
> (2) Prevention and control of the pollution of streams and other waters
> (3) Regulation of the use of land in stream channels and other areas required for the accomplishment of the conservation plan
> (4) Prevention, control and correction of the erosion of soils, beaches, and shores
> (5) Protection of watersheds
> (6) The location, quantity and quality of the rock, sand and gravel resources
> (7) Flood control
>
> Gov't Code § 65302(d)

This provision requires cooperation between water purveyor and land use planner, although how the general plan is to address the information once collaboration has occurred is not clear.

Some general plans use an optional public facilities or infrastructure element to examine the availability of water supply. While successful in addressing water needs and potential projects and supplies, this strategy may not relate to the general plan's policies for land use or resource conservation. Several general plans contain what are commonly known as "concurrency" policies for various types of infrastructure. These policies typically state that new development can proceed only after demonstrating adequate capacity in roads, sewer, water, schools, and other required systems. Concurrency polices are in use in many areas where water supplies are of concern, including Sacramento (*see* sidebar), Santa Cruz, and Santa Barbara counties.

Optional Water Element. Water is such a critical resource to the economic and environmental well-being of California, that some communities have created a separate water element to integrate the various components of the hydrologic system and highlight the value of the resource. A water element can guide future land use decisions, provide the needed data and assumptions about water, and offer information in a publicly accessible document. In the most recent version of the General Plan Guidelines (2002), the components of an optional water element are described (*see* sidebar, facing page).

Imperial County has developed a water element that emphasizes adequate supplies for urban and agricultural needs, protection of surface water resources, and water quality protection. Other jurisdictions, such as Santa Barbara County, have in-depth water resource policies including a separate chapter for local groundwater resources. Several other counties are considering water elements in light of recent legislative requirements to link water and land use. The University of California at Davis has developed a simple model as part of its campus planning (*see* sidebar). Sonoma County is in the process of preparing a comprehensive water element for its general plan.

Specific Plans

A specific plan is a more precise land use and infrastructure plan for a specified land area that becomes part of the community's general plan. Gov't Code § 65450. By statute, a specific plan must include text and maps or diagrams specifying:

- The proposed distribution, location, and extent of land use, including open space within the area covered by the plan
- The proposed distribution, location, and extent and intensity of major components of public and private transportation, sewage, water, drainage, solid waste disposal, energy, and other essential facilities that may be located within the area covered by the plan and needed to support the land uses the plan describes

Sacramento County's Concurrency Policies

Sacramento County's general plan contains three policies that require suitable water infrastructure prior to development approval. Many parts of Sacramento County presently are served by groundwater. The basins are stressed and may experience overdraft. The county is working with other entities, notably the City of Sacramento and the East Bay Municipal Utilities District (which has significant available surface water), to replace some of the county's groundwater use with surface sources. Concurrency policies described in the general plan include the following:

- For new development areas (identified on a map), entitlements for urban development shall not be granted until the Board of Supervisors adopts a master plan for water supply and all agreements and financing for supplemental water are in place. The land use planning process may then proceed, and specific plans and rezoning may be approved.

- The master plan shall include three planning objectives: consider alternate conservation measures, achieve safe yield of groundwater supply in conjunction with development in new urban growth areas, and formulate a five-year monitoring program to review water plan progress.

- Development entitlements shall not be granted in areas where no groundwater exists and water purveyors have reached their capacity to deliver treated water, unless all necessary agreements and financing to obtain additional water supply are secured.

University of California, Davis Water Management Plan

Several years ago the University of California, Davis developed a "one-stop" document that considers the role of water in its campus planning. A university campus is not required to adopt a general plan, nor are campuses subject to the general plans in their adjacent communities. However, U.C. campuses prepare what is called a Long-Range Development Plan, which is not unlike a community plan.

In 1997, U.C. Davis prepared a Water Management Plan to help guide its thinking about water use, conservation, drainage, and wastewater treatment. The plan brought together, in one document, the following topics and campus policies:

• Water budget

• Water demands, including assessment of low and high use

• Potential water sources, both external and internal, and the actions required to secure use of the sources

• A management structure to ensure future decisionmaking

• Water quality compliance requirements

• Drainage and flood control elements of the campus

• Stewardship of creek resources

• Water conservation policies and programs

• Contingency planning and coordination with outside agencies and others

A variation of this model could be applied to cities and counties, enabling various water planning documents and the general plan to be linked. ■

• Standards and criteria by which development will proceed and standards for conservation, development, and utilization of natural resources, where applicable

• A program of measures with regulations, programs, public works projects, and financing measures necessary to implement the plan

Common uses for specific plans include:

• Large undeveloped land areas designated for future development, often with multiple land owners and a lack of basic infrastructure

• Downtown areas and redevelopment districts and neighborhoods

• Areas where there is substantial controversy over how and where to allow development

• Areas where special design standards or resource protection measures may be needed

Because the land use diagram in a specific plan provides a relatively precise level of detail, the specific plan is an appropriate vehicle for addressing water resources issues. Unlike general plans, specific plans require an analysis of infrastructure needs, as well as an analysis of timing, phasing, and financing.

Specific plans that create major development potential (*i.e.*, greater than 500 residential units or the equivalent of other land use types) are subject to the recent provisions of the California Water Code and require a separate water supply assessment (*see* pages 67–68).

Integrating Water Demand and Supply Analysis into General and Specific Plans. The most direct way to account for water supply issues in a general plan or a specific plan is during the initial development or a substantial amendment of the land use map. This process is described in detail in chapters 4 and 5. The basic approach is to:

• Determine existing water use patterns

• Establish water use factors for each land use

• Map the community's existing and potential land uses, including both infill/intensification and new developed land to be added

• Determine total future water demands based on the water use factors (with water conservation assumptions built in)

• Provide the basis for comparing future water needs against future supplies

This approach may require considerable research and analysis, particularly in a community where the water purveyor does not have a well developed Urban Water Management Plan, integrated resources plan, water master plan, or supply-demand balance on which to rely. In communities having a relatively recent, detailed water demand-and-supply evaluation, the general plan can incorporate this work by reference and rely on it to determine the amount of growth that can be accommodated. This approach offers an initial level of detail for assessing availability of water supply. Other factors that are relevant, even at the general plan level, include the timing and provision of adequate physical infrastructure, dry year scenarios, and potential threats to water sources.

Developing a comprehensive water plan at the same time the general plan or specific plan is revised can ensure consistency and accuracy between the documents. The City of Woodland undertook such an effort, linking the city's general plan update to master plans for water, wastewater, and drainage.

Subdivision Map Act

The Subdivision Map Act (Gov't Code § 66410 *et seq.*) vests in a city or county the power to regulate and control the design and improvement of the subdivision of land within its boundaries.[5] Although the basic requirements are codified in state law, a local jurisdiction adopts its own subdivision ordinance to govern the process. The local subdivision ordinance generally ensures that the land is developed in an orderly manner, spelling out conditions that may be applied to subdivision applicants so that needed improvements in infrastructure can be funded. Like all planning implementation measures, the subdivision of land must be consistent with a community's general plan.

In the past, water supply was not an explicit part of subdivision regulation. However, with the passage of SB 221 in 2001 (Gov't Code § 66473), cities and counties can no longer approve a tentative subdivision map (or a development agreement including land subdivision) of more than 500 housing units unless the water supplier verifies in writing that a sufficient and reliable water supply will be available prior to project completion. This requirement also applies to smaller subdivisions if the project represents 10 percent or more of the total number of connections for a smaller water purveyor (one with fewer than 5,000 connections). Certain types of subdivisions, including projects surrounded by urban uses (*i.e.,* urban infill) and affordable housing projects, are exempted from these requirements.[6]

When approving a tentative map for a proposed subdivision, the city or county must make a finding that sufficient water will be available. In this case, "sufficient" means enough water to serve the project during average, dry, and multiple dry years without affecting existing and projected water customers. Like other similar requirements, cities and counties can place

Land Use Planners and Water Purveyors Need to Communicate

As a result of the passage of Senate Bill 221 in 2001, land use planners will have to become more familiar with the issues of water supply and demand Likewise, water purveyors will have to become more involved in development applications than they may have been in the past.

With only 90 days to provide data, land use planners and water purveyors should work cooperatively in advance to develop streamlined procedures and data-sharing arrangements. Thereafter, when subdivision requests occur, the procedures will be in place, the information flow will be efficient, and timelines can be met.

For a coordination process that was developed in the Sacramento region, *see* page 69. ■

---

5. *See also* D. Curtin, Jr., and R. Merritt, *Subdivision Map Act Manual,* Solano Press 2003.

6. Urban infill is not explicitly defined in the law and may eventually form the basis for either a legislative "clean-up" or a court providing an interpretation of infill. Affordable housing projects are clearly defined as residential projects exclusively for very low- and/or low-income households as defined by state law.

conditions on a tentative map stating that the water must be available when the final map is recorded. This gives the water purveyor and the applicant time to ensure an adequate water supply source. To make the finding, local jurisdictions must identify the potential water purveyor and request written verification that water supplies are available, giving the water purveyor 90 days to provide the data, with the possibility of a 30-day extension.

Senate Bill 221 is viewed as a "backstop" when long-range water supply planning has not occurred prior to subdivision of the land. Should written verification indicate that water supplies are not adequate to serve the project, the city or county may still approve the subdivision, but only after making a formal finding, supported by substantial evidence, that other water supplies can be made available. The local jurisdiction may work with the applicant and the water purveyor to seek these new sources of water. The test for determining the adequacy of future or planned water supplies is rigorous. To demonstrate "sufficient water supply," the purveyor (or, alternatively, the city or county) must show valid water entitlements, water infrastructure financing, and all major permits and approvals. Paper water or speculative sources will not suffice.[7]

For many large subdivisions, the most direct approach to demonstrating sufficient water supply is to rely on an approved Urban Water Management Plan. The plan should clearly indicate that the land in question was intended to be served, and that the water supply is adequate. Following the land use method for water demand analysis described in chapter 4 is essential to this approach.

Local Ordinances to Address Water Availability

When addressing water supply and land use decisions, local jurisdictions with actual or perceived shortages occasionally seek their own remedies. Ordinances developed locally often combine water availability with other community issues, such as slowing growth or reducing environmental impact. Some ordinances link the demands that result from urban development specifically to the availability of water, while others mitigate existing water problems by generating funding or requiring improvement in local systems. For examples of local ordinances aimed at protection of water quality or specific landscape features (such as streams), *see* chapter 7.

Comprehensive Development Fee. In the early 1990s, Watsonville, a small coastal city heavily dependent on the rich agricultural economy of the Pajaro

---

7. The California Department of Water Resources and the OPR have developed a guidebook to assist land use planning agencies and water purveyors in understanding how to comply with these requirements. *The Guidebook for Implementation of Senate Bill 610 and Senate Bill 221 of 2001 to Assist Water Suppliers, Cities and Counties in Integrating Water and Land Use Planning*, 2003, available at www.dwr.water.ca.gov.

Valley in southern Santa Cruz County, developed a water management ordinance as part of its comprehensive water conservation and use program. Although debate about the magnitude and nature of its groundwater problems continues, the consensus is that the local aquifer has been severely overdrafted, primarily from many years of agricultural pumping. The situation became so acute that intrusion of seawater was evident along the coastal plain, pulling some of the rich artichoke and strawberry fields out of production. In 1984, the Pajaro Valley Groundwater Management Agency was formed to address these problems on a regional scale.

The City of Watsonville relies primarily on groundwater for its water supply. And while urban use is only a fraction of the total groundwater withdrawal, the city recognized that new development leads to additional groundwater extraction, resulting in a further overdraft of the basin. In fact, in the city's CEQA analyses, even negligible increases in water use were considered significant cumulative adverse impacts.

So Watsonville adopted a comprehensive water management ordinance for all new development and any redevelopment that required additional water service. The ordinance added a surcharge to the water connection fee and subsequent water rates to fund various improvements in water management, including conservation and efficiency programs, studies of recycled sources, improved locations for wells, and related activities to reduce the impact on the groundwater basin. The city also increased its charges for existing water users to augment the new development funding, arguing that all water users should bear some of the burden for improving the groundwater situation. The city continues to work with the Pajaro Valley Water Management Agency and others to secure additional water sources for the future.

Water Use Off-Set. Water budgeting is another approach used by water-short communities. During the 1980s, in the small community of Morro Bay along California's central coast, groundwater supplies had been tapped and available surface supplies were stretched to their limits. In response, the city instituted a program where new development could only receive approval for additional water supply if an applicant could demonstrate, through a conservation offset, that the existing water demand had been reduced by an amount equivalent to twice the water required by the project. The concept was relatively simple. A developer of a new project would petition the city for water service, and the city

Focusing a Specific Plan on Stream Protection—The Soquel Village Specific Plan

In 1990, the County of Santa Cruz embarked on a unique land use planning process for one of its small urbanized communities in the central part of the county. The bucolic village of Soquel, an unincorporated mix of residential, commercial, and public uses, occupies a low valley site with Soquel Creek at the center of the community. In fact, a sizable portion of the urbanized village is within the creek's 100-year floodplain. In addition to flooding problems, Soquel sought a land use planning process to stimulate local business without sacrificing the historic character of its downtown and to relieve traffic congestion problems without widening the main road through town.

A specific plan was selected as the most appropriate planning vehicle because it combined flexibility with requirements for a detailed physical design and infrastructure planning. The use of a highly inclusive public process proved to be an excellent model for reaching consensus. Open workshops were held to define the issues, with residents and business owners sketching potential solutions on maps and arriving at an agreed-upon set of public and private improvements that met the objectives.

The resulting plan focused significant attention on the creek. Setback requirements for new construction were developed first, and then a long-term strategy was crafted to phase out relatively low-value urban uses—through redevelopment purchase as they became available—to allow parts of the floodplain to be restored to more natural conditions. A recreational system was proposed that involves trails, interpretive areas, and bridges and restored habitats along the creek. Some urban structures may use their proximity to the creek for visual enhancement, at the same time offering structural flood protection. ■

would provide a list of businesses and residences wishing to retrofit older, inefficient plumbing, or in some cases landscaping. The development project applicant would then pay for the retrofit, and had to demonstrate that the offset was adequate to more than cover the proposed new demand. Morro Bay supported this program for several years, until additional long-term water sources were developed.

Water Budgeting Approach. A community in New Mexico has used a phasing program to address the problem of water availability. Concerned about growth and limited resources, Santa Fe drafted an ordinance linking annual growth rates to its municipal water budget.

Santa Fe's municipal ordinance limits total new water demand from urban development to 190 acre-feet per year, budgeting 145 acre-feet for future residential use and 45 acre-feet for commercial and industrial use, with a maximum of 15 acre-feet for tourist-related development. Approximately 10 percent of the budgeted water is available for use outside current city limits, thereby emphasizing infill and compact city growth without eliminating projects on the city's edge. To implement the ordinance, Santa Fe is establishing a Water System Allocation Permit for all new development projects.

Role of the Local Agency Formation Commission

LAFCO = Local Agency Formation Commission

A Local Agency Formation Commission (LAFCO) ensures the orderly growth of cities, and the orderly, efficient provision of public services, by deciding how California's jurisdictional boundaries are created or modified. Each county's LAFCO decides on proposed annexations to cities or services districts and whether district or agency boundaries can be expanded or changed. LAFCOs define the limits of a city or service district and the sphere of influence for each city and local public service agency in the state.

Every county has a LAFCO, typically made up of two county representatives, two representatives from the cities within the county, and one at-large member (although membership may vary). Often staffed by an executive officer who also may have a role in county planning, LAFCOs historically have had a limited role focused on ensuring logical growth patterns and acceptable fiscal negotiations between cities and counties (or districts). This was in part due to the focus of their work and in part because major decisions and analyses (general plan amendments, specific plans, environmental studies) typically occur at the city or county level before reaching the LAFCO.

As of 2001, new state legislation gave LAFCOs an expanded, more rigorous role that increased their visibility and required them to address water supply issues. Known as the Cortese-Knox-Hertzberg Local Government Reorganization Act of 2000, the law expanded the requirements for LAFCO public service reviews for annexations and sphere-of-influence changes. These reviews must include written determinations for each of the following:

- Infrastructure needs or deficiencies
- Growth and population projections for the area
- Financing constraints and opportunities
- Cost-avoidance opportunities
- Opportunities for rate restructuring
- Opportunities for shared facilities
- Government structure options, including consolidation or reorganization
- Evaluation of management efficiencies
- Local accountability and governance

As a result, LAFCOs must now address all infrastructure needs and deficiencies in more detail, including cost implications, shared facility options, and opportunities for district restructuring. This suggests a more rigorous look at water supplies and demand. The California Association of LAFCOs is in the process of developing guidelines to implement the requirements. While the practical ramifications of these changes are not yet known, it is likely that future LAFCO decisions will require more detailed and sophisticated water supply-and-demand analyses than in previous years.

Water Resources Planning and CEQA

Unless expressly exempted, local and state government actions are subject to the California Environmental Quality Act, including general plan amendments, specific plans, development projects, and water supply plans and projects.[8]

As a result, planners and citizens often utilize the CEQA process to address the issue of water resources, and more specifically availability of water supply. Many of these analyses are quite comprehensive and find their way into negative declarations (NDs), environmental impact reports (EIRs), and related documents. Water supply analyses through CEQA can play a major role in the decision-making process for a project or plan.[9]

EIR = Environmental impact report
ND = Negative declaration

8. Several types of water-related plans and projects are listed as "statutory exemptions," meaning that the legislature has exempted them explicitly from CEQA review. These include temporary water transfers up to one year in duration; piping, redesign, or use of reclaimed water for certain specified irrigation and industrial uses; minor alterations to comply with public water systems' fluoridation requirements; and preparation of Urban Water Management Plans. Additionally, routine and minor construction, maintenance, and operations of water facilities are "categorically exempt" from CEQA requirements.

9. The CEQA process is well documented in Bass, Herson, and Bogdan, *The CEQA Deskbook* (2001), and Remy, Thomas, Moose, and Yeates, *Guide to the California Environmental Quality Act* (1999–2000), both published by Solano Press.

CEQA in a Nutshell

The California Environmental Quality Act has the following basic objectives:

- Disclosure of environmental impacts
- Identification and prevention of environmental damage
- Disclosure of agency decisionmaking
- Enhancement of public participation
- Fostering intergovernmental coordination

In its simplest form, the CEQA process has the following generalized steps:

- The lead agency (typically the jurisdiction making the decision or proposing the project or plan) defines the project or action and determines if CEQA applies or if an exemption is warranted. The lead agency also consults with other agencies.

- If CEQA applies, the lead agency prepares an initial study that assesses the likelihood of the project having significant environmental effects. If the project may have such effects, the lead agency must prepare an environmental impact report. If the project will not result in significant environmental effects, or if the effects can be mitigated (avoided or reduced to levels less than significant), and the project applicant agrees to include mitigation measures in the project, then a Negative Declaration or Mitigated Negative Declaration is prepared.

- The lead agency prepares the draft ND, MND, or EIR and sends it out for public review.

- The public and other agencies comment on the draft EIR verbally or in writing, and the lead agency responds to the comments in the final EIR, which is also available for the public to review.

- The lead agency holds a public hearing (or several) and makes a determination of the adequacy of the environmental documentation.

Only then can the lead agency make its decision on the action, project, plan, or program that was subject to environmental review. ■

CEQA provides limited substantive guidance on the issue of water resources or water supply. Typical questions addressed in a CEQA review of a proposed plan or project include:

- Is water supply a potentially significant issue or an important public concern? If so, what level of detail for water supply/demand analysis is appropriate for the project?

- What reliable data and analyses are already available within an Urban Water Management Plan, water master plan, or other document? If information is not available, which entity will supply the area with water, and who can best provide the analysis?

- Is the proposed plan or project likely to have a significant effect on water resources?

- If so, what mitigation measures or alternative project/plan options are available to address shortages in the future?

To determine an adequate information base, process, and standard of review for water issues, it is instructive to look at the state's CEQA Guidelines and recent state legislation, as well as several recent court decisions.

CEQA Guidelines. A useful starting place is to examine those environmental effects that "may be considered significant under CEQA" (Appendix G, *California Environmental Quality Act Guidelines*, California Resources Agency, 1999). A project, plan, or action has a significant environmental effect on water if it:

- Violates a water quality standard
- Substantially degrades groundwater supplies or interferes with recharge
- Substantially alters existing drainage patterns resulting in erosion, runoff, and flooding
- Creates runoff that exceeds the drainage system capacity
- Substantially degrades water quality
- Places housing in a 100-year flood hazard area
- Impedes or redirects flood flows within a 100-year flood hazard area
- Exposes people or structures to significant risk from flooding
- Exceeds existing water supplies
- Exceeds existing wastewater capacity
- Fails to comply with wastewater treatment requirements
- Requires construction of new or expanded wastewater or water treatment facilities or stormwater drainage facilities

As lead agency, each jurisdiction may have its own issues and its own thresholds regarding what constitutes a significant impact to water resources.

Water Supply and Land Use Legislation. Senate Bill 610 of 2001[10] sets forth requirements for CEQA documents that address water supply for larger plans and projects. Cities and counties must incorporate water supply assessments into any CEQA document (EIR, MND, or ND) for development projects that exceed the following thresholds:

EIR = Environmental Impact Report
MND = Mitigated Negative Declaration
ND = Negative Declaration

- Residential use of more than 500 units
- Retail use of more than 500,000 square feet
- Office use of more than 250,000 square feet
- Hotel/motel use of more than 500 rooms
- Industrial use of more than 40 acres or 650,000 square feet
- A mixed use project that includes any use or combination as large as any of the above, or
- Any project that would demand water greater than the equivalent of 500 dwelling units

The thresholds are quite high, and for many communities will rarely be reached. Numerous smaller projects and plans could well have cumulative water demands that are significant. These can be accounted for in an Urban Water Management Plan or a water master plan, but do not require a water supply assessment based on recent law.[11]

The city or county initiates the procedure by identifying the appropriate water purveyor for a proposed development project and then determining how the project will be handled. If it is clearly accounted for under the latest Urban Water Management Plan (UWMP) or a comparable water supply assessment, this information can be incorporated directly into the CEQA review. If the project was not accounted for (or if there is no UWMP), the city or county requests a water supply assessment from the water purveyor. The assessment must cover a 20-year projection of water demands and supplies in normal, dry, and multiple dry years, including existing and planned future water users. If the project requires new water, these sources must be documented. For a new source to be considered, the assessment must demonstrate that the water purveyor has secured water rights, can obtain capital funding for the infrastructure, and can identify and secure the required regulatory permits and approvals. Similar information is needed if a project will rely on groundwater. The purveyor has 90 days to supply this information, with a

UWMP = Urban Water Management Plan

10. California Water Code §§ 10631, 10656, 10910, 10912, 10915, and 10657.
11. Many analysts believe that even for projects and plans below these thresholds, water supply information requirements under CEQA will be expanded. CEQA documents are subject to public review, and it is possible that the kind of scrutiny and review SB 610 requires eventually will be expected by the public for smaller projects when water supply is a potential concern.

Historical Background for Linking Water Supply and Land Use for Development Projects

We Can and Will Serve

Local water agencies exercise considerable authority to plan for, develop, and distribute water for present and future needs. Water suppliers in California have traditionally understood themselves to be subject to a "duty to serve" new development. Language in various water district enabling statutes, as well as in court cases, reinforces this perception. *See* Water Code §§ 31020 and 22075.

Refusal to serve is highly unusual and exercised only in limited circumstances. California Water Code section 350 states that a purveyor can refuse service only if it:

> [F]inds and declares that the ordinary demands and requirements of water customers cannot be satisfied without depleting the water supply of the distributor to the extent that there would be insufficient water for human consumption, sanitation and fire protection.

The duty to serve is often viewed as the first, foremost, and perhaps only mission of a water-purveying agency. For many years, the vehicle for carrying out this duty has been the "can and will serve letter." This is a written declaration by the public or private purveyor stating that the water supply is sufficient to accommodate a new proposed development. It is generally submitted at the subdivision or building permit stage, well down the line from any fundamental planning or land use decisions. Most land use planners understand the can-and-will-serve letter to be formulaic and not subject to discussion or discretion.

As described throughout this text, during the 1990s, both the legislature and the courts began to reconsider the relationship between water supply and land use decisions. The can-and-will-serve approach was thought to be inadequate to address a growing concern that new development was often approved with less than reliable water service. During average or wet years the water supply might be adequate, but in times of drought, or when supplies are threatened, it might be inadequate for existing, planned, and newly approved uses.

The State Legislature Acts

The California Legislature's initial contribution to the land use/water supply issue was the passage of Senate Bill 901 in 1995. SB 901 was sponsored by the East Bay Municipal Utilities District, as a result of a long-standing issue regarding serving water outside its current boundaries.

In 1993, EBMUD sued Contra Costa County over a proposed 11,000-unit residential development in Dougherty Valley, about twenty miles east of San Francisco Bay. Alleging that the county failed to consider water supply when it approved the development, EBMUD did not want to be forced to expand its service boundaries, in part because existing customers might be left with less reliable water. EBMUD prevailed at the trial court level, but the developers appealed. Ultimately, the case was settled when the developers, the county, EBMUD, and Zone 7 of the Alameda County Water District agreed to a water service plan for the new growth area. Zone 7, whose water is contingent on transfer from agricultural contractors, would become the project's primary water purveyor, and EBMUD would serve as the back-up if the Zone 7 water sources proved inadequate.

Senate Bill 901 required that cities and counties obtain long-term water planning information from the purveyors serving proposed development. Generally included in environmental review documents, this information was to be part of the documentation for land use decisionmakers. The class of projects subject to SB 901 was limited to large-scale land development proposals involving a new specific plan or a revision or amendment to the community's general plan or an adopted specific plan. The process required land use agencies and water purveyors to exchange data, but did not dictate a substantive result, nor is it enforceable. A survey conducted in 2000 indicated that few jurisdictions followed the law, noting that only two percent of those surveyed complied with all elements of the statute. For many, SB 901 was a start, but little else.

However, it paved the way for the Senate Bills 610 and 221, passed in 2001. Also shaped and advocated by EBMUD, these bills had much broader support and impact. ∎

possible 30-day extension. Once provided, the information becomes part of the CEQA review, and the city or county has to make a formal determination about the adequacy of long-term water supplies.[12]

If it finds that long-term water supplies are inadequate, the local jurisdiction must include plans for augmenting the existing supply. These plans must identify specific projects, costs, approvals and permits required, funding sources, and related data. It is the responsibility of the land use agency to make findings regarding the availability of water supply and include the findings in the public record when making project decisions and determining the adequacy of the CEQA document. Like all CEQA reviews, the lead agency must either approve or disapprove the plan or project.

The practical significance of this requirement will be much higher visibility for water supply-and-demand studies, and much more coordination required between land use agencies and water purveyors (or between land use planners and their public works counterparts) in plans and development projects.

Court Decisions. In several cases, the courts have attempted to sort out issues related to the adequacy of CEQA review with respect to long-term water supply planning.

Stanislaus Natural Heritage Project v. County of Stanislaus (1996) 48 Cal. App. 4th 182. In *Stanislaus*, an EIR for a proposed specific plan was prepared for a 5,000 unit, 29,500-acre residential and resort development to be built in phases over a 25-year period. The project identified a secure water source for the first five years of the plan, but failed to determine a water source for subsequent phases. Instead, the EIR treated the long-term lack of water supply as a significant, unavoidable impact. Proposed mitigation included a commitment that construction beyond the first five years could not proceed until a secure water source had been identified. The EIR also indicated that additional environmental review would be required at that time.

Previously, this line of reasoning may have been considered adequate. However, in this case the Court of Appeal invalidated the EIR because it lacked adequate information regarding potential water supply sources for the entire project. The court stated:

> The County knew neither the source of the water the project would use beyond the first five years, nor what significant environmental effects might be expected when the as yet unknown water source (or sources) is ultimately used.

The court concluded that the "project" was the entire specific plan and that it contemplated construction of the whole plan. Therefore, some analysis

12. *See The Guidebook for Implementation of Senate Bill 610 and Senate Bill 221 of 2001 to Assist Water Suppliers, Cities and Counties in Integrating Water and Land Use Planning, 2002,* available at www.dwr.water.ca.gov.

of the water supply, perhaps even a broad evaluation of future options and associated impacts, was needed.

As a practical matter, a city or county and its land use planners, with insufficient data and limited expertise in water supply and related issues, may find this task difficult. To avoid this possibility, the land use planner and water purveyor should review the plan at the earliest stage of a project.

***County of Amador v. El Dorado County Water Agency* (1999) 76 Cal. App. 4th 931.** In *Amador,* the Court of Appeal invalidated an El Dorado Water Agency decision to certify an EIR and approve a water supply project designed to serve future population growth that was detailed in El Dorado County's Draft General Plan. The water supply strategy included an allocation of 17,000 acre-feet of surface water per year from the American River watershed. Concluding that the water purveyor had made water projections based on invalid demands contained in the county's *draft* general plan, the court reasoned as follows:

> Had a general plan reflecting population and development policies been adopted, a water project to meet those needs would certainly have been appropriate. Here, however, the new general plan had not been adopted. The proposed water project was not designed to be compatible with the existing general plan, but with the draft plan. This sequence of events–approving a water program before adopting a general plan–precludes any proper review of significant growth issues.

The court went on to argue for what it believed should be the proper sequence of planning:

> Instead of proceeding from a more general project to more specific ones, as is commonplace in tiering, the exact opposite occurs (here): a specific water project drives the general plan process. The issues become circular: water supply projects are adopted to meet growth plans outlined in a draft general plan, and the general plan is then adopted because an adequate water supply exists for the outlined development plans.

These and other related CEQA cases suggest some practical advice for land use and water planners:

- Water supply should not be overlooked as an important issue under CEQA.
- Analysis of long-term water supply and demand should be part of the information disclosed in the CEQA process, even if the water information is not precisely known.
- Water supplies must be identified for the entire plan or project, even when a long planning horizon makes it difficult to accurately represent the needs of plan build-out.
- Direct and indirect effects should be addressed, as well as cumulative and growth-inducing effects.

- Adopted growth plans, usually in the form of local general plans, are the most acceptable basis for projecting future demands and evaluating future scenarios.
- The effects of water supply should be evaluated using an appropriate historical baseline.

Integrating Water Supply Issues into the Day-to-Day Development Review Process

Once a community has sound water policies embedded in long-term plans, ordinances, and CEQA procedures, the policies need to be implemented as each development project is proposed. This requires careful project review and ongoing monitoring to track water use and supply over time. Because conditions can change and new information may become available, it is best to be flexible when implementing a comprehensive program. The Sacramento region has begun to create a consistent approach as part of a regional water supply and environmental protection program (*see* sidebar and Figure 3-2).

To implement a water budgeting and accounting procedure, a jurisdiction must rigorously document new water demands and report these findings periodically. Because planning departments and water purveyors are typically not set up to

The Water Forum Successor Effort Water Accounting Procedures

The Sacramento Water Forum, described in detail in chapter 8, is a collaborative policy process made up of more than 40 representatives including water, business, public, and environmental interests. In the year 2000, after six years of negotiations, these interests entered into an historic accord known as the Water Forum Agreement. The Agreement seeks to protect and restore the resources and habitat of the lower American River (the local river that many of the purveyors use as their primary water source), while providing for a safe and reliable water supply for all of the planned growth in the region for the next three decades.

The Agreement specifies how much water and the type of supply each of the area's water purveyors can use over the next 30 years. As part of the initial agreement, the parties agreed to create a procedure to track water supply and demand and formally integrate land use planning and water supply decisions on a "real time" basis. The Water Forum Successor Effort has carried this work forward and has established a tracking procedure for water purveyors and land use agencies.

The procedure involves exchanging the best available water supply-and-demand information whenever a major development project is proposed or when a county or any of the cities in the Sacramento region develop a new or revised general or specific plan. It also applies to

LAFCO decisions regarding annexation or sphere-of-influence changes. The procedure allows for a regional entity, in this case the Water Forum, to compile water demand and supply on an annual basis to ensure that agreed-upon limits on the use of American River water and groundwater are respected. Simple spreadsheets catalog total demand, and this amount is then added to the baseline assessment.

The information exchange includes the Urban Water Management Plan of the affected water supplier, background data from the Water Forum process, and up-to-date water supply-and-demand data for each project or plan and each purveyor. Progress in water conservation, new sources or facilities, and other supply improvements are included. When a development proposal or plan is considered by a city council or county board of supervisors, the assessment is reviewed. These procedures do not tie the hands of land use agencies regarding their approval or denial of plans and projects, but ensure that up-to-date water information is; part of the decision-making process.

The procedure also allows the various Water Forum stakeholders to contribute to the discussion. High-profile projects that may require unanticipated water supply arrangements can be discussed in a neutral forum. As conditions change, these multi-party discussions can be revisited.

Figure 3-2
Sacramento Water Forum Procedure for Incorporating
Water Supply Information into Development Proposals

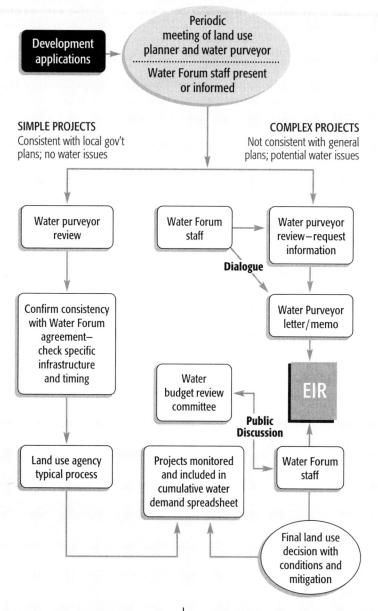

Business, environmental, public, and water interests are all at the table to weigh in on questions regarding water use and its potential effects. And a dispute resolution process is available if the parties cannot reach agreement.

Figure 3-2 illustrates how a major development project is handled. It is worth noting that the Water Forum procedures were being developed prior to passage of Senate Bills 221 and 610; however, their requirements have been integrated. ■

conduct this level of cumulative assessment, tracking water demands on a continuous basis, additional staff resources may be necessary.

The advantages of a comprehensive process are clear. City councils and boards of supervisors required to make decisions on land use approvals are aware of the effects a particular project or plan will have on overall water supply and how quickly an area may be reaching its limit or threshold. The land use-based approach for calculating water demands, outlined in chapter 4, establishes the baseline for addressing subsequent development proposals.

What This Means for Land Use and Water Planners

Taken together, legislative requirements, court cases, and existing laws and practices will greatly expand the role of water supply, demand, and future projections in decisions about land use planning and growth. Urban water management plans and water master plans will take on more significance for city and county decisionmakers, which suggests that land use planners should become involved in their preparation, review, and use. Water supply analyses will be conducted more frequently, in greater detail, and with heightened public scrutiny. Land use planners will have to understand and communicate to the public the details of complex water supply projects, multi-agency arrangements, and transfers. Coordination between land use and water use planners will increase, and, in some cases, land use planners may be asked to work directly with developers to verify new water supply sources that may be counter to or unknown by local water agencies. Over time, the technical state of the art for water supply and demand forecasting and planning will likely improve.

For a comprehensive, detailed, and defensible methodology for assessing water demands and supplies and linking them directly to land use and growth plans, *see* chapters 4, 5, and 6.

The Development Pipeline

One of the thorniest issues for planners is how to account for development applications that are in process—the so-called development pipeline. Every local government has projects like these—major and minor applications in midstream, often well known to the community and potentially controversial.

The total water demands of the development pipeline may not represent a significant portion of overall demand. Because of their visibility, however, it's important to establish credible assumptions for these projects, and these may be difficult to define. The mix and magnitude of land uses change frequently, especially when a project is in the final stages of negotiation before coming before the decision-making body. Some projects are withdrawn.

Complications notwithstanding, it's useful to select a date and calculate the cumulative water demand from a credible list of projects. And it is essential to be transparent about which applications to accept into the pipeline. The most speculative—major general plan amendments, for example—should either be excluded or put in a separate category. A range of possible demands can be used, and projects with future water demands that are more certain can be detailed more precisely.

A simple spreadsheet that is updated regularly can serve as the cumulative assessment. By keeping the list timely and making it available to the public and other agencies (including water districts), the value and credibility of the analysis is strengthened. Many planning departments track pending development projects and periodically report their findings. Adding water demand or other infrastructure needs can enhance these matrices. A list of these projects can also serve as a consistent database for required CEQA analysis of pending and cumulative projects. ■

CHAPTER 4

Analyzing Water Demands

Projecting future water demands accurately is the primary linkage between urban growth and water supply planning. To ensure defensible results and reduce the perception that water projects are growth inducing, the projections must be linked to planned land uses that have undergone environmental review. Water demands should be based on water use factors developed from actual consumption data, with the methodology for forecasting clearly presented and easily understood.

Many of the required programs that chapters 2 and 3 address rely on the development of water demands configured for a specific purpose. Essential to the process is a detailed database of existing and future water demands based on the land use approach this chapter presents (*i.e.,* mapping land uses and applying a water use factor to each). This allows planners to aggregate the demands for a variety of purposes while relying on the same assumptions, source data, and open processes so important in developing water demands today.

This chapter compares approaches to demand projections and presents a detailed guide to developing existing and projected water demands using a land use-based methodology. The chapter also discusses the importance of phasing demands over time, and approaches for dealing with conflicting land use and water supply planning horizons. An important component of any water demand analysis is the assumption of demand management savings; water savings that should be built into the projections are discussed along with more aggressive programs that could reduce the need for future supplies.

An important component of any water demand analysis is the assumption of demand management savings that should be built into the projections, along with more aggressive programs that could reduce the need for future supplies.

Need for Accurate Estimating– Existing Demands

The foundation for comprehensive water supply planning is an accurate analysis of present and future water demands. Often water supply studies project future

A detailed assessment of current use is the critical building block for a variety of analyses.

demands, but pay little attention to the methods and accuracy of calculating current water use. However, a detailed assessment of current use is the critical building block for a variety of analyses.

For example, determining water demands for each land use type requires a detailed picture of existing demand usage. Examining the constraints of water system facility capacity requires a careful analysis of existing demands by small geographic areas within a water service area. Estimating potential water savings for specific conservation measures requires detailed assessments of existing uses by land use type. Projecting water demands into the future relies on existing water use patterns.

Need for Accurate Estimating— Projected Demands

Demand projections are required for long-range supply planning, sizing and scheduling of water distribution system facilities, revenue forecasts for rate studies, hydraulic modeling of infrastructure improvements, conservation planning, and risk and reliability analyses. As discussed in chapter 3, recent California legislative and court actions require that the water needs of certain proposed land use development projects be measured against the supplies available to the water purveyor. If the forecasted demands used in the purveyor's supply planning are detailed and based on planned land uses, responding to these various needs can be relatively straightforward.

Demand projections for future water supplies and for building and phasing new facilities must be as accurate as possible. If projections are too low, additional water supplies and facilities will be needed earlier than planned, and facilities may be undersized and unable to meet demand. Moreover, a dry year can trigger emergency shortages and rationing, inconveniencing existing customers and possibly resulting in economic impacts. New water supplies, especially new surface rights, are difficult to obtain and usually require a lead time of many years. During California's recent droughts (from 1976 to 1977 and from 1987 to 1992), many communities were ill prepared to respond to the shortages.

If demand projections are too high, the need for water supplies and new facilities may not be warranted for some time. This may result in facilities that are oversized and inefficient, and could lead to unnecessary environmental or community impacts and degradation of water quality. In addition, the lower-than-estimated rates or connection charges may not be adequate to repay the cost of building the facility in an appropriate time frame.

When developing demand estimates and projections, applying a greater level of detail initially will permit accurate estimating for a greater number of uses (*see* sidebar). This greater level of detail will also ensure consistency between the various uses. Water demands should be developed at a sufficient

Water Demand Database

A detailed database can provide a consistent framework for developing the following types of water demands:

- Average annual
- Seasonal
- Dry versus wet year
- Maximum day
- Peak hour
- By land use, user groups, and sectors
- Potable versus nonpotable
- Indoor versus outdoor
- Industrial use mandatory for operations
- System losses
- Geographic by node polygon and pressure zone

level of detail to permit their aggregation, thus providing a consistent basis for all infrastructure analyses. Providing one detailed source of demands will actually save the purveyor the cost of preparing a separate set of demand projections for other purposes.

Methods Used to Determine Water Demands

Three methods are typically used to determine water demands: population projections, socioeconomic or econometric models, and land use-based models.

Population-Based Projections

Because census and other population data are readily available, population projections have traditionally been the most widely used. This method applies a per capita water use coefficient to a projected service area population, and typically assumes that nonresidential water consumption will maintain the same relationship or ratio to residential population. Methods relying on the number of connections or customer classifications used for billing purposes are similar, but depend on more accurate data obtained from water purveyors for each user group.

Unfortunately, the easily accessible, straightforward population projection method has no direct connection with land use, and often no publicly accepted basis for the forecast. And because it is so generalized, population projections cannot be easily disaggregated for more detailed analyses. A per capita approach also assumes that current consumption patterns will continue into the future and that the ratio of nonresidential uses to residential uses will not change. Moreover, per capita projections are incapable of producing precise estimates of the effectiveness of conservation savings. On the other hand, population projection-based demands are relatively inexpensive to forecast, and can be of value as a single number for an entire city, if the city has fairly homogenous resdential land uses and expects no variation in the future land use mix.

Socioeconomic Modeling

Socioeconomic modeling relies on detailed computer analyses and extensive amounts of economic and demographic data. When the data are available, this method is superior to population projections because its rigor yields a greater level of accuracy. Water consumption estimates can be tied to population, as well as employees, thus accounting for nonresidential demands.

Like population projections, however, socioeconomic models have no direct connection to planned land uses, and there is no publicly accepted basis for the forecast. Often they cannot be used to predict the impact of factors

When the data are available, socioeconomic modeling is superior to population projections because its rigor yields a greater level of accuracy.

affecting demands that are not reflected in the historical data, such as improved conservation technology. Because they are highly complex, socioeconomic models have a "black box" reputation that is not readily understood by elected decisionmakers or the public, rendering the approach difficult to use in the public participation processes that are increasingly required for water supply projects.

On the other hand, a socioeconomic model may be appropriate if a large geographical area, such as the state of California, requires a projection of demands. When using an econometric model, data should be developed that utilize existing and planned land uses wherever possible. Assumptions must be clearly explained, preferably by relying on a stakeholder process. Adding these steps will help obtain support for the results. For more information on these models, *see Forecasting Urban Water Demand,* R.B. Billings and C.V. Jones, American Water Works Association (AWWA), 1996.

Land Use Method

The land use methodology is based on mapping land uses and then applying a water use factor to each category. If not already available, the existing land uses are mapped by interpreting aerial photographs and designating each land use based on a developed list of categories. Future land uses are identified from the general plan land use map, as well as from those areas where infill developments or increased densities are planned to occur. The study boundary is typically the water purveyor's designated sphere of influence. Unit demands for each land use are derived from consumption data that have been "normalized," and adjustments made to future unit demands to reflect changing conditions. The unit demands are then applied to the mapped land uses to calculate the demand per land use throughout the study area.

The land use-based approach to estimate and project demands is the most accurate, versatile, and defensible in today's environment of political and environmental sensitivity. Accuracy is enhanced by the development of demands at a fine level of detail (for a hydraulic model, for example) that can then be aggregated and used for system-wide supply projections. Since future demands are based on planned and allowable densities of land uses, this approach reduces the growth-inducing implications that arise when unplanned urban development is assumed in calculating future demands.

Coordination with Land Use Planning Efforts

When projecting defensible water demands, it is important to rely on the local planning agency to provide a clear picture of planned land uses. Water demands should represent the future land uses contemplated by each local government planning agency with land use authority. As described in chapter 3, the land use element of the general plan not only represents the land that can accommodate future growth, but has also undergone an environmental documentation process under CEQA, as well as public review and input. After land uses are mapped and labeled according to the planned uses (discussed later in this chapter), the maps should be presented to local agency land use planning staff for review, confirmation, and updating.

CEQA = California Environmental Quality Act
EIR = Environmental impact report

When evaluating the environmental effects of water supply and infrastructure facilities that rely on the water demand projections, the general plan EIR can be relied on for the primary and secondary environmental impacts associated with the planned development of land. This is a key advantage of a land use-based approach to forecasting demands. Other forecasting methods require a new analysis that describes how water demands reflect the growth a community is planning. If a correlation with the general plan land use element cannot be made, the environmental analysis must identify and address any growth-related impacts associated with the development of lands assumed to accommodate the population and employee projections used in the water demand forecast.

Developing Land Use-Based Water Demands

With a land use-based approach, it is necessary to identify study boundaries, existing and projected land uses, and existing and future unit water demands. Unit demands are then applied to the land uses, and existing unit demands are adjusted to reflect future conditions. The land use method is described more extensively below and throughout this chapter. For a list of the steps undertaken to develop existing and projected demands, *see* Figure 4-1.

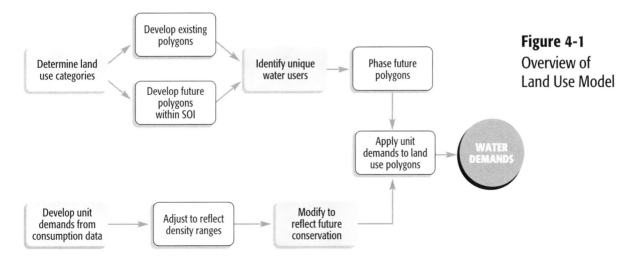

Figure 4-1
Overview of Land Use Model

Boundaries

Every city and special district in California has two boundaries established by the county's LAFCO: the city limit (for a city) or service area (for a special district), and a sphere of influence (SOI) (*see* chapter 3 for a detailed discussion of LAFCOs). LAFCO approval may be required to amend boundaries where cities have urban services boundaries but provide services to other communities (sanitary sewage collection or water service, for example). The only water purveyors that are exempt from LAFCO jurisdiction are private water companies whose boundaries are established by the California Public Utilities Commission.

The service area or city limit boundary is typically used when developing maps of existing land use, and the sphere of influence is the outer geographic boundary for projecting demands. Because the SOI boundary has been reviewed in a public CEQA process and reflects the area theoretically planned for growth, its use can greatly reduce the perception of growth inducement (of the unplanned use of land).

In addition to the SOI, some communities may use an ultimate service boundary, ultimate growth boundary, or urban limit line for infrastructure planning. This permits sizing of facilities, when initially constructed, to accommodate the planned needs of the future growth areas.

It is important to maintain the distinction between the areas within and outside the SOI boundary. First, the demand projections should reflect the land uses the community is planning through its general plan process, ensuring that the uses form the basis for sizing and phasing of infrastructure improvements. Second, the general plan environmental documentation should maintain a distinction between the SOI and any boundaries beyond (such as a planning area or ultimate service boundary) with regard to the level of environmental analysis undertaken. Subsequent analysis of growth-related impacts associated with development of lands between the two boundaries may also be necessary. Additional environmental review is required when the SOI is to be extended, which is often the case when a general plan amendment or infrastructure project relies on the growth and water demands associated with the area.

Existing Land Uses

Most analyses require that existing water demands be identified either for their own use or as a starting point for accurately projecting future demands. Existing demands can be obtained simply by determining the production requirements of the surface water treatment plant or groundwater wells. However, this "snapshot in time" must be adjusted to reflect normalized demands, so that weather and other factors do not affect the particular year chosen for study

---

Dougherty Valley

The East Bay Municipal Utility District (EBMUD) used its sphere of influence to develop the Water Supply Management Program water demands. When the Contra Costa County Board of Supervisors approved an 11,000-unit subdivision outside EBMUD's SOI, EBMUD countered that it could not guarantee a water supply to that area through an extended drought. Although the builder filed suit, EBMUD prevailed, thus establishing the validity of this approach. ∎

EBMUD = East Bay Municipal
Utility District

LAFCO = Local Agency
Formation Commission

SOI = Sphere of influence

Figure 4-2

Methodology for Distributing
Existing Contra Costa Water District
Treated Water Demands

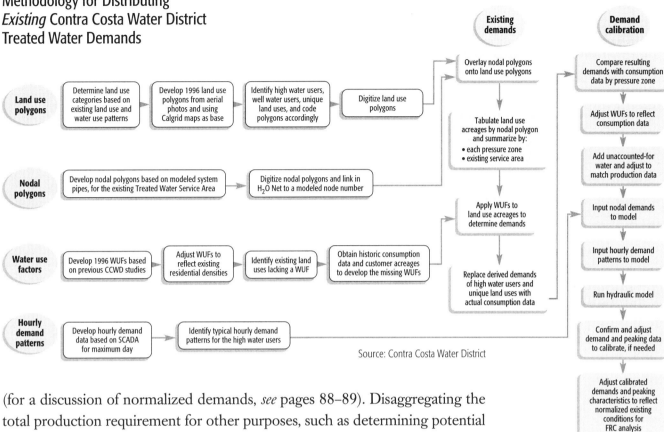

Source: Contra Costa Water District

(for a discussion of normalized demands, *see* pages 88–89). Disaggregating the total production requirement for other purposes, such as determining potential conservation savings associated with specific land uses or estimating the demand in a particular geographic area, can be challenging.

The best approach to determining existing demands is to use the steps presented in Figure 4-2. The first step is to list land use categories and densities that reflect existing land uses, taking into consideration the categories used in the general plan land use element and the purveyor's billing data.

After selecting the appropriate land use categories, the next step is to develop a map of existing land use polygons by interpreting aerial photographs and/or digital orthophotographs. The land use polygons are then digitized to become a map layer. Water distribution system maps can help define the areal extent of the existing system to be mapped, but it is also important to identify developable lands if the map will be used later to develop future water demands.

Although a computerized mapping program, such as a geographic information system (GIS), is the most efficient tool for this process, maps prepared using computer-aided design (CAD) and spreadsheet databases can also be used. Most GIS software can be used for this relatively simple application. For an example of the types of map layers needed for a water demand analysis, *see* Figure 4-3.

A certain level of skill and care is required to interpret aerial photographs accurately. Some land uses may appear to be undeveloped in aerial photos, but

CAD = Computer-aided design
CCWD = Contra Costa Water District
GIS = Geographic information system

Figure 4-3
GIS Layers Needed
for Demand Estimating

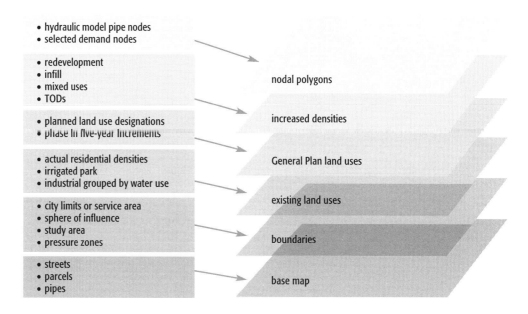

- hydraulic model pipe nodes
- selected demand nodes

nodal polygons

- redevelopment
- infill
- mixed uses
- TODs

increased densities

- planned land use designations
- phase in five-year increments

General Plan land uses

- actual residential densities
- irrigated park
- industrial grouped by water use

existing land uses

- city limits or service area
- sphere of influence
- study area
- pressure zones

boundaries

- streets
- parcels
- pipes

base map

TOD = Transit oriented
development

Distribution System Hydraulic Model

With a "real-time" Distribution System Hydraulic Model, water purveyors can simulate water distribution, analyzing deficiencies such as pressure problems, capacity constraints, and water quality conditions.

The system can also be used to study project alternatives and future needs—such as facilities and sizing—to help make capital improvement decisions. The most commonly used program in the industry is called H$_2$ONET. ■

in fact may be irrigated park land or apartment/condominium common areas. Site visits and review of billing data can confirm whether the land should be identified as "irrigated turf" or "unirrigated open space." Suburban two-story apartment buildings and small offices may also be difficult to distinguish (and have different water requirements), although apartment complexes can often be identified by their unique covered parking characteristics. Occasionally, an agency will have a detailed, up-to-date inventory of existing land uses that can be used in conjunction with the aerial photographic analysis, if the land use categories reflect water use patterns. Since the aerial photographs may be out of date, matching water demands and production with the appropriate time frame of the aerials is essential.

Highways, wide streets, and transit corridors require their own land use classification and polygons, so that the unit demands of adjoining land uses are not diluted. This is particularly important if irrigation within these polygons can be accounted for separately, and if the potential for conservation or use of nonpotable or recycled water is to be assessed for future demands. It is important to be consistent in developing polygons for each land use. Since transportation routes often account for more than ten percent of the gross acreage within a community, when polygon boundaries are being digitized, major transportation corridors should preferably all have their own polygon. Or the polygon line should be drawn down the center of the corridor, depending on the net or gross acreage approach chosen.

For an example of a digital orthophotograph illustrating mapped layers of polygons for existing land uses, *see* Figure 4-4. This example also contains a layer identifying the water meter for each customer (shown as dots). Consumption data from billing records associated with each meter are later used to determine

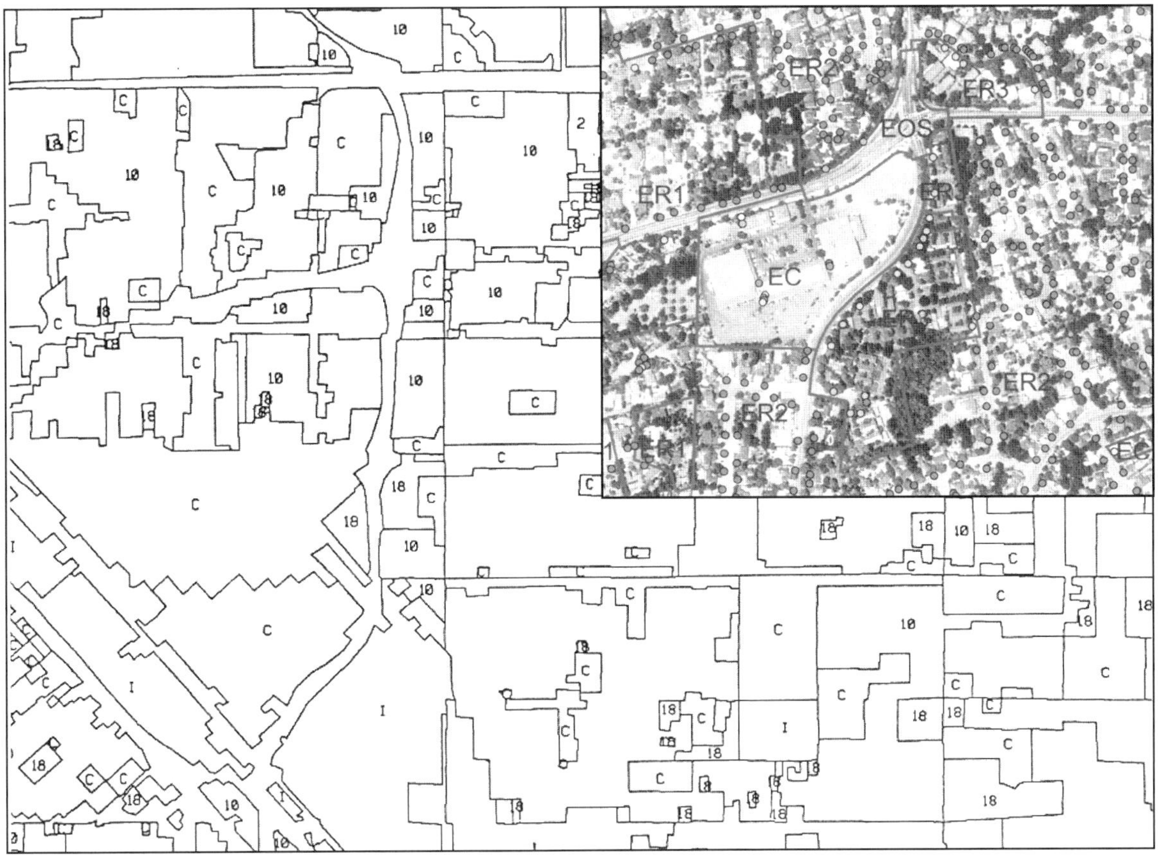

Figure 4-4
Existing Land
Use Layers

the unit demands associated with each land use category. The availability of the billing data permits a high level of accuracy. However, the accuracy depends in part on the interpretation of the consumption data as it relates to unit demands per land use category (discussed below).

Future Land Uses

For purposes of water planning, the future land use database is comprised of the following components:

- Mapped "existing land use" polygons
- Vacant lands within urbanized areas that are planned for growth
- Planned growth areas outside the urbanized areas, but within the SOI
- Potential growth areas outside the SOI
- Existing land uses that may be converted to a different land use in the future
- Underutilized lands that may increase in density with infill or redevelopment
- Specialized unique water users

The first step is to determine whether additional categories may be required for uses other than those described above. Then, a map is digitized, distinctive from the existing land use map, representing all land use polygons within the SOI or other designated boundary that are vacant, undeveloped, or underdeveloped with the potential for increased densities, and future growth areas.

The Los Vaqueros Reservoir

In 1989, prior to the common use of GIS technology, the Contra Costa Water District undertook a thorough analysis of projected water demands for use in sizing a new reservoir. The study area included the existing CCWD service area and sphere of influence, the SOIs for the raw and treated water customers, as well as lands outside the SOI that may require domestic service in the future, thus accommodating long-range supply planning in eastern Contra Costa County. The treated and raw water service area includes all of the cities of Antioch, Clayton, Concord, Martinez, Oakley, and Pittsburg, and part of the cities of Pleasant Hill and Walnut Creek.

Water demand within CCWD's SOI was projected using a methodology that relied on land uses designated in the general plans adopted by each city and the county. Anticipated major industrial demand was based on industrial customers within CCWD's service area. The study area included one city immediately adjacent to the SOI whose general plan land uses became part of the projections. For rural lands outside that city's SOI, several growth scenarios were developed demonstrating water demand under various future land use conditions.

Planned land uses were identified and mapped, and unit demands were developed. Savings resulting from long-term conservation measures by individual water purveyors within the study area were addressed. Total demands were projected separately for areas within and outside the CCWD SOI. For the reservoir sizing criteria, the CCWD Board of Directors selected the demand that reflected planned land uses within the District's SOI. By maintaining separate analyses, the Board had the flexibility to pursue various options and fully understand the implications of each scenario. ■

The 100,000 acre-foot Los Vaqueros Reservoir stores Delta water during times of high water quality.

To identify the possibility of higher-intensity development, conduct interviews with staff from the local land use planning authority (city or county community development or planning department, military, port, or airport authority, etc.) to identify current development that is underutilized, undergoing redevelopment, or experiencing intensification. These areas are then mapped and labeled by category on the "future land use" map, with the anticipated date of development generally represented in five-year increments. This is labor-intensive, but important, particularly in light of an emerging "smart growth," development style that emphasizes infill, redevelopment, and a mix of uses.

An underlying principle of smart growth is the encouragement of mixed use and higher density in targeted urban areas with established infrastructure. The result is higher unit water demand per acre, but often much lower water demand per capita, at least for residential use. This is because higher density requires less outdoor irrigation water per resident. A water system must be planned for urban infill at higher densities and per-acre water demands to prevent the possibility of low pressure from undersized pipelines and inadequate reservoir capacity.

Since a general plan land use map is typically used to identify the planned uses for new growth areas, infill areas, and vacant lands, the local planning staff should confirm current land use designations for these polygons. The planning staff should also estimate the timing of development in five-year increments to allow for phasing projected water demands.

It is imperative that future land use designations represent planned land use consistent with the community's general plan. Infrastructure planning should reflect the appropriate planning authority's anticipated land uses or, ideally, be conducted in conjunction with the general plan revision process. As discussed above, this process not only includes extensive public review, but is subject to CEQA analysis. Under this approach, water demands, and

Figure 4-5

Methodology for Projecting *Future* CCWD Treated Water Demands

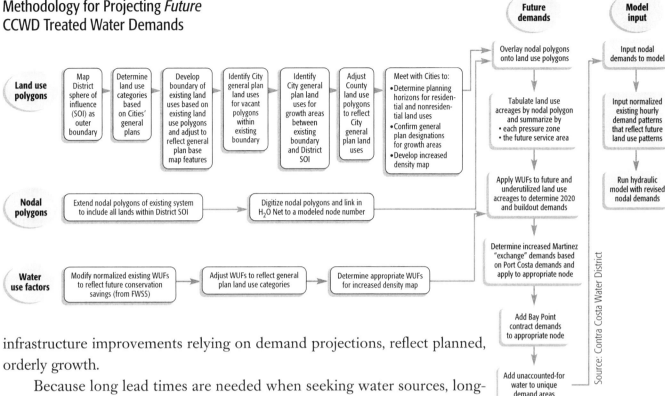

Source: Contra Costa Water District

infrastructure improvements relying on demand projections, reflect planned, orderly growth.

Because long lead times are needed when seeking water sources, long-range water supply needs may extend beyond the local jurisdiction's SOI and general plan horizon. In this case, a generalized approach is preferable, and working with the land use planning authority to obtain the most reliable data will ensure defensible results. For unplanned future demands, the areas of developable lands and the likely mix of land uses for the planning horizon year should be estimated by land use planners. To give decisionmakers clear information, these later phased land uses, and their demand projections, should be kept separate from the overall demand projections for planned growth.

This process recommended for projecting future demands requires an extensive level of detail (Figure 4-5), corresponding to the level of detail described in the discussion of a distribution system hydraulic model.

Land Use Unit Demands

Land use unit demands (LUDs) are also called water use factors (WUFs) or water duties. Usually developed in units of acre-feet per acre per year (af/ac/yr), or in gallons per day per acre (gpd/ac), they are applied to existing and future land use polygons on a per-acre basis. Sometimes figures in acre-feet of water per housing unit or per 1,000 square feet of commercial use are developed.

Unit demands are usually derived from water consumption or sales data. The more detailed the data, the more accurate the unit demands. Consumption data are typically available from the water purveyor's finance department

---

Acre-Foot

An acre-foot is 325,900 gallons, or the amount of water covering one acre of land one foot deep.

---

af/ac/yr = Acre-feet per acre per year
gpd/ac = Gallons per day per acre
LUD = Land use unit demand
WUF = Water use factor

on a monthly, bimonthly, or annual basis by billing classification for each customer and for the entire system. Some systems have data available by subareas such as hydraulic pressure zones. The data must be adjusted to reflect the selected land use categories. For example, if billing information is available for single- and multi-family residential categories and the land use categories of the demand analysis rely on different density levels, the data must be converted to unit demands for ranges of dwelling units per acre to reflect these demand patterns.

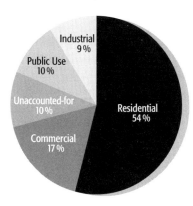

Figure 4-6

Urban Applied Water Use by Sector

Source: DWR Bulletin 160-98

UFW = Unaccounted-for water

Approximately 55 percent of total urban demands in California is classified residential, 25 percent commercial and industrial, 10 percent public, and the remaining 10 percent is unaccounted-for (Figure 4-6). To ensure the highest degree of accuracy, substantial emphasis should be given to residential use. Knowing a community's specific land use characteristics is also important in focusing the level of effort to determine existing and future water demands and the most effective techniques for demand management (*e.g.,* conservation).

In communities with unmetered uses or unread meters, like many in California's Central Valley, unit demand data can usually be obtained from a nearby community or geographic area with similar socioeconomic and demographic conditions, as well as similar soil and weather patterns. However, it may be necessary to adjust the unit demands of unmetered uses to reflect higher consumption patterns because consumption is not affected by price sensitivity. Another source of data might be an unmetered community that has conducted a test case or audit to estimate the conservation potential of single-family residential use. Yet another approach would be to calibrate the derived demands for existing uses that have consumption data (discussed below), and then calculate the demands of unmetered uses using the remaining quantities. Although newer development must now be metered, the meters are not always read.

For land use categories lacking a specific billing data category, common in residential use, unit demands can be derived by identifying and calculating the acreage of land uses that are similar to the density desired. Two to three years of billing data for individuals within the designated density range can be averaged to arrive at an annual quantity, and the total use can then be calculated per acre.

Consumption patterns may differ between pressure zones and service areas due to slope, age and type of vegetation, socioeconomic conditions (income), and wind and other climatic conditions. Current use of other sources, such as private wells and recycled water, or areas other water purveyors serve should be considered as the land use inventory is being developed so that these demands can be calculated separately. Water rates can influence demands, as demonstrated by unmetered residential use and households in neighborhoods with high income, both of which generally have the highest per capita demand in the state. Other factors to consider include adding the use of unaccounted-for water (UFW) to the unit demands, and how to represent high-volume users.

Table 4-1 summarizes unit demands for various urban land use categories for an agency in the inner San Francisco Bay Area. While the unit demands are based on actual consumption, the residential unit demands have been normalized, and a 10 percent UFW factor has been applied. These unit demands are lower than for most communities within the state, and even within the Bay Area, due to the area's cooler climate, large areas of currently underutilized commercial and industrial lands, residential densities with small areas dedicated to landscaping, and older, established landscaping that requires less water for irrigation.

Unaccounted-for Water

Often the data for overall consumption and production quantities differ. Consumption data reflect the amount of water passing through a customer's meter at or near the point of use, and production quantities reflect the metered supply of water entering or exiting a treatment plant or production well. The difference between the two, usually called unmeasured or unaccounted-for water, is accommodated in accurate demand estimating.

Unaccounted-for water may represent a system problem, such as a pipeline leak or loss at a treatment plant or reservoir. Or it may reflect a known use that is not billed, such as water used by a municipal facility. UFW also comes from meter errors, fire hydrant flushing, theft, construction, and the public's non-metered use (Figure 4-7). In a well-managed system, UFW should add up to no more than 10 to 15 percent of the total (Jim Angers, AWWA Small Systems Helpline Specialist, AWWA *Opflow* July 2001). Losses exceeding 15 percent are typical of older communities with aging water supply systems.

An estimate of unaccounted-for water can be made by comparing total production data to total consumption or billing data. For an example of this, *see* Table 4-2. To calculate unit demands, the estimated percentage of UFW is added to each consumption-based unit demand, arriving at a more accurate estimate of total existing water demands. Unless efforts are made

LAND USE CATEGORY	UNIT DEMAND*
Residential	
Low-density residential (0.1–2.9 du/ac)	0.6
Medium-density residential (3–9.9 du/ac)	1.9
High-density residential (10–19.9 du/ac)	4.9
Very high-density residential (20–50 du/ac)	10.7
Commercial/Industrial	
Industrial low volume	0.7
General commercial/industrial	2.1
Office and industrial	2.1
High-density office	4.8
High-volume users (top ten for two years)	Specific to each use
Public and Other Uses	
Public and quasi-public	1.5
Irrigated parks/turf areas	0.5
Schools	1.0
Open space and vacant lands	No water demands

Table 4-1. Average Unit Demands for a Moderate Climate Area

* af/ac/yr

Figure 4-7
Sources of Unaccounted-for Water

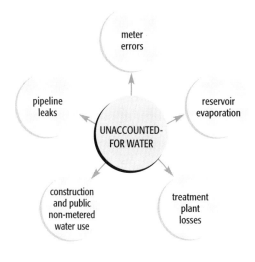

Table 4-2. Unaccounted-for Water in millions of gallons				
YEAR	TOTAL PRODUCTION	TOTAL CONSUMPTION	WATER LOSS	UFW PERCENTAGE
1987	12,776	11,571	1,201	9.4
1988	11,839	11,738	101	0.9
1989	11,981	11,388	593	4.9
1990	12,107	11,686	421	3.5
1991	9,226	8,487	739	8.0
1992	10,594	9,514	1,080	8.7
1993	10,950	9,993	957	8.7
1994	11,430	10,306	1,124	9.8
1995	10,923	10,065	858	7.9
1996	11,708	10,799	909	7.8

The analysis of unaccounted-for water can be applied by pressure zone to determine ranges of unaccounted-for water within the system and specific areas of higher UFW.

to reduce the UFW, this percentage can also be applied to future unit demands. Moreover, the analysis can be applied by pressure zone to determine ranges of unaccounted-for water within the system and specific areas of higher UFW.

Estimating the causes and quantities of UFW loss involves several steps:

- Reviewing water purveyor meter data, meter routes, and billing cycle data, and evaluating its accuracy
- Reviewing production data and evaluating the accuracy of consumption and production data by pressure zone, when available
- Determining areas of high unaccounted-for water use and identifying known water use; investigating construction use, known leaks, tank drainage or overflows, line flushing and hydrant tests, use in fire suppression, public uses such as street cleaning and unmetered parks, and other uses
- Identifying possible causes of system loss such as leaks, meter errors, and illegal usage
- Conducting leak detection testing, if warranted, in various areas representative of the distribution system to quantify potential UFW associated with leaks throughout the system

Cost-effective solutions, such as pipe replacement programs, to reduce or manage system loss, should be recommended. For more information about estimating and reducing system losses from leaks, *see Water Audits and Leak Detection* (Manual 36), AWWA 1999.

High-Volume Water Users

In the development of land use inventories and unit demands, land use maps should have a separate classification for high-volume water users, indicating their areal coverage as a polygon. Several years of consumption data can be retrieved for the top five to ten water users identified as separate polygons, and averaged to derive the typical annual water consumption per year on a per-acre basis. Each high-volume water user should be labeled separately so that its existing water demands are not included in the average for its respective land use.

Users that consistently show up on a list of high-volume water use should be treated individually. For smaller, primarily residential communities, five to ten high-volume water users are typical. For larger water districts with extensive industrial uses, as many as 20 may be typical. High-volume users include refineries, food processing industries, golf courses, hospitals, and unique users with single meters like universities and government institutions. Sorting annual water consumption records in descending order will typically reveal a natural breakpoint that separates the highest-volume users from the others, and the difference may be an order of magnitude (*e.g.,* 1,000 versus 100).

Sorting annual water consumption records in descending order will typically reveal a natural breakpoint that separates the highest-volume users from the others, and the difference may be an order of magnitude.

Applying Unit Demands to Land Uses

Before using existing unit demands to forecast future unit demands, several adjustments must be made. First, apply unit demands to existing land uses to calibrate the unit demands, ensuring that actual conditions are reflected. Then normalize the calibrated demands to remove any weather conditions that might influence unit demands (*e.g.,* above or below normal rainfall). Finally, apply the variables described below by land use category and geographic region to reflect anticipated future water demand conditions.

When applying unit demands to an existing land use database, select the boundary map layers reflecting the geographic area of interest, starting with the outside boundary. The outside boundary could be the city limits or its sphere of influence. Within the outer boundary, another boundary map is then created for the demand polygons.

Demand polygons, which consist of smaller divisions of interest within the study area, can vary significantly in size. Typical demand polygons include small junction (node) polygons for use in a hydraulic model, service area that might reflect groups of meter routes, areas of responsibility for a Board of Directors, zones with varying water rates, a city or special district boundary, a special hydraulic study area for capacity analyses, and so forth.

Unit demands are applied to the acreage of each land use within the demand polygon. In Table 4-3, the demand polygons represent pressure zones. The maps for the outer boundary and the demand polygons are combined

Table 4-3. Calculating Demands				
PRESSURE ZONE	BUSINESS PARK acres : af/ac/yr	RETAIL COMMERCIAL acres : af/ac/yr	LOW-DENSITY RESIDENTIAL* acres : af/ac/yr	TOTAL DEMANDS acre-feet / year
10	298 : 1.47	317 : 2.48	1,083 : 1.76	3,130
20	10 : 1.47	117 : 2.48	1,892 : 1.85	3,805

* Low Density Residential
   (3–6 dwelling units / acre)

with the map(s) for the land use polygons. Acreages by land use calculated for each demand polygon are stored in a land use inventory or spreadsheet that identifies the total number of acres per land use (in this instance, a simple GIS calculation can save a lot of time).

Unit demands are then applied to the acreage of each land use within each demand polygon. Using this method, a land use inventory spreadsheet can be developed for any geographic area (*e.g.,* pressure zone or meter reading route) with its own boundary map and the desired water demands determined for the area.

The water demands may be for an entire service area or for a small special study area. A distribution system hydraulic model requires a detailed knowledge of water demands along most of the pipes in the system and at each node or pipe junction. A nodal polygon map consisting of thousands of demand polygons can be superimposed on a land use polygon map to create a land use inventory, with unit demands applied to each of the land uses within each demand polygon.

The resulting demand polygon data can then serve as input files for a distribution system hydraulic model. Some agencies like EBMUD have even developed their own hydraulic model program with a direct link to a separately developed, land use-based water demand database. GIS calculations can be easily linked to a hydraulic model using software such as H$_2$OMAP. In fact, with the H$_2$OMAP Allocator program, stored customer meter data and hydraulic models are linked directly, a feature that will likely be commonplace for all future distribution system models.

Calibrating and Normalizing Existing Demands

After unit demands are applied to the land use inventory, it is possible to calibrate the resulting existing demands. First, compare total production and consumption to the calculated demands. The production total for water treatment plant(s) and/or well production is usually available from the operations department. The consumption total reflects the amount of water billed to customers in the system, but does not reflect unaccounted-for water, discussed previously. When unit demands are based on billing data, consumption should match calculated water demands. If an estimate of unaccounted-for water has been applied to unit demands, then the total calculated demand should be compared to production data.

When total production or consumption differs from the calculated demands, the following questions should be asked:

- If consumption totals are lower than calculated demands, was an estimate of unaccounted-for water added to the unit demands?
- Is there a match between the production data and land use inventory timeframes?
- Is there a match between the production and consumption timeframes?
- Were high-volume water users assigned their own land use category?
- Do unit demands reflect actual existing densities? Don't assume that because an area has a general plan designation of a particular density, that is the existing density.

If these questions have been answered satisfactorily and the information still doesn't match, review unit demands for variability. Focusing first on residential demand (since residential comprises the predominant land use), adjust the unit factors until the calculated demands correspond to consumption data. This may involve obtaining specific customer consumption records, and the land use acreage associated with the consumption quantity, to derive additional unit demand data. The more specific the data, the greater the level of accuracy. If this information is not available and calculated demands are being compared to total production, an estimate of unaccounted-for water should be added to the unit demands at this point rather than after calibration.

When the calculated demands match with the annual production or consumption data, calibration for that year is complete. Unit demands can then be normalized for typical existing conditions. If developed from only one year of data, existing unit demands must be normalized to remove climatic, drought, drought recovery, and/or economic variables, so that unit demands reflect typical or average conditions. Any part of the unit demands associated with outdoor irrigation is directly affected by weather conditions. If the consumption data are from a wet or dry year, unit demands associated with land uses that include irrigation–single-family residential, parks, schools, etc.–should be adjusted accordingly. Another method for normalizing data is to average several years of consumption data. Once normalized, existing unit demands are used to estimate future conditions, described below.

Surface Water Supply Update for Western Placer County

In 2001, the Placer County Water Agency, a water provider serving Placer County, produced a useful public dialogue tool related to long-term water supply and demands. Specifically targeting local land use jurisdictions and those interested in the interactions between development decisions and availability of water supply, Placer County's report was described as a work in progress, designed to elicit dialogue and discussion. However, it is more than a discussion paper. It is a highly accessible analysis of the long-term Water Demand/Supply Balance.

Several elements in the document are noteworthy. Its demand assumptions are based on the adopted general plans of each of the four cities in the western part of the county, and on the county general plan, which is further divided into nine separate area/ community plans. This level of detail and common-sense breakdown of buildout areas makes the analysis easy to follow.

The general plan maps are consolidated on a single map that is, like all of the information in the document, available on compact disc as an interactive graphic. It also establishes land use-based water demands for nine separate land use categories. The document looks at spheres of influence, rural water demands, and environmental water needs and examines several future scenarios based on different growth rate projections. ■

Future Land Use Unit Demands

Factors to Consider When Deriving *Future* Unit Demands from *Existing* Demands

- Short- and long-term conservation savings
- State plumbing and other codes with mandatory conservation devices
- Office vacancy rate changes
- Intensification of redeveloped or reused lands throughout the community, not just in targeted areas
- Trends in household sizes
- Age of established versus new landscaping
- New development utilizing larger footprint (less landscaping) or more stories
- New development built at upper end of allowable density range

After calibrating and normalizing existing unit demands, future demands can be derived for future land use categories. Even when the categories themselves do not change, the existing unit demands may have to change to reflect future unit demands. Adjustments are needed to reflect changing conditions in areas of new growth, such as new development at the upper end of an allowable density range, conservation savings associated with plumbing code changes, and so forth (*see* sidebar).

These projections require an understanding of regional trends in land use planning. More an art than a science since data are not always available, future land use trends are difficult to predict. But through careful observation of changes over time, an experienced land use or water resources planner can generalize from demographic and land use development trends to make judgments about the following:

- Availability and value of land in the community and region
- Historic versus anticipated density
- Community land use policies, such as encouraging compact growth versus sprawl
- The nature of the local economy and its impact on income and sensitivity to water rates
- Business trends that might affect patterns of water use, including changes in the number of employees versus total square footage changes
- Jobs and housing balance within the community and region
- Commercial changes within specific neighborhoods
- Demographic trends, including the number of people and appliances per household, or increased use of appliances
- Higher housing prices that encourage remodeling, resulting in the acquisition of additional appliances, bathrooms, and automatic watering systems
- Value of land and related factors

If you have sufficient time and resources, a sensitivity analysis of each factor will reveal trends. Savings from conservation and from plumbing code requirements are standard assessments that all California water purveyors have developed, although the impact on overall demands is difficult to prove.

Future land use unit demands must reflect any savings anticipated from planned future efforts to manage water demand, such as programs to conserve water and reduce unaccounted-for use. Accurately applying estimates of conservation savings to unit demands is important. How conservation programs can affect demand projections is described below.

For a land use polygon representing a potential for infill and increased density, a new unit demand is required that reflects the use of more water per

EBMUD's Land Use-Based Approach to Demands

The primary objective of EBMUD's "District-wide Update of Water Demand Projections" was to develop tools that would enable the district to evaluate various water system demands on a macro and micro level using a common database with a high level of accuracy.

At the macro level, water demands were calculated for land within the Ultimate Service Boundary (for supply planning purposes) and by region within the district (since climatic and demographic conditions on the east side of the Oakland hills vary significantly from those on the west side).

At the micro level, demands were calculated by nodal demand polygon (for use in a distribution system hydraulic model) and can be used in the future for individual land use categories (to evaluate water conservation). The project was uniquely accurate in determining water use factors (referred to as Land Use Unit Demands) and the distribution of existing demands, because many assumptions that had typically been crafted from experience and

The water demands reflect very different densities of land use.

professional judgment relied on actual data. The result is an industry model that represents a new level of land use-based demand projections.

Key features of the EBMUD example include:

- Land uses in a geographic information system are linked electronically with a water consumption database, and electronic calculation tools are developed
- The district's ultimate service boundary (USB) and the LAFCO sphere of influence are used as boundaries
- Actual land uses and actual consumption data are reflected
- Twenty-two land use planning agencies were consulted for future growth data from the general plans
- Planning agencies identify phasing of new growth
- Infill and redevelopment are accommodated

- District conservation goals are included
- Results are more easily explained and defended than with other approaches, and assumptions are clearly presented and transparent
- Results can be disaggregated for multiple uses while relying on the same data

For the approach used to develop existing and projected demands and the calculation tools necessary for updates, *see* Figure 4-8.

The methodology selected was land use-based demand projections and two GIS tools developed specifically to simplify calculations for such a vast quantity of generated data. A GIS for existing and future land uses within the district USB helped create the land use databases. The development of existing and future land use polygons relied on the following steps:

- Identification of appropriate land use categories
- Determination and digitizing of existing land use based on interpretation of digital orthophotographs and field surveys
- A thorough calibration analysis of existing land use and demands
- Development and digitizing of future land use based on input provided by local planning agencies

An electronic mapping program was used to create land use polygons for each cluster of parcels with a similar use. Attributes were assigned to each polygon

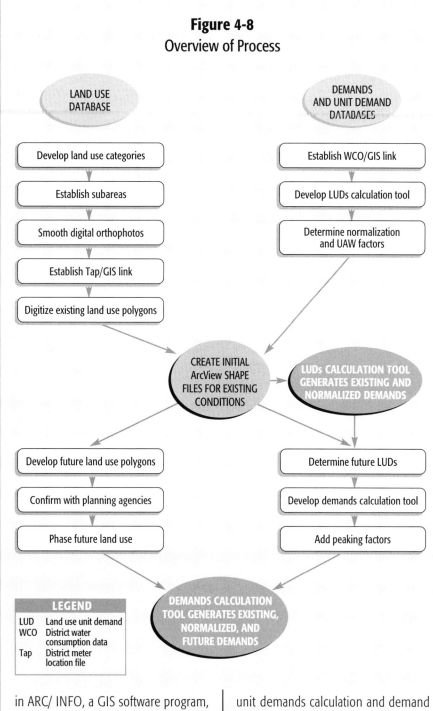

Figure 4-8
Overview of Process

LAND USE DATABASE

- Develop land use categories
- Establish subareas
- Smooth digital orthophotos
- Establish Tap/GIS link
- Digitize existing land use polygons

DEMANDS AND UNIT DEMAND DATABASES

- Establish WCO/GIS link
- Develop LUDs calculation tool
- Determine normalization and UAW factors

CREATE INITIAL ArcView SHAPE FILES FOR EXISTING CONDITIONS

LUDs CALCULATION TOOL GENERATES EXISTING AND NORMALIZED DEMANDS

- Develop future land use polygons
- Confirm with planning agencies
- Phase future land use

- Determine future LUDs
- Develop demands calculation tool
- Add peaking factors

DEMANDS CALCULATION TOOL GENERATES EXISTING, NORMALIZED, AND FUTURE DEMANDS

LEGEND

LUD	Land use unit demand
WCO	District water consumption data
Tap	District meter location file

in ARC/ INFO, a GIS software program, with a land use classification and subarea designation.

These graphic representations were converted into ArcView, another more user-friendly GIS program. The shape files then became a source of data for the unit demands calculation and demand calculation tools discussed below.

A unique advantage of the project was the availability of EBMUD's billing records, representing a customer consumption database (called Water Consumption Oracle or WCO database), that were linked

acre. This can be based on consumption data from specifically identified customers with patterns of similar usage or may be available from neighboring communities already experiencing more intense land use patterns.

When a thorough analysis of existing demands cannot be conducted prior to analyzing future demands, the focus should be placed on identifying future water use factors. These should be based on consumption data that have been adapted for future land use categories to reflect changing demographic and land use pattern changes, as discussed above.

Phasing Demands and Planning Horizons

Coordination with land use planning authorities includes the probable phasing of development for future land uses. Phasing indicates the timing of water service for a particular area, with forecasts for water demands typically developed in 5-year increments for the first 20 years, and in 10-year increments to the planning horizon.

Most general plans are based on a buildout date of about 20 years (although no specific time horizon is required by law). Many of the planned land uses are not necessarily expected to occur in that timeframe, but are assumed to develop for the purpose of holding capacity and environmental analyses. Land use planning authorities

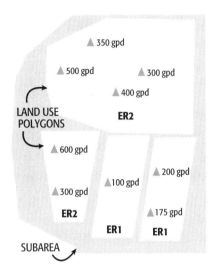

Figure 4-9
Calculation of Existing LUDs

Subarea Shape File Data			
UNITS	ACREAGE	DEMANDS	SUBAREA LUD
ER1	0.75	475	630
ER2	1.9	2650	1400

Source: MWH

electronically to another database that included each customer's meter (known as the "Tap" coordinates database). The customer meters were spatially located in a GIS file linked to the digitized land use polygon and boundary GIS files developed in ARC/INFO for this project. Customer water meters are represented as dots in Figure 4-4.

Consumption information was extracted using a GIS-based LUD Calculation Tool and used to populate the land use polygons (shape files). The consumption data for each land use polygon were then totalled and divided by total polygon acreage, resulting in unit demands per land use polygon. For a simplified example of this approach, *see* Figure 4-9.

The Calculation Tool is of particular importance because water demand varies widely within EBMUD's large service area due to climate, topography, pattern of land use, etc. The tool easily calculates the LUD for each polygon and for the subarea in which the polygon is located, based on actual consumption data for a given year. It also calculates the normalized subarea LUD, using formulas that remove unusual weather factors, for use in developing a future LUD. It adds in the estimates of unaccounted-for water that reflect production requirements versus consumption characteristics. Thus, the existing LUDs relied on actual consumption data and became the basis for future LUDs.

Future LUDs, relying on land uses designated in the general plan and discussions with each of the 22 land use planning agencies in EBMUD's service area, were then developed for the following land use characteristics:

- Vacant lands within the urbanized areas larger than one-half acre

- Growth areas outside the urbanized area but within the urban service boundary and LAFCO-designated sphere of influence

- Existing land uses anticipated to be converted to a different land use in the future

- Distinctive areas of underutilized lands anticipated to increase in density

The GIS shape files for future land uses indicate the amount of water needed to serve a particular area in five-year increments, based on input the planning agencies provided. The shape files for the existing land use polygons contain attributes indicating the year the land use will change and its anticipated classification.

Once the the LUD Calculation Tool identified existing and normalized use factors (in gpd per acre for each land use polygon), normalized LUDs were adjusted to reflect anticipated future consumption and land use patterns, including planned water conservation savings. Adjustments reflect the construction of new development at densities higher than historic levels but within the allowable general plan range, as well as the changing number of people per household, anticipated office vacancy rates, and other urban trends that are difficult to quantify but must be accounted for.

Adjustments were made to the normalized LUDs for each land use by subarea to determine future LUDs. A second ARC/INFO GIS tool, called the Demands Calculation Tool, was developed to populate the existing and future land use polygon attributes in the shape files with LUDs to calculate demands within any given boundary. The Demands Calculation tool multiplies the acreage of each polygon by the appropriate LUD to determine future demands, storing the information for each land use polygon in five-year increments through the year 2030. Thus, it's possible to project total demands for any given time period by defining the area of interest and adding up the demands for each land use polygon. All the information is linked directly to the hydraulic model for an accurate representation of future demands in the distribution system. ■

usually have a fairly reliable indication of developer interest and community intent when asked to estimate the timing of new growth and redevelopment.

The planning horizon for water demand projections typically extends beyond 20 years for supply planning and about 20 years for planning major facilities.

The planning horizon for water demand projections typically extends beyond 20 years for supply planning and about 20 years for planning major facilities. Thus, land use planning authorities should provide realistic (versus hypothetical) projections when phasing development beyond the general plan horizon.

To accommodate a planning horizon of 40 to 50 years, which is often well beyond the planning horizon of a general plan, land use demands projected within the sphere of influence must be clearly distinguished from estimates made beyond that boundary. Staging water supplies and facilities based on demands inside the SOI boundary (for an initial phase) should be distinguished from facilities staged on demands outside the SOI.

Typically, the environmental review for a general plan addresses environmental impacts associated with the full development of all planned land uses within the SOI. As a result, the environmental impacts need only be referred to in the environmental documentation required for new water supplies and facilities. A project-level EIR should still be prepared for the facilities and supplies needed to serve development within the SOI, which can then be combined with a program-level analysis of facilities expansion and acquisition of additional supplies. The program-level analysis would address the water needs of lands outside the SOI.

In cases addressing the long range supply needs–for lands beyond those specified in the community's general plan–a project-level EIR may be needed because the acquisition lead time is so long. Representing the demand (or need) assumptions spatially can make environmental analysis less difficult. The primary and secondary impacts (construction and increased traffic, respectively) associated with growth can then be adequately addressed.

Demand Management

Managing demands can take the form of pricing water service, reducing the amount of unaccounted-for or lost water, lowering pressure within the distribution system, and implementing conservation measures. Demand management options are often evaluated before or in parallel with identification of alternative water supply sources.

Rate structures and pricing strategies that encourage conservation include inclining block rates, seasonal pricing, surcharges for excess use, new metering (as long as a consumption-related rate structure is implemented), and incentive fees that act as surcharges until a property owner retrofits with water-saving fixtures. Demand reductions tied to rate structure changes depend on a variety of factors unrelated to price, such as weather, household income, number and age of occupants, and irrigated land. For more information on rate structures, *see*

Designing, Evaluating, and Implementing Conservation Rate Structures, A Handbook Sponsored by California Urban Water Conservation Council, July 1997; "Long Term Effects of Conservation Rates," American Water Works Association Research Foundation, AWWA 2000; and *Water-Supply Planning, Issues, Concepts & Risks*, D. Prasifka, Van Nostrand Reinhold Company, 1988.

Various sources of unaccounted-for water use have been described previously, but it's worth noting that developing countries sometimes experience huge losses after constructing a new pump or water treatment plant with higher pressure. Although not a preferred strategy, installing pressure-reducing valves can decrease consumption and unaccounted-for loss associated with system leaks.

Long-term conservation savings can range from implementing state or local plumbing codes that require low water use fixtures to conservation measures targeted for emergency drought management.

Benefits of Conservation

The benefits of conservation include reduced operation and maintenance costs, particularly for energy and chemicals, reduced capital costs, and the ability to serve customers with less resource impact. Capital cost savings from water supply projects can result from deferring, reducing the size of, or eliminating capital projects. This may also produce environmental benefits by forestalling facilities that could affect stream flows or groundwater levels. In addition to savings for the water user and purveyor, conservation can also benefit other entities, such as the wastewater treatment provider. While conservation alone cannot solve all supply-related problems, reduced demands through conservation can significantly contribute to meeting needs.

From the perspective of deferring or reducing proposed capital improvement projects, reducing the amount of water used during the summer season is very effective. Peaking factors representing variations from average day demands–typically recorded for maximum day, peak hour, and minimum month water demands–are used to project capacity needs for infrastructure improvement, including facilities for treatment, distribution, and treated water storage. Although not a major focus, minimum monthly water demands are important because they generally represent indoor consumption or use that is not weather related, which is more difficult to reduce. For an illustration of a seasonal hydrograph showing the quantities required for above- and below-average months for residential land use, *see* Figure 4-10.

When trying to lower peak water demands, a prime target is exterior use by single-family homes and public agencies. Water conservation for

> **Conservation-Encouraging Rate Structures**
>
> **Inclining Block Rate.** The price per unit increases as the quantity purchased increases.
>
> **Seasonal Pricing.** The price per unit increases during summer months and is reduced during winter months.
>
> **Excess Use Surcharge.** A surcharge is applied if the total quantity purchased exceeds a pre-established limit.

Figure 4-10
Typical Seasonal Hydrograph–Urban Water Demand

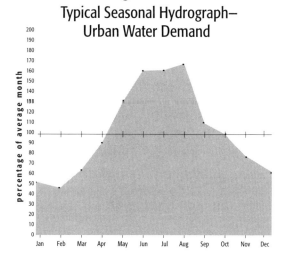

BMP = Best management practice
CUWCC = California Urban Water Conservation Council
MOU = Memorandum of understanding
ULFT = Ultra low flow toilet

Best Management Practice

A BMP is a policy, program, rule, regulation, or ordinance—or the use of devices, equipment, or facilities—that water purveyors generally employ to use water efficiently.

Table 4-4. Urban BMPs

① Water Survey Program for single- and multi-family residential customers
② Residential plumbing retrofit
③ Distribution system water audits, leak detection, repair
④ Metering with commodity rates
⑤ Large landscape conservation programs/incentives
⑥ High-efficiency washing machine rebate programs
⑦ Public information programs
⑧ School education programs
⑨ Commercial/industrial/institutional conservation programs
⑩ Wholesale agency assistance programs
⑪ Conservation pricing
⑫ Conservation coordinator
⑬ Water waste prohibition
⑭ Residential ULFT replacement programs

Source: California Urban Water Conservation Council, March 2001

irrigated turf associated with parks, playing fields, and schools can save a significant amount. Priority should also be given to residential land use of low to medium density that usually accounts for the largest total quantity of water use, with a large portion related to outdoor irrigation. Commercial and industrial water consumption, as well as consumption for large multi-family land uses with irrigated common areas, are also good candidates for conservation.

The downside is that conservation reduces a utility's revenue, which was the case in California when two severe droughts required conservation and rationing. Another disadvantage is that a "hardening" of demand limits a utility's ability to achieve significant reductions during a future drought.

A potential side effect of a formally adopted conservation program is the public perception that saving water will accommodate additional growth. This concern actually caused EBMUD's Board of Directors to delay becoming a signatory party to the Urban Water Conservation Best Management Practices Memorandum of Understanding (MOU), discussed below.

Conservation Best Management Practices

In 1991, water agencies, cities, counties, state agencies, and public interest groups throughout California crafted an agreement committing water suppliers to implement aggressive water conservation measures. This historic agreement was called the Urban Water Conservation Best Management Practices Memorandum of Understanding. State and federal regulatory agencies have incorporated many of the MOU conditions into their reviews and approvals for new water projects or stream diversion requests.

The MOU developed fourteen conservation Best Management Practices (BMPs) that signatories must implement to the extent that the implementation is economically sound (*see* chapter 2). The BMPs are listed in Table 4-4 and described in more detail in Appendix C.

The DWR Division of Planning and Local Assistance and the California Urban Water Conservation Council have a number of up-to-date water conservation publications ranging from how to evaluate BMPs for a conservation program to implementing a particular BMP. For more information, contact the DWR Publications Office (916/653-1097) or CUWCC (916/552-5885 or www.cuwcc.org).

Designing a Conservation Program

A water conservation program should be based on need and benefits, with measures targeted at those land uses with the highest demand or where the greatest savings can be achieved in a cost-effective manner.

Plumbing Code Upgrades. To estimate water savings resulting from plumbing code upgrades, multiply the number of homes expected to convert to ultra low-flow toilets by the number of flushes per home. Homes constructed or remodeled prior to 1980 typically require 5 to 7 gallons per flush; those built between 1980 and 1994 typically use 3.5 gallons; and those sold in California since 1994 need 1.6 gallons. The conservation analysis should include an assumption of total saturation, meaning that all homes contain water-efficient fixtures. The projected water savings per dwelling unit can be derived from plumbing end use studies and from demographic data. Savings for a specific land use can then be estimated per acre, and that number can be used to adjust future unit demands.

Screening. In evaluating best management practices, first screen all potential conservation measures for appropriateness. Qualitative criteria representing non-monetary factors should be developed prior to launching an assessment of potential savings or a cost-benefit analysis for each measure. *See* the sidebar for examples. Disaggregated demand data from the land use-based approach can be particularly helpful when identifying uses that might produce effective water savings and best accommodate BMPs. After screening, the BMPs are analyzed for cost-effectiveness.

Potential Water Savings. Quantifying the savings associated with water conservation can be difficult. However, with a land use-based approach for estimating and projecting demands, trends can be easily identified and tracked before and after a measure is implemented. This information can be useful when periodically evaluating a measure's effectiveness. Because weather and other hydrologic conditions can mask annual savings, monitoring for an initial period of several years may be needed to produce an accurate estimate of conservation effectiveness.

Consumption data are analyzed to estimate indoor versus outdoor consumption for each land use, with indoor usually determined by the lowest monthly consumption (during winter or rainy months). For single-family residential land use, the majority is applied outdoors (40 to 60 percent depending on climate, soils, lot size, and other conditions), followed by water for toilets and washing machines (Figure 4-11). Commercial use is primarily for restrooms, followed by cooling and heating, and landscaping. Industrial use of water is primarily for rinsing, followed by fume scrubbers and cooling systems, with a small portion associated with water treatment, landscaping, and restrooms.

Examples of Initial BMP Screening Criteria

- Already implemented
- Sufficient data for evaluation
- Technical feasibility
- Environmental impacts
- Implementation difficulty
- Customer acceptance
- Better measure available

Figure 4-11
Typical Single-Family Residential Water Usage

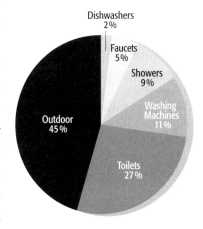

Dishwashers 2%
Faucets 5%
Showers 9%
Washing Machines 11%
Outdoor 45%
Toilets 27%

Source: DWR Bulletin 160-98

Urban Water Conservation Certification

In recent years, a working group of stakeholders and water conservation specialists was established to develop a mechanism for certifying that water purveyors with a connection to the CALFED Bay-Delta Program follow the best management practices set forth in the Urban Water Conservation MOU. The result is to be a standard procedure to certify that a water provider has met and continues to practice BMPs for water use efficiency—providing a set of incentives for those who are certified and potential penalties for those who fall short.

Proponents stress that the certification process would give federal and state funding agencies a common standard for assessing the conservation efforts of each purveyor and would enable the public to identify purveyors who take conservation seriously. Moreover, proponents suggest, an accepted measurement standard would reduce the need for prolonged debate and analysis of conservation for each water supply or integrated resource plan.

Opponents stress that each water system has its own unique weather, soils, demographic, and economic characteristics that reflect whether a BMP is cost effective to initiate or continue practicing, and that the process is just another requirement for agencies already burdened with legislative mandates.

One approach that has been proposed is for the State Water Resources Control Board to rely on input, oversight, technical advice, and studies of specific BMPs from the California Urban Water Conservation Council to make enforcement decisions regarding water supplier certification. These decisions would be integrated with the requirements of the CVPIA and Urban Water Management Plans. Smaller water purveyors (with fewer than 3,000 connections) would not have to be certified. Mid-size purveyors (3,000 to 20,000 connections) would file reports on their BMP-related activities at prescribed intervals that are coordinated with UWMPs. Larger purveyors (20,000 connections or more) would have an additional monitoring and reporting requirement. The working group is exploring various incentives and penalties that might be applied to ensure compliance.

This group continues to refine its approach. The end result may be state legislation or possibly administrative rulemaking for various state water programs. ■

Once water usage data are established for each land use, estimated savings associated with each conservation measure can be evaluated. Estimates of savings associated with a particular measure, including the retention rate, are usually based on field data for large samples. In the absence of specific historical data for the study area, it's necessary to rely on published water savings data relevant to the study area's specific conditions. *Residential End Uses of Water*, American Water Works Association Research Foundation 1999, is an excellent reference for residential land use. *Commercial and Institutional End Uses of Water* (also by AWWARF 2000) is another good reference. Variables of the study area may include such conditions as weather, land use and density, irrigated areas associated with land uses, demographics such as household size, and socioeconomic factors. Water savings often develop slowly, reaching full maturity after maximum market penetration has been achieved, five to ten years after the start of a program.

Benefits. Benefits from conserving water include the reduced costs of operation and maintenance, as well as reduced capital and supply requirements in the future. While the cost of providing water is generally fixed, some costs are reduced when production is reduced. These include power for pumping and chemicals for treatment to enhance the quality of drinking water. To estimate this amount, divide the annual cost of an item affected by demand (pumping, for example) by the total production volume associated with the item. Reduction in water production leads to a straight-line or proportional reduction. If the benefits of saving water exceed what it costs to generate those benefits, then the measure is considered cost effective (*see* adjacent sidebar).

A benefit can also result from the deferral, downsizing, or elimination of future capital projects, including obtaining new supplies. Figure 4-12 demonstrates how conservation savings can affect the

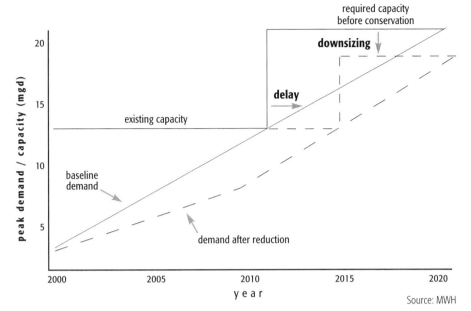

Figure 4-12
Conservation Effects
on Facilities Planning

timing or need for new capacity or facilities. Long lead times are often required to plan major capital improvements. If the need for a new project can be delayed due to predicted conservation savings, you must monitor the program's effectiveness and make adjustments corresponding to capital improvement plans.

As shown in Figure 4-13, avoided costs are associated with reduced annual operating expenses, as well as the capital costs saved from project delay. Total savings are based on costs that have been avoided as well as water savings associated with the selected conservation measures.

Costs. The costs of water conservation are usually associated with the costs an agency incurs to implement a particular measure or program. It may be possible to share some program expenses with other public or private entities, thus reducing individual agency costs. When preparing the estimate, use the full period required to implement the plan (typically ten years), along with the average annual cost over the same timeframe.

Benefit-Cost Analysis. To prepare a benefit-cost analysis, compare the present value of benefits with costs. Since the timing of the costs to implement a conservation program do not usually match the timing of a benefit from conservation (*i.e.,* investment is made at a project's beginning while the benefit is often achieved later), bringing them to their present value places all costs and benefits on an equal footing.

The present value of the benefits over the timeframe of the value of the benefits is compared to the present value of costs over the same period to determine the benefit-cost ratio (present value of benefits divided by the present value of costs). When the ratio is greater than

---

**Cost-Benefit
Evaluation Parameters**

- Total water savings over program life
- Maximum annual savings
- Cost per acre-foot of savings
- Cost savings of delayed capacity improvements
- Present value of program costs
- Present value of revenue losses to program

Figure 4-13
Definition of Cost Savings for Conservation Analyses

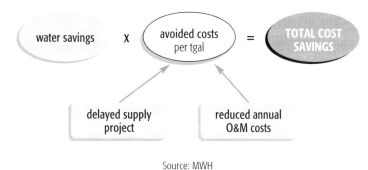

Source: MWH

1.0, the measure is economically effective; if it is less than 1.0, it is not typically considered economically effective. However, sometimes the extra water savings, public relations, or non-economic benefits derived from a particular measure may be so great that it is worth considering. Conservation programs can then be designed around the highest priority BMPs.

The total estimated savings associated with plumbing code and other regulations are applied to existing and projected demands to form baseline water projections. For alternative demand management strategies, estimate a range of savings or target reductions, from a low level of demand management to an aggressive level of effort. Providing a range allows for flexibility when incorporating demand management strategies into integrated resource plans (discussed in chapter 6).

If the actual savings achieved do not reflect the utility's projections, the conservation efforts can be modified (by increasing or decreasing implementation measures), or the timing of a particular capital improvement can be changed (for example, build sooner or delay construction).

"Water Conservation News," the monthly newsletter published by the California Department of Water Resources, provides up-to-date information on developments in water use efficiency (www.dpla.water.ca.gov/cgi-bin/publications/pubs/main.pl).

Dealing with Uncertainty

All water resource planners understand that demand projections are inherently uncertain. No data are available to support what the future will look like, only trends and plans. Because it's impossible to know how land use and consumption patterns will change over time, demand projections and conservation models rely on assumptions. However, the accuracy of the assumptions can be refined, depending on the availability of detail and the methodology used for analysis.

It is also important to understand the sources of uncertainty in a given projection. This sharpens the focus and emphasizes which actual demands should be monitored over time. Effectively identifying data weakness and uncertainty depends largely on developing the greatest level of water demand detail to allow maximum disaggregation of the data. This, in turn, allows the focus on monitoring to be where it is most needed.

Effectively identifying data weakness and uncertainty depends largely on developing the greatest level of water demand detail to allow maximum disaggregation of the data.

When using these projections, flexibility and adaptability are important. Presenting the upper and lower bounds of a range of projections can be helpful for supply planning. For example, the acquisition of new supplies should be based on the upper end of the projection range, while financial projections use the more conservative lower bounds. Facilities planning may require a specific "build-out" demand for a pipeline design, but the construction of pump stations and treatment plants are usually phased to reflect the increasing demands over time.

Other Applications of the Land Use-Based Approach

The land use-based method presented in this chapter can be modified to be used in estimating sanitary sewer, storm drainage flows, and related studies and plans. Modifications might include the development of land use categories that also reflect impervious surfaces and patterns of wastewater generation. To do this type of work requires the development of a map layer depicting watershed drainage or catchment area (versus water demand) polygons is required. Utilizing the same mapped database of planned land uses for each of the utility demand or flow projections provides for consistency between projections and a clearer understanding of the assumptions each product uses.

CHAPTER 5

Evaluating Water Supplies

As California's growing water demands confront a finite resource, the linkage between water supply and urban land use becomes increasingly important. Water supply is stretched, conservation is either in place or being implemented, and public scrutiny is high, making development of new sources and siting of facilities difficult. Providing the quality of water appropriate for each land use has become a priority, in contrast to using precious treated drinking water for all uses. And where increasing urban development threatens reservoirs and aquifers with runoff and pollution, watersheds and wellheads must be protected (*see* chapter 7).

This chapter examines the state's water supply opportunities and offers managers and planners an understanding of the factors to consider when evaluating existing supplies and developing new supplies to meet pressing urban demands. It also suggests new management techniques and explains how to redistribute water from where it is found to where it is needed. According to the DWR, approximately 70 percent of California's average annual runoff is from watersheds north of and including Sacramento. And about 75 percent of the state's urban and agricultural demands for water are south of Sacramento, with roughly half the population living in the South Coast region.

DWR = Department of Water Resources
maf = Million acre-feet

Supply Sources in California

By the year 2020, California's population will increase by 12 million to about 46 million (www.dof.ca.gov.doc), dominated by the counties of the San Joaquin Valley and Southern California's Inland Empire. Many of the groundwater basins in these areas are (and in some cases have been for some time) in a state of overdraft, with many of the purveyors already experiencing water shortages during sequential dry years. Continued urban growth in these areas will stretch available supplies and add pressure for agricultural transfers.

In addition to demand-related shortages, several statewide events that occurred in the past decade or so affect availability. These include implementation of the Central Valley Project Improvement Act (CVPIA), the 1993 U.S. Fish and Wildlife Service (USFWS) Biological Opinion on the winter-run chinook salmon (as well as other USFWS actions under the Endangered Species Act), the Monterey Agreement, the Bay-Delta Accord, and the loss of some Colorado River water. Some local actions have either limited or capped future surface diversions in an effort to maintain or restore habitat for fisheries (*e.g.,* the lower American River). For more information on each of these actions, *see The California Water Plan Update, Bulletin 160-03,* DWR 2003.

Forecasted shortages, particularly during dry years, highlight the need to develop new water management programs and build new facilities. Urban conservation programs can help reduce demands, but make only a partial contribution to total state need. This is particularly the case since two major droughts in the past 30 years have brought about a hardening of demands, making it more difficult to reduce demands.

The next section presents a general discussion of California's three primary sources of supply–groundwater, surface water, and to a much lesser extent, recycled or reclaimed water.

Groundwater

Most drinking water in the United States and California comes from groundwater that is stored in underground basins or aquifers (natural underground reservoirs or water-bearing formations). These aquifers are replenished mainly by precipitation, infiltration from streambeds, deep percolation resulting from irrigation, seepage from unlined water conveyance facilities, and to a lesser extent artificial recharge. Figure 5-1 illustrates the interrelationships between surface and groundwater, as well as the natural and human methods for recharging the groundwater basin.

California's net groundwater usage by hydrologic region is shown in Table 5-1. Note the difference between average year and drought year conditions. An increase in demand during dry years is often a function of higher temperatures and the lack of rainfall applied naturally to outdoor vegetation. Increased use of groundwater to offset reduction in the

Millerton Reservoir on the San Joaquin River diverts water to the Madera and the Friant-Kern canals.

availability of surface water is a typical pattern during dry year or drought conditions. As long as the groundwater basin is replenished during wetter years, this seldom results in long-term impacts. Indeed, water supplies are purposefully managed in this manner in conjunctive use systems, described in detail later in this chapter.

Under average conditions, California uses approximately 12.5 maf of groundwater annually. This includes the amount of groundwater exceeding the replenishment or inflow capability of various aquifers throughout the state, resulting in an overdraft condition of approximately one to two million acre-feet per year (mafy). Overdraft is not a measure of annual fluctuation, but rather represents a long-term trend associated with fluctuations that can have serious consequences.

At a local level, overdraft may result in higher extraction costs or a loss of supply to adjacent well owners and could affect existing surface water rights. Overdraft can also quickly mobilize contaminant plumes, requiring aggressive containment measures. In the case of coastal aquifers, overdraft can cause the intrusion of salinity, thus lowering the quality of the water and

Table 5-1. Annual Agricultural and Municipal Water Demands Met by Groundwater

HYDROLOGIC REGION	Total demand volume taf	Demand met by groundwater taf	Demand met by groundwater %
North Coast	1,063	263	25
San Francisco Bay	1,353	68	5
Central Coast	1,263	1,045	63
South Coast	5,124	1,177	23
Sacramento River	8,720	2,672	31
San Joaquin River	7,361	2,195	30
Tulare Lake	10,556	4,340	41
North Lahontan	568	157	28
South Lahontan	480	239	50
Colorado River	4,467	337	8

Source: DWR Bulletin 160-98

mafy = million acre-feet per year

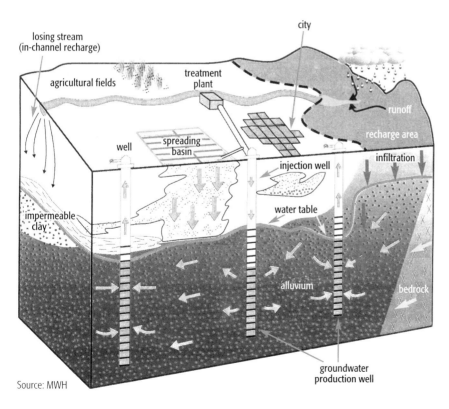

Figure 5-1
Groundwater Use and Recharge

Source: MWH

Groundwater Recharge

Groundwater recharge, or replenishment, involves pumping or percolating (natural or artificial) stormwater runoff or imported water into an aquifer to replenish its supplies.

Overdraft

Overdraft is an undesirable condition where the amount of water withdrawn from a groundwater basin exceeds the amount that will replenish it over a long period of time.

Adjudication

Adjudication is a judicial proceeding that assigns a priority to an appropriation of surface or groundwater, resulting in a court decree that defines the rights to or use of that water.

Water Year

In California, the water year begins on October 1 of the previous year and continues through September 30 of the current year. For example, the 1986 to 1992 drought actually began in early 1987 and ended in the middle of the 1992 water year.

WTP = Water treatment plant
DHS = Department of Health Services

necessitating either abandonment of coastal wells or desalination technology to make the supply potable.

In California, groundwater rights are not subject to statewide regulation. An overlying right is based on ownership—all property owners above an aquifer possess a shared right to its use. However, an overlying user may not take an unlimited quantity without regard to the needs of others. While groundwater can be appropriated by pumping and transporting for use on non-overlying lands, the right of an appropriator is subordinate to an overlying right.[1]

While local and regional purveyors often manage California's groundwater basins (see chapter 2), the majority of groundwater users are individual well owners. Groundwater basins, which underlie 40 percent of the land surface, are typically complex systems comprised of layers of aquifers separated by confining layers of impermeable material such as clay. The aquifers cannot be specifically measured in terms of capacity, areal extent, and inflow, and their extractions and outflow cannot be precisely quantified.

Because groundwater is not visible and basins are complex, capturing the attention of the public and regulators can be difficult when overdraft conditions occur. If competing claims for diminishing water resources pose a serious problem, the state may appoint a water master to adjudicate the issue. Court adjudications have established pumping limits for 18 of the 450 groundwater basins throughout California, with Los Angeles and San Bernardino Counties having the greatest number of adjudicated basins. As discussed in chapter 2, many forms of locally-based groundwater management ordinances used throughout the state address overdraft, protect water quality, or regulate potential export of groundwater.

Surface Supplies

Surface water supply whose origin is precipitation or snow pack, when not diverted directly for use, is stored in natural lakes, human-made reservoirs, or aquifers. Surface water supply is either diverted from a water body (such as a stream, river, or lake) located within or near the service area or is imported from another watershed. Most surface supply systems store these diversions in reservoirs during conditions of snow melt, precipitation, and

1. Three types of groundwater rights are recognized in California's complex system of case-law driven groundwater law. An overlying or correlative right is granted automatically to any landowner overlying an aquifer and extracting groundwater. An appropriative right is where "surplus" water is extracted and transported for use. A public entity only may seek a "prescriptive" right by active, continuous use of groundwater for a period of five years. Public utilities like cities and water districts can acquire a prescriptive right with a priority over private land owners, but private parties cannot acquire a prescriptive right.

high runoff. Stored water is then available during other times of the year as needed.

Facilities. Most surface water from a river, lake, or reservoir is withdrawn through an intake structure and conveyed to a storage facility close to the service area that allows the supply to be diverted when available and stored until needed. Typically, the conveyance facilities also deliver the supply directly to a water treatment plant (WTP).

Another less common intake method uses infiltration galleries, commonly called "Ranney Well Collectors," to transport water. These facilities are below the surface in thin alluvial deposits adjacent to streambeds. Surface water is filtered naturally through the soil and withdrawn as groundwater or, if already groundwater, in formations that are not deep enough to accommodate wells. Infiltration galleries are particularly useful for water supplies that are difficult to develop or generate a minimal yield. Streambed supply captured by infiltration galleries, considered by the State Department of Health Services (DHS) to be "groundwater under the influence of surface water," is subject to surface water treatment requirements.

All surface water is subject to treatment requirements established by DHS (www.dhs.ca.gov), the primacy agency that implements the federal Safe Drinking Water Act in concert with the USEPA. WTPs are ideally located along the perimeter of a service area at a relatively high elevation so that gravity can convey the water to customers and to storage tanks and reservoirs throughout the distribution system.

Water Rights. In California, surface water rights are based on both riparian and appropriative rights.[2] Riparian rights–which are derived from English common law and may not be transferred–provide water to landowners on the banks of waterways, but are limited to parcels adjacent to waterways. If the land is subdivided, newly created parcels not adjacent to the waterway lose these rights. While each rightholder is entitled to a reasonable

2. Other types of surface water rights under California's complex water law include Tribal Water Rights, pre-1914 water rights, and rights to springs. *See* California Water, Littleworth and Garner (1995, new edition scheduled Winter 2004) for more details on these types of water rights.

Land Subsidence from Overdrafting

Land subsidence is typically associated with an alluvial groundwater basin that is overdrafted. Most noticeable in the San Joaquin Valley where elevation dropped significantly over the past 75 years, subsidence occurs when the subsurface clay soil is dewatered. The clay soil then compresses under pressure and becomes permanently deformed. Loss of water storage associated with clay soil is usually not significant relative to the amount of water that is stored in sand and gravel lenses.

Source: U.S. Geological Survey

share of the resource, the water may be subject to other claims. Riparian rights are often imprecisely defined, particularly during a shortage.

By contrast, appropriative rights, which originated in the mining camps of California, are well defined. Since 1914, the state has required that a permit be obtained before appropriating water, with the permit and license specifying the place and purpose of use, quantities, point of diversion, and ability to store the water. Appropriative rights are created by use and lost by non-use. Water diverted and used prior to 1914 is afforded higher priority, and the right is not subject to permit and license, but can be taken away through non-use.

Permitted appropriative water rights (or post-1914) are not limited to a parcel, but rather to a defined service area or place of use, for a specified amount and set of conditions. The water right must be for a beneficial use, and a senior appropriator may exhaust the resource to the exclusion of a junior rightholder.

The State Water Resources Control Board (SWRCB), Division of Water Rights, grants appropriative permits. The SWRCB also can declare that a particular river or stream is fully appropriated, meaning that no further water rights are available from this resource. Physically, particularly in dry years, this may well be the case for many of California's rivers.

Primary Water Purveyors. The federal agency with a right to the greatest quantity of water in California is the United States Bureau of Reclamation (USBR). The USBR owns and operates the Central Valley Project (CVP) and contracts its water to local and regional water purveyors. DWR, the state agency with a right to a high quantity of water, owns and operates the State Water Project (SWP) and also contracts its water supply to local and regional water purveyors.

California's largest regional water purveyor, the Metropolitan Water District of Southern California (MWD), contracts for state water and Colorado River water to meet the full or partial needs of local agencies in six Southern California counties serving a population of over 17 million. The San Francisco Public Utilities Commission (SFPUC), another large regional urban water agency with rights to the Tuolumne River in the Sierra Nevada as well as local sources, meets all or part of the needs of 29 agencies in 4 counties serving a population of over 2.4 million in the San Francisco Bay Area.

The Los Angeles Department of Water and Power (LADWP), which has water rights in the Owens and Mono River basins as well as local supplies, contracts with MWD for a portion of its needs. The San Diego County Water Authority (SDCWA) serving 3 million customers, has its own local sources, but also contracts for MWD and Colorado River water. The Santa Clara Valley Water District (SCVWD) manages its own local surface supplies and the groundwater basin, but contracts for state and federal water. EBMUD, serving more than 1.3 million on the east side of San Francisco Bay, has water rights to the Mokelumne and American Rivers in the Sierra Nevada as well as local sources.

Beneficial Use

Beneficial use refers to the purpose accomplished when water is diverted for good reason and without waste.

CVP   = Central Valley Project
EBMUD = East Bay Municipal
              Utility District
LADWP = Los Angeles Department
              of Water and Power
MWD   = Metropolitan Water District
              of Southern California
SCVWD = Santa Clara Valley
              Water District
SDCWA = San Diego County
              Water Authority
SFPUC   = San Francisco Public
              Utilities Commission
SWP   = State Water Project
SWRCB = State Water Resources
              Control Board
USBR   = United States Bureau
              of Reclamation
USEPA   = United States Environmental
              Protection Agency

Recycled Water

Most recycled water in California is used for agricultural irrigation, groundwater recharge, irrigated turf and other landscape applications (primarily golf courses and parks), and industrial uses such as process cooling. The level of treatment required is based on the reclamation source and the land uses receiving the supply. For treatment requirements, *see* the DHS website. Although the subject of some debate, recycled water can be stored in groundwater basins where percolation into the aquifer adds additional filtering.

Recycled water must have a dedicated distribution system, and the pipes are often the color purple to distinguish them from pipes for drinking water and sanitary sewers. When used within a commercial building for toilet flushing, a dual internal plumbing system separates recycled water from potable supplies. These systems are more typical of new construction, found primarily in Southern California, since retrofitting an existing building can be expensive.

A reclamation facility is usually located at a wastewater treatment plant (WWTP), at the lowest elevation of the collection system. This is necessary because sewers generally rely on gravity to convey wastewater to a WWTP, with the effluent usually discharged to a waterbody such as the ocean, a river, or an export pipeline. In recent years, satellite reclamation facilities have become popular in new growth areas. These facilities are sited upstream from a WWTP, usually in conjunction with large-scale development, to minimize conveyance and pumping requirements.

The reuse of municipal wastewater is becoming more common as costs associated with new surface supplies increase and new treatment technologies lower the cost of recycled water. Other motivations, such as discharge limitations, contribute as well. The City of San Jose began recycling its wastewater in part because treated effluent was adding too much fresh water to the salt marshes, which are critical habitat for the salt marsh harvest mouse and other sensitive wetland species, located near the effluent discharge at the southern end of San Francisco Bay.

Indirect Potable Reuse. Recycled water has also been used successfully for indirect potable reuse (IPR). DHS specifies minimum detention times (in an aquifer or a surface water reservoir) before the recycled water blended with either groundwater or surface water can be used as a potable supply. IPR applications include groundwater recharge and blending recycled water with surface water in storage reservoirs.

IPR for groundwater augmentation is becoming increasingly common. For example, nearly all of the water flowing into Orange County through the Santa Ana River consists of treated effluent from San Bernardino and Riverside Counties. The Orange County Water District (OCWD) captures this water as part of its Santa Ana River groundwater basin recharge program. The

> ### Recycled Water
> Recycled water is municipal and/or industrial wastewater treated to a sufficiently high level that it can be reused.

IPR = Indirect potable reuse
OCWD = Orange County Water District
WWTP = Wastewater treatment plant

> ### Indirect Potable Reuse
> Indirect potable reuse refers to the purpose accomplished when previously used water has been treated, blended, and stored to make it suitable for human consumption. It is indirect because recycled water has been blended with surface or groundwater and stored, for a short period, in an aquifer or reservoir.

LPP = Local Projects Program
VVWRA = Victor Valley Wastewater
Reclamation Authority

OCWD, in conjunction with the Orange County Sanitation District, is proceeding with a $600 million project to produce up to 140,000 acre-feet of recycled wastewater to recharge aquifers. This treated effluent will be conveyed to spreading basins where it will blend with other sources of supply: the Santa Ana River water discussed above, SWP water, and water from the Colorado River Aqueduct.

Although IPR had not yet been used for surface water augmentation, the City of San Diego recently attempted to implement the state's first indirect potable reuse project of this kind. Proposing a high level of tertiary treatment, the city wanted to filter the water through granular media, using microfiltration, reverse osmosis, ion exchange, ozone, and chlorine. The treated recycled water, a blend with 50 percent potable water from local runoff and imports, would be stored in the San Vincente Reservoir. DHS specified a minimum storage period of one year, after which the stored water would be treated conventionally. But because it was seen as a "toilets-to-tap" proposal, the project lost public support and was halted in the final stages. Variations of this project are still under discussion.

Seawater Barrier. Along the coast of California, recycled water can be used as a seawater intrusion barrier, with recycled water recharging the aquifers through spreading basins or injection wells. OCWD has used recycled water as a sea water barrier to protect its aquifers since the 1970s.

Third-Party Impacts. When planning the use of recycled water, third-party impacts must be considered. Recycled wastewater that is not discharged to a river or stream, or whose volume of return flow is reduced, might affect existing surface or groundwater users. Not unlike a third-party impact associated with some water marketing situations discussed later in the chapter, if the effluent originally augmented downstream flows, moving the recycled wastewater location could adversely affect the environment and the water supply.

For example, the Victor Valley Wastewater Reclamation Authority (VVWRA) discharges treated effluent into the Mojave River, where much of it finds its way into the groundwater basin. The VVWRA proposed to alter the discharge so that the City of Victorville could use the water for irrigation, thus reducing the amount that could be extracted from the overdrafted Mojave groundwater basin. Water producers and the California Department of Fish and Game filed protests, asserting that the project will reduce the stream flow (California Water Law and Policy Reporter, Volume 11, Number 3, December 2000). Consequently, to compensate for the reduction, the purveyors had to obtain additional supplies.

Water quality is an emerging concern associated with the use of recycled water for irrigation that infiltrates into the groundwater basin. Newly discovered contaminants that are not yet regulated, or treatment processes that have not been upgraded to address new contaminants of concern, could have significant implications to supply availability of groundwater basins. As water supplies become stressed, third-party impacts associated with recycled water use may also be scrutinized more carefully.

For more information about recycled water, *see* the Water ReUse Association website (www.watereuse.org). Visit the DHS website (www.dhs.ca.gov) for information about laws related to recycled water and specifically "California Health Laws Related to Recycled Water ("The Purple Book"), June 2001 Update (www.dhs.ca.gov/ps/ddwem/publications/waterrecycling/index).

Determining the Availability of Supply

When evaluating the availability of a community's existing and projected sources of water supply, planners should consider a number of factors:

- Long-term average year supplies
- Dry year and seasonal availability
- Potable and non-potable supplies
- Emergency supplies available following catastrophic and other events

Long-Term, Average-Year Supplies

Existing supplies of groundwater and surface water must be evaluated for their ability to meet projected annual water demands.

Groundwater. Many terms are used to define the amount of water that can be reliably extracted from a groundwater basin over the long term, such as perennial yield, safe yield, operational yield, and production yield. (*See* sidebars.) Because groundwater cannot be seen and does not flow in a defined channel, but can exist in various geologic layers with varying transport and recharge conditions, an assessment of yield can be difficult. And because an aquifer does not have an ownership boundary, pumping by one party can affect the availability of supply to another agency or landowner.

To develop a water budget for groundwater supply, calculate the average annual inflow to an aquifer minus average annual outflow. Inflow includes recharge from precipitation and streams that are losing flow to the aquifer, inflow from other aquifers, water applied through irrigation, and artificial recharge (*e.g.,* infiltration basins and injection wells). Outflow includes groundwater lost to streams that are gaining flow, as well as springs, pumping, and outflow to other aquifers. When outflow is greater than inflow, an overdraft condition may be occurring.

Individual well capacities are determined to quantify the available supply to a water purveyor. The well's future availability should also be determined, based

Perennial Yield

Perennial yield is the amount of groundwater that can be extracted annually on a sustained, long-term basis from an aquifer or basin without adverse effects. Generally, it is where long-term extraction equals long-term average replenishment.

Safe Yield

Safe yield is the maximum quantity of water from a groundwater basin that can be maintained indefinitely or diverted from a stream without adverse effect.

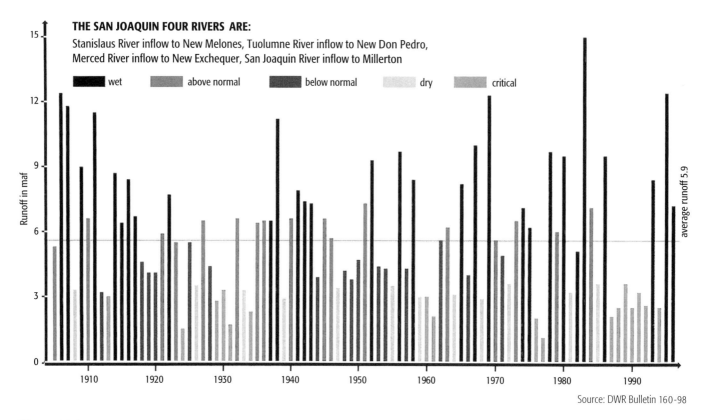

THE SAN JOAQUIN FOUR RIVERS ARE:

Stanislaus River inflow to New Melones, Tuolumne River inflow to New Don Pedro,
Merced River inflow to New Exchequer, San Joaquin River inflow to Millerton

■ wet   ▨ above normal   ▨ below normal   ░ dry   ▨ critical

Source: DWR Bulletin 160-98

Figure 5-2
San Joaquin Rivers
Unimpaired Runoff Data

Operational Yield

Operational yield is the groundwater use that can be sustained
over the long term to meet specified management objectives.

---

on the replacement schedule, water quality conditions that future drinking water regulations may affect, and impacts from other wells.

Land use practices affect the availability of groundwater supply through increased demands and differing natural recharge rates that can affect an aquifer's yield. Availability may also be significantly limited by a contaminated aquifer or if a plume of contamination is heading toward a production well.

The water budget method described above uses a very simple formula to determine an aquifer's annual overdraft, but it does not reflect sustainable pumpage. Evaluating long-term groundwater yield requires that an aquifer's characteristics be analyzed through a long hydrologic sequence to reflect variations in average annual conditions. A groundwater model can be a useful tool for this analysis. For an example of the uses and data required for a groundwater model, *see* Table 5-2.

Surface Water. Surface water supplies are typically assessed for long-term availability under average year conditions. A thorough assessment determines how frequently the upper limit and seasonal quantities specified in a water rights permit or water contract can be diverted. Water rights typically specify quantity in total annual and seasonal limits and maximum rate of diversion.

As with groundwater supplies, average year deliveries are evaluated over a long hydrologic sequence based on 75 or more years of data, if available. This information—along with snowpack data, storage assessments, and projected water demands on the system from more senior water rights holders—is used to estimate the water supply that can be reliably delivered to meet system demands under extended drought conditions (or the "firm delivery capability"). For an example of 100 years of annual unimpaired runoff data, *see* Figure 5-2.

Including the potential for recycled water in the assessment will free up potable water to meet potable water demands. To identify recycled water use potential, an analyst begins with land use data developed for the water demand projections discussed in chapter 4. Land uses that can accept recycled water are identified and assessed for feasibility, taking into account proximity to a wastewater treatment plant and to candidate land uses that ensure the efficient alignment for conveyance facilities.

To determine the most efficient quantity of recycled water, compare demands to daily and seasonal recycled water availability along with any specific needs for infrastructure. For example, according to DHS, parks must be irrigated with recycled water at night, yet WWTPs produce the greatest quantity during the day as it is generated. In this instance, a local storage facility would make it possible to balance demand with supply.

Comparing Supplies with Demands. Each water supply should be assessed separately for average annual availability. Comparing available supply to projected demands will anticipate any average annual deficiencies that may arise (*see* the left side of Figure 5-3).

Dry-Year and Seasonal Availability

Variable climatic conditions can affect the availability of water supplies year to year, particularly with surface water. If a wholesale agency such as Metropolitan, USBR, or DWR is the supplier, it is advisable to understand their assumptions of reliability in all hydrologic conditions.

Type of Year. A drought can be defined as two or more consecutive dry years. A drought planning period, also called a design drought, which is commonly used to assess a supply's firm yield, is usually six to eight continuous dry years. For Urban Water Management Plans (and perhaps compliance with SB 610 and

USE	DATA REQUIRED
Basin planning and management	Area coverage and subregion boundaries
Agriculture and urban water use	Stream locations and data
Regional and site-specific analysis	Peripheral watersheds
Seawater intrusion analysis	Precipitation data
Groundwater availability	Aquifer characteristics
Conjunctive use operations	Land uses–historic, short-term projection, long-term projection
Vulnerability assessments	Calibration period

Table 5-2. Hydrologic Model Uses and Data Requirements

Folsom Reservoir during the 1987–1992 drought

Figure 5-3
Annual Demands and
Supply Availability

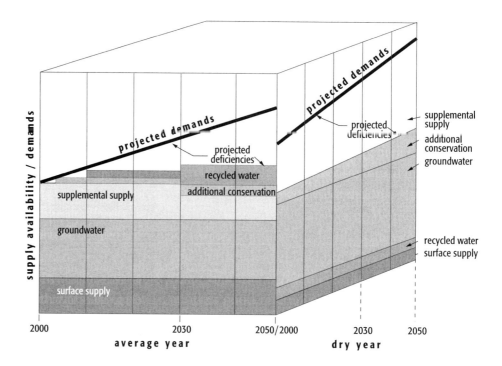

SB 221), three water years, based on the driest three-year historic sequence for the purveyor's water supply, should be used.

A drought in California that exceeds three years is uncommon, but does occur, as shown in Figure 5-4. To ensure a conservative assessment of the yield for purposes of drought planning, a period extending more than three years is used. The level of water supply reliability a community desires is related to the level of risk it is willing to take, balanced against the cost of providing that increased level of reliability.

Surface Water. Assessing the firm yield of surface supplies relies on the historic stream flow record (*see* the example provided in Figure 5-2), taking into account several complex factors. These include whether it is a primary or junior water right, contract limitations for shortages, available storage capacity, limitations of the Endangered Species Act (or other environmental constraints), other demands on the supply, and the ability to identify a drought early on and invoke conservation efforts that would save stored water.

To assess the availability of surface supply for a dry year and for multiple dry years, develop stream flow data for each supply source the purveyor manages (Figure 5-2). For single dry years, compare annual stream flow data to DWR determinations of the type of water year (wet, above normal, below normal, dry, critically dry) for specific watershed units throughout the state. When assessing availability of streamflow during multiple dry years, compare the same data to that of a multi-year dry period (Figure 5-4). Of course, the long-term availability of these supply sources must take into account increased demands on the supply by others.

Supply Reliability

Defined by the magnitude and frequency of delivery deficiencies in dry years, supply reliability is a function of hydrology, system storage, and system demands.

Source: Water Supply Master Plan, SFPUC, April 2000 (www.ci.sf.ca.us)

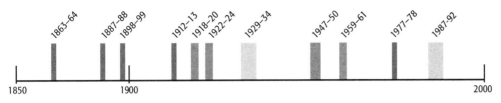

Figure 5-4
California's Multi-Year
Historical Dry Periods
(1850–present)*

* Dry periods prior to 1900 estimated from limited data   Source: DWR

To assess the availability of a recycled water supply for multiple dry years, it is important to consider that, as conservation programs and rationing are implemented during a drought, indoor water use decreases, and the quantity of wastewater decreases. Therefore, if the majority of wastewater is being treated for recycled use, the quantity during multiple dry years may be reduced.

Seasonally, the production of recycled water is somewhat consistent, unlike a land use with an outdoor component that causes peaks in the summer (Figure 4-10). A park with high demands during the summer may need very little water in winter and spring as a result of precipitation. On the other hand, the use of recycled water for industrial processing is attractive because demand is consistent and not dependent on weather. When planning recycled water production, take into account variability of demand based on land use. The Alameda County Flood Control and Water Conservation District-Zone 7 (Zone 7 Water Agency), which provides water for Pleasanton, Livermore, and Dublin, is reclaiming sand and gravel quarries for use as storage facilities. One may be used for recycled water to accommodate seasonal fluctuation.

Groundwater. Dry seasons and dry years depend on the pumping capacity of the basin and individual wells, as well as an assessment of their ability to withstand short- or long-term conditions of overdraft. Susceptibility to land subsidence and the possibility of seawater intrusion or water quality contamination are other factors that can affect yield.

Comparing Supplies with Demands. Determining the probability of a water shortage for the projected level of demands is essential to a thorough assessment of supplies. Comparing available supplies to demands projected for a dry year may reveal deficiencies (*see* the right side of Figure 5-3). Without conservation or rationing, a dry year will naturally result in greater water use due to increased evapotranspiration rates and consumption requirements, and a decreased level of precipitation.

By using more surface supply in a wet period and relying on groundwater during a dry one (operating surface and groundwater conjunctively), it is possible to meet demands for various types of years (Figure 5-5). Supply can then be augmented during dry years by increasing conservation efforts and the imposition of rationing, or, for critically dry years, by obtaining a new supply, such as a drought bank purchase. Note, however, that a supply purchased during a wet year may not be available in a dry year (Figure 5-5).

In addition to a dry-year deficiency, seasonal variations in both demands and supplies can result in seasonal deficiencies. The increased demand for water during the summer is due primarily to land uses that require outdoor irrigation (*see* the right side of Figure 5-5). Meeting seasonal peaks depends both on availability of supply (including raw water storage) and facility capacities that are designed for maximum-day demands (involving storage tanks and treatment plants) or water demands for peak-hour conditions (involving pipeline capacity).

Potable and Non-Potable Supplies

Another measure of supply is the availability of potable versus non-potable water. Since some demands—for example, what is needed to irrigate turf—do not need to meet drinking water standards, the use of alternatives to the highest and best quality water diversifies supplies and reduces the cost of treatment. In this case, the quality of the non-potable supply (recycled water and surface or groundwater that does not meet drinking water standards without treatment) is evaluated, and a separate distribution system is developed. For example, groundwater supplies with naturally-occurring radon or arsenic levels that exceed drinking water standards can be used safely for certain uses without treatment, if a separate distribution system is available.

Non-Potable Water

Raw and non-potable refers to water not used directly for human consumption because of water quality considerations.

In general, raw water has not been treated to drinking water standards or is used for agriculture. Non-potable typically refers to water not intended for direct human consumption, and can include raw or recycled water that is not treated for purposes of indirect potable reuse.

Figure 5-5
Supply Availability—
Selected Year

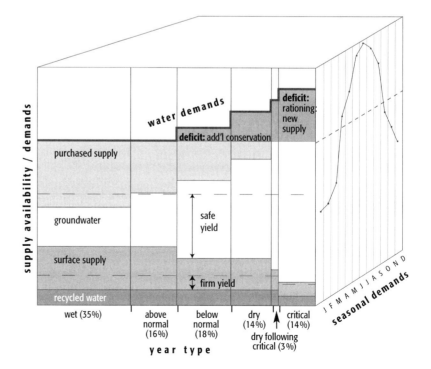

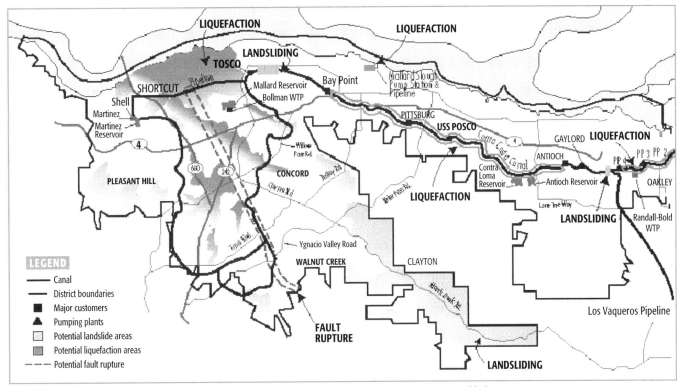

System Reliability Following Catastrophic and Other Events

Incorporating a level of reliability and risk assessment into supply planning is critical. Although a catastrophic event cannot be predicted or prevented, it is possible to anticipate and minimize its effects. A natural or human-induced event that increases risk to short- and long-term water supplies, in addition to the risk and reliability issues that dry years and a drought might present, include the following catastrophic and slow-occurring events:

- Seismic vulnerability
- Flooding contamination
- Intrusion of seawater
- Chemical contamination
- Wildfire
- Terrorism

In 2001, the AWWA (www.awwa.org) published "Emergency Planning for Water Utility Management" (AWWA Manual M19, 2001), a book that offers guidance for preparing an emergency plan.

AWWA = American Water Works Association

Seismic Vulnerability. The vulnerability of a water system to a seismic event has become an important consideration in water system planning. As geologists and engineers gain a greater understanding of the likelihood of and the impacts resulting from a catastrophic event, particularly in an urban area, water agencies

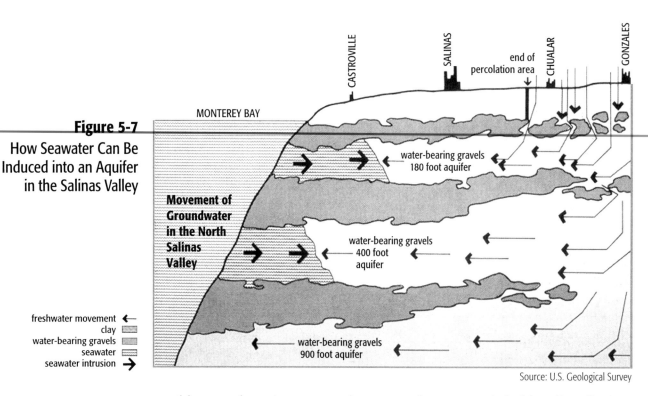

Figure 5-7

How Seawater Can Be Induced into an Aquifer in the Salinas Valley

CASTROVILLE
SALINAS
end of percolation area
CHUALAR
GONZALES

MONTEREY BAY

water-bearing gravels 180 foot aquifer

Movement of Groundwater in the North Salinas Valley

water-bearing gravels 400 foot aquifer

freshwater movement ←—
clay
water-bearing gravels
seawater
seawater intrusion →

water-bearing gravels 900 foot aquifer

Source: U.S. Geological Survey

are able to evaluate impacts to the system from ground shaking, liquefaction, fault rupture, earthquake-induced landslides, and fires or energy loss that can follow. Figure 5-6 presents the results of a vulnerability assessment for the Contra Costa Water District that identified its most vulnerable geographic areas. The assessment also addressed the possible effects of a major event on water distribution over time following the event. Implementation of recommendations resulting from these assessments, as CCWD is doing, can improve a system's reliability and minimize the amount of down time due to repairs.

Flooding Contamination. Flooding can seriously compromise drinking water supply reliability. Flood waters contain viruses, bacteria, and chemicals, particularly in rural communities, and the entire distribution system must be flushed out and disinfected before potable water can be conveyed again. Several weeks after flood waters have receded may pass before a notice to boil water can be lifted.

Seawater Intrusion. Overdrafting of coastal aquifers has resulted in seawater intrusion along the California coast, particularly in Southern California and Monterey Bay (*see* Figure 5-7). Seawater intrusion creates brackish water unsuitable for drinking water or agricultural use without desalination or demineralization treatment. Pumping and treating the water can also increase the rate of intrusion, depending on local conditions. By minimizing overdraft, or by injecting or recharging non-saline water into the aquifer to act as a barrier, intrusion can usually be prevented. In Southern California, several water management agencies have been creating such barriers with recycled water for years. And in the Castroville area, the Monterey County Water Resources Agency has

Brackish Water

Brackish refers to a mixture of fresh water and saltwater.

developed a recycled water supply and distribution system to reduce reliance on coastal agricultural wells that have been contributing to seawater intrusion.

Chemical Contamination. Contamination can eliminate or greatly reduce long-term availability of drinking water. In some communities, chemical contamination has been chronic, with cleanup efforts focused on groundwater treatment and redistribution of drinking water. Overdrafting the aquifer can also exacerbate the problem by drawing contaminated water towards a supply well.

The City of Fresno has had to shut down more than twenty percent of its wells (almost 50 of about 240) due to contamination from dibromochloropropane (DBCP), an agricultural pesticide. This has resulted in efforts to redistribute the available high-quality groundwater supply. The city is also building a facility for the treatment of surface water, once solely used to recharge the groundwater basin, so that it can be used directly for domestic supply.

DBCP = Dibromochloropropane

Wildfires. Wildfires that occur within the watershed of a drinking water supply can seriously affect its quality. Wildfires destroy vegetative cover that can create erosion during the next rainfall, rendering a waterbody useless for months or years due to excessive turbidity. High turbidity levels can also create a number of water treatment and health-related concerns. For further discussion of water quality protection, *see* chapter 7.

Terrorism. In the last several years, water agencies have greatly increased their analysis and security regarding potential terrorism and related actions that could threaten components of their water supply systems.

New Opportunities for Water Supplies and Supply Management

Developing new water supplies can be very difficult, often requiring 5 to 20 years of planning before the supply is needed, depending on the difficulty in obtaining the supply. Although the supplies can be introduced in phases, conducting feasibility and engineering studies, environmental analyses, and obtaining permits and approvals in advance, can help prevent undesirable effects on both the community and the environment. This not only minimizes the effort required during later phases, but presents the entire project to the regulatory agencies and the public.

As the costs of new supplies increase and the public is more willing to consider creative options such as water recycling and desalination, new management techniques and technologies are becoming easier to implement (for the overall process and evaluation criteria for assessing water supply alternatives, *see* chapter 6). Some options include:

- Demand management—water conservation, leak detection, etc. (*see* chapter 4)
- Conjunctive use of ground and surface waters

Conjunctive Use

Conjunctive use refers to the combined use of surface and groundwater supplies.

- Water purchases, transfers, and banking
- Desalination and demineralization
- Off-stream storage and expansion of existing reservoirs
- Gray water
- Watershed management for source protection (*see* chapter 7)

Conjunctive Use of Ground and Surface Waters

Surface water is often used to recharge the groundwater basin.

Managing groundwater is critical for maintaining the reliability of supply. Basic management techniques include monitoring water quality conditions and trends, stabilizing the basin, and protecting natural recharge areas. To enhance the groundwater supply, recharge programs for storing recycled and imported water can be implemented. Cooperative planning of aquifer management is also important, since usually more than one purveyor relies on the aquifer for supply.

If a community is fortunate enough to be above a groundwater basin and have surface supplies, managing the basin conjunctively can greatly increase reliability and provide flexibility to meet needs. Figure 5-8 illustrates a typical conjunctive use strategy for various types of years. The basic premise is that more surface water is used during wetter years when it is available, and use of groundwater is increased during drier years. The same strategy is applied seasonally by providing more surface water during the winter months and more groundwater during summer months.

Rarely available during dry periods when needed, new surface supplies may be available for wet years and during winter or spring. A conjunctive use plan would store in the aquifer any

Figure 5-8
Conjunctive Use
Operating Strategy

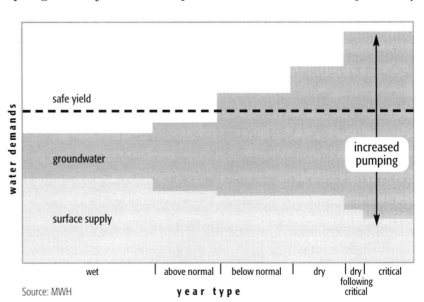

Source: MWH

excess surface water supplies obtained during wet periods to be drawn upon during dry seasons or dry years.

A typical conjunctive use program relies on the natural recharge of an aquifer during wet years and wet seasons, or–in the case of artificial storage and recovery programs–on the artificial recharge of surface supplies through spreading basins or more commonly through well injections. Groundwater can then be withdrawn year-round, but it is particularly useful during summer months to meet peak demands and in dry years and other times of shortage, while maintaining the aquifer's perennial yield. In another version of conjunctive use, a water purveyor works cooperatively with other agencies to utilize an off-site aquifer (discussed below under Water Marketing and Banking).

Developing a sustainable supply through a conjunctive use program depends on several factors. These include an aquifer's available storage capacity; water supply available to recharge the basin, either naturally or artificially; the ability to extract water (*e.g.,* extraction facilities, wells); and the wheeling capacity for conveyance facilities. Financial agreements and institutional arrangements between parties for additional surface water supplies, sharing of aquifers, and use of conveyance facilities are also important. And because groundwater has always been considered a property right of an overlying property owner, any impact a water purveyor causes by extracting water from an existing individual well must be addressed.

To ensure that overdraft does not occur, a conjunctive use program usually includes wells to monitor groundwater, providing information about the direction the water is moving, levels, quality, and other relevant data. Underground conditions are complex, however, and accounting for stored water in groundwater basins can be difficult.

Conjunctive use is not new. The number of districts and agencies actively pursuing conjunctive use programs has grown rapidly in recent years, especially with the availability of state funds from propositions and through the California Bay-Delta Authority program (formerly CALFED). One interesting example of a regional water purveyor that encouraged development of conjunctive use on a local level is the MWD program. MWD solicited grant proposals from Southern California water purveyors for groundwater storage programs, ranging from feasibility studies to construction projects. Among the eligible projects were direct recharge facilities with spreading basins, injection and extraction wells, and facilities pertaining to in lieu recharging operations, discussed below. Nine projects were selected, based on evaluation criteria that included regional and local benefits, water quality impacts, local support, and financial integrity. The cost per project ranged from $500,000 to $15 million, and an additional 64,000 afy will be made available to the region during drought years. *California Water Law & Policy Reporter,* Volume 11, Number 9, June 2001.

Groundwater Banking

In groundwater banking, surface water is stored in groundwater basins in times of surplus, through recharge or injection, for withdrawal during shortage. Banking can also involve the use of available surface water in lieu of groundwater to enable recharge to occur and water levels and storage to recover.

Artificial Storage and Recovery

ASR is the human addition of water to the groundwater basin through actions such as irrigation, induced infiltration and spreading basins, or well injection. This water, or a portion, is then recovered or pumped for use at a later date.

Wheeling

Wheeling is the transfer of water through unused capacity in a conveyance facility by an entity other than its owner.

afy = acre-feet per year
ASR = Artificial Storage and Recovery
SGA = Sacramento Groundwater Authority

Sacramento Groundwater Authority Conjunctive Use Program

The Sacramento Groundwater Authority (SGA) was formed in 2000 as part a collaborative effort to manage regional groundwater resources. A joint powers agency made up of 18 of the water purveyors in the area north of the American River, SGA serves as the entity to develop programs to conjunctively utilize the surface water of the American River (and possibly the Sacramento River), along with local aquifers.

SGA has a major role to play in stabilizing the groundwater basin, and in fashioning a regional solution to river restoration for the lower American River. Put simply, SGA will develop a conjunctive use program that involves taking river water—already used and contracted for by the purveyors—during high river flows and storing it in a large aquifer in northern Sacramento. Then, during dry periods, the purveyors will take less or no water from the river, thereby leaving the water for fish and aquatic resources. Purveyors' needs will be satisfied by groundwater that has been stored and banked in the aquifer, with new infrastructure for withdrawal and conveyance.

Implementation of the conjunctive use program is already underway. As one of its first efforts, SGA has banked water provided by five of its member agencies (four water districts and the City of Sacramento) and then sold it to the Bureau of Reclamation on behalf of the Bay Delta Environmental Water Account. The banked water is being used to enhance fisheries within the Delta system, an environmentally-related beneficial use. Revenue resulting from the water sale will help fund the facilities and infrastructure needed to implement the regional conjunctive use project.

Numerous details still need to be worked out: most notably, how to accurately measure the extractions and ensure that the water is used for the purposes intended. SGA intends to account for the water by measuring the groundwater extraction each of the member agencies deposited into the groundwater bank. ∎

Water Purchases, Transfers, and Banking

According to DWR, about 80 percent of the total applied water use in the state is for agriculture. In recent years, some agricultural water users have sold their water rights or contracts to urban agencies, or reduced production during drought years in order to sell water on a temporary basis. Changing practices that make agricultural water available, permanently or during droughts, include fallowing or retiring land, substituting crops that require less water, and replacing surface water with groundwater supplies in agricultural operations. Conserving water through improved operational efficiency (such as adding linings to unlined canals) can also produce an additional permanent supply.

Because most of California's population and its agricultural land are in the drier southern half of the state, and much of the water is in the north, the engineered water system moves water on a daily basis from where it originates to where it is needed. Water purchases, transfers, and banking agreements can also be done this way to meet local or regional needs. Transferring supplies between willing sellers and buyers is commonly called water marketing.

Water Marketing and Banking. True water marketing—where a free market exists with multiple buyers and sellers, and without fixed prices—may be difficult to implement because of the complexities inherent in marketable water. In part, the difficulty lies in the meaning of entitlement for an existing water right and contract holder (*e.g.*, upper limit versus actual use). Other problems can result from permitting requirements, third-party or secondary impacts, Delta pumping restrictions, allowable transfers from a county or water district, wheeling arrangements, and effects of energy deregulation.

Short-term transfers can include purchases made from the state's emergency Drought Water Bank or the CVPIA Interim Water Acquisition Program, or through spot purchases from another agency. According to DWR, temporary withdrawal from a reservoir, where existing supply is stored until there is an urgent need, is another source of transfer. Future high runoff that creates surplus flow refills what has been withdrawn. This method requires available capacity in the reservoir.

Long-term agreements for new supplies may include the purchase or lease of a water right or a contractor's entitlement (*e.g.*, CVP or SWP water) and agreements for storage or banking in an aquifer for later use. When working with a contractor, agreement must be obtained from the agency holding the right, such as the USBR or DWR, and/or the agency that contracts directly with the water right holder, such as a regional purveyor.

Wheeling agreements must also be obtained from agencies that own the required conveyance facilities. For more information on provisions for water wheeling, *see* Water Code sections 1810–1814.

An example of a contract water sale involves the Kern County Water Agency (KCWA), a large wholesaler with customers in both urban and agricultural districts. The KCWA sold 25,000 acre-feet of its SWP entitlement to the Mojave Water Agency and 7,000 acre-feet to the Zone 7 Water Agency. Because it holds both the rights to the water and the rights to the conveyance facilities, DWR approval was required.

Third-Party Impacts. Unlike new storage facilities or some configurations of water banking, water marketing does not add a new supply to California's overall system, but redistributes the use of an existing supply. Third-party impacts associated with water marketing can result when water is no longer conveyed to a particular location that has historically applied this water to the land.

For example, transferring supplies out of a watershed can affect the land and diverters that rely on this water. Groundwater levels may decline if infiltration is reduced, and fallowing lands may affect aquatic and terrestrial species and habitat dependent on applied water and agricultural return flow. A region with fallowed land may also experience economic repercussions due to the loss of jobs, reduced property taxes, and impacts to agriculture-related businesses.

If surface water users switch to groundwater supply, overdraft of groundwater may occur or be exacerbated. This in turn can result in reduced streamflow that not only has an impact on aquatic and terrestrial species and habitat but can also harm downstream diverters that depend on return flow. Reductions in agricultural return flow draining into the Salton Sea, for example, would result in higher salinity levels, thus altering the sensitive balance of species in that habitat. Where the supply consists of new water, created by reducing irrecoverable losses or outflow to the ocean during extremely high runoff periods, storage and banking does not contribute to impacts on third parties.

Water Marketing Approvals. The steps required to implement water transfers include obtaining agency approvals; commissioning studies to assess environmental and operational impacts; entering into agreements for conveyance,

---

Fallowing

Fallowing, by paying a farmer not to grow a crop, is a method used to conserve water. Water not used for irrigation becomes available for urban or environmental use or is stored for future use.

Water Banking

Water banking refers to temporary or long-term physical storage of water through a negotiated agreement.

Water Marketing

Water marketing is the process of purchasing or leasing water rights or a contractual right to a supply in order to gain access to the supply on a temporary or permanent basis.

IID   = Imperial Irrigation District
KCWA = Kern County Water Agency
PVID = Palo Verde Irrigation District

Water Banking

Several agricultural water districts in Kern County have marketed their banking capabilities. The Semitropic Water Storage District, Kern Delta Water District, and Arvin-Edison Water Storage District, all located in the southern San Joaquin Valley near the California Aqueduct, are currently banking water for other State Water Project contractors.

Semitropic developed one million acre-feet of storage capacity for a groundwater storage program. MWD and SCVWD both have agreements with Semitropic to deliver SWP water in wet years to Semitropic for in lieu groundwater recharge, described below, of up to 350 taf of storage each. Alameda County Water District (ACWD) also has an agreement with Semitropic for 50 taf, and the Zone 7 Water Agency has an agreement for 43 taf.

Under these arrangements, the contractor pays a one-time charge, plus a charge for every acre-foot of water stored, and pays the pumping costs for every acre-foot retrieved. Because Semitropic farmers have access to California Aqueduct water, pumping is reduced when water is stored in the aquifer. At the contractor's request during dry years, Semitropic would release its SWP allocation to the contractor, in lieu of pumping groundwater from the aquifer. In the case of agencies located downstream of Semitropic, Semitropic could pump groundwater into the California Aqueduct for delivery.

Under the Kern Delta/Arvin-Edison program, MWD purchases 40,000 to 75,000 afy and stores 250,000 to 350,000 ac-ft of SWP water in the underlying aquifer. During dry years and at MWD's request, Kern Delta/Arvin Edison returns up to 50,000 afy of the stored water through an exchange of stored SWP or other local surface water deliverable through the California Aqueduct, or pumping of groundwater into the California Aqueduct via other existing or new connecting facilities. ∎

operation, and exchange or purchase; and identifying available storage or conveyance facilities (*see* sidebar, page 122).[3]

Conservation Savings Sales. A creative way to develop a new water supply is illustrated by the MWD-Imperial Irrigation District (IID) conservation program. Under this program, IID will improve the conveyance system–lining part of the All American Canal to reduce loss from leakage. This in turn will lead to IID reducing its Colorado River diversions, permitting the U.S. Bureau of Reclamation to make the water available to MWD. The process leading up to this apparently simple program was actually very complex and is a fascinating story told by Norris Hundley, Jr., in *The Great Thirst, Californians and Water, a History*, published by the University of California Press in 2001. Two of the complexities involved verifying the actual water savings associated with conservation and negotiating a market rate.

Exchange Agreements. An example of an exchange agreement is provided by the Coachella Valley Water District and the Desert Water Agency, two Southern California SWP contractors that do not have conveyance facilities to receive water directly from the SWP. Instead, they have entered into an agreement with MWD, whereby MWD releases water from its Colorado River Aqueduct into the Whitewater River for storage in the upper Coachella Valley groundwater basin. In exchange, MWD takes delivery of an equal amount of the agencies' SWP water.

Land Fallowing. In 2001, MWD developed a 35-year arrangement with farmers in the Palo Verde Irrigation District, in eastern Riverside County along the Colorado River, to pay them not to grow crops on up to 29 percent of their land. Because these farmers have water rights dating back to 1877, the Palo Verde Irrigation District (PVID) has the highest priority of receiving its supply before any other water agency in Southern California can divert from the Colorado River. MWD is seeking the additional supplies in preparation for the state's five percent

3. For additional information, *see Layperson's Guide to Water Marketing*, published by the Water Education Foundation (www.watereducation.org) in 2000; *A Guide to Water Transfers,* July 1999 Draft, published by SWRCB (www.waterrights.ca.gov); and the Bay-Delta Authority's website (http://ontap.ca.gov), which also includes a database of water transfer activities listing the quantities, duration, and processes agencies used for each transaction.

reduction in its allocation of Colorado River water when Arizona takes its full allocated share anticipated to occur around 2015.

With the new arrangement, MWD would pay an immediate fee per acre to every farm operator willing to leave up to 29 percent of his or her land fallow in any year. In addition, farmers would be compensated for each acre fallowed each year when requested. In return, MWD would receive up to 111,000 acre-feet of water per year, leaving as many as 26,500 acres fallow. The water would be conveyed through the Colorado River Aqueduct for immediate use or storage.

The MWD-PVID fallowing arrangement led to a number of questions about third-party impacts: among them, that small businesses dependent on farming might fail, or that the loss of farm labor jobs could result in higher unemployment and lower sales tax revenues in an area of the state already struggling. To address these concerns, MWD compensated feed and farm implement dealers along with merchants in related businesses for possible loss of income.

From the perspective of statewide public policy, loss of agricultural productivity that might cause economic dislocation raises significant issues. Many believe that the state should not only protect its agricultural land, but also the agricultural economy that sustains many communities. Others believe that certain regions in the state, such as the dry Imperial Valley or the poorly drained Westlands Water District lands in the western San Joaquin Valley, are not well suited to sustainable irrigated farming and perhaps should be irrigated less.

Agriculture is critical to the economy and the environment, and to California's heritage. Any permanent transfers of water should only be undertaken after carefully weighing third-party impacts, environmental and economic issues, and the future of agriculture in the region. But given anticipated urban growth and the lack of significant new supplies of water and its economic value, some level of reduced agricultural production in order to provide urban water is inevitable.

Desalination and Demineralization

As membrane and other treatment technologies become more cost-effective, demineralization and desalination will be used more frequently. These processes can lower the mineral content in groundwater and reduce the levels of TDS found in sea water, bay water, brackish groundwater, and supplies having high percentages of agricultural runoff or wastewater.

However, implementing desalination can be problematic, not only technologically or economically, but because coastal communities are often highly sensitive to the perception of a potentially unlimited water supply leading to growth-related impacts. Moreover, operating a desalination facility can be costly in terms of energy requirements.

Steps Required for Water Transfers

Approvals

- SWRCB approval of any changes to water rights
- USBR or DWR contract modifications
- Local regulatory agency requirements

Studies

- CEQA compliance
- Operations studies, yield reliability, costs, mitigations identified and addressed, including third-party effects

Agreements

- Conveyance capacity wheeling and repayment
- Exchange or purchase agreement with seller
- Operational changes

Facilities

- Conveyance from source or storage facility
- Temporary storage
- Long-term storage

EWA = Environmental Water Account
TDS = Total dissolved solids

Desalination, Desalting, Demineralization

Desalination, desalting, and demineralization are treatment processes that make seawater or brackish water available for potable or non-potable use. While considerably less saline than seawater, brackish water contains dissolved minerals in amounts that exceed normally acceptable levels for potable and non-potable use.

California Bay-Delta
Environmental Water Account

The CALFED Bay-Delta Program (now administered by the California Bay Delta Authority) is a long-term comprehensive program to restore ecological health and improve various water management activities for beneficial uses in the San Francisco Bay/Sacramento-San Joaquin Delta (Delta) system (for additional information on this program, *see* chapter 8). The plan was developed by the CALFED lead agencies (primarily federal and state resource and water agencies), responsible agencies, and stakeholders as a framework or starting point for a series of specific actions related to ecosystem quality, water quality, water supply reliability, and levee system integrity.

Creation of the Environmental Water Account (EWA), initiated in 2000, is one of the actions undertaken to promote flexible water management in order to provide additional protection and recovery for fisheries in the Delta. EWA is cooperatively administered by the U.S. Fish and Wildlife Service, NOAA Fisheries, California Department of Fish and Game, the DWR and its State Water Project, and the Bureau of Reclamation and its Central Valley Project. These agencies have primary responsibility for managing the EWA water assets and exercising biological judgment to determine which SWP and CVP operational changes are beneficial for the long-term survival and recovery of fish species. In other words, EWA is in the business of buying water from some part of the state or federal "plumbing" system, sometimes storing it in surface or groundwater reservoirs, and providing that water where it is needed for environmental purposes.

EWA does not create any new water for the state, and will purchase water only from willing sellers north and south of the Delta who have demonstrated that local water needs are not impaired as a result of the transaction. Water can be purchased for short periods of time (for a single year or a season) or for longer periods. EWA water will be used primarily to meet the requirements of the federal and state endangered species acts. Specific uses include the following:

• Augmenting stream flows and Delta outflows

• Modifying exports to provide fisheries benefits during critical stages of life history

• Replacing project water supply interrupted by modifications to project operations

Specific actions that may be taken to make water available for the EWA include banking, borrowing, or transferring water supplies, selling water, arranging for conveyance of EWA assets (*i.e.*, water), and making operational changes in the SWP and CVP. For example, the EWA might provide replacement water for SWP contractors to allow for reduced pumping of Delta water when fish are in the vicinity of the Tracy and Banks pumps. During summer months of June and July, EWA water would be used to reduce the export of Delta water to avoid high salvage of sensitive fish species such as the Delta smelt or Sacramento splittail. EWA water would be used to compensate for these export reductions. Other actions might include upstream water releases to improve instream flows for anadromous fish migration, spawning, rearing, and similar activities. EWA is also working with local agencies to store water in groundwater basins during wet or normal years to use for environmental purposes when fisheries could benefit.

In 2000, approximately 480,000 acre-feet of water was purchased from willing sellers in Northern and Southern California, and significant storage capacity was leased in Southern California groundwater basins (see Winternitz and White, 2001). To ensure biological justification for the use of EWA assets, a Science Advisory Board has been established to review recommendations from the Management Agencies and suggest long-term studies to evaluate and monitor the biological effects resulting from the EWA. EWA is scheduled to operate on a trial basis through 2005.

According to Winternitz and White (2001):

Establishing the EWA is an historic achievement. For the first time ever, state and federal resource agencies have been provided an acquired water supply to manage for the benefit of aquatic assets. Regardless of whether the EWA is continued, it has caused a change in the way business is conducted by the state and federal fish and water agencies in California....

Treatment technologies used are either a membrane or thermal process. Since treatment plants are usually located near the source, by the ocean or along a bay, new pipelines and pumping facilities are required to integrate this source into the existing distribution system. The energy requirements, brine disposal, and construction can be expensive, and coastal areas often have ecosystems sensitive to construction impacts. Discharging the brine to a wastewater discharge outfall is one of the easier solutions that can actually improve the quality of effluent by increasing the level of salinity.

A desalination facility constructed in Santa Barbara, but only used as a back-up supply.

In Oceanside, the city owns and operates the Mission Basin Groundwater Desalting Facility, which treats brackish groundwater through a process of reverse osmosis. This local supply source not only reduces the city's reliance on imported water, but increases the reliability of its water supply following an event such as an earthquake.

In the inland city of Corona, the 10 mgd Temescal Desalter treats groundwater and discharges the basin's contaminants through the Santa Ana Regional Interceptor, thus allowing for treatment of the brine. Supplying drinking water that is lower in salt also benefits Corona's wastewater treatment system. This new water source allows the city to meet RWQCB wastewater discharge requirements for TDS. And the cycle of increased groundwater pumping to the desalter, coupled with higher quality wastewater discharged back into the basin and creek, improves the water quality of the Temescal Basin and the Santa Ana River.

Off-Stream Storage and Expansion of Existing Reservoirs

Reservoirs constructed on rivers can result in ecological damage to aquatic and riparian species and habitat typically found in streams, riparian corridors, and valleys. Due to heightened public and agency concern about ecological disruption and the difficulty of mitigating the damage, the only new storage reservoirs that are likely to be built in the future are off-stream reservoirs. Constructed in valleys with intermittent streamflows and minimal or no riparian habitat, off-stream reservoirs are filled with water that has been diverted and pumped from another watershed. Several large reservoirs have recently been constructed in California, including MWD's 800,000 acre-foot Diamond Valley Lake located near Hemet in Riverside County, Contra Costa Water District's 100,000 acre-foot Los Vaqueros Reservoir in Contra Costa County, and the San Diego County Water Authority's 24,000 acre-foot Oliveheim, all of which are off-stream facilities.

Enlarging an existing reservoir to capture excess stream flow available primarily during periods of high precipitation has recently attracted some interest. In fact, expanding capacity to capture flow from flooding can serve a dual purpose by reducing the impact downstream. In this respect, the USBR is studying the enlargement of Shasta and Friant dams, and several other facilities.

Developing additional storage capacity allows an agency to capture supplies during a high runoff period for use when the water is in demand. As dry year supplies become more valuable, capturing wet year flows in excess of what is needed for environmental use (*e.g.,* maintaining stream flows for fisheries) can be an effective way to avoid acquiring new, less reliable supplies. For example, the peaks of the highest annual runoff, above what is needed for other uses, such as fish and wildlife, etc., could be stored in an off-stream reservoir (Figure 5-2). This water can not only be for urban and agricultural uses, but also released in dry years for aquatic and riparian needs.

Since capturing and storing water from high stream flow in off-stream facilities could solve many of California's supply problems, additional off-stream storage facilities and the expansion of existing facilities will likely be constructed in the future.

Gray Water

Gray water is made up of bath, shower, or washing machine water, typically associated with residential use, that can be applied to subsurface irrigation of lawns, trees, and shrubs. Gray water is most beneficial on large lots with extensive landscaping and permeable soils. Separate plumbing systems are required to separate the gray water from other discharges for distribution to the end use.

In 1992, the California state legislature amended the Water Code to allow gray water systems to be installed in residential buildings with the approval of local health departments. Because installing and maintaining these systems can be expensive, and local jurisdictions are concerned about the health implications, gray water has not yet received a high rate of acceptance. At present, gray water is not thought to be a significant potential source of new water supply.

Graywater – DHS Definition

Graywater refers to untreated wastewater that has not been contaminated by any toilet discharge, has not been affected by infectious, contaminated, or unhealthy bodily wastes, and does not present a threat of contamination by unhealthful processing, manufacturing, or operating wastes.

Graywater includes wastewater from bathtubs, showers, bathroom basins, washing machines, and laundry tubs, but does not include wastewater from kitchen sinks or dishwashers.

California Water Code, Chapter 22, Section 14876

CHAPTER 6

Preparing an Integrated Water Resources Plan

Changes in the policy arena over the past two decades have presented a challenge to the traditional approach to water supply planning, resulting in a more holistic process. Some of the significant changes include:

- Two serious droughts leading to severe water shortages
- Greater awareness of dry-year planning and water-reliability issues
- Substantial growth in areas short of water
- Awareness of and legislation addressing environmental issues associated with water resources
- The public's increased sophistication and involvement in planning and decisionmaking

As a result of these changes, a more comprehensive approach to water resources and system planning–known as integrated water resource planning–has emerged. This chapter shows how to integrate water supply, demand, and an alternatives evaluation process to prepare an integrated resource plan (IRP). We also describe how this approach can meet current requirements for linking growth with water supply reliability. Methods for establishing and linking goals and objectives to evaluation criteria and using the process to develop, screen, and evaluate alternative solutions are also suggested. In addition, we present the essential components of an implementation plan to ensure a successful integrated planning effort.

Integrated Water Resources Planning

An integrated approach typically results in an integrated resources plan (IRP), an integrated water resources plan (IWRP), or a similar product. In the past, a water system master plan focused primarily on known water supplies and the resulting water system facility needs (*see* sidebar, page 130). By contrast, an IRP

Gentlemen, you are piling up a heritage of conflict, for there is not enough water to supply the land!

– John Wesley Powell, addressing the Irrigation Congress in 1893

IRP = Integrated resources plan
IWRP = Integrated water resources plan

Historic water tower in Fresno

includes the establishment of goals and objectives, and involves a comprehensive assessment of demands, supplies, and alternatives to meet facility needs, as well as variables such as environmental effects. This is not to say that a facilities master plan is no longer needed, but its content may now reflect more components of the IRP process. For a typical IRP process, *see* Figure 6-1.

Each IRP reflects the specific needs and supply conditions of its own agency, and throughout the process stakeholders are involved. An IRP may include various local, regional, state, and even federal agencies, along with local land use planning authorities and the local wastewater agency.

At key junctures, an IRP also should include the public in development of goals and/or objectives, development of alternatives, establishment of evaluation criteria, and evaluating the alternatives. For methods involving stakeholders and examples of public processes, *see* chapter 8.

Environmental Compliance Considerations

Traditional water master planning does not incorporate environmental quality considerations into the development of alternatives, but rather considers environmental review a compliance step to be tackled at the end of the process. In a traditional master plan, separate environmental documents are usually prepared to implement each recommendation for a project (construction of facilities, for example) as needed.

When preparing an IRP, environmental considerations, a key component of the recommended strategy, should be woven into the development of broad goals and objectives and the analysis of supply and demand alternatives from the outset. IRPs can lead directly to the preparation of a program-level environmental impact report (EIR) on the recommended plan–and/or an environmental impact study (EIS) if a federal action is involved–followed by project-level environmental review of specific components. The programmatic document addresses both the context and need for the project. A program EIR can evaluate focused, project-level infrastructure components planned for the near term that can then be followed by a subsequent project EIR or a Negative Declaration for long-term components.

A comprehensive evaluation should integrate other applicable requirements of the California Environmental Quality Act (CEQA), the National Environmental Policy Act (NEPA), and the Endangered Species Act that might be relevant so that they all become part of the plan design and the criteria for evaluating options. Similarly, the Army Corps of Engineers 404 permit requirements–under the Clean Water Act for any agency filling or having an impact on "waters of the United States"–and other water-related permits should be part of the plan. *See* chapter 2 for details on these laws.[1]

While NEPA requires that an EIS contain an alternatives analysis with each alternative under consideration evaluated equally, CEQA states only that the alternatives to the preferred project should reflect a "reasonable range" and receive a comparative evaluation. An IRP can readily fulfill both of these information and analysis needs.

Identifying the anticipated need for environmental compliance early affects how an IRP might be written. If a per capita method (based on population projections) instead of a land use-based method is used to project water demands, for example, the public might conclude that the capital projects are growth-inducing. This concern may arise from limited public involvement in developing population projections compounded by an absence of environmental documentation revealing the assumptions on which the plan relied. For a discussion of the use of other documents, such as general plan-designated land uses (to project water demands and determine where new infrastructure is needed), general plan EIRs, and LAFCO-designated spheres of influence, *see* chapter 4.

The public perception of growth issues and environmental impacts varies significantly throughout

Figure 6-1
Integrated Resource Plan Process

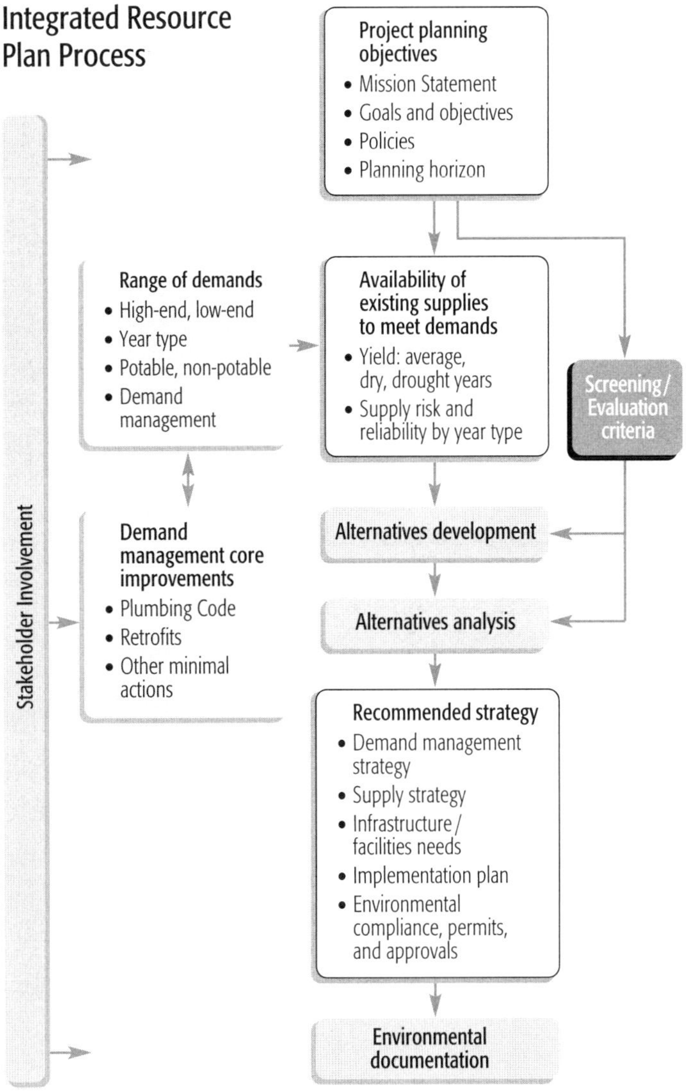

Army Corps of Engineers Section 404 Permit

A permit from the U.S. Army Corps of Engineers is required by Section 404 of the federal Clean Water Act for any applicant who seeks to "dredge or fill" waters of the United States, which includes various wetlands and marshes.

1. Suggestions for integrating environmental laws and requirements into the planning process are available in The NEPA Book and the CEQA Deskbook, published by Solano Press. For CEQA and NEPA process flow charts, *see* Appendix D.

Definition of Terms

Problem Statement. Statement of primary issues to be addressed.

Mission (or Vision) Statement. Summary of future desired condition that offers overall direction for the IRP process. It may seek to balance a community's need for water with its desire for environmental quality and other variables.

Goals. Defines mission statement more specifically, but not as precisely as an objective. Broad but realistic statement describing a desired condition rather than a narrowly defined outcome. Can be short- and long-term and may apply to particular components of an IRP: for example, new supplies, conservation, cost effectiveness, or environmental quality.

Objectives. More specific subset of the goals that are used to guide and evaluate the selection of a specific implementing action. Should be time-oriented, quantifiable, and directed toward a particular entity to allow for measurement of success over time. An objective can form the basis for adaptively managing a plan.

Actions. Specific activity that will result in or contribute to achieving an objective or goal. Moves an agency toward a desired condition identified in mission statement. Should specify who is responsible; when it must be completed; constraints, costs, and/or studies required; and any appropriate monitoring.

BAWSCA = Bay Area Water Supply and Conservation Agency
BAWUA = Bay Area Water Users Association
MWD = Metropolitan Water District
SCVWD = Santa Clara Valley Water District
SFPUC = San Francisco Public Utilities Commission

the state. Some water-related projects in environmentally sensitive areas are subject to intense public scrutiny while other communities have more neutral attitudes with less concern about growth and the environment. Despite this variation, any IRP that will be closely scrutinized should provide a thorough explanation of its assumptions and the methodology employed.

Why Integrated System Planning Makes Sense

An integrated approach to assessing water demands and supplies not only results in more defensible implementation actions, but accommodates changing conditions such as land use patterns and weather variability. Integrated water system planning considers the limitations of supply, particularly during dry years, the management of demands, and how demands and supplies are interrelated. Because water projects are expensive, communities are insisting on more accountability when planning for future facilities and supplies. A more rigorous approach to developing and analyzing alternatives, often with public involvement, can result in a greater level of community support for expensive capital improvements. More work up front can save time and costs later in the process or during project implementation.

Establishing Goals

When working with stakeholders (whether it is an internal project management team, a public advisory, technical, or steering committee, or a less structured public involvement process), the first steps are to establish a mission (or vision) statement, goals, and objectives. This is particularly valuable because of the complexity of water supply planning, the huge capital outlays required, and possible environmental impacts. Working together to identify a project's common goals not only prevents basic misunderstandings, but can foster feelings of ownership in the process. Moreover, it fulfills the primary purpose of providing an agreed-upon framework for decisionmaking.

Although definitions may vary, an IRP should not be limited by semantics. Water planners should be internally consistent and tailor the terms used to what is needed to communicate effectively. The word "goals," for example can encompass a problem statement, a mission statement, objectives, and actions (*see* sidebar for a definition of terms used in this discussion).

Establishing the mission statement, goals, and objectives early on will aid in the development of alternatives and criteria for an alternatives analysis later in the process. Goals and objectives used to guide integrated resource planning are typically established for the following purposes:

- Rate impacts
- Environmental effects or future restoration

- Water quality
- Long-term reliability of water supply
- Operational reliability
- Long-term decision-making process and public interaction
- Other potential topics

An example of a mission statement and accompanying goals for a water supply master plan is provided by the San Francisco Public Utilities Commission (SFPUC) and its partner in the process, the Bay Area Water Users Association (BAWUA). BAWUA (now called Bay Area Water Supply and Conservation Agency or BAWSCA) represents the 29 retail water agencies and a water company that purchase water from the SFPUC.

To accomplish the mission statement, the SFPUC Water Supply Master Plan Steering Committee (composed of the various internal operating groups of the partners) worked diligently to identify the following goals:

- **Provide Desired Supply Reliability.** Configure and operate the SFPUC system to optimize use of its Sierra and local water resources to satisfy the expressed needs of the customers
- **Protect Economic Interest.** Protect the long term economic interest of all SFPUC ratepayers and the financial investments of the SFPUC and its wholesale customers
- **Protect Environmental Resources.** Implement system modifications and improvements so as to protect important environmental resources
- **Provide High-Quality Water.** Preserve the highest quality water for potable uses and other appropriate customer needs

As another example, the Board of Directors of the Santa Clara Valley Water District (SCVWD) initially developed a set of 13 draft goals and corresponding criteria for its last IWRP. External stakeholders then reviewed and refined the statements, expanding the list to 15. The goals were refined even further and were used to evaluate water supply alternatives (*see* sidebar).

For an example of quantifiable objectives, *see* MWD's IRP guidelines in the sidebar on page 134.

Alternatives Development

The key to developing alternatives is to establish evaluation criteria reflecting an agency's mission statement, goals, and/or objectives that have been agreed upon by various interests and stakeholders. Broad screening criteria are often applied before evaluation criteria to screen out or eliminate alternatives with a fatal flaw.

SFPUC Water Supply Master Plan Mission Statement

To provide SFPUC customers with alternative water supply and management options for SFPUC system use, characterized in terms of reliability, cost, water quality, operational flexibility, and environmental impacts, and to develop a framework for decisionmaking by the SFPUC and its customers leading to appropriate agreements and an implementation plan.

Goals of Santa Clara Valley Water District's IWRP

Operational

- Provide equal reliability of water throughout the county
- Maximize system flexibility
- Maximize effective use of water supply
- Maximize multi-purpose potential for integrating district functions
- Meet level of service

Risk

- Minimize risk of providing supplies
- Maximize ability to respond to changing conditions

Economic

- Minimize total district costs
- Minimize rate impacts

Community

- Protect economic well-being of county by minimizing costs to the community
- Include public involvement and maximize public acceptance
- Maximize opportunities for recreation and environmental uses
- Maximize the quality and treatability of source water
- Promote efficient water use

Environmental

- Avoid or minimize adverse impacts to habitats or ecosystems

Supply and/or infrastructure alternatives should be configured in sufficient detail to apply the evaluation criteria. The need for, along with the sizing and staging of, any recommended facilities should be premised on demand projections that are clearly explained and based on land use.

Evaluation Criteria

Typical evaluation criteria to meet an agency's goals may include the following topics:

- Supply availability and reliability
- Costs
- Water quality
- Environmental impacts
- Risk and uncertainty of supply
- System reliability
- Public support
- Public health and safety
- Flexibility
- Institutional issues
- Ease of implementation
- Agency control
- Impacts on local economy
- Third-party impacts
- Customers' ability to pay

When using these topics as evaluation criteria, it is important to define each one clearly so that, when applied, the alternatives can be compared. For example, with a goal of "improving (annual and seasonal) water supply reliability," the actual criterion might be "to provide the highest level of supply reliability." For a goal of "providing high quality drinking water," the criterion might be "to meet or improve all state and federal drinking water standards on a consistent basis." Established criteria must also be applied when an Army Corps of Engineers' 404 Permit is required or another regulatory framework must be addressed.

A simplified version of the evaluation criteria can be used to screen out fatal flaws so that a particular alternative is not carried forward any further. The screening process will also help explain why an alternative is eliminated (which the environmental documentation process requires).

Developing Alternatives

A variety of solutions should be identified that reflect established goals and criteria. Before dismissing an alternative, it is useful to wait until the screening

---

Metropolitan Water District's IRP Guidelines

- One hundred percent reliability during the next ten years, even under a worst-case drought.
- MWD shall maintain a resource mix that balances investments in additional imported water with investments in local resource development and conservation.
- An untreated water rate not to increase for ten years and average water costs of about $414 per acre-foot by the year 2005, less than a one percent annual increase.
- MWD commits to a resource development and financial strategy that is flexible and provides financial security for MWD and its member agencies.

criteria have been applied. If no solution satisfies the criteria, the goals may be unrealistic. At that point, either review and redefine each goal, or search for new alternatives.

Once existing supplies have been measured against projected demands, the system needs must be determined. Sources of alternative supplies may range from using more of what already exists, such as groundwater, to the acquisition of new sources. Focus on alternative supplies and the specific treatment, storage, and transmission needs that may be required for these supplies. If transfer water is an alternative, the following questions should be addressed:

- What is the quality of the water?
- Is it necessary to modify the treatment plant for a different quality?
- When is the transfer water available?
- Is storage required?
- Do the transmission facilities have sufficient capacity?
- Is it necessary to address significant third-party economic or environmental effects?

If it's necessary to identify and site new facilities for the additional supply, the specific alternative should describe each component required (Figure 6-3).

After defining an alternative, develop the data necessary to measure it against the evaluation criteria. For example, assume that a project goal is "improving (annual and seasonal) water supply reliability," with the corresponding criterion "to provide the highest level of supply reliability." In this case, information projecting the frequency of annual and seasonal shortages would make it possible to assess the performance of each alternative.

Information summarizing the cost of a particular alternative should reflect its present

Distribution System Hydraulic Models

A distribution system hydraulic model can be a useful tool for developing and assessing alternative supply and system components. With a hydraulic model, it's possible to identify deficiencies of the existing and future water distribution system, quantify available capacity, plan the most cost-effective integration of new facilities into the system, and store important data such as physical characteristics and a maintenance history of existing facilities.

The speed and graphic capabilities have improved so much in recent years that stakeholder workshops use hydraulic models to describe assumptions and assess alternatives in real time. Recent improvements to hydraulic models for distribution systems also allow water quality conditions to be characterized, which is helpful when planning a system to meet drinking water regulations.

Figure 6-2
Link Between Master Plan and Planning Data

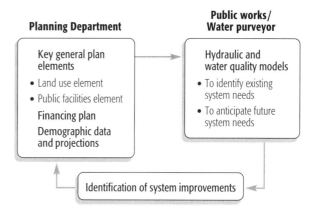

A distribution system hydraulic model can also help link land use planning and utilities planning functions. Land use, demographics, and phasing assumptions used for water demand in the hydraulic model are rooted in general plans and other planning data that have withstood public scrutiny (*see* Figure 6-2 and previous information in chapter 4).

Hydraulic model output shows existing and alternative future system improvements and phasing that can be iteratively coordinated with the development of the general plan and financial planning, thus providing consistent and defensible system planning documents and results. ■

Figure 6-3

An Example of Supply
Planning Project Components

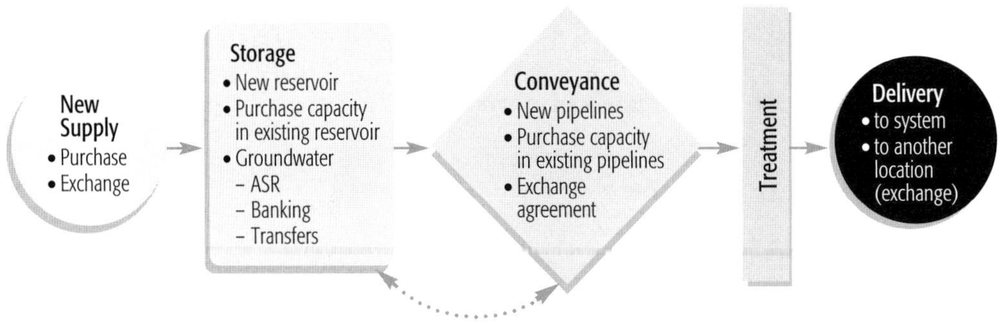

value, capital requirements, annual operation and maintenance, and/or a benefit-cost analysis. Water quality information might include a comparison, by parameters of concern, to existing supplies, any variability associated with differing supplies, the supply's treatability, or any associated risk of pathogens. Environmental information might include possible significant effects, such as the presence of a special status species, costly or difficult mitigation requirements (that may actually be built into an alternative project description), or the environmental benefits associated with each alternative project.

Evaluating Alternatives

Nowhere in the water supply and system planning process is the need for stakeholder involvement more valuable than when evaluating alternatives. Various methods can be employed, ranging from simple high, medium, and low rankings against the criteria to more complex computer-decision models.

A high-medium-low ranking method is an appropriate tool for comparing alternatives that are distinguishable, non-controversial projects involving a small group of stakeholders such as internal agency staff (*see* Table 6-1). Although apparently quite simple, the approach relies on detailed information developed for each alternative.

While it is common to quantify the rankings (Table 6-2), this method can foster a perception that decisions based on numeric ranking reflect a greater level of accuracy than actually exists. Quantifying in this manner often assumes that criteria have equal weight, which may or may not be the case. Some stakeholders may be troubled by an approach whose analyses and decisions are not immediately understandable and transparent.

A computer model is often used to quantify the decision-making process inherent in every evaluation. Using a decision model, such as the popular Criteria Decision Plus software, criteria and subcriteria are weighted, and the alternatives are compared to the criteria. Because one can easily quantify and apply a wide range of criteria to

Justification or Need for Project

When developing the environmental documents for improvements to the war system, it is important to demonstrate how the water demands were estimated. This will help explain why the project is needed and clarify discussion of growth-related issues.

Since water demands typically drive the sizing and timing of a project, present the analysis early in the process and tie it to the development of improvements (by using a distribution system hydraulic model, as presented in Figure 6-4, for example). ■

Table 6-1. Comparing Alternatives Against Criteria				
ALTERNATIVE	**E V A L U A T I O N C R I T E R I A**			
	MINIMIZE COSTS	MAXIMIZE RELIABILITY	MINIMIZE ENVIRONMENTAL IMPACT	PUBLIC SUPPORT
A	Medium	Medium	Highest	Highest
B	Low	Highest	Lowest	Medium
C	High	Lowest	Medium	Lowest

Table 6-2. Quantifying Alternatives Against Criteria				
STEP ONE ALTERNATIVE	**E V A L U A T I O N C R I T E R I A**			
	COST	MAXIMIZE RELIABILITY	MINIMIZE ENVIRONMENTAL IMPACT	PUBLIC SUPPORT
A	$1M	50%	90	35
B	$2M	100%	75	25
C	$0.5M	20%	85	10
STEP TWO RANKING	**R A N K I N G O F A L T E R N A T I V E S**			
	LOWEST COST	HIGHEST RELIABILITY	LOWEST ENVIRONMENTAL IMPACT	PUBLIC SUPPORT
1	C	B	A	A
2	A	A	C	B
3	B	C	B	C

an unlimited number of alternatives, a decision model can be an effective tool for a complex project. It can also contribute to the stakeholder process where various participants rank each criterion to measure the alternatives against non-cost criteria that is difficult to quantify. As with any evaluation process, however, it's important to describe the methodology carefully so that stakeholders can fully understand the results.

Strategies for Water Supply and Demand

Rather than selecting only one alternative to meet a project's objectives, a hybrid or mix-and-match strategy can reflect the best components of each alternative. This strategy may include a new supply source along with various other core improvements, such as the use of conservation or recycled water. The key is to establish a goal for core improvements, while remaining flexible to changing

Figure 6-4

Land Use Data Are Important to an Accurate Hydraulic Model

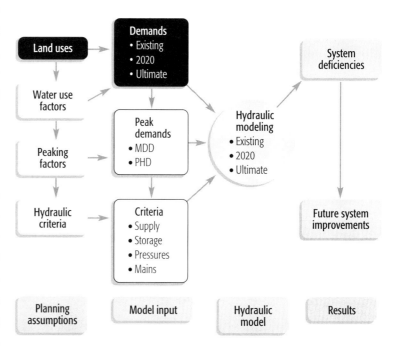

Metropolitan Water District Strategy

- Diamond Valley Lake, an 800,000 acre-foot off-stream reservoir near Hemet that doubled the region's surface water storage for drought protection, emergency reserves, and seasonal regulation

- Semitropic Storage Program, a 350,000 acre-foot program storing water in a San Joaquin Valley aquifer for use during a drought

- North Las Posas Groundwater Project with Calleguas Metropolitan Water District, a 100,000 acre-foot storage program

- Signed agreements with member agencies for 23 local water recycling and groundwater recovery projects, that provide a total contract amount of 116,000 afy

- Signed agreements with member agencies for about 200 conservation programs that provide an estimated savings of at least 40,000 afy

- A water banking and transfer program with Arvin-Edison Water Storage District that will provide up to 350,000 acre-feet of dry year water supplies

- A conjunctive use storage program with Raymond Basin agencies, similar to the North Las Posas program, for 75,000 acre-feet

Source: MWD 2001 (www.mwd.dst.ca.us)

conditions. If the new supply being developed is not available at the quantities originally anticipated, for example, the strategy's upper range of water conservation may need to be implemented to meet the shortfall.

The IWRP of the Santa Clara Valley Water District resulted in a water supply strategy that was based on an array of components. Strategies for demand and supply management included aggressive water conservation measures and use of recycled water for outdoor irrigation in new developments. A groundwater banking program is also underway. In wet years, SCVWD stores water with the Semitropic Water Storage District in Kern County for use in dry years (*see* chapter 5). In addition, SCVWD is pursuing long-term transfer agreements with other Central Valley agencies.

The Metropolitan Water District also put together a resource strategy based on a balanced approach to developing imported and local resources. The strategy relied on the maximum use of surface and groundwater storage available in the region, with additional supplies added in order of ascending cost. Resource options identified to meet the gap between existing firm water supplies and future demand are illustrated in Figure 6-5, where each option is ranked by the total cost of each unit and the amount of water it could provide.

MWD chose a resource mix made up of different levels of these options based on the goals listed below. *See Southern California's Integrated Water Resources Plan, Executive Summary*, MWD, March 1996. The projects MWD selected (*see* sidebar) have been or

EBMUD = East Bay Municipal Utility District

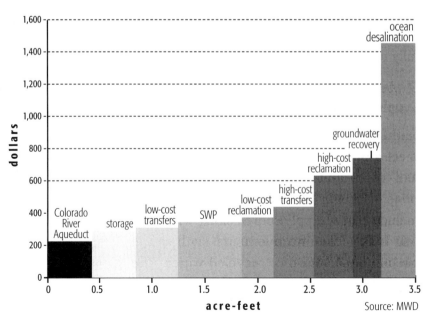

Figure 6-5
Average Unit Cost of Alternatives ($/af)

Source: MWD

are being implemented, and several are described in chapter 5.

- Maximize the availability of low-cost water that the Colorado River Aqueduct (CRA) delivers
- Provide adequate State Water Project supplies to meet requirements for reliability and water quality
- Fully utilize the existing potential for local groundwater conjunctive use and surface storage
- Implement water recycling and groundwater recovery projects identified by member agencies and other water providers as cost effective
- Utilize voluntary water transfers needed for dry years and storage replenishment

The East Bay Municipal Utilities District (EBMUD) has taken a unique approach to supply options. Due to the complexities of implementing a large water project, EBMUD chose to develop three different projects in parallel, assuming that the one capable of full implementation would become apparent over time. All EBMUD projects are being pursued simultaneously, in addition to core improvements in conservation and recycling. All three projects are undergoing full environmental review and documentation.

Assessing the Risk of Shortage versus Developing New Supply

In 2002, the City of Santa Cruz embarked on an innovative study designed to test the effects of shortages and gauge the reaction of its primary customers to different levels of projected water shortage. Santa Cruz relies primarily on local surface water sources supplying the needs of nearly 90,000 residents, as well as businesses, recreation, and industrial users. The city maintains an Urban Water Management Plan and an up-to-date Drought Contingency Plan. A key question asked was how much and how often the community is willing to tolerate cutbacks in water service and what actual and perceived impacts might be created by different cutback levels. According to Goddard and Fiske, the city has determined that:

> [I]t is willing to accept some degree of use curtailment in order to minimize the size, expense, and potential environmental impacts of developing new sources of water. This is because local community values strongly favor environmental protection and preserving the small town character of the City, and because many (including elected officials) perceive the need for water supply improvements only as contributing to unwanted growth in the region....

The study examined six projected drought scenarios, from a 10 percent cutback to a dramatic 60 percent system-wide cutback that the city experienced during the 1976–77 drought. Interviews, focus groups, and surveys were conducted to examine the reactions of each major customer group to a specified level of water shortage. The testing method was tailored for residents, businesses, and specialized water-using industries such as resorts/golf courses and others. Results suggest that each group responds differently under the various scenarios.

Residential customers indicated a relatively modest hardship at a shortage level below 20 percent and a shift to significant hardship at a level of 30 percent and above. At the highest level (50 percent and above), hardship is expected to be severe, with considerable conflict among citizens and between citizens and the city. Business and industrial customers generally followed this pattern, with several notable exceptions. The landscape industry felt serious economic hardship much sooner (with cutbacks of 15 to 20 percent). Restaurants, hotels, hospitals, and some high-technology manufacturing businesses also faced economic hardships at relatively low cutback levels.

While specific results for any given community may vary, the significant lesson is that such a methodology can help test the effects of shortages and establish appropriate policies for drought planning. Certain users can better withstand cutbacks than others. Water purveyors must fairly administer cutbacks, but valid public policy reasons exist for examining the effects on different types of customers.

The City of Santa Cruz intends to use these findings in its future supply and demand planning to assess the policy trade-off between new water supply sources and the risk of shortages on existing customers. ■

Source: *Impacts of Municipal Water Shortages*, Goddard and Fiske, 2002, City of Santa Cruz

- Divert American River water to Mokelumne aqueducts. One option involved developing a new Sacramento River intake at Freeport, in partnership with the County of Sacramento and the Bureau of Reclamation, a treatment plant, and a pipeline to the aqueducts to use a water contract for American River water.
- Negotiate a conjunctive use program with San Joaquin County interests to store water from the American or Mokelumne Rivers during wet years in San Joaquin County aquifer(s). The overdrafted aquifer would be recharged as water levels improve over time. EBMUD would then pump a negotiated percentage of the recharged water during dry years and pay a storage charge.
- Pursue additional Mokelumne River storage by raising the existing dam at Pardee Reservoir.

As this book goes to press, EBMUD is pursuing all three projects, and the Freeport Project is successfully progressing. For more information on the Freeport Project, *see* www.freeportproject.org.

Moving from Project Planning to Implementation

Once the conceptual strategies have been selected, an implementation plan is needed to provide a greater level of detail for project execution. Although the plans may differ, many components are shared. Early stakeholder involvement, for example, is critical to the success of any plan. The following components are usually included in an implementation plan, with a varying degree of detail:

- New water supply and supply management strategy with detailed implementation steps
- Supplies requiring further investigation
- Demand strategy with conservation goals
- Comparison of project objectives with recommended plan of prioritized improvements
- Demonstration that the solution is the best way to achieve project's objectives
- Specific capital and operational improvements
- Phasing of facilities
- Detailed cost estimates
- Water rate and financing plan
- Description of environmental compliance and permitting requirements
- Stakeholder involvement process (*see* chapter 8)

Many of these components were discussed previously; the remaining components (prioritizing recommendations, phasing, financing, environmental compliance, and stakeholders involvement) are discussed in the following section.

Criteria for Establishing Priority Recommendations

A recommendation is given high priority by establishing specific criteria that demonstrate its importance. Unlike the criteria used to evaluate an alternative, criteria specific to setting priorities among implementation choices are tailored to each situation and may include the following:

- Vulnerability of the system
- Need for improvements based on projected demands
- Greatest benefit for the cost
- Funding availability (grants or loans to implement, revenue generation, etc.)
- Uncertainties associated with availability of a new supply
- Ability to implement (difficulty obtaining agreements with other agencies, anticipated public controversy, etc.)
- Lead time required for implementation
- Agency policies, such as one requiring more utilization of existing supplies through storage prior to adding new supply

Often, water purveyors set priorities among the criteria, although the process can be tailored for a public group or decisionmakers. The recommended improvements are then ranked according to how they reflect the ranking criteria. While a computer decision model can help conduct this process in a group setting, prioritization can also be kept simple enough to avoid the need for a high level of decision-making support tools.

Phasing and Scheduling Plan

The timing required to implement a plan's recommended components should reflect the priorities discussed above. A comprehensive schedule encompasses financing, institutional and permit negotiations to pursue new supplies, and any environmental compliance necessary to obtain approvals and permits for new supplies and facilities. Where appropriate, permits and approvals can be obtained for the entire project, even if this expands the amount of time projected for this phase. The schedule should also be flexible enough to accommodate any changes in conditions that require rapid implementation or delay. Some of the variables that might arise could relate to changes in demand projections resulting from economic conditions or from actual versus predicted savings associated with a conservation program, or from the fact that the availability of imported water may be greater or less than that anticipated.

Financing Plan

If recommended capital improvements rely upon land use-based water demand projections, the financing plan can easily reflect costs that are associated with

Central Coast Water Authority pipeline, the last significant SWP conveyance construction project

existing versus new development. That portion of supply or infrastructure capacity improvements needed for existing customers, for example, can be quantified and the water rates for the area increased to reflect marginal costs. The portion of the improvements associated with meeting future demands is typically paid for through connection charges. With disaggregated land use-based demands, water rates can reflect geographic regions having patterns of higher consumption that would be affected by an inclining rate structure. Disaggregated demands can also help distinguish costs associated with large areas experiencing infill, reuse, and increased density.

Environmental Compliance and Permitting Requirements

After identifying recommended supplies, the implementation plan should state any additional environmental compliance needed to satisfy CEQA and/or NEPA along with a description of actions that trigger the analysis. For flow charts of the CEQA and NEPA processes, *see* Appendix D.

The implementation plan should list and briefly describe the various permits and project approvals required. Since EIRs and environmentally-related permits have very detailed requirements, the IRP implementation plan should identify the need for these actions to ensure that the environmental documentation requirements are addressed early in the planning process for each individual component or facility.

Some agencies publish permit handbooks or summaries for the initial identification of potential permits and approvals associated with a project. These can be patterned after the State of California Governor's Office of Planning and Research Permit Handbook or the permit and regulatory requirements produced by the CALFED Bay-Delta Program. The implementation plan can incorporate a summary chart of potential permits and approvals, with a brief description of the action that triggers the need and each agency's application requirements. Estimating the amount of time necessary to obtain each permit can help the engineering staff incorporate environmental compliance requirements into the overall schedule. A permit implementation plan of this type is appropriate at the stage of project planning (feasibility/predesign), but is replaced with actual negotiations and detailed scheduling tasks during project design.

As an example, the permits and approvals typically required for water treatment plants in California are listed below. Each of these should be confirmed, and their requirements should be described in the implementation plan.

- Air Quality Board permits for liquid chlorine and ozone generators and destruct/scrubber units and nonemergency energy generators (see size requirements)
- Department of Health Services Permit to Construct and Authority to Operate (a treatment plant)
- Regional Water Quality Control Board Waste Discharge or other National Pollution Discharge Elimination System permit requirements
- Local fire department risk management plan
- Local road department or Caltrans easements and rights-of-way for pipelines in and out of a plant
- CEQA and potentially NEPA requirements
- Any other permits relevant to site-specific conditions

Permits for water supply acquisitions are much more complex, and can trigger a federal action if the project has an impact on wetlands, aquatic species and habitat, riparian habitat, or threatened, rare, or endangered species. Federal agencies typically involved with water supply projects include the U.S. Army Corps of Engineers, U.S. Environmental Protection Agency, U.S. Fish and Wildlife Service, and NOAA Fisheries. Numerous state agencies may also be involved in water supply projects, including the State Water Resources Control Board, the Department of Fish and Game, the Department of Health Services, to name a few.

Involvement of a particular agency is dependent on site-specific conditions. A modification of a water rights permit from the State Water Resources Control Board, for example, typically involves renegotiation of the original permit. This may result in a requirement for water releases for fisheries purposes if it is determined that stream flows are inadequate.

Stakeholder Involvement

Obtaining broad support for the water supply and system planning implementation effort is critical to to the process. Building support can lead to stakeholders helping to implement elements of the plan or otherwise contributing to its success. For a complete discussion of stakeholder involvement methods and several case studies, *see* chapter 8.

A stakeholder is anyone with an interest in the project, ranging from internal staff, to the general public being asked to implement conservation measures, to regulatory agencies approving a permit. As described in Figure 6-1, formal opportunities for stakeholder involvement should be offered throughout the entire planning process.

To gain additional public support, public education should be integrated into the various stakeholder efforts. This could be as simple as adding an informational insert describing the project to a water or sewer bill, preparing a video for a target audience, or holding a calendar and billboard contest for kids.

When building consensus for a solution to a regional water problem, it is imperative that the process be stakeholder driven. In addition to water purveyors, the plan must involve the environmental, recreational, business, and other interests of the public so that the plan reflects the community as a whole. Techniques for making the stakeholder process work are discussed in chapter 8.

CHAPTER 7

Linking Water Quality Protection with Land Use

Water quality for beneficial uses can play as great a role in water system planning as water quantity. When groundwater contamination threatens well water, purveyors are forced to seek alternative entitlements and sources. When excessive erosion or pollutants from runoff degrade sources of surface water, not only do treatment requirements and costs increase, but the result may be an increased risk to public health. When state or federal drinking water standards are made more stringent to protect public health, additional treatment or new sources are required. Requirements to maintain water quality standards in the San Francisco Bay and the Sacramento River-San Joaquin River Delta have dramatic and far-reaching implications for hundreds of diversions on the various streams and rivers feeding the Bay and Delta. For many, water quality, not quantity, will be the primary battleground for California's "water wars" of the years ahead.

As the drinking water industry learns more about the implications of new and well-established water quality constituents of concern, addressing water source protection has become essential. The approaches and tools in this chapter can apply to watershed management for point and nonpoint source discharges, as well as flood control, timber management, ecosystem restoration, and range management. This chapter uses a watershed-based approach to focus on some of the critical water quality issues facing water planners today. It also describes ways of linking different land uses with water quality protection, particularly as they are related to drinking water source protection. This chapter does not address water treatment technologies in detail.

Various techniques described in this chapter can assist in integrated watershed planning:

- How to characterize a watershed for land uses and activities relevant to the goals and objectives of the plan

Protecting drinking water sources includes protecting conveyance facilities.

- How to prioritize contaminants and sources
- How to assess conditions of susceptibility or vulnerability

Finally, the chapter offers innovative solutions for implementing land use-related controls and urban site design techniques to protect water quality.

What Is Watershed Planning?

Ask ten people the meaning of watershed management and you will likely be given ten different answers. As described in this book, watershed management is a proactive, broad-based method for resolving a specific water issue by comprehensively linking land use and water resources within a drainage basin. Linkage between land use and the associated impacts of water quality and flow—and between natural and human elements—is a part of this approach. Once the linkage is made, problems related to water quality and flow are easier to solve through source control and flow management. Fixing a problem at its source with an integrated ecosystem approach is preferable, and far less costly than mitigating individual water quality issues after they become a problem. A watershed management approach can also help integrate goals for long-term ecosystem health and economic sustainability.

Drinking Water Source Protection

Regulatory emphasis on raw water quality and corresponding drinking water treatment requirements is increasing. Treatment costs continue to accelerate along with the complexity of day-to-day operations. As treatment plants become more challenging to design and operate, human error and inadequate treatment process performance may lead to regulatory violations that will affect public health and the environment. And as our knowledge of water quality contaminants grows through the use of improved analytical tools and techniques for measuring trace pollutants and evaluating health effects, the drinking water industry will be required to continue to improve water treatment processes and operations.

One example of increased industry knowledge is the presence of the protozoa *Cryptosporidium parvum*. Relatively unknown a few decades ago, in 1993 a major outbreak of a waterborne illness in Milwaukee was associated with *Cryptosporidium*. While the Milwaukee water treatment plant had adequate filtration and disinfection, a change in process chemicals intended to reduce corrosivity may have allowed *Cryptosporidium*—possibly originating in a slaughterhouse—to survive. The resulting outbreak of cryptosporidisis sickened 400,000 people and killed nearly 100. *Cryptosporidium* poses a substantial treatment challenge. One viable option is to monitor raw water quality at its source in an effort to control the level of treatment required. As these new parameters emerge, watershed source control will become an increasingly important approach to manage water quality and limit treatment costs.

Another example of the industry's growing knowledge base is in suspected carcinogens formed during the process of disinfection. Chlorine, used as a disinfectant, produces disinfection byproducts, or DBPs, that have serious implications for human health. The DBP trihalomethanes, or THMs, are carcinogenic compounds that are formed when chlorine is mixed with the organic carbon found naturally in waters with decayed organic matter. Bromate, another DBP, can be formed by mixing a naturally-occurring bromide from a salty water source with ozone (used as a disinfectant). During certain times of the year, bromide is present in the state's primary municipal surface water supply from the Sacramento River-San Joaquin River Delta.

DBP = Disinfection byproduct
THM = Trihalomethane

Another important factor driving source protection is the high cost of complying with new regulations that address these parameters. Due to financial limitations, small systems find it particularly expensive to comply with the regulations. In California, large systems provide drinking water to 26 million residents, but nearly 10 million are served by small systems, some of which may find it difficult to meet increasing standards.[1]

Source protection is the first barrier to water quality degradation.

To ensure adequate drinking water quality in the future, a multiple barrier approach is needed: source protection, water treatment, and disinfectant residual. Utilities relying on surface water must have management tools that allow for strengthening the first barrier to water quality degradation, their reservoir watersheds. However, utilities using groundwater must have also protection tools in place since groundwater systems, implicated in nearly half of all outbreaks of waterborne disease, are responsible for 85 percent of coliform violations.[2]

DHS's Drinking Water Source Assessment and Protection (DWSAP) Program, which fulfills the federal watershed assessment requirements under the Safe Drinking Water Act (SDWA), is briefly described in chapter 2. DHS also requires a Watershed Sanitary Survey for surface waters.

DWSAP = Drinking Water Source Assessment and Protection
SDWA = Safe Drinking Water Act

Other Watershed Trends

In addition to concerns about the treatment of drinking water, other trends argue for a more integrated approach to watershed planning that overlaps with water quality source protection. The Clean Water Act amendments of 1995 (National Pollutant Discharge Elimination System) and the waste discharge requirements of the California Porter-Cologne Act mean that nonpoint source discharge requirements are becoming nearly as stringent as point source discharge requirements, though much more difficult to manage. A

1. Alexis Strauss, Director of EPA Region IX Water Division, Western Water, February 2001.
2. B.A. Macler and F.W. Pontius, Update on the Ground Water Disinfection Rule, Journal, AWWA, 89:17, 1997.

watershed management approach is becoming increasingly necessary to address non-point source issues.

Some communities and regulators are taking a systems approach that integrates ecosystem protection with sustainable development. State funds are available to restore urban streams in an effort to solve flooding and erosion problems and enhance a stream's natural value. Responding to a disaster after the fact can be very costly. Therefore, communities are trying an ecosystem approach, such as a wider floodway with habitat restoration and wetlands enhancement, to address flooding and increase available habitat. And finally, the public expects greater accountability for costly public works projects, resulting in nontraditional, nonstructural solutions for multiple and overlapping watershed problems.

Integrating Multiple Goals in Watershed Planning

Watershed plans use a comprehensive systems approach to deal with significant drainage basin issues. However, in trying to resolve numerous issues simultaneously, there will be conflicting interests and potentially conflicting solutions.

Developing a watershed plan that addresses numerous primary issues can require several years to complete. To involve many interests and agencies can also be time-consuming and expensive. The most successful plans try to solve a clearly stated primary problem–drinking water protection, flood management, or habitat enhancement–while allowing related issues to be addressed as secondary priorities. The solutions to the primary problem can then be supported by demonstrating the mutual benefit for other issues and/or how it can minimize conflicts with another issues.

Multiple Goals

Watershed planning is also a process that can be used to address complex stakeholder and drainage interest group issues in a comprehensive way. If each stakeholder understands and appreciates the plan's primary purpose, or the major problem it is addressing, the inclusion of additional goals can result in a plan that achieves widespread support.

USBR's New Melones Lake Resource Management Plan is an example of a successful plan where potentially conflicting issues led to multiple goals (*see* the case study in chapter 8). This particular watershed plan had as a primary goal the mitigation of recreational conflicts associated with fluctuating (New Melones Lake) reservoir levels. A secondary objective was to enhance the ecological resources of lands surrounding the reservoir. By involving key stakeholders from within and adjacent to the watershed, USBR was able to successfully manage multiple goals and resolve potentially conflicting goals for the management plan. Ad Hoc Work Group members (stakeholders representing various watershed interests) dedicated substantial personal time to the review of materials prior to meetings, and constructively accepted solutions benefiting more than their individual interests. Before agreeing to be involved, the stakeholders understood the primary problems USBR hoped to resolve. The process of having multiple goals, exemplified by the New Melones experience, applies equally to drinking water source protection. For discussion of public participation models to address water resources management, *see* chapter 8.

Conflicting Goals

Developing multiple, clear goals for a watershed plan increases the possibility of identifying and resolving conflicting issues. One example of conflicting goals for a watershed can be found with in-reservoir water management.

Multipurpose Reservoirs. Multipurpose reservoirs were historically built for 'water supply, flood control, and/or hydropower generation. Total storage capacity is allocated for water supply, flood control, hydropower generation, and operational fluctuations (and more recently to include fish and wildlife enhancement and water quality management). Water levels in a reservoir are typically lowered by the end of the calendar year to provide capacity for flood flows (from winter rains or snow melt), which can result in a shortage of water supply if the winter snowpack or spring rains are at lower than normal levels. The quick release of water is difficult during a large storm due to downstream channel constraints and urban development in floodplains, thus flooding can result.

To minimize conflicts between the goals of water supply and flood capacity within a watershed, agencies monitor anticipated storms carefully and release water prior to a predicted major storm. To minimize the conflict further, agencies provide additional storage so that a greater percentage of reservoir allocation will be dedicated to flood control. This can be accomplished by making more off-stream storage available to multiple users, or by storing high winter flows in groundwater basins for withdrawal in the summer or during dry years.[3]

Reservoir Operations and Habitat. Conflicting goals can also occur where sensitive habitat is present in the upper reaches of a water storage reservoir. Often relatively flat, this land has years of accumulated sediment and may have wetlands and substantial riparian vegetation. Reservoir levels that fluctuate based on water supply needs often conflict with habitat that depends on a relatively constant surface water elevation. The Sweetwater Authority (SWA) has vegetation in the upper reaches of the Sweetwater Reservoir that provides suitable habitat for the endangered Least Bell's Vireo. Reclaiming an old sand mining site, SWA developed a large amount of new habitat for the vireo. After

SWA = Sweetwater Authority

3. Additional information on flood control conflicts and solutions can be found in *On Borrowed Land: Public Policies for Floodplains*, S. Faber, Lincoln Institute of Land Policy, 1996.

Leakage from old flumes can create wetlands that must be maintained.

DWSAP = Drinking Water Source
Assessment and Protection
THM = Triholomethanes
TOC = Total organic carbon

extensive monitoring, SWA confirmed that the birds used the new lands, and the remnant habitat in the reservoir could be used for water storage purposes with less impact on the species.

Wetlands Created from Leakage. Old flumes or canals that leak while conveying water from the source to the users is another example of conflicting goals. These leaks often create isolated wetlands that rely on leaking water. As water supplies have become more valuable, however, water purveyors have been repairing or replacing the old flumes to reduce system loss and improve water use efficiency. However, this conflicts with the Department of Fish and Game requirement that wetlands be maintained or mitigated. Replacement wetlands or other mitigations are needed in these instances to allow for conservation of critical potable supplies. Placer County Water Agency is analyzing leakage and conservation issues in their aging canals and flumes.

Detention Basins and Organic Pollutant Loadings. Where a detention basin is present within a drinking water watershed, another conflict can occur. Although the basin is intended to minimize loadings of contaminants, such as soil from an eroding slope, decayed vegetation within the basin can increase the amount and concentration of total organic carbon (TOC) loadings to the drinking water reservoir. Organic carbon mixed with treatment plant disinfectants can create THMs, which are carcinogenic. Managing the release of basin water to minimize TOC loadings presents a difficult and costly management effort involving increased maintenance and careful design. Similarly, detention basins that also serve to attract waterfowl and other wildlife can increase local coliform levels.[4]

Watershed Planning Process

The following basic watershed planning steps can be adapted to address almost any kind of watershed problem. Remember to weave public education and stakeholder communication into each step of the process. These steps take the Department of Health Services DWSAP a step further in recommending the development of goals and objectives that can be used throughout the process, from identifying and assessing management options to formulating plan recommendations and identifying techniques for implementation.

- Identify and assess stakeholders and their interests
- Define problems and establish goals and objectives

4. For more information on TOC loading, *see* Reservoir Management for Water Quality and THM Precursor Control, G.D. Cook and R. Carlson, AWWARF, 1989.

- **Delineate and characterize** the watershed in terms relevant to the objectives
- **Prioritize** water quality parameters of concern and their sources
- **Assess and analyze** watershed conditions and threats
- **Identify and evaluate** management options (source control and flow management)
- **Provide recommendations** for management and develop implementation techniques

Methods to identify and assess stakeholder interests are discussed in more detail in chapter 8. Defining the problems and establishing a mission statement, goals, and objectives are discussed in chapter 6. Watershed planning tools and methods for the remaining key tasks are provided in the following sections.

Characterizing a Watershed

Delineating and characterizing a watershed involves the use and storage of large amounts of spatial and temporal data. The detail may range from a simple USGS topographic map with data layers to a complex database with multiple attributes. It is important to establish a data management system appropriate for the level of detail desired to facilitate efficient storage, retrieval, and use of the data.

Delineating a surface water watershed, as discussed here, differs greatly from delineating groundwater recharge zones. Due to the wide range and detail of available data, characterizing a watershed or aquifer, unless carefully managed, can result in unnecessary costs. The characterization should focus on land uses and activities that affect the program's goal. If drinking water protection is the underlying goal, for example, data collection and watershed characterization should focus on activities and monitoring related to drinking water standards.

Data Management

The level of detail for the watershed analyses will be determined by the ultimate uses of the plan, its geographic scale, and an appropriate time frame (in the case of travel time, for example, whether the contaminant of concern will reach the water supply in a few days or a few years). Projects that involve either a large watershed or a significant amount of detail are best managed with an electronic data management system for mapping with a linked database, such as a geographic information system (GIS). Data typically used are discussed below.

For most watershed analyses, a GIS is a necessary tool because it can store an extensive amount of spatial and temporal data, which it can then analyze and composit to create new information and new management tools. By selecting individual mapped layers of data and overlaying key characteristics, maps analyzing composited data can be developed (Figure 7-1).

GIS = Geographic information system
USGS = United States Geological Survey

Organizing a Data Management System

- Identify data needs and required format, by subject
- Catalog available data, including:
  – Sources
  – Description
  – Format
  – Coverage
  – Date
- Highlight gaps in data and develop an alternative approach, if unavailable
- Obtain and code data to a master catalog

Figure 7-1
Composited Data Used
for Watershed Analysis

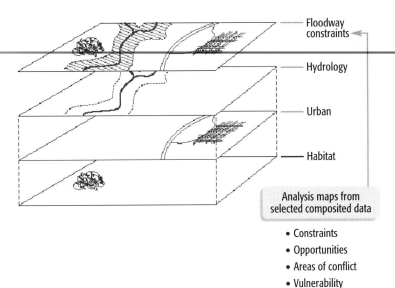

- Floodway constraints
- Hydrology
- Urban
- Habitat

Analysis maps from selected composited data

- Constraints
- Opportunities
- Areas of conflict
- Vulnerability

Figure 7-2
Watershed Delineation

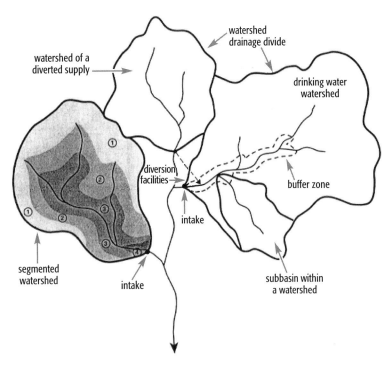

watershed of a diverted supply

watershed drainage divide

drinking water watershed

diversion facilities

buffer zone

intake

segmented watershed

intake

subbasin within a watershed

Delineation of a Watershed or Groundwater Protection Zone

Surface Water. A watershed is generally bounded by a major ridgeline—an area of land from which water drains into a river or system of interconnected streams. A hydrologic basin is the drainage area upstream from a given point on a stream. For drinking water purposes, the given point on the stream is often the water system intake. A typical stream system with the watershed drainage divide as its outermost boundary is illustrated by Figure 7-2. Topographic maps can be used to indicate the drainage divide by following the highest elevation between streams draining in different directions that are not connected hydrologically.

A large watershed can be divided into subwatersheds, as needed, for a more cost-effective inventory of contaminant sources and susceptibility analyses. Varying geographic boundaries, used for different levels of analysis, can include a subbasin within the main hydrologic basin, a buffer zone paralleling the waterbody within a hydrologic basin, a separate hydrologic basin that conveys water to the primary watershed through a diversion intake and pipeline, and a segmented watershed prioritizing the lands proximate to the waterbody (Figure 7-2).

Groundwater. For groundwater supplies, all nonpoint sources of contaminants in an aquifer recharge area can potentially affect the quality of the groundwater. Therefore, wellhead protection zones are typically used to focus the assessment in a cost-effective manner. The purpose of this delineation is to detect and mitigate a spill, allow enough time to elapse for a microbe to die, or allow for contaminant concentrations to diminish during transport. For the DHS DWSAP, groundwater delineation can use one of the following methods:

- Arbitrary fixed radius
- Calculated fixed radius
- Simplified variable shapes
- Analytical methods
- Hydrogeologic mapping
- Numerical flow or transport models

For more information on groundwater delineation methods, *see* DHS's Drinking Water Source Assessment and Protection Program requirements at www.dhs.cahwnet.gov. If the groundwater is "under the influence of surface water," as defined by DHS, the surface water watershed delineation is also used.

Linkage Between Land Uses/Activities and Water Quality Impacts

When viewed as a source of potential water contamination, natural and human land uses and activities take on a different perspective. Every aspect of a particular land use or activity can be broken down and analyzed to identify the various levels of potential impact (Figure 7-3). Understanding the linkage between these activities and their effect on water quality is essential when trying to identify the source of a water quality problem. A watershed can then be characterized in terms relevant to the program's goals. Natural and human watershed characteristics and activities relevant to surface water watersheds, and many of the human activities also applicable to groundwater recharge or wellhead protection zones, are described below.

Natural Watershed Characteristics. Natural watershed characteristics that influence water quality–topography, vegetation, soils, nutrients, geologic conditions, intensity of rainfall, wildlife, and potential for wildfire–can be classified by whether they contribute contaminants to or help move them toward a

Figure 7-3

Example of a Relationship Between a Land Use and Water Quality

EXISTING/ POTENTIAL LAND USES AND ACTIVITIES	Land Use/Activity – CAMPGROUND					
	ACTIVITY IMPACT	AREAL EXTENT	LOADINGS	DURATION	IMPACTED WATER BODY SIZE	RISK LEVEL
Grazing	Increase in impervious surfaces	Square feet	Additional runoff (cfs)	Storm event (months)	Creek to reservoir	To be determined • High • Medium • Low
Roads						
Septic Systems	Contaminant runoff from paved surfaces	Square feet	Oil and grease (lbs/sf)	Storm event (months)	Creek to reservoir	
CAMPGROUND →						
Residential	Landscaping fertilizers	Square feet	Nutrients (lbs/sf)	Storm event (months)	Creek to reservoir	
Business Park						
Trails	Sewage hauling spill	Point source	Gallons	Spill in reservoir (months)	Creek to reservoir	
Fishing						
Golf Courses				Spill on land (years)		
Industrial						

waterbody. **Topography** and slopes directly affect how contaminants are moved; the steeper the slope, the greater the acceleration of transport.

Vegetation in a watershed can be of concern, depending on its proximity to a waterbody and its nutrient contribution. Vegetation can also be valuable in trapping sediments, reducing erosion, absorbing pollutants, and providing habitat. Debris can protect soils from the erosive impact of rainfall, but if excessive nutrients are released into a waterbody, which occurs particularly with decayed macrophyte debris (debris from plants that grow along the shallow reaches of waterbodies, like tules), high levels of organic carbon will reach the water treatment plant. As discussed previously, organic carbon mixed with disinfectants can cause DBPs. High nutrient levels during warm weather can also result in algae growth that will clog water intake facilities and treatment plant filters, cause taste and odor problems, and contribute additional organic carbon upon decay. Nutrient sources include decayed vegetative matter, animal waste, fertilizer, septic system leachate, wastewater effluent discharge, and erosion.

Since it's made up of light particles, clay **soils** do not settle easily during aqueous transport, but remain suspended and result in turbidity that must be filtered out of the drinking water supply. Turbidity itself is not a specific public health concern, but other constituents of concern can adhere or adsorb onto the surfaces or into the pores of the particulates. These contaminants are then transported in the watershed and through the treatment process. Microorganisms in particular have been known to survive disinfection during treatment by being lodged within the pores of particulates.

In contrast, the counterpart to clay soils–gravels and gravelly loams– cause sedimentation problems during transport. These heavier soils settle more quickly than clay, changing the morphology of a stream, adversely affecting aquatic habitat, and decreasing the capacity of a reservoir.

As with vegetation debris, the nutrient content in soils–specifically nitrogen and phosphorus–can encourage the growth of algae, thus reducing oxygen levels for fish, resulting in taste and odor problems in drinking water. The erosional process carries organic material from the land into a waterbody, and aquatic plant and algae growth contributes organic matter, a DBP concern.

Some **geologic conditions** can be considered contaminant sources. Exposed minerals can be leached either through a natural erosional process or through human activities such as applied irrigation water, road cuts, and abandoned mines. A prime example is the poisoning of wildlife at Kesterson Wildlife Refuge in the 1980s. Kesterson is located

Clay soils can increase turbidity levels while gravelly soils can cause sedimentation problems.

downstream of the Panoche Fan, a natural alluvial fan on the west side of the San Joaquin Valley. When the Panoche Fan was irrigated for agriculture, the water leached naturally-occurring selenium from the soils that were transported to the reservoir, resulting in birth deformities and the death of wildlife. In high concentrations, selenium is also lethal to humans. Other examples of geologic conditions as contaminant sources can be found in mines, abandoned prior to the requirement for restoration plans, that are now leaching metals and draining into major drinking water supplies.

A more common geologic problem occurs with the arsenic and radon found throughout California in the groundwater supply. In fact, the aquifers in the southern San Joaquin Valley have some of the highest arsenic levels in the country. Typical of certain geologic formations, these naturally-occurring elements are creating problems for water purveyors due to the recent and anticipated regulations restricting the levels of these constituents in drinking water.

Rainfall intensity has a greater influence on water quality than total quantity of rainfall. During rainfall events, intense rainfall causes soils to move more quickly. Excessive rainfall causes flooding, which then carries contaminants into a waterbody. Following a major storm, the quality of water is degraded by inorganic and organic solids and associated adsorbed contaminants–metals, nutrients, pesticides, and herbicides–that are resuspended or introduced in runoff. If a sewage system or septic tank is flooded, sewage can contaminate a drinking water source and the distribution system. More than half of all the outbreaks of waterborne disease in the United States during the last half century have followed a period of heavy rainfall.

Wildlife not only carry microorganisms, but move nutrients and pathogens closer to a waterbody. Microorganisms, particularly *Cryptosporidium* and *Giardia*, are the water quality parameters of greatest concern due to the health risk and difficulty of treatment. In addition, some animals, such as feral pigs, can cause extreme damage to a riparian corridor by rooting, trampling a stream bank, and compacting soil, all of which increase the rate of erosion.

Wildfire is a concern for water quality because it changes the watershed's vegetative cover, increasing erosion and DBP precursors. A natural or human-caused fire followed by rainfall can often cause serious erosion that will render a waterbody useless for months or years due to excessive turbidity levels. The fine ash particles a wildfire produces are difficult to remove with conventional water treatment processes and can change the water's pH. Moreover, when erosion occurs, microbes, organics, and inorganics that adhere to particulates are transported into the waterbody as well, contributing to degradation of source water quality. Where utilities have experienced wildland fire within a drinking water supply watershed, the resulting high turbidities have created a number of water treatment and health-related concerns.

Road runoff and livestock waste are potential contaminant sources in drinking water watersheds.

MTBE = Methyl tertiary butyl ether
SOC = Synthetic organic chemical
VOC = Volatile organic chemical

Human Watershed Characteristics. Almost all land uses and human activities, if in high concentrations or near a waterbody, can be characterized as contaminant sources for a drinking water supply. Drinking water quality concerns associated with some of the more common land uses–road corridors, sanitation facilities, livestock operations, chemical usage, and impervious surfaces–are described below.

Highways, streets, and parking lots contribute hydrocarbons (gasoline, motor oil), heavy metals (lead, chromium, copper), and herbicide applied during roadside maintenance, as well as chemicals spilled in an accident. If a road cut is not graded properly, or an automobile does not stay on the pavement, the resulting erosion leads to increased particulate transport and turbidity.

Small-scale **sanitation facilities** that collect, treat, and dispose of human waste can pose a variety of water quality risks when the facilities fail or are operated improperly. This failure can introduce disease-causing microorganisms into the raw water supply and cause an increase in nutrient loading, particularly nitrogen, for a watershed reservoir. Rural residential development and older residential neighborhoods are often on community or septic systems that can fail or leak pathogens and hazardous material into a groundwater or surface water supply. A community sewage treatment facility that discharges directly into a reservoir or creek can cause potential contamination, as can pond failure, overflowing manholes, and malfunctioning pumping equipment. A septic system can contaminate the water supply if the leachfield or septic tank becomes clogged and the sewage percolates through the soil into a nearby creek or reservoir. In households with septic systems, improperly disposing of household chemicals–including substances containing metals, pesticides, or herbicides–can lead to contamination from the leachfields.

Livestock grazing can contribute pathogens and nutrients through fecal matter and, if not properly managed, can cause soil disturbance (through compaction resulting in increased runoff and erosion or by streambed disturbance). On the other hand, livestock grazing can reduce fuel loadings, which can assist in wildfire protection.

Synthetic organic **chemicals** (SOCs) and volatile organic chemicals (VOCs) represent the largest group of drinking water quality parameters currently regulated. Many VOCs and some SOCs are formulated for or result from an industrial process. One VOC of particular concern from a watershed protection perspective is methyl tertiary butyl ether (MBTE). An additive in reformulated gasoline originally intended to reduce vehicle emissions, MBTE has found its way into groundwater through leaking underground storage tanks and into surface waters through fuel spillage or leakage and from the use of two-stroke gasoline engines.

Pesticides and herbicides are specifically formulated for their toxic effects on animals and plants. From a public health perspective, these organics have been identified as–or are suspected of being–carcinogens, mutagens, or teratogens. Herbicides and pesticides enter a waterbody directly from overspraying, from transport by the wind when applied, or through runoff from the land into the source water. A heavy metal such as mercury or dioxin–that primarily derives from minerals and municipal and industrial wastes–can have a toxic effect on human health if the concentration in the water or in fish consumed by humans is sufficiently high.

Urban development increases the amount of **impervious surfaces**, thus increasing stormwater runoff that, under natural conditions, would percolate into the soil. The result is not only total increased runoff volume, but also increased flow rates, thus increasing pollutant loads. Besides the metal and hydrocarbons from automobile corridors discussed above, urban land uses and activities contribute a variety of contaminants such as chemicals and nutrients from landscaping, hazardous material from improper disposal, and pathogens from pets and livestock. When excessive quantities are applied, fertilizers and pesticides from irrigated turf at parks and golf courses contribute contaminants. These are only a few examples of the contaminants resulting from urban land use.

For an overview of the relationship between potential contamination sources of concern and water quality parameter groups, see Table 7-1. This table and the above discussion provide a very basic understanding of the concerns associated with human and natural characteristics of a watershed.

Table 7-1. Relationship Between Contaminant Sources and Water Quality Concerns

PRINCIPAL ACTIVITIES	MICROORGANISMS	DBP PRECURSORS	TURBIDITY/PARTICULATE	SOCs, PESTICIDES & METALS
Agricultural crop land			•	•
Agricultural livestock uses	•	•	•	
Automobile corridors and parking lots			•	•
Erosion and landslides		•	•	
Herbicide and pesticide use				•
Recreation, body contact	•	•	•	
Sanitation facilities	•	•	•	•
Urban runoff, mixed uses	•	•	•	•
Wildfires		•	•	
Wildlife	•	•	•	

Source: MWH

Prioritizing Contaminants and Sources

Criteria for Setting Priorities for Water Quality Parameters of Concern

- Risk to public health (carcinogens, prevalence in waterbody, etc.)
- Ability to treat (for example, pathogens are more difficult to treat than hydrocarbons)
- Potential for byproducts of treatment (DBPs, etc.)
- Public acceptance (taste, odor, etc.)

To keep the watershed management plan focused on issues relevant to the program goals, each parameter of concern (DBP, pathogen, SOC, etc.) should be identified and prioritized according to its importance (*see* sidebar). This process can also address other watershed concerns such as aquatic ecosystems, whose prioritization criteria might include reduced oxygen, increased temperature, pH levels, and fluctuating flow and quality conditions.

Once the parameters are established and the link between a contaminant source and water quality parameters are clearly understood, it's possible to identify and prioritize the source of each parameter—land uses or activities. Any step that links land uses and activities to a water quality concern will, of course, reduce the number of *unknown* sources of a water quality problem. Contaminant sources should be prioritized by factors most relevant to the individual watershed conditions (*see* sidebar).

Assessing Watershed Susceptibility Conditions

Criteria for Setting Priorities for Contaminant Sources

- Source of high-priority water quality parameter
- Risk to users (for example, carcinogenic versus aesthetic concern)
- Proximity to waterbody (for example, adjacent to waterbody versus ridgeline of watershed)
- Ability to manage source (livestock versus wildlife, etc.)

Assessing watershed conditions to determine a water system's susceptibility to contamination is more effective once the water quality parameters and sources of contaminants are known. Focusing on the identified contaminant sources of concern will reduce the level of effort required as well as the overall cost, keeping the assessment process manageable. Since a watershed assessment may also result in important political and economic decisions that can affect the public and become controversial, the susceptibility assessment should be based on a credible scientific evaluation.

A key step in assessing watershed conditions is to define the nature and extent of each prioritized contaminant source. A typical template for this assessment is presented in Figure 7-3 (see page 151). The first step should be to determine the magnitude of the contribution of loadings along with the duration of impact and the size of the waterbody affected. The level of risk posed by the contaminant getting into the waterbody should be considered, along with any cumulative effects, particularly as the contaminants contribute to future loadings.

Computer models can be used to assess a watershed's vulnerability or susceptibility to contaminant transport. For assessing groundwater systems, hydrogeologic models are available.

Identifying opportunities and constraints for future management actions is important to the process. To determine the watershed characteristics required to support a plan's goals and objectives, an analysis of land suitability is often conducted. Land suitability criteria help determine physical constraints, identifying areas vulnerable to impact or that may contribute contaminant loadings, for example. For the steps involved in developing an opportunities and constraints analysis, *see* the sidebar at right.

By overlaying resource maps and interpreting the results (Figure 7-1, see page 150), it is possible to map a project's constraints, opportunities, vulnerabilities, and areas of conflict for the composited data. Composited data layers can identify land areas that can be developed for multiple goals–such as lands developed for urban or recreational uses that are not in conflict with habitat enhancement and restoration opportunities. The San Francisco Public Utilities Commission has developed a complex constraints and opportunities analysis to protect drinking water by creating water quality vulnerability zones for its local watershed lands (Figures 7-4 and 7-5). The methodology is summarized in the sidebar on pages 158–159 and described more fully in Appendix E.

Utilizing Land Management and Institutional Controls

Several methods can be used to protect water quality within a watershed: source reduction, management of pollutant flows, treatment controls, and institutional controls. Controlling the source is particularly attractive because a contaminant is then reduced or eliminated before it enters the hydrologic system. Flow management and treatment either prevent pollutants from reaching a waterbody or treat them after they have combined with runoff from stormwater. Institutional controls include governmental actions that regulate land use or development policies and actions to institute water quality controls.[5]

Land Management for Source Reduction, Flow Controls, and Treatment

When it rains, stormwater runoff from saturated soils or impervious surfaces transports contaminants into receiving waterbodies. Preventing pollution–versus controlling the flow once it's contaminated–is preferred, but not always possible. Once released, managing and treating stormwater flow is the next step in minimizing the impact on a receiving waterbody. Source reduction and flow management and treatment, along with specific examples showing how to incorporate these techniques into site development, are discussed in the following section.

---

5. For additional information on source reduction, flow control, and treatment, *see* California Storm Water Best Management Practices Handbook (for Municipal, Industrial, and Construction Activities) prepared for the SWRCB Stormwater Quality Task Force in 1993 (**www. swrcb.ca.gov/ stormwtr/docs/bmp**). Other sources of information include Erosion and Sediment Control Handbook by Steven Goldman *et al.* 1986, and Stormwater Best Management Practices Including Detention by B.R. Urbonas and P. Stahre, 1993.

Identifying Constraints and Opportunities in a Watershed

- Determine specific watershed characteristics required to support the plan's goals and objectives

- Apply watershed characteristics criteria to the study area to disclose and map all potential opportunities

- Overlay the mapped opportunities for multiple objectives to determine constraints or compatible opportunities

- Conduct field visits to confirm viability of opportunities and constraints

- Finalize the opportunities and constraints

SWRCB = State Water Resources Control Board

San Francisco Water Quality Vulnerability Zone Development

The San Francisco Public Utilities Commission prepared two watershed management plans for its five local reservoir watersheds located in San Mateo and Alameda counties. The primary goal of the program is to "maintain and improve source water quality to protect public health and safety." Identifying source areas that contribute drinking water contaminants along with areas susceptible to transporting contaminants to a waterbody is one of the unique aspects of the plan.

As a part of the overall plan (Figure 7-4), the physical characteristics of the 63,000 acres comprising the watersheds were put into a relational database and analyzed. The information was then used to study source and transport vulnerability for five groups of water quality parameters: particulates, disinfection byproduct precursors, microorganisms, nutrient loading (nitrogen and phosphorus), and synthetic organic chemicals and pesticides.

Vulnerability zones were developed and mapped using a GIS database.

Each water quality vulnerability zone map was developed based on five watershed physical characteristics—soils, slope, vegetation, wildlife concentrations, and proximity to waterbodies—and their relationships to each of the five groups of water quality parameters. For example, soils were evaluated according to their density, organic carbon content, moisture content, nutrient content, and adsorption capacity. These results were then correlated with the five groups of water quality parameters, respectively. A similar type of analysis was conducted in order to develop relationships between the other four watershed physical characteristics and the five groups of water quality parameters.

An approach was defined and verified to incorporate the watershed physical characteristics information into the five water quality vulnerability zone maps. The composite approach was based in part on information gathered from existing watershed management plans throughout the country. (The American Water Works Association Research Foundation report *Effective Watershed Management for Surface Water Supplies,* Robbins *et al.,* AWWARF, 1991, is a useful source of information on drinking water source protection.) Verification of the composited approach was achieved through the use of the universal soil loss equation and the forestry industry's hazard rating index. Once verified, high-, medium-, and low-vulnerability zones were defined for each group of water quality parameters. The resulting composited water quality vulnerability zones are presented in Figure 7-5.

Water quality vulnerability zones were identified to determine management strategies regarding future activities in the watersheds, as well as corresponding mitigation activities that must be pursued to ➡

Figure 7-4
San Francisco Watershed Management Planning Process

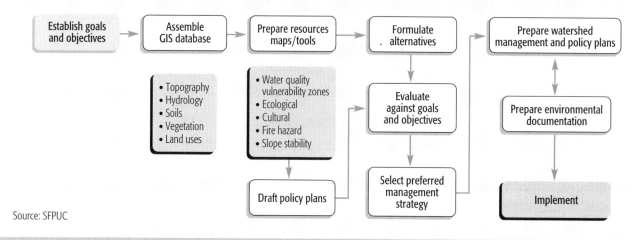

Source: SFPUC

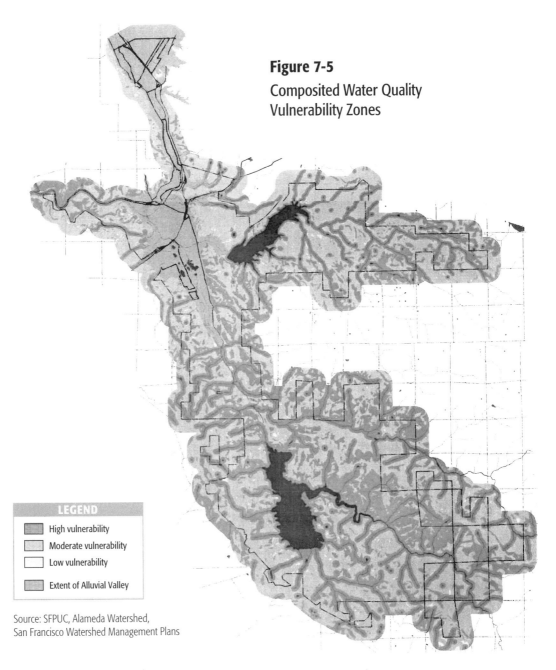

Figure 7-5

Composited Water Quality Vulnerability Zones

LEGEND

High vulnerability

Moderate vulnerability

Low vulnerability

Extent of Alluvial Valley

Source: SFPUC, Alameda Watershed, San Francisco Watershed Management Plans

maintain or enhance current water quality. Water utilities can use this method to begin the task of evaluating the physical characteristics of its watersheds and determine how specifically these lands may be contributing contaminant sources. This information in turn, can be related to current and future watershed activities, and used as a tool to identify areas of high vulnerability which may require different protection and management policies. It can also be used in reviewing development or access requests, and can contribute to the fulfillment of source water assessment and protection program delineation and assessment tasks, as required by the State Department of Health Services. Water quality vulnerability zones also can be used to establish pertinent watershed baseline and special monitoring programs essential to understanding the relationships between physical characteristics, watershed activities, and water quality effects. ▪

Adapted from AWWA Journal, *Protecting Water Quality in the Watershed,* C. James, K. Johnson, and E. Stewart, August 1994.

Source Reduction. Controlling the source of contamination in stormwater by incorporating pollution prevention activities in the first place is usually more cost-effective than managing or treating contaminated water. To accomplish this, implementing public education and participation programs and encouraging good housekeeping practices by individuals, businesses, and government agencies is required.

A good example of a source reduction technique can be found at the SFPUC Alameda watershed. Livestock grazing in the drinking water watershed affected water quality and riparian vegetation, particularly when the cattle drank from a stream or the reservoir's edge. To eliminate this source of contamination, SFPUC encouraged the cattle to move away from the reservoirs and streams by installing a remotely-operated, solar-powered pump that fills a water tank and nearby cattle watering trough located away from the waterbodies. Known as the McGuire Peaks water tank, it also provides water for fire fighting in this remote location. *Watershed Watch*, Issue 7, Summer 2001, SFPUC. *See* the sidebar for other source reduction techniques.

Flow Management and Treatment. As regulations addressing nonpoint pollution sources expand and the need for water quality protection increases, a carefully planned and designed urban stormwater system is critical. The traditional approach has been to "get rid of the water" as fast as possible. As it hits rooftops, streets, sidewalks, and other impervious urban surfaces, rainfall collects a variety of pollutants and flows into stormwater facilities far more quickly than under natural conditions. Surface runoff then travels into impervious gutters and a network of impervious underground pipes, channels, and culverts to a discharge point in a river, stream, lake, wetland, or other natural waterbody. Along the way, the conveyance system becomes larger and larger as runoff accumulates from the surrounding urban area, carrying suspended pollutants and sediments to the discharge point. Although providing protection from local flooding, a system of this type does not take advantage of the urban landscape to convey, infiltrate, treat, and store water, thus creating water quality problems downstream.

If pollutants cannot be reduced at the source, flow can be managed by diverting water away from sensitive waterbodies (e.g., out of the watershed) or by applying different types of treatment. One treatment uses vegetation to filter contaminants from the runoff. Another uses constructed wetlands to treat urban stormwater, providing multiple benefits, such as ecosystem restoration and open space enhancement, making it more popular than the use of structural facilities. Catch basins can capture large debris, but require high levels of maintenance.

The Tahoe Regional Planning Agency (TRPA), in conjunction with the U.S. Natural Resources Conservation Service, has been innovative in requiring and developing pollutant flow management and treatment techniques to prevent further degradation in the clarity of Lake Tahoe. The traditional use of a gravel infiltration trench is being replaced with a new recycled plastic technology that takes up far less space. For more information on TRPA's best management practices for flow management and treatment, *see* www.trpa.org/BMPInfo/bmp.html.

The Sweetwater Authority in southern San Diego County has developed an interesting project for managing flow. The Sweetwater Reservoir is within one of the most urbanized drinking water watersheds in California, with additional development planned. To manage contaminated runoff from urbanized land, SWA has implemented an Urban Runoff Diversion System designed to collect stormwater and allow runoff either to drain directly into the reservoir or be captured and pumped. When the first-flush runoff contains high levels of total dissolved solids (TDS), before entering the drinking water reservoir the flow is pumped out of the watershed and discharged downstream of the dam into the Sweetwater River. Once in the river's lower reach, the diverted water recharges the aquifer and becomes a supply source for the Richard A. Reynolds Groundwater Demineralization Facility. Runoff with acceptable TDS levels is allowed to flow into the reservoir, and the water is then treated at a surface water treatment plant before entering the distribution system.

The Urban Runoff Diversion System allows SWA to minimize TDS levels in the reservoir, thereby minimizing treatment requirements. No water is lost to the system, however, because the diverted water flowing in the Sweetwater River is picked up by the demineralization facility. For more information about the system, see the SWA website (www.sweetwater.org).

Urban Design Solutions. Designing urban development around natural drainage and incorporating flow management techniques, such as vegetated swale biofilters and runoff detention basins, is an effective approach to remove nutrients, particulates, and metals and reduce peak flows. The following discussion offers examples of flow management techniques that can provide numerous benefits.

Several communities such as the City of Davis have developed retention basins to manage flow and serve a number of purposes simultaneously (Figure 7-6). First and foremost, the basins serve drainage and flood control needs where water can be slowed and retained (with some infiltration into the upper, nonpotable aquifer). Some sediment also settles out, and debris is captured at the outlet structures. Second, the basins serve as a visual and recreational resource, with trails, bikeways, and green spaces developed along the edges. As an indication of the design's effect on economic value, many of the adjacent residential lots have sold for nearly twice the cost of a lot in the interior of the subdivision. And, finally, the ponds have been carefully designed by biologists and landscape architects to attract and sustain populations of

First Flush

First flush is water that falls on lands containing the highest concentration of contaminants from lawn fertilizers, car oil, pet waste, and other pollutants that have been accumulating on paved surfaces and landscaping for months since the previous rainfall. This concentrated runoff is typically conveyed into storm drains and other waterways and usually ends up in a waterbody.

Education Efforts in Santa Cruz County

The County of Santa Cruz instituted an information campaign to encourage creekside property owners to take care of riparian corridors, improving erosion control and reducing downstream sedimentation. The county developed a simple, but compelling illustrated publication showing 11 basic techniques to ensure a more ecologically healthy stream system. A publication is mailed to every creekside property owner in the county, and follow-up education is conducted in selected areas. Strictly voluntary, the program has reduced sediment and led to increased awareness and improved stewardship of streams. ■

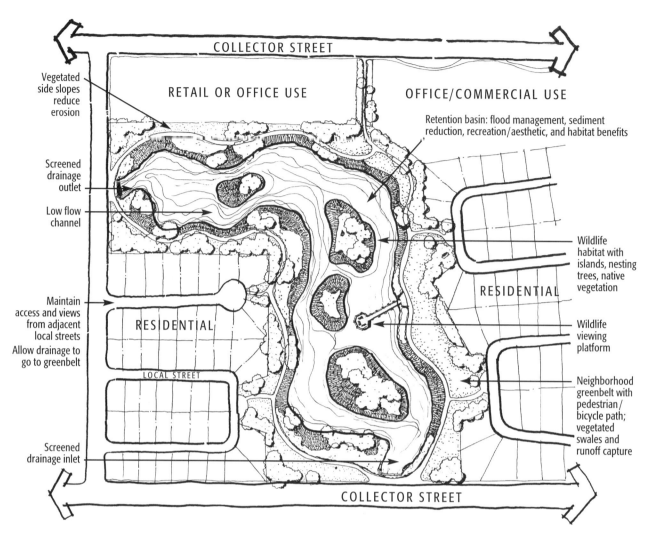

COLLECTOR STREET

RETAIL OR OFFICE USE

OFFICE/COMMERCIAL USE

Vegetated side slopes reduce erosion

Retention basin: flood management, sediment reduction, recreation/aesthetic, and habitat benefits

Screened drainage outlet

Low flow channel

Wildlife habitat with islands, nesting trees, native vegetation

RESIDENTIAL

Maintain access and views from adjacent local streets

Allow drainage to go to greenbelt

RESIDENTIAL

LOCAL STREET

Wildlife viewing platform

Neighborhood greenbelt with pedestrian/bicycle path; vegetated swales and runoff capture

Screened drainage inlet

COLLECTOR STREET

Figure 7-6
Residential Neighborhood Design with Multiple Use Retention Basin

Multi-use retention, flood control, and recreation basin in Visalia, California

wildlife species, including ducks and geese, shorebirds, egrets, owls and other raptors, small mammals and many invertebrates, freshwater wetland and upland plants, and other species. The ponds feature wildlife viewing platforms and walkways, and have become a major attraction for the community's neighborhoods. In addition, local schools take advantage of the ponds for educational purposes. A low-flow channel–replenished by a former agricultural well that pumps water from the upper, nonpotable aquifer–has been designed into the ponds to keep water available to wildlife year-round.

These basins are not without challenges. Ponds require considerable maintenance, particularly to clean sediment traps and debris screens and to ensure viable vegetation and habitat (although community volunteers can do some of this work). A pond also requires a large amount of valuable urban land, so a higher-density situation may make it impractical. And while water does infiltrate into the upper aquifer, it arrives with a number of urban contaminants, potentially rendering it unsuitable for potable purposes. Although they have a highly visible and prized urban wildlife population, the ponds do not constitute fully restored natural habitat. Islands are often used to protect species from domestic pets, and see-through fencing keeps residents out of the channels and the ponds for safety and wildlife protection, but allows viewing. Finally, before embarking on such a plan, it's necessary to make sure that the soils have sufficient capacity to absorb runoff and accommodate stormwater.

Other communities, such as Fresno and Visalia, have long used detention basins that also serve active recreational needs. During a storm event, the sports fields are unusable, but serve instead to retain and absorb stormwater, filtering out some sediment and debris. These fields function very well as recreational amenities, but require maintenance, especially after a major storm.

A water quality monitoring program should accompany all projects that control flow and treatment. Ongoing monitoring is necessary to determine if the project is effectively reducing or eliminating the contaminant of concern.

Integrating Protection of Stormwater Quality into Site Design. For almost any type and scale of urban development, so-called "low-impact" design features can be planned and developed as part of the project to better manage urban (and rural) stormwater. These design measures can restore runoff control by replacing storage volume and increasing infiltration, save infrastructure and drainage costs, reduce contaminants in source and drain water, and, in some instances, recharge aquifers. They can also provide recreational, aesthetic, and habitat benefits.[6]

Beginning at the level of an individual lot, sidewalk, and street, a project can incorporate design features that reduce peak flow, retain and infiltrate runoff, and assist in water quality filtration. The primary purpose is to maximize permeability of the site, and mimic a more natural runoff regime.

A single-family or duplex residential site designed for maximum permeability (Figure 7-7) could include the following features:

6. For a thorough discussion of these design concepts, *see* Start at the Source, Bay Area Stormwater Management Agencies Association, January 1997, Low-Impact Development Design Strategies, prepared by Prince George's County, Maryland, Department of Environmental Resources, June 1999, and Low Impact Development (LID): A Literature Review, U.S. Environmental Protection Agency, Office of Water, EPA-841-B-00-005, October 2000.

Two views of multi-purpose retention and flood management ponds in an urban environment: one at low flow, one following a storm.

Low Impact Development for Water Management

For the purposes of water management, low impact development (LID) is the planning and engineering of a site to mimic the natural water cycle functions and watershed relationships. LID can be used to manage stormwater creatively and with less impact.

LID = Low impact development

Figure 7-7
Residential Site Designed for Maximum Permeability

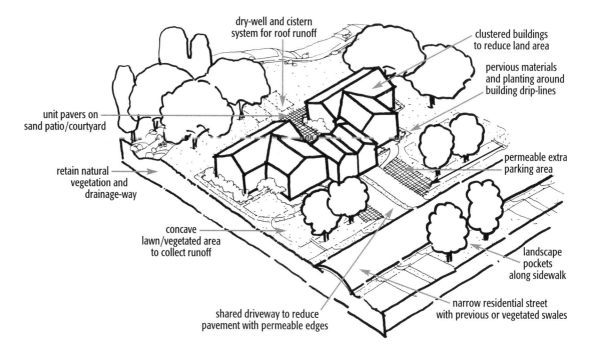

dry-well and cistern system for roof runoff

clustered buildings to reduce land area

pervious materials and planting around building drip-lines

unit pavers on sand patio/courtyard

permeable extra parking area

retain natural vegetation and drainage-way

landscape pockets along sidewalk

concave lawn/vegetated area to collect runoff

narrow residential street with previous or vegetated swales

shared driveway to reduce pavement with permeable edges

- Reduced pavement through the use of narrower residential streets
- Shared or narrow driveways
- Clustered buildings that preserve land area for landscaping
- Use of permeable materials, where practical–pervious concrete, porous asphalt, turf block, brick, natural stone, gravel, unit pavers, etc.
- Protection/enhancement of existing natural landscape

The building itself can be designed to conserve runoff with vegetation, dry well, or pervious surfaces at the roof dripline. Once it reaches a driveway, water does not need to be connected directly to the impervious street-and-gutter system; instead, a grass, mulch, or vegetated buffer can intercept the runoff.

For multi-family and higher-density housing and commercial sites, many pervious materials may not be practical or what local planning or engineering standards permit. However, a specialized parking lot design can add a significant amount of permeable area for drainage. For a smaller infill lot, a hybrid of pervious and impervious materials can capture runoff (Figure 7-8). Larger residential projects, can use a parking bay and tree/landscape clusters. In even larger lots and commercial projects, an overflow parking area and/or extensive underground drainage and collection systems can be used.

For streets, the main issues are the total pavement surface and connectivity to buffers and green spaces for filtering water. In a residential

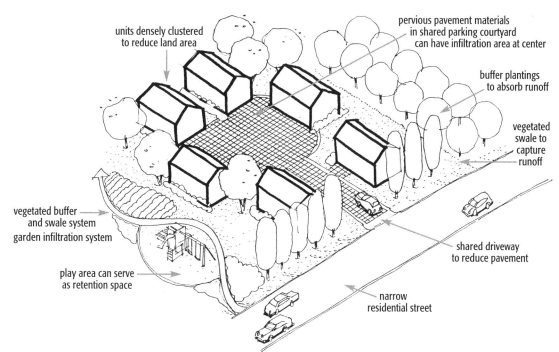

Figure 7-8

Residential Infill
Site Showing
Low-Impact
Stormwater
Management
Features

In the figure:
- units densely clustered to reduce land area
- pervious pavement materials in shared parking courtyard can have infiltration area at center
- buffer plantings to absorb runoff
- vegetated swale to capture runoff
- shared driveway to reduce pavement
- narrow residential street
- play area can serve as retention space
- vegetated buffer and swale system garden infiltration system

development, streets and sidewalks can comprise 60 to 70 percent of the total impervious surface. Many of the pollutants in runoff come from these surfaces. One of the best ways to reduce runoff and pollutants is to reduce the overall street width. Using a planting strip or gravel/pervious edge along a street can provide a buffer for runoff as well as a safe haven for pedestrians. Similarly, an urban curb and swale system can capture and infiltrate runoff. A concave vegetated swale conveys water, while allowing infiltration and landscape surface. Finally, at a cul-de-sac, a permeable or vegetated central feature can add visual interest, slow traffic, and provide a place for runoff (Figure 7-9).

For a modest-sized infill site, many of the same principles apply, but typically with less overall space and more need to create joint solutions for drainage. For a variety of features that might apply in a more urban residential context, *see* Figure 7-8. Community open spaces and gardens can serve as buffers that accommodate swales and channels. A concave lawn could serve as a basin that slows or dampens runoff. A common drive and walkway can have pervious elements, offering both an aesthetic and recreational opportunity.

On a neighborhood scale, various elements can be combined by adding an area-wide retention basin that captures, retains, and filters water. Such a basin can also serve as a visual and recreational amenity and as habitat for urban wildlife. For many of the features that can be integrated into new neighborhood design, *see* Figure 7-10.

A neighborhood or community-scale retention facility can combine urban wildlife habitat or recreational space with drainage, flood

Figure 7-9

Use of a Vegetated Concave
Island to Absorb Stormwater in
a Small Residential Cul-de-Sac

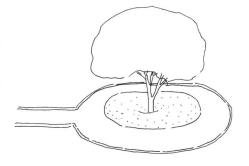

Figure 7-10

Neighborhood-Scale Ideas for Stormwater Management

agricultural land edge; drainage and recharge

retention basin and groundwater recharge

residential site
• clustered housing preserves open space
• narrow streets and path system
• community gardens/open space

stream setback/flood plain with recreation trail connecting adjacent land uses

use of play fields as retention space

vegetated buffers at edges of housing area

greenbelt used to collect and retain runoff from streets and houses

school with vegetated buffers

narrow local and collector streets

The use of pervious pavement

control, and water quality improvement (*see* Figure 7-6). In either case, ensuring the existence of adequate measures for safety, water quality, and maintenance is important. Safety usually involves a form of transparent fencing around an area of a basin that might be inundated during a storm, and can also mean a gentle side slope to prevent accidents and reduce erosion. Water quality protection typically implies a debris screen and some form of sediment trap near an outlet to limit the amount of pollutants leaving the basin. A careful monitoring and testing protocol is also recommended to ensure that water quality is maintained at an acceptable level for an urban area. Unless a low flow channel or similar design feature is employed for the benefit of wildlife, stormwater will reside for a very short period. Maintenance requirements may include clean up after a major storm and the rainy season, monitoring of water quality, planting and landscape maintenance, and related activities.

Some basins are designed specifically to meet local wildlife objectives and are likely to have limited public access. Trails and bikeways are typically designed around the perimeter to protect habitat and to ensure safety during a storm event.

A basin used for recreation offers different challenges. Side slopes must be carefully designed and planted for safety, aesthetics, and erosion control. Vehicle and pedestrian/bicycle access must be planned to allow for use and maintenance. If a basin is

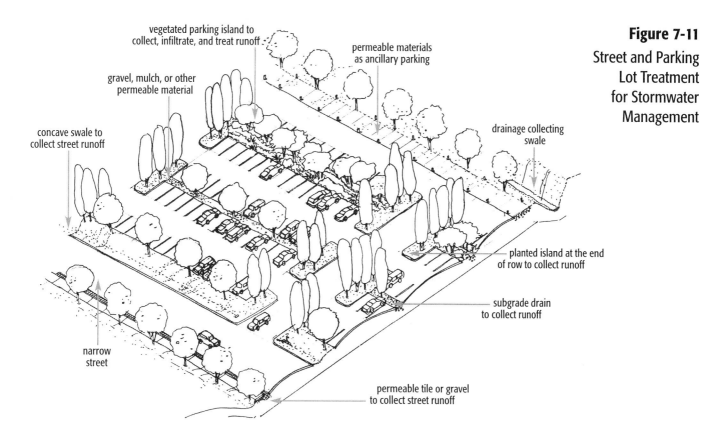

Figure 7-11
Street and Parking Lot Treatment for Stormwater Management

vegetated parking island to collect, infiltrate, and treat runoff

permeable materials as ancillary parking

gravel, mulch, or other permeable material

drainage collecting swale

concave swale to collect street runoff

planted island at the end of row to collect runoff

subgrade drain to collect runoff

narrow street

permeable tile or gravel to collect street runoff

used for sports, as in many communities, the field must be graded and constructed to withstand the additional drainage.

Institutional Controls

The innovative urban design treatments discussed in this chapter are not yet typical of development projects. Nor are they typically allowed in local public works standards for streets, sidewalks, and drainage systems. Figure 7-11 shows innovative storm drainage features for roads and parking areas. So, how can a planning agency make innovative design a reality?

One approach is to codify a set of flexible drainage standards as an alternative to a community's traditional engineering design requirements, giving a developer/applicant a choice between the two. Similarly, a community might place innovative drainage solutions within its adopted design guidelines, allowing an applicant to choose the preferred method to meet the requirements. Another option might permit planned development zoning for large-scale projects where an infiltration approach to site or neighborhood design is feasible. Planned development zoning allows a developer/applicant to propose innovative ways to meet community zoning standards. Yet another option would require innovative standards through a specific plan or development agreement (*see* chapter 3). This would be most appropriate where terrain,

Naturalized drainage-way in a residential area

Village Homes'
Innovative Drainage Design

The Village Homes residential and commercial subdivision in the City of Davis uses a unique method for stormwater runoff. Davis is a university-oriented community with a population of approximately 65,000 in California's Central Valley about 15 miles from Sacramento. The terrain is generally flat, the community is surrounded by farmland, and the soil offers varying levels of drainage and infiltration capacity.

Proposed in the mid-1970s as an ecologically and socially unique subdivision, Village Homes features narrow streets, an extensive bikeway and pedestrian system, solar-oriented homes on small lots, generous open spaces and community gardens connected throughout the neighborhood, and an above-ground, non-structural stormwater system.

Runoff either infiltrates into the ground or is captured in grassy or sandy swales that crisscross the subdivision. The swales serve as common open space, separators between homes, and recreational space

The Village Homes residential project in Davis uses all above-ground, natural storm drainage.

during much of the year. During a storm event, the swales and channels fill with water and gradually release the runoff into the city's stormwater detention ponds and then into channels heading for the Sacramento River to the east. The onsite system, which has performed as well as any in the city, requires relatively minimal maintenance other than landscape trimming and cleaning of culverts under pathways and roads. The system was less expensive than a conventional drainage and pipe system. The swales and channels provide an aesthetic and recreational benefit and help shape the neighborhood, while performing stormwater functions well.

This and other innovations in the subdivision were not accomplished without major debates with the city. When the project was first proposed, many of the ecological ideas ran counter to established public works standards and practices. These requirements

were modified through a planned development procedure to allow for, among other things, the innovative drainage system. In subsequent years, learning from the Village Homes project, the City of Davis has incorporated some (but not all) of the innovations into its typical subdivision planning. However, the unique drainage system used by the community remains unique, although other developers have tried components of the system.

The Village Homes community has not only survived, but thrives. In recent years, a commercial and office component has been added, and it continues to command some of the highest-per-square-foot home values in the area. Many urban planners and designers view the project as a model of ecological site design. For more information on Village Homes and its designers and developers, see *A Better Place to Live* by Judith and Michael Corbett, Island Press 2000. The Corbetts designed and developed this unique project. ■

hydrology, and stormwater needs create appropriate conditions for a low-impact approach.

General Plans, Specific Plans, Ordinances, and Other Land Development Controls. Using a general plan or specific plan, the planning authority can designate priority watershed lands or recharge areas on a land use map and adopt policies ensuring water quality protection. The priority watershed lands can be required to have special approvals, and other development control requirements associated with proposed development activity or modification to existing development. Establishing a water quality protection plan would be the first step to implement the plan before land use controls are established.

Land use and development requirements for priority watershed lands or recharge areas could include open space or conservation easements, low-impact development, clustering of urban uses, allowing for higher land use densities with strategies for flow management and treatment, and stricter zoning and other development standards. Formation of these special planning areas with stricter development standards may include requirements such as performance zoning, buffer zones, reduced impervious surfaces, mitigation of past problems, stricter construction site runoff controls, alternative pollutant flow treatment-type landscaping, and other structural and nonstructural treatments.

General plans, specific plans, and local (city and county) implementing ordinances can also be used for stream, reservoir, wetland, and floodplain protection. These measures typically are designed to achieve numerous objectives. For example, a stream setback can help keep urban development out of the floodplain, protect valuable riparian habitat (and maintain a tree canopy to shade streams), provide for groundwater recharge, and offer a vegetated natural buffer through which runoff water can be filtered as it drains toward the water course.

At the building permit stage, measures for water quality protection can be applied. For example, contaminated runoff, the primary source of beach closures nationwide, is becoming a major issue along southern California's urbanized coastline. A draft ruling by the State Water Resources Control Board upholds a decision by the Los Angeles region's Regional Water Quality Control Board (RWQCB) requiring cities to use their land use authority to address urban runoff at the source. Land use authorities can incorporate specific measures for stormwater control into the building permit process. When applying for a permit, a builder would be required to

Typical parking lot without drainage innovations or landscape treatment

Parking lot median used to collect, filter, and retain runoff

RWQCB = Regional Water Quality Control Board
TMDL = Total maximum daily load

Erosion Control
in the Wine Country

Napa County has been working on a planning and regulation system designed to reduce erosion and sediment-related impacts from intensive agricultural development for wine production. Napa Valley is world-renowned for high-quality wine. The county and its citizenry have strong policies to protect most of the productive land in use for agriculture. The area also has a severe water quality problem. This is particularly true of the Napa River, flowing through the center of the valley and several of its largest urban areas, including the City of Napa. In fact, the State Water Resources Control Board lists the Napa River as an "impaired" waterbody for sediment under its Section 303(b) planning process.

In the last two decades, winery and vineyard development has accelerated, often on steeper, more erosive hillside locations. This has led the county to propose various measures for controlling erosion and sedimentation and to address related issues of habitat and visual impact. In 1991, Napa County passed one of the most far-reaching ordinances  in the country to reduce erosion from hillside vineyard use. Called the Conservation Ordinance, the legislation essentially requires best management practices for new hillside vineyards, implemented through carefully reviewed plans for managing erosion control. The ordinance has been applied to several hundred projects, and modeling data indicates that erosion rates have been significantly reduced.

However, in the late 1990s erosion and other watershed-related problems again became an issue in the county. Citizen concern, plus discussions with the Regional Water Quality Control Board about the Napa River's impaired status and an impending TMDL (total maximum daily load) study, prompted the Napa County Board of Supervisors to initiate a review of the Conservation Ordinance to seek a more comprehensive watershed-based solution.

After meeting for several years, dedicated stakeholders representing every side of the issue were able to resolve some of the many issues they faced. Several solutions emerged that were quite unique. The group decided to form a Countywide Watershed Conservancy to facilitate the acquisition and restoration of key watershed sites to protect habitat and add buffers along streams. The group also recommended a number of other projects, including a Watershed Information Center that over the long term would serve as a public clearinghouse for water quality, habitat, and watershed-related data. While the various interests have widely divergent

Hillside vineyard. Note the mosaic of preserved oak woodland and the drainage engineering features.

objectives, the group agreed that monitoring and careful data collection over the long term are critical to managing the watershed and returning the River to unimpaired status.

The stakeholders and the county continue to struggle over proposed regulations that might affect the wine industry. Going well beyond simply erosion and sediment control, the proposed regulations address biological issues, peak runoff control, and management of native vegetation. Recommendations included requiring setbacks from a creek and stream (even for an existing vineyard), contributions to restore buffer strips that are valuable to habitat and water filtering, additional best management practices for controlling erosion, and BMPs to reduce off-site increases in surface runoff. ∎

include plans for on-site treatment to prevent contaminated runoff from leaving the property. A treatment facility can range from a detention basin that captures and slowly releases runoff, to a basket-size fabric net filled with special absorbent granules that hang inside a storm drain inlet to filter out oils and grease from a parking lot.

The San Diego RWQCB's draft NPDES stormwater permit also requires that local land use authorities ensure that new development does not contribute contaminants to stormwater. Builders would be required to install facilities capable of capturing and treating runoff generated by the first three-fifths (.6) of an inch of rain in a 24-hour period. The rules apply to housing developments with 10 or more units, parking lots with 25 spaces or more, commercial developments of at least 100,000 square feet, auto repair shops, gas stations, restaurants, and homes on hills, among others.

The Tahoe Regional Planning Agency requires that all new construction have water quality best management practices for stormwater. For example, infiltration BMPs are required to infiltrate and store a 20-year rain event, so that the structure can treat runoff at a rate of one inch per hour. For more information on land development requirements and permits in the Tahoe Basin, *see* www.trpa.org.

Stream and Riparian Setbacks and Buffer Zones. Many jurisdictions require a setback from a stream or creek for new or expanded urban development activity, an approach that has many benefits. A setback provides a measure of flood protection, as well as reduced investment in flood insurance and the cost of clean-up. However, to construct a setback levee, an overflow zone, or any other nonstructural flood management measure, a very wide setback is needed. A setback can protect established healthy riparian habitat, frequently home to a diverse plant and animal community. Setbacks allow space for future habitat restoration or recreational trails and parkways. A setback can also create a buffer strip for runoff approaching a creek or stream. Sediment, solids, oil and grease, and some organic materials can be filtered from runoff draining through natural vegetation. A setback can also create a recharge area for groundwater if surface runoff and groundwater are directly connected.

For a low order stream, a setback may be as narrow as 10 to 25 feet. For major streams, communities have established setbacks as wide as 200 to 300 feet. A typical local government ordinance or planning policy may call for a 100-foot setback from a defined channel. A setback is usually measured from the top of a defined bank, but, for a major stream, the top may be difficult to determine and require an area-specific definition. For an example of how a buffer zone can be

City of Oakland's Creek Protection Ordinance

The City of Oakland has embarked on a comprehensive program to protect its creeks and streams and move toward restoration. In 1997, the city adopted a Creek Protection Ordinance to integrate its approach to creeks and riparian areas and clarify the activities and permit levels required. Developed with substantial public interaction, the ordinance is designed to ensure that construction or management work done on a public or private creekside property will minimize impacts to the creek, riparian corridor, and to water flow and quality.

The ordinance carefully defines "creek" and spells out permit requirements, outlining what is needed for a creek protection plan and the criteria used to make the decision. It also explains mitigation and restoration requirements, detailing what is and is not allowed. The program specifies when additional clearances from other agencies such as the California Department of Fish and Game or the RWQCB may be required.

According to the city, the ordinance is working well as a comprehensive tool to address the smaller swales, creeks, drainages, and riparian areas not protected directly by the state or other processes. ■

BMP   = Best Management Practice
NPDES = National Pollutant Discharge Elimination System

A simple landscaped swale to convey, percolate, and filter stormwater

Daylighting

Daylighting generally means opening a watercourse that has been previously confined in a culvert or pipe, and restoring the natural bank topography and vegetation to pre-developed conditions.

sized and used to identify watershed vulnerability zones for a rural drinking water watershed, *see* Appendix E.

A shortcoming of this approach is that the urban area setback generally applies only to new development. In some cases, an urban area has reclaimed a creek or stream that is "lost" or paved over. The City of Berkeley, for example, has daylighted several creeks including parts of Strawberry Creek running from the Berkeley Hills toward the San Francisco Bay, and has restored open space and parkland along the newly opened banks. The City of San Luis Obispo has successfully daylighted a creek running through the heart of its downtown. A restoration or daylighting project cannot completely restore the natural watershed functions to an urbanized area, but can offer educational, recreational, and aesthetic benefits, and create or protect remnant habitat.

Effluent Trading. Another example of an institutional control for water quality protection is effluent trading. Watershed-based effluent trading describes any agreement between parties contributing pollutants to a waterbody that affects the allocation of pollution control responsibilities among dischargers. The product being traded is pollutant reductions or improvements to water quality. Conditions may favor trading within a watershed if, for example, discharger A can achieve pollutant reductions at a significantly lower cost than discharger B. Discharger B might then purchase pollutant reductions from discharger A (say, on a dollar-per-pound basis) such that the same or greater reductions are achieved at a lower overall cost. Potential trades may include point-to-point source trading, point-to-nonpoint source trading, nonpoint-to-nonpoint source trading, intraplan trading (among multiple discharge points from a facility, for example), and pretreatment trading (between industrial dischargers to a collection system, etc.). Regulators may require that a TMDL evaluation or similar mass loading allocation be in place for a watershed, at least for the parameters of concern, before allowing trading to occur between pollutant sources.

The potential advantages of effluent trading include reduced costs for an individual source, economies of scale for a treatment process, incentives for all sources to maximize pollutant reduction, encouragement of innovative technology; facilitation of permit compliance for point sources, and accommodation of growth when pollutant reductions are obtained elsewhere within the watershed. Disadvantages might include a potential acute impact at a discharge location while pollution reduction is shifted elsewhere, point sources bearing much of the burden for nonpoint source pollution control, and imperfect information leading to an inappropriate trade. As more data are gathered about the cost-effectiveness of nonpoint source controls, effluent trading may become more commonplace.

CHAPTER 8

Towards Collaborative Water Planning

The major trends in water policy today suggest a participatory or collaborative approach to developing and implementing water plans. Relying on multiple sources of water requires the cooperation of agencies and communities beyond the boundaries of any one purveyor. Conjunctive use of surface water and groundwater, for example, could mean working with several agencies, private landowners, and the state and federal water projects to achieve a reliable and cost-effective supply. Requirements to identify and analyze environmental effects and third-party impacts from water decisions brings in diverse interests and identifies connections and potential problems beyond those that one purveyor or agency can solve. Requirements to address endangered species issues and environmental water needs lead to a whole new set of involved parties. Mixing land use and growth issues with water supply decisions introduces yet another set of interests. Interdependence is indeed the wave of the present.

Interdependence is indeed the wave of the present.

The water planning processes described in this book are designed to be transparent to the public and encourage collaboration, so that members of interest groups, government agencies, and the general public can understand the analysis and make a meaningful contribution to policy and decision-making. Integrated resource planning (discussed in chapter 6) incorporates dialogue from the very beginning so that the community understands and accepts technical demand projections as the basis for planning, seriously considers a variety of water supply choices, and evaluates packages of water service alternatives from the perspective of reliability, cost, and environmental impact.

Relying on a community's general plan, specific plans, and local ordinances to address water issues leads to public consultation. Not only does the process require interaction and review, but in many communities engenders an intense level of debate. An urban water management plan has a formal requirement for public consultation. Groundwater management plans require public and agency involvement. And environmental impact assessment–either through the National Environmental Policy Act or the California Environmental Quality Act–has requirements and procedures for public review and disclosure. Participation by those with differing points-of-view is in part how planning operates. The various groups and individuals interested in water issues are sophisticated and involved, and expect to participate.

The Traditional Approach

Historically, a single water purveyor would seek new supplies with interaction only as necessary from federal or state regulators or water rights holders such as the Bureau of Reclamation or the Department of Water Resources. A water resources planner and engineer would develop and present technically sound options to management and ultimately to water agency decisionmakers, and public interaction would be limited to environmental review at the CEQA or NEPA stage. It is, in short, a traditional "top-down" model where technical solutions are available for public review, but the data, methods, options, evaluation, and selection are all completed without active collaboration.

All too often this approach has resulted in a stalemate, either between competing water interests or among environmental, water, and development interests. In the Sacramento region, for example, litigating water projects was the norm for nearly 30 years prior to the Water Forum discussed in detail later in this chapter. In the various plans and projects surrounding Bay-Delta issues, litigation and political fighting were the norm for many years. In other parts of the state, litigation, citizen referenda, or initiatives have become a common result.

These stalemates are costly. Lawsuits and political campaigns are expensive and time-consuming, and can lead to divisiveness. While the battle is being waged, objective planning and analysis may not be moving forward and new solutions may receive limited attention. In the past decade, many water planners and decisionmakers have concluded that these stalemates are too costly and a better process is needed.

Dozens of formats for public participation are appropriate at various stages in the water planning process. Ranging from simple public outreach in the form of a web site or a newsletter to an elaborate, formal, and lengthy mediation effort, public participation might involve a few key interests or broadly inclusive collaboration with 50 to 100 separate parties at the table. A town hall meeting or open house where broad membership of the community can be solicited for general input might be appropriate, or, at another

CEQA = California Environmental Quality Act

NEPA = National Environmental Policy Act

In the past decade, many water planners and decisionmakers have concluded that these stalemates are too costly and a better process is needed.

stage, a carefully selected stakeholder committee that focuses for months on technical issues and detailed written agreements might be preferable.[1]

In this chapter, we concentrate on a style of collaborative policy development known as "interest-based" negotiation, specifically examining how this approach can be applied to integrated water resources planning as outlined in chapters 4–6. Particularly appropriate for water resources planning, this model can accommodate a high degree of controversy; solutions require considerable technical understanding; and complex alternatives often involve environmental, water supply, and economic development interests that are readily identifiable. Other styles of public involvement are also valuable, and their techniques can be used to supplement the interest-based approach documented here.

This chapter can only offer a thumbnail sketch of the theories, tools, and techniques for collaborative policy development. For a more thorough understanding of the subject, *see* Managing Public Disputes: A Practical Guide to Handling Conflict and Reaching Agreements by S. Carpenter and W.J.D. Kennedy, 1988, and The Consensus-Building Handbook, edited by L. Susskind, S. McKearnan, and J. Thomas-Larmer, 1999. For more information about methods and techniques for facilitating collaborative workshops and meetings, *see* Facilitator's Guide to Participatory Decision-Making, S. Kaner, 1996; Meeting of the Minds by D. Iacofano, 2001, and Making Meetings Work by M. Doyle and D. Strauss, 1993.

A Primer on Collaborative Public Policy Development

Definitions and Principles

Collaborative Policy Development. For purposes of this book, collaborative policy development is defined as bringing together all of the appropriate stakeholders in a structured process to work cooperatively to resolve a public policy question or develop a plan, in this case related to water resources. Definitions of stakeholder, interest, and facilitator/mediator are in the adjacent sidebars. A collaborative approach to water planning has the following benefits:

- Allows water or land use agencies to fulfill legal and procedural requirements for public review and participation, and may also be valuable when seeking subsequent permits from state and federal environmental regulatory agencies

> **Stakeholder**
>
> A stakeholder is any person who has a direct interest in the outcome of a policy or planning decision. The stake may be a direct or indirect financial interest or may involve a policy or value interest such as protecting an environmental resource.

1. Whatever type of participatory process is used, federal, state, and local governments (including public water purveyors) need to be aware of the various open meeting laws that govern participation, how agendas and notices are handled, how advisory bodies must operate, etc. The three laws with the most wide-ranging effects are the Federal Advisory Committee Act (FACA) for federal agency work, the Bagley-Keene Open Meeting Act for state agency work, and the Ralph M. Brown Act, which governs conduct of local government meetings in California. Be sure to consult appropriate counsel if there are any uncertainties about the application of these requirements.

FACA = Federal Advisory Committee Act

Interest

An *interest* is the value choice of an individual stakeholder or group of stakeholders related to a specific issue. The interest of a water agency, for example, may be to provide the community with a reliable source of water over the long term. This is distinguished from a *position* or *posture*, the formal or informal stance an individual or group might take on a specific issue or policy question. For example, that same water agency may take the official position that, to meet its interest, a certain amount of water must be secured from a new reservoir project. The distinctions between interest and position are further outlined in the text.

Facilitator and Mediator

A *facilitator* is one who helps a group of stakeholders or diverse interests understand and frame the issues, working through differences of opinion to achieve some level of agreement. A facilitator is thought to be neutral and objective on policy matters. Facilitation may cover a broad spectrum of issues and be effective for small or large groups, but may not always lead to a detailed agreement when conflict is significant.

A *mediator* is also a neutral and objective professional who attempts to help resolve a policy issue among competing interests. A more focused process, mediation is designed to resolve an active, definable dispute between specific identifiable parties with a high level of conflict or controversy.

- Can tap into specialized knowledge or political contacts of stakeholders that can be brought into negotiations
- Can lead to innovative, and sometimes unexpected, solutions by bringing together divergent viewpoints in a creative problem-solving environment
- Can reduce the potential for stalemate and litigation by allowing all viewpoints to be presented and help craft a solution
- Can educate all interests on technical and policy issues
- Can create or improve personal relationships and trust among different interests that can help in times of conflict and carry over from the issue at hand to future interactions
- Can expand opportunities for potential funding and resources by bringing other players into the plan or project
- Is open, inclusive, and democratic (when done well), and can lead to a solution that has strengthened support and justification

A collaborative policy process is by no means a panacea. Just because it's extensive does not make a process effective or suggest that conflict or litigation can be avoided. A public process can be long, tiring, and expensive. In fact, each case study described in this chapter lasted many years and required significant resources from agencies and stakeholders. Some interests may be reluctant to compromise, seek a new solution, or even participate in the process at all. Participants in the workshops or negotiations may reach an agreement or a have a deeper understanding of the issues, but constituents outside the process may receive only limited information or may never agree with the solutions. And when the process is allowed to degrade into a battle of opinions and values with no grounding in technical data, expert information may not be given adequate attention. Since a collaborative process is frequently advisory to a formal decision-making body, the ultimate policymakers may not fully support the advisory group's recommendations. By using effective techniques during the interactive process, however, each of these pitfalls can be overcome. The key is *effective* collaboration, not just more of it.

Five Typical Stages of a Collaborative Process

The collaborative planning process can be expressed as a simple, but effective model with five basic stages:

- Assessment and Planning
- Organization and Process Design
- Education

- Negotiation and Agreements
- Implementation[2]

In any interaction, large or small, short-term or long, the various stages of the model can be played out. For a comprehensive public process, each step is followed deliberately and carefully to ensure that the approach is organized and effective. But even for a single meeting or interaction, assessing the situation, planning and organizing the meeting, educating all interests about the issues, and then (and only then) negotiating or seeking agreement is a useful discipline.

- **Assessment and planning.** Typically this stage begins by interviewing key stakeholders and reviewing background information to determine whether the planning or policy problem is appropriate for collaboration and, if so, who should be involved. Once it's clear that a collaboration process may have merit, the agency identifies and interviews stakeholders more formally, gathering information about the nature of the water resource issues and other matters of concern to each stakeholder. These can range from a potential conflict to options and choices for solving the policy problem. At this stage it is useful to assess the technical complexity of the problem, identifying the data and analysis in hand (or that may be needed) and the resources and time available to collect relevant information.

  It is critical to ascertain who should take part in the negotiations, what the key issues are, and whether stakeholders are willing to participate, along with the type of information each one believes is necessary to address the issues. This initial stage can be extensive. In a recent example of managing groundwater in an unregulated basin, project coordinators interviewed more than 100 key stakeholders over a one-year period. Assessing the best way to design a successful process requires a thorough understanding of the problem. Often, the assessment results in a formal report that summarizes findings and sets direction without attributing specific comments or ideas to an individual stakeholder.

- **Organization and process design.** In this stage, a suitable process is organized and designed, based on information gathered in the assessment. While every process is unique, in water planning the educational phase can be extensive because the technical and regulatory/legal issues are complex. And a considerable amount of time should be devoted to formulating and evaluating alternatives as well.

  Products of an organizational phase typically include a schedule or flow chart mapping the steps required, a clear path or scope of work identifying

Figure 8-1
Five Typical Stages of the Collaborative Process

Assessment and planning

Organization and process design

Education

Negotiation and agreements

Implementation

2. The five-stage model is adapted from the work of the Center for Collaborative Policy (www.csus.edu/ccp), a joint program of California State University, Sacramento, and McGeorge School of Law, University of the Pacific. The Center was founded in 1992 by Executive Director Susan Sherry to further collaborative problem-solving for local, regional, state, and federal government policy issues.

Not every situation is ripe for collaboration. The following conditions should be present in some form to ensure a successful process:

- Multiple issues and potential solutions allow for trade-offs when crafting an agreement

- Primary parties are identifiable and willing to participate

- All parties have a legitimate spokesperson(s) and have shown a commitment to see the process through and respond to their constituencies

- Stakeholders have a relative balance of power (the eventual decisionmaker may have legal authority, but major stakeholders who can block or influence the ultimate decision also have legitimate power)

- Interested parties are likely to have future dealings with one another on future issues

- No party can achieve everything desired through a new law or some other channel (a so-called alternative to a negotiated agreement)

- An external pressure (e.g., a funding deadline, regulatory process, or statutory or legal deadline) requires that an agreement be reached

- Sufficient time and funding are available to work through the issues collaboratively with funding committed so that the process can be coordinated professionally

Source: Adapted from a list developed in 2001 by Susan Sherry and Susan Carpenter for the Center for Collaborative Policy (www.csus.edu/ccp), a Joint Program of California State University Sacramento and McGeorge School of Law, Pacific University.

tasks and milestones, a charter and/or set of ground rules for stakeholders, and committed funds and resources to conduct the process. While the initial design should reflect as much of the overall planning effort as possible, diversions, changes, and revisions will doubtless occur. Collaboration is dynamic. Stakeholders may leave or be added, a new issue or potential solution may surface, and a new question may be posed that requires new data. The process design must respond to these changes, but charting a comprehensive course from the beginning will make that task easier.

- **Education.** Formal and informal education occurs throughout the process. This book has addressed the kinds of data gathering, modeling, analysis, and documentation needed for comprehensive water planning. In a collaborative process the key is to link technical information with a policy issue that must be resolved and the underlying interest of each participant. Every issue may require a different type of education.

  For example, framing a policy question succinctly so that every stakeholder can understand it may be more difficult than settling a technical dispute about the amount of water that can be safely withdrawn from a groundwater basin. A common pitfall in a collaborative process is spending too little time on education, and proceeding to discuss and negotiate a solution or agreement without a common understanding of the problem, alternative solutions, and their consequences.

- **Negotiation and agreements.** Most people consider this stage the essence of a public process. However, negotiating or reaching an agreement may occur at any stage. Early in the process, for example, participants are typically asked to agree on the rules of engagement (often called "ground rules," or more elaborate versions called "charters"). Later, after preliminary education, participants may be ready to accept broad principles or goals to guide solutions. At various stages in the educational process, participants may be asked to agree on fundamental information (e.g., levels of groundwater overdraft or existing water demands) or study methodologies to enable the alternatives to move forward.

- **Implementation.** Implementing the proposed plan or policy is the final stage of a collaborative process. While an advisory group or committee may often stop its work at the plan stage, implementation and monitoring should be built into the agreement. To be sustainable, an agreement must assure participants that every agreed-upon issue will be addressed and that commitments will be kept. For example, an environmental group seeking higher levels of water conservation in the future will need assurances that the actions will occur, with periodic monitoring demonstrating the level of compliance and mechanisms to correct deficiencies. Building in assurances, monitoring, funding, and some ongoing venue for discussion and evaluation are essential to a plan's long-term success.

A Few Common Principles

Several principles that are common to most participatory interactions merit brief review.

Representation and Inclusiveness. For a water planning project, typical representation includes the local water purveyor, any other agencies or water rights holders that might assist in securing or conveying water, environmental groups (possibly representing numerous environmental interests such as river protection, land use issues, or groundwater contamination), local cities and county representation, community groups such as ratepayer/taxpayer organizations or neighborhood groups, local landowners, and business and development interests, particularly those that are significant present or future water users. Depending on the scope of the project, others who are formal stakeholders or in a partnership capacity may join the process. Partners might include federal and state regulatory or resource agencies (*e.g.,* California Department of Fish and Game, U.S. Fish and Wildlife Service, Regional Water Quality Control Board), LAFCO representatives, neighboring water agencies, flood control districts, and others. The key is to be inclusive, so that every substantive interest is represented at the table.

DWR = Department of Water Resources

LAFCO = Local Agency Formation Commission

The key is to be inclusive, so that every substantive interest is represented at the table.

Selection and organization of stakeholder representation can vary. In the CALFED-Bay Delta process, for example, primary representatives from more than 20 federal and state agencies are involved in regulating environmental and water resources and agencies responsible for the major water projects (*e.g.,* DWR, Bureau of Reclamation). However, a formal stakeholder committee– consisting of more than 30 individuals representing water use, energy, flood control, agriculture, business, community, and environmental interests throughout the state–also advises the agency representatives. Various other stakeholder and technical working groups have been formed to address water use efficiency in agriculture, restoration of the Delta ecosystem, etc., and broad public involvement and outreach are also part of the CALFED process.

Charters and Ground Rules. Every collaborative group needs rules of engagement to conduct business and proceed efficiently toward agreements. The overall direction and operating approach for a collaborative group is called a **charter,** and might include the group's mission, representation, timeline or expected milestones, and legal or statutory boundaries (referred to as "sideboards" or the legal boundaries of possible solutions). It might also include the stakeholder structure or organization, its leadership, anticipated products, how collaborative interactions are to be conducted and decisions are made, guidelines for dealing with the media, and related topics. The entire group generally agrees to a charter early in the process, reviews its contents when necessary to stay on track and correct unproductive activity.

Ground rules typically focus on meeting decorum and conduct; procedures for decisionmaking, recordkeeping, and feedback.

Ground rules, while similar, typically focus on meeting decorum and conduct; procedures for decisionmaking, recordkeeping, and feedback. It is not uncommon for a large collaborative exercise to have an overall charter to guide the process and specific ground rules to help with day-to-day workshop/meeting issues. In more modest situations, a simple set of ground rules will suffice to ensure a civil, effective process.

Two important rules of engagement that are often ignored are central to a successful process. Participants must agree on a decision-making structure and procedure before addressing a difficult policy decision. Will the group operate by consensus? If so, what does that mean? Typically, consensus means all parties either agree to or can live with a decision and do not wish to block a proposal. Does the group operate with less than a consensus? Some groups, for example, striving for consensus can call for a two-thirds or three-quarters vote after exhausting debate. Whatever the procedure, and no matter how hotly debated, agreement on some decision-making procedure is essential. Once in place, a decision procedure is seldom needed, except in rare instances where consensus cannot be achieved. It may even be viewed as a sign of failure or lack of creative problem-solving to fall back on a decision procedure.[3]

Each member of a committee or task force should be actively involved in developing relationships with and educating other stakeholders.

Reporting back to constituents, decisionmakers, and colleagues is a second issue that is often overlooked. Each member of a committee or task force should be actively involved in developing relationships with and educating other stakeholders. Because relationship-building cannot easily be duplicated "outside the room," each member involved in the collaborative process should frequently take progress reports back to their respective board, commission, or other constituents and consult with colleagues on important issues or policy choices. Without a formal process for communicating with constituents, an outcome may not be supported by the broader public the collaborative is supposed to represent.

3. While rules for decisionmaking vary, some form of consensus-based approach, with the ability to agree or stand aside, usually works best. It may also be advisable to have a provision for reporting the dissenting view, as well as the one that prevails. The Sacramento-based Water Forum developed a unique approach where each of four formal, interest-based caucuses have to reach 75 percent agreement, so that no interest—business, water, public, environmental—could be entirely left out of any major decision. It is noteworthy that after eight years of working together, the Forum has never had to resort to a formal "vote."

Separating Interests from Positions or Postures. A fundamental principle in interest-based negotiating is that stakeholders should be encouraged to define their underlying interests, as distinct from any positions their organizations might take on a particular issue, and make the interests known to all participants in a non-threatening way. Consider, for example, the possibility of developing an off-stream reservoir. If one participant cannot support an off-stream project of any kind, while another participant vows to have the project constructed at all costs, negotiating a solution is impossible. But if the facilitator can uncover the first participant's underlying interest–to protect and restore the stream reach and avoid any impact to local vistas–and the underlying interest of the other group–to have additional reliable water at a reasonable cost–there may be room to negotiate, because these "interests" allow for mutual gain.

Many techniques can help move from positional to interest-based thinking. One is the simple act of respectfully asking a participant "why." What leads you to that conclusion? What part of the proposal troubles you or threatens your interest? A second technique is to have participants, either as individuals or in like-minded caucuses, express their underlying interests. These written statements are shared and discussed without judgment or without initially trying to resolve the dispute. Often a participant who assumes an opponent's position based on previous interactions is surprised to find their real underlying interest.

Inventing Options for Mutual Gain and Interdependent/Linked Agreements. Once you have reached the solution and negotiation stage, it is important to recognize that sustainable agreements are typically those whose primary solutions are linked together. In other words, each interest has a part of the solution, and each interest is dependent on the other's success. In the water resources arena, this often means that a water supply project can move forward, but only if it is linked directly to commensurate environmental protection and restoration goals. Or, an agreement to develop a new water source and serve a new area is linked to an aggressive water conservation program with assurances of success. These types of interdependent agreements; sometimes referred to as "gives and gets" enable all interests to see their solutions reflected, and provide assurance that the solutions will occur. Such interdependent solutions tend to be more lasting because all of the stakeholders have a vested interest in seeing everyone's solution move forward.

During the discussion, participants or facilitators should be searching for options that serve multiple interests, or mutual gain. Solutions that can be identified and framed as having benefit to several (or even all) of the interests stand a much better chance of success. The more we

Understanding Alternatives to Negotiation–Napa River Watershed Plan

In a group (comprised of more than 20 members) negotiating watershed management solutions to hillside erosion issues in California's Napa Valley, the essential policy question was how to increase protection for the hillsides surrounding the valley and minimize water-quality degradation on the Napa River and its tributaries. At the same time, local business interests wanted to continue developing vineyards and wineries in the fertile and lucrative soil in the valley and hillsides.

From the beginning, litigation to compel change was an option for the environmental groups, and political pressure on the local board was an option for the winery interests. Despite these options, each party recognized the value of reaching agreement. The interactive process moved forward, even surviving a lawsuit that one of the parties filed. ∎

Groundwater in Goleta

The Goleta Water District is a water purveyor north of the City of Santa Barbara that relies heavily on groundwater. For many years debate raged over whether the groundwater basin was in a condition of long-term overdraft. Numerous technical studies were conducted, reviewed, conducted again, and restudied. Conclusions were controversial and hotly debated.

For environmental interests, overdraft was evident, and no further water should be drawn from the basin to support increased growth and water demands. For interests that were development-oriented, the groundwater aquifer had available capacity, and carefully planned extractions could be increased without harm.

On several occasions, land use and water planners tried to meet and consider policy options for future water supply. However, technical debates about groundwater use, depletion, overdraft, and safe yield prevented any type of productive discussion. Finally, with leadership from both the county government and water district board, a representative committee of technical stakeholders was assembled to examine the various studies. Through careful facilitation, the group was able to reach agreement on data and trends for the groundwater basin. The policy issues and choices were still debated vigorously within the community, but with a common grounding in the technical parameters. ■

can be trained to think in terms of solutions that provide mutual gain, the more robust and lasting the agreements will be.

Alternatives to a Negotiated Solution. An important element of collaboration is to openly recognize that every participant has options that go well beyond the process. In other words, if people can achieve their objectives in some other fashion, they are likely to do so. Sometimes that route may be litigation. Or it may be new legislation or funding that supports one position over another. A collaborative process works because the possibility of achieving a lasting solution increases when people work together to reach consensus. Participants are encouraged to identify and analyze their options and those of opponents realistically. This capacity for acknowledging reality strengthens the collaboration and assists in eventual decisionmaking.

Organizing a Process with Adequate Time, Resources, and a Communication Strategy. To succeed, a well-organized process requires adequate time, funding, and a thoughtful communications strategy. It is not enough to provide participants with meeting notes about issues and agreements. Written feedback should be concise, accurate, focused, and delivered in a timely fashion. It should be given to participants as well as decisionmakers and any constituent who can influence the eventual outcome. Some attention should be devoted to keeping the final decisionmakers apprised of progress. In water planning this is typically the water agency's management and board. Leadership must support the project from the outset. As the collaborative progresses, any wavering of support must be addressed.

Common Issues in Water Resources Planning

Resolving Technical Disputes

Water planning involves complex hydrologic issues and the use of extensive data, technical methodologies, and computer models. It also requires assumptions about water consumption for each land use type, levels of water conservation that might be achieved in the future, or the likelihood of a particular water supply option being available at a given time. This type of information, which can be problematic in a public process, requires considerable education and study. A discussion or debate can be stymied unless basic data issues are resolved.

To reach agreement on the direction of water policy, a group must have a common understanding of the problem and common facts and models on which to base decisions. Some call the process of establishing a common information base the education phase or joint fact-finding.

In the process of joint fact-finding, stakeholders agree on the information needed, how it's obtained, the experts to enlist, and how the data should be analyzed. A subcommittee of a larger group representing each of the major interests often handles the process. After working with the appropriate technical data and experts, the subcommittee returns to the full group with a recommended course of action. Panels of experts representing different viewpoints or experience can be useful. Having stakeholders identify and agree on what constitutes an expert–that is, who has technical or scientific credibility with the group–is also valuable.

When negotiating a technical dispute, one pitfall that should be avoided is yielding to the temptation for endless collection of data. Although it may further the interest of some participants to use data to slow the process or impede a decision, the group must decide the level of detail needed to answer the policy question, even though the data may not necessarily be all that one might ever want.

Settling Disagreements over Assumptions, Baseline Conditions, and Methods

Water supply and demand analysis requires forecasting, which in turn requires developing assumptions and models. Gaining agreement on assumptions and models or analysis to forecast the future can prevent dissension later in the process. For example, potential water conservation should be addressed prior to formally choosing water supply options. Some participants may argue that no new supplies are needed until a water provider has wrung every drop out of conservation. A realistic assessment of how much water can be conserved and at what cost is critical.

Similarly, modeling future water demands requires that participants agree on a common basis for future land uses. If a community's general plan is uncertain or is being debated, agreeing about future water needs will be difficult.

What appears to be a simple matter can, and has, led to extensive debate. All participants may not necessarily agree on the baseline for water use. This is particularly true when the State Water Project (SWP) or the Central Valley Project (CVP) are involved. Large amounts of water and high levels of variability from one year to the next make projection of consumption problematic and the use of unmetered water difficult to assess. Beyond that, conflicting interpretations of environmental laws or court rulings can lead to vastly different assumptions about the amount of baseline water available for consumptive use. It is worth the time and effort to design an education and negotiation process that sorts out these technical matters to make sure all participants are starting at the same point.

CVP = Central Valley Project
SWP = State Water Project

The Importance of Goals, Objectives, or Principles

Reaching conceptual agreements early in the process demonstrates the value of collaboration and establishes the basis for more detailed problem-solving.

Reaching conceptual agreements early in the process demonstrates the value of collaboration and establishes the basis for more detailed problem-solving. Broad principles or goals provide this foundation. Often the goals try to balance one interest with another: reliable water supply, while protecting environmental values. Or, they attempt to achieve multiple objectives: maintaining economic development, improving water quality, and restoring the river's natural ecosystem.

Agreeing to even broadly stated goals can be difficult. A participant may struggle over a specific choice of words and push for more or less specificity. However, once a participant's interests have been defined, agreement on a conceptual statement is often possible. The power of common goals that express the basic aspirations of the collaborative in a few sentences is valuable throughout the process. They help a planner suggest measurable objectives, criteria for evaluating alternatives, and a basis for negotiating detailed agreements.

Developing, Evaluating, and Packaging Alternatives

The heart of integrated resource planning (*see* chapter 6) is the development and evaluation of alternatives designed to meet water resources goals and objectives. Considering complex alternatives in a public process, however, requires a carefully designed approach.

Evaluation criteria should be defined and agreed upon prior to developing alternatives. Criteria are typically derived from the plan's initial goals or objectives and should reflect the underlying interests of the stakeholders. Other issues to discuss prior to negotiating alternatives are how criteria should be measured, the appropriate level of detail, and methods for testing alternatives. It is useful to systematically list the advantages and disadvantages of each alternative, and weigh each criterion in a public forum. This exercise, especially when accompanied by graphics, can demonstrate the trade-offs that are possible, highlighting how various interests can be served by each choice.

The development and presentation of alternatives can play a role in the acceptance of a final choice.

The development and presentation of alternatives can play a role in the acceptance of a final choice. One suggestion is to define what is fixed as a "given" or "backbone" of every alternative. For example, all participants may accept a certain level of water conservation that may be common to all alternatives. It's also important to ensure that each alternative meets the basic planning objectives. While one alternative may favor one objective over another, no feasible choice should completely ignore an interest or value. And finally, avoid an array of choices and themes that appears simplistic: "environmental protection option" or "maximize water reliability option." Alternatives like this tend to polarize participants. Ultimately, the consensus solution will likely be a hybrid, a combination, or a variation of the original options.

Finding a package of agreements that satisfies the interests and values of each participant can result in a lasting agreement. One approach is to make different elements of a solution interdependent. For example, a collaborative project undertaken for California's Napa Valley addressed flood management concerns in the Napa River watershed. Although all parties believed that a solution was needed, single-purpose flood control solutions that had been proposed for nearly 30 years failed to win local support. Through a facilitated effort involving more than 50 stakeholders (23 agencies and many local and regional interests), a package of interrelated agreements was accepted. The flood management elements contain benefits for wildlife habitat and river restoration. The environmental enhancements cannot be achieved without funds from the flood control projects. Solutions to flooding include urban design improvements desired by communities through which the river passes. Should any one of these elements be eliminated or modified, the others are affected. The selected alternatives are interdependent and so too are the stakeholders.

Participants in the Sacramento area Water Forum

The selected alternatives are interdependent and so too are the stakeholders.

An agreement in concept or a framework agreement can be helpful when some of the components have been settled, but other issues are unresolved. A framework agreement typically establishes a follow-up process for arriving at a detailed solution, and includes objectives to be met, ways to judge whether solutions address the issues raised, and a procedure for completing negotiations.

Assurances and Monitoring

A water plan covers a lengthy time horizon. Many projects and programs will be phased in when demand warrants or environmental monitoring suggests a need to mitigate or restore. It is critical that every agreement contain mechanisms to track progress and assurances that commitments will be kept.

An assurance is essentially a point of leverage promising a participant that an interest or objective will be met. For example, a commitment to reduce stream diversions to protect fisheries can be incorporated into an agency's water rights permit or into a regulatory permit from a resource agency. Without this external legal backing, a participant may place less trust in long-term agreements to protect resources. Similarly, signing a memorandum of understanding or creating a joint powers authority to complete infrastructure for shared water supply may be required to ensure that all parties are comfortable with future commitments. These assurances should be built directly into an agreement.

Summary

Detailed comparative research and evaluation of collaborative efforts in water policy are just beginning to emerge. One such analysis, conducted by Sarah Connick and Judith Innes from the University of California, Berkeley, reviewed the Water Forum, CALFED, and the San Francisco Bay Estuary Project (two of which are described in this text). Connick and Innes conclude.

> We have seen from our studies of collaborative dialogues focusing on water policy making in California that these efforts have produced robust and lasting outcomes that extend well beyond the resolution of specific disputes. Together these and other examples demonstrate how such dialogues have profoundly transformed the policy-making practices, as well as the way in which day-to-day decisions about on-the-ground management and operations are made. The California water policy arena has been a notoriously conflictual environment, in which parties frequently were at odds with one another on multiple fronts simultaneously, fighting one another through regulatory and resource management agencies, the courts, Congress and the legislature, and the voters. Today, however, these diverse parties are engaging in collaborative dialogues, focusing on joint problem solving rather than mutual destruction, and more often than not going to the legislative bodies and voters with one voice in seeking remedies to their problems.

> Connick and Innes, 2001, *Outcomes of Collaborative Water Policy Making: Applying Complexity Thinking to Evaluation, U.C. Berkeley Institute of Urban and Regional Development Working Paper 2001-8.*[4]

Case Studies

The case studies on the following pages illustrate how these principles have been applied in three separate contexts. Although relatively large-scale and broad in scope, these examples represent what collaborative water policy can deliver. The Water Forum is a regional planning project intended to provide adequate water supplies while protecting the environmental resources of the lower American River. The CALFED-Bay Delta program is an example of a statewide effort to restore Delta habitat, while improving the reliability of the water supply, flood protection, levee stability, and water quality. The New Melones Lake Resource Management Plan is an example of a stakeholder group

---

4. Other excellent comparative and analytical studies of collaboration in watershed management or water resources have been written. Two broad literature reviews are noteworthy: W.D. Leach and N.W. Pelkey, (2001), "Making Watershed Partnerships Work: A Review of the Empirical Literature," Journal of Water Resources Planning and Management, November/December, Volume 127, No. 6, pp. 378–385. Kenny *et al.* (2000), "The New Watershed Source Book: A Directory and Review of Watershed Initiatives in the Western United States." Natural Resources Law Center, University of Colorado School of Law, Boulder, Colorado.

that balanced recreational opportunities and habitat protection in a situation where significant controversy and acrimony had preceded the collaboration.

Water Forum

For many decades, the biggest stumbling block to balanced water solutions in the Sacramento region was that individual groups–water purveyors, environmentalists, local governments, citizen groups–independently pursued their own water interests with limited success. The Water Forum brought together a diverse group of 40 business and development leaders, citizen groups, water purveyors, environmentalists, and local governments in Sacramento County and the surrounding region (water managers in El Dorado and Placer counties joined the Forum in 1995). Initiated by the City and County of Sacramento, the Forum was organized in 1993 to seek collaborative and regional solutions to a series of water resources problems focused primarily (although not exclusively) on the Lower American River from Folsom Lake, a Bureau of Reclamation reservoir, to the confluence of the American and Sacramento rivers.

The Water Forum brought together a diverse group of 40 business and development leaders, citizen groups, purveyors, environmentalists, and local governments in Sacramento County and the surrounding region.

The collaborative process. The Water Forum process was based on the methods and principles described in the beginning of this chapter. The Center for Collaborative Policy (formerly called the California Center for Public Dispute Resolution) served as facilitator and mediator, moving the process from initial assessment and organization through detailed phases of education, negotiation, and implementation.

Organized into four major interest-based caucuses (business, environment, public, and water), Forum participants met frequently in caucus, plenary, and small groups to assess their interests and respond to issues and solutions. Specialized subcommittees were formed to address various technical and policy issues such as a "Surface Water Team" for analyzing and negotiating specific water diversions from the American River and a "Demand Conservation Team" that addressed issues of water use efficiency standards and progress. In every case, subgroups included representatives from each interest and participants who had sufficient expertise to work through complex technical issues.

After extensive discussions, data collection, and fact-finding, the Water Forum focused on the key interrelated problems that needed to be resolved:

One "co-equal" objective of the Water Forum is to preserve the natural resources of the American River.

Another "co-equal" objective is to provide a reliable water supply for planned growth in the region through 2030.

- Regional water shortages, particularly during drought conditions
- Protection of the recreational and environmental resources of the Lower American River (including various wetlands and tributaries that derive water from the American River)
- Lowered groundwater tables and contaminated groundwater in the region
- Water reliability risks

Water Forum participants devoted tens of thousands of hours to researching problems, suggesting and testing alternatives, developing principles to guide agreements, and negotiating regional solutions to achieve two co-equal objectives:

- **Provide a reliable and safe** water supply for the region's economic health and planned development to the year 2030
- **Preserve the fishery,** wildlife, recreational, and aesthetic values of the Lower American River

Signed by all 40 signatory parties and published in January 2000, the Water Forum Agreement contains seven inter-related elements, each of which is necessary for a regional solution.

The agreement. Signed by all 40 signatory parties and published in January 2000, the Water Forum Agreement contains seven interrelated elements, each of which is necessary for a regional solution. For one element to proceed, the signatories must agree to their responsibilities in each of the other seven elements. This deliberate packaging enables participants to see their interests represented, but only if others' interests are also served.

- **Increased surface water diversions.** All signatories will support the surface water diversions agreed to for each water supplier and the facilities needed to divert, treat, and distribute the water. These supplies were forecast out to year 2030, based on land development planned in each community's general plan. These agreements are very specific, describing baseline water usage, 2030 diversion amounts and sources in average, drier, and driest years, timing of diversions, and any specific requirements to secure the source. To date, many of the water purveyors have built significant facilities, and each of the interests, including the environmental groups, has actively supported the projects.

- **Actions to meet customers' needs while reducing diversion impacts in drier years.** The agreement envisions increasing possible diversion from the American River from the current level of 216,500 AFY to 481,000 AFY. With adequate mitigation, these diversions can be accomplished without adverse impacts to the Lower American River in wet and average years. However, in dry years, to avoid impact to recreational, fishery, wildlife, or aesthetic values of the river, purveyors agreed to dry year cutbacks in diversion. To continue meeting water customer demand, water supply alternatives will need to be developed. These include conjunctive use of groundwater and surface water, reoperation of reservoirs on the Middle Fork of the American River, and increased conservation and recycling. The dry year cutbacks are in the process of being secured through either water contracts with the Bureau of Reclamation or water rights conditions.

- **An improved pattern of fishery flow releases from Folsom Reservoir.** This element provides a pattern of water releases from Folsom Reservoir that more closely matches the needs of anadromous fish, in particular fall run Chinook salmon and steelhead. The Water Forum convened a Fish Biologists Working Session to focus agency and other fisheries experts on this issue. The Water Forum is working with technical experts, the Bureau of Reclamation, U.S. Fish and Wildlife Service and NOAA Fisheries, and all of the stakeholders to implement fish-friendly standards on a permanent basis. This new standard is to be ensured through a revised State Water Resources Control Board water rights permit for the Bureau's water. This complex exercise involves managing levels of river flow and water temperatures to meet environmental objectives under varying year types and in varying times of each year. To date, the technical aspects of this element have made it difficult to complete. However, the new flow management standard that is emerging includes a "prescriptive" component of water that will be always be available to fisheries in all types of water years and all months. In addition, an adaptive management group (called the River Management Group) will meet regularly to augment the minimum flow with additional water designed to meet specific fish needs as they arise, or to reduce flows to conserve cold water for achieving temperature objectives in dry years.

- **Lower American River Habitat management element (including recreation).** This element contains five components to address the water flow, temperature, physical habitat, and recreational issues for the Lower American River. The five components include a habitat management plan (funded by many of the signatory agencies), 22 specific fisheries improvement projects identified by the CALFED program and co-funded by various signatory agencies, monitoring and evaluation, project-specific mitigation, and Lower American River recreational projects. Recreation projects include trails, land acquisition, and facility improvements.

- **Water conservation.** Water conservation is designed to stretch the region's supplies, to reduce impacts on groundwater pumping, and to demonstrate to state and federal agencies

Water flowing from Folsom Reservoir on the American River

Groundwater management is a key principle in the Water Forum Agreement.

SGA = Sacramento Groundwater Authority

that the region is using water efficiently. Residential water meters, Urban Water Conservation Best Management Practices, public involvement and education, water conservation plans, and agricultural water conservation are all included. Each water purveyor has a conservation plan tailored to its needs and capabilities. A regional monitoring and reporting program is tracking how well purveyors are meeting their conservation schedules.

- **Groundwater management.** The groundwater element includes monitoring of water withdrawn, water levels and storage volumes, and conjunctive use of surface and groundwater. Sustainable yields are in place for each of three identifiable groundwater basins. The Sacramento Groundwater Authority (SGA) was created using a joint powers agreement among the cities of Sacramento, Citrus Heights, and Folsom, the County of Sacramento, and numerous water purveyors to manage the north basin. The Authority is facilitating a conjunctive use program, including assisting in creating infrastructure capacity, conducting detailed monitoring and management programs, and ensuring that the groundwater yield is not exceeded. Recently, on the strength of the SGA's partnerships, the California Bay Delta Authority provided a $22 million grant for improved infrastructure to allow for conjunctive use. The SGA can also establish regulatory fees based on zones of benefit. A separate collaborative dialogue is currently in progress to determine how to manage the south and central basins.

- **Water Forum successor effort.** Once the Agreement was finalized, the signatories recognized that the collaborative model was the only way to ensure fair and consistent implementation. They agreed to an ongoing successor effort to complete detailed agreements (many of the initial agreements were still in conceptual form), oversee, monitor, and report progress as actions occur, and respond to changing circumstances over the next three decades. Essential to this effort is an early-warning system to ensure that all organizations are aware of changes that must be addressed, specific projects that must be reviewed for conformance with the overall agreement, and questions and issues that might result in disagreement or conflict. The successor effort includes one subgroup devoted to developing a detailed plan for river and fisheries habitat restoration, another subgroup devoted to groundwater issues in south-central Sacramento County, and another group to develop explicit procedures to ensure that future land use decisions rendered by each local government are consistent with the water supply planning and procedures contained in the framework.

In addition to the formal stakeholders, cooperation with state and federal agencies is necessary to ensure implementation of the agreement.

In particular, the Bureau of Reclamation will be called upon to support an updated flow standard in the Lower American River and to enter into diversion agreements with upstream Water Forum purveyors diverting water above Folsom Lake. The State Water Resources Control Board will be asked to adopt an updated flow standard as part of a water rights condition. Any Water Forum decisions will have to dovetail with water quality and water supply projects and decisions of the California Bay Delta Authority. To accomplish this, the Water Forum staff and key stakeholders continue to meet regularly with the Bureau, State Water Resources Control Board, California Department of Fish and Game, U.S. Fish and Wildlife service, California Department of Water Resources, and the California Bay-Delta Authority.

Conclusions. A series of factors have contributed to the success of the Water Forum. Among the most important is the working relationships and trust that developed amongst participants. Former combatants and litigants worked together for seven years to develop the framework, and now continue to work toward implementation. They can, as one participant has observed, "finish each other's sentences." Stakeholders have chosen to address their long-standing differences as a formal mediation process, and continue to rely on an interest-based approach in seeking creative solutions. The Forum has also helped facilitate changes in institutional relationships, and a new regional groundwater management authority has been formed. Several long-standing lawsuits have been resolved,[5] and new plans have been developed to guide the future actions of local, regional, and state agencies.

Like other multi-jurisdictional and multi-interest collaborative efforts, the Water Forum has been time-consuming and complex. What sets it apart is the level of specificity in its agreements, and, at least thus far, its success in preventing costly litigation and conflict. For each water purveyor, for example, the agreement spells out how much water can be diverted in average, drier, and driest years through the planning period of 2030, and the facilities and improvements needed to achieve that supply. Additionally, each stakeholder has a list of specific agreements, commitments, and requirements to follow in order to comply with the overall framework. Some of these fall under the rubric of water contracts and legal agreements, along with a willingness to provide funds, an openness to projects the Forum might otherwise oppose, or a willingness to participate with other stakeholders in planning, cost-sharing, or lobbying.

---

5. East Bay Municipal Utility District had been in litigation with environmental groups and Sacramento County for more than 20 years over EBMUD's claim to American River water. With support and hard work from Water Forum members of all interests, the legal wrangling ended, with EBMUD agreeing to divert its water from a point downstream on the Sacramento River where there would be minimal impact to American River fisheries.

Realistically grappling with each other's interests may be frustrating, but far better–and less costly–than previous battles.

What also sets the Water Forum apart are the ongoing successor effort and a shared understanding that realistically grappling with each other's interests may be frustrating, but far better–and less costly–than previous battles. In many of the organizations the cultures have begun to change, reflecting the need to mediate and resolve disputes as a matter of business as usual. In the future, it's likely that many public policy and natural resource arenas will require this shift in culture.

CALFED Bay-Delta Program

The CALFED Bay-Delta Program[6] is an unprecedented effort to create a framework for managing California's water resources and addressing a wide range of issues related to the Sacramento River-San Joaquin River-San Francisco Bay Delta (Delta). CALFED is a collaborative program of more than 20 state and federal agencies with environmental management, regulatory, or water supply responsibility in the Delta (Table 8-1). The CALFED program also includes extensive participation from agricultural, urban, environmental, fishing, and business interests, as well as Native American tribes and local governments (especially rural counties) across the state in the form of a 30-member Bay-Delta Advisory Council and numerous specific work groups and various public participation sessions.

The Delta is the largest estuary on the West Coast with unsurpassed ecological importance.

A region of critical importance, the Delta is the largest estuary on the West Coast with unsurpassed ecological importance for anadromous fish and migratory waterfowl–in total more than 750 species of plants and animals. It also supplies or conveys drinking water to two-thirds of the people of California and irrigation water for over 7 million acres of farmland. As the hub of the SWP and CVP, the Delta includes more than 7,000 permitted water diverters and has complex water-quality problems. It has had to withstand the introduction of many non-native species, and relies on an extensive flood protection system serving much of the Central Valley, protecting both urban and rural land.

In June 1994, under the direction of Secretary of the Interior Bruce Babbitt and California's Governor Gray Davis, state and federal agencies addressed Delta-related problems by signing an historic agreement to:

- Coordinate state and federal actions to meet water-quality standards
- Coordinate the operation of the SWP and CVP to meet environmental mandates
- Establish a long-term solution to ecosystem restoration, water quality, reliability of water supply, and levee system integrity in the Delta

This agreement provided the foundation for the CALFED Bay-Delta Program.

6. In 2002, the state legislature created the California Bay Delta Authority (CBDA) to manage and oversee the CALFED programs. For simplicity and historical continuity, we will continue to use the short-hand term "CALFED" in this section of the book.

Table 8-1. CALFED-Bay Delta Agencies partial list

STATE AGENCIES	FEDERAL AGENCIES
Resources Agency • Department of Water Resources • Department of Fish and Game • Reclamation Board • Delta Protection Commission • Department of Conservation • San Francisco Bay Conservation and Development Commission	**U.S. Department of the Interior** • Bureau of Reclamation • Fish and Wildlife Service • Bureau of Land Management • U.S. Geological Survey
California Environmental Protection Agency • State Water Resources Control Board	**U.S. Environmental Protection Agency** **U.S. Department of Commerce** • NOAA Fisheries
Department of Food and Agriculture	**U.S. Department of Agriculture** • Natural Resources Conservation Service • U.S. Forest Service
Delta Protection Commission	**Western Area Power Administration**
Department of Health Services	**U.S. Army Corps of Engineers**

The collaborative process. While state and federal agencies and technical experts have assumed a leadership role throughout the process, hundreds of stakeholders have spent thousands of hours discussing, debating, and negotiating long-term restoration and management plans for the Delta and California's water. CALFED included (and continues to include) some form of public/stakeholder interaction in every component of its work. Formal mediation efforts, work groups and advisory groups, public workshops and meetings, technical and scientific review panels, newsletters and information pieces (often on CD-ROM), a web site, and other tools are employed to maintain the flow of information on what is a very large and complex undertaking.

For example, during the environmental review process for CALFED's Programmatic EIR/EIS (required under CEQA and NEPA), 17 formal public hearings and numerous workshops were held, over 4,000 written comments were received and responded to, and more than 1,200 people spoke on the program.

EIR = Environmental impact report
EIS = Environmental impact statement

This more traditional format, however, should not overshadow the collaborative process that helped inform CALFED and under which various components of the program now operate. The CALFED process is not simply one stakeholder collaborative, but a network of interrelated processes, each with its own tasks, representatives, and issues. One such effort has been focusing on ecosystem restoration, another on the efficient use of agricultural water. Yet another, the Integrated Storage Investigation, deals with the storage of surface water, groundwater storage and conjunctive use, how to evaluate power facilities, and the possible removal of barriers to fish migration. In each program, CALFED has relied on interest-based groups, as well as technical stakeholders whose role is to improve the use of science in the process and look toward innovative approaches for resolving long-standing problems. Each process used a different participatory strategy and style of facilitation, but has relied on the basic principles of inclusiveness, dialogue, and consensus-building.

BDAC = Bay Delta Advisory Council

The Bay-Delta Advisory Council (BDAC)–a federally-chartered advisory committee[7] made up of more than 30 members from agriculture, business, water, environmental, tribal, urban, fishing, and other interests–provides public oversight. BDAC continues to advise the agencies on policy matters, responding to products and programs, and addressing process questions.[8]

The CALFED program. The primary objectives of CALFED are to:

- **Provide good water quality** for all beneficial uses
- **Improve and increase** aquatic and terrestrial habitats and improve ecological functions in the Bay-Delta to support sustainable populations of diverse and valuable plant and animal species
- **Reduce the mismatch** between Bay-Delta water supplies and current and projected beneficial uses dependent on the system
- **Reduce the risk** to land use and associated economic activities, water supply, infrastructure, and the ecosystem from catastrophic breaching of Delta levees

The CALFED program is now implementing the various components packaged into the Record of Decision, issued in 2000. CALFED describes itself as "a forum through which agencies coordinate their actions and evaluate their progress. By working together from a single plan and coordinating actions, each independent agency can meet its objectives more efficiently."

During most of its initial development, CALFED was not an agency, but a program that relied on voluntary and continuous cooperation (and funding and staff) from each agency. It also served as a focal point for public and stakeholder interaction through the BDAC and specific work groups and stakeholder processes. In 2002, the state legislature passed a bill creating the California Bay Delta Authority, thus providing an administrative "home" for the program in state government. Still, the program relies heavily on its many agency partners for implementation.

CALFED's substantive program is organized to simultaneously resolve four interrelated issues: ecosystem restoration, water-quality improvement, levee system improvement, and water management. For an illustration of the various components of the CALFED program that contribute to its four fundamental strategies, *see* Figure 8-2.

Figure 8-2
Program Elements

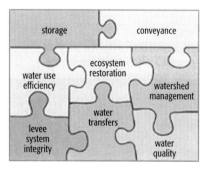

7. As a federally-chartered advisory committee, it has a formal charter, accepted by Congress, and certain operating requirements mandated by the Federal Advisory Committee Act.

8. As a result of state legislation in 2002, the California Bay Delta Authority was created to serve as CALFED's administrative home. As part of this transition, a high level advisory board has been established to provide overall direction.

Each strategy contains goals and measurable objectives, specific programs, hundreds of actions by many different organizations or agencies, and a plan for monitoring, assessing progress, and adaptively managing. Each strategy also contains funding priorities and a timeline. As an example, the Water Use Efficiency Program builds on the work of the existing Agricultural Water Management Council and the California Urban Water Conservation Council by providing technical support and targeted financial incentives (in the form of grants and loans) for water conservation, conjunctive use, and related programs. The Ecosystem Restoration Program (ERP), yet another example, is designed to achieve or contribute to the recovery of listed species found in the Delta and reduce conflicts between environmental and other beneficial water uses. Since 1994, ERP has begun funding the early implementation of restoration programs to jump-start the activity. In its first five years, CALFED's ERP received more than 900 proposals and funded 271 projects worth approximately $250 million. Projects ranged from fish ladders to land acquisition to habitat restoration. To appreciate its many elements, *see* the CALFED Bay-Delta Program, Record of Decision, 2000, or visit the CALFED web site (www.calfed.water.ca.gov).

Much of CALFED's work will be to provide funding and incentives for local, regional, state, and federal agencies that can help achieve its objectives. These funds come directly from state and federal appropriations, various state bond measures, and from individual agency budgets and funding sources. The estimate for the first stage of CALFED's activities is approximately $8.5 billion.

Conclusions. Like the Water Forum, CALFED (and now the California Bay Delta Authority) is a success not only for its substantive gains, but for building relationships among former combatants and for changing and creating institutions. As a direct result of the process, parties traditionally opposed to one another jointly developed and publicly backed two major statewide ballot propositions designed to raise nearly $3 billion for environmental restoration, water-quality improvement, water use efficiency, and facilities for water supply. These two measures, supported by more than two-thirds of the state's voters, are fueling much of the early implementation of the CALFED process.

Of particular interest are the innovative approaches to water management that have resulted from these interactions. One such innovative program is the Environmental Water Account (EWA)

Meandering channels in the Sacramento River-San JoaquinRiver Delta

ERP = Ecosystem Restoration Program
EWA = Environmental Water Account

CALFED (and now the California Bay Delta Authority) is a success not only for its substantive gains, but for building relationships among former combatants and for changing and creating institutions.

described on pages 124–125. With the EWA, California now has a water provider actively purchasing water on the market and devoting it to fisheries and other habitat problems, as needed. An Operations Group–made up of key players from the SWP, CVP, and the state and federal fish and wildlife agencies and technical advisors–has been used to make timely decisions about using the many components of California's two water systems to maximize environmental benefits without sacrificing needed supplies. Information on fisheries status, water quality, flows and temperatures, likely future weather conditions, and other variables are assessed and responded to with specific actions.

Another program is moving toward a Statewide Water Transfer Information Clearinghouse to explain proposed transfers and improve understanding of the process. The program also intends to create statewide standards for transfers and streamline the process, providing various tools to monitor and assist appropriate projects. Another innovation is the Science Program, which is designed to offer new information and scientific interpretation necessary to implement and monitor progress and measure success.

Some critics argue that CALFED has not resolved the almost insurmountable political problem of moving more water around, through, or past the Delta to support the water needs of southern California and the San Joaquin Valley–or that direct solutions for new water supplies or storage opportunities are still in the discussion stage. Others suggest that significant funds–including federal appropriations–are not forthcoming and may not be realized. Given the magnitude of the problems being addressed, few can argue that CALFED has not been a major force in changing how water is managed and how people relate to one another. Connick and Innes (2001) conclude:

> The overall approach of CALFED has moved toward institutionalizing a new approach to water management, which is both flexible and outcome oriented, rather than like the bureaucratic model, which is inflexible and input oriented.

New Melones Lake
Resource Management Plan

Construction of the New Melones Dam on the Stanislaus River in the western foothills of the Sierra Nevada in 1978 involved a long and divisive battle spanning several decades. Even after the final authorization was received, an activist chained himself to a

Low reservoir levels during dry years triggered the need for new management strategies.

New Melones Reservoir

rock along the river canyon in a last attempt to stop the reservoir from being filled. While the original controversy subsided many years later, planning for federally-owned watershed lands adjacent to the reservoir had the potentially to rekindle old controversies and create a host of new ones.

The upper Stanislaus River is in a deeply incised, steep-sided canyon. While the perimeter of the watershed is characterized by flat-topped, cliff-sided ridges, part of the Table Mountain formation, the remaining terrain ranges from mountainous in the upper watershed to round-topped ridges and broad valleys closer to the reservoir. Along the river, the area contains unique geologic features including caves of soluble limestone, as well as extensive mineral resources, including gold.

RMP = Resource Management Plan

Managing the unique watershed lands presents a variety of challenging issues. The area contains more than 600 historic and prehistoric sites representing 10,000 years of human habitation, and the caves have considerable biological, paleontological, archaeological, and recreational value. Extensive recreational opportunities are available, but some activities rely on maintaining water levels at opposite extremes for reservoir function. When water levels are low, boating is severely restricted, but low levels allow the use of the upper river canyon for whitewater rafting. The lake levels experience wide fluctuations because this federal facility has operational policies that include storage of water and releases to meet downstream water quality standards on the San Joaquin River.

The New Melones Lake Resource Management Plan (RMP) was designed to establish a consistent framework of integrated policies and actions for responsibly managing public resources. The plan was also supposed to balance the management of conflicting uses, at the same time gaining acceptance from the public. A policy statement and specific goals were developed through extensive public workshops designed to ensure representation by those interested in the reservoir and the surrounding land. The program provided a mechanism for building community consensus and incorporating the public's views into the design. Early in the process, stakeholders defined issues relevant to the overall land stewardship policy that were refined throughout its development. These issues became the basis for formulating the RMP's management elements.

The most critical factor contributing to the RMP's success was the involvement of an Ad Hoc Work Group, made up of stakeholders who represented a broad range of public interests and concerns that would function in an advisory capacity to the Bureau of Reclamation. Solicited at an initial set of open public workshops, potential members of the group were recommended by community leaders and interviewed by Bureau of Reclamation staff responsible for maintaining the facilities. The group consisted of 20 members reflecting the comprehensive and often conflicting interests of the surrounding communities–ranching, boating, caving, environmental protection, whitewater rafting, sport fishing, local economic development, cultural resources, and law enforcement.

The Ad Hoc Work Group donated many hours each month to reviewing issues, interests, and technical materials, debating sensitive topics, and attending general public workshops and bi-monthly meetings. Because of their high level of involvement, group members made a meaningful contribution at every stage of the project, which included the following:

- **Identification** of issues
- **Development** of goals and objectives
- **Identification** of recreational siting and ecological opportunities and constraints
- **Definition and evaluation** of management plan alternatives
- **Selection** of a preferred plan
- **Consideration** of implementation elements

The RMP management direction is organized by resource element. The resource management elements, listed below, provide a balanced approach to stewardship of the natural and cultural resources, and provide for water-based recreational opportunities under safe, well-managed conditions.

Resource Management Elements for the New Melones Reservoir. Each element of the Resource Management Plan (*see* sidebar) includes policies and specific action items. A policy of the Wildlife Element, for example, indicates that all habitat improvements should be coordinated with appropriate state and federal agencies, and a related action item identifies the development of artificial osprey nest structures to supplement nests that are inundated or proximate to boaters when water levels are high.

Because the New Melones Lake watershed contains such diverse ecological and recreational opportunities and constraints, the Ad Hoc Work Group, the Bureau of Reclamation, and the consultant team developed additional geographically-based action items. These items reflect the needs of each planning area while remaining consistent with overall management policies. For example, numerous recreational improvements were included that accommodated current and anticipated fluctuation of reservoir water levels and also reduced existing conflicts from incompatible use. Boat ramps extending to lower water levels were designed for high-demand planning areas, and shoreline swimming areas were moved to locations nearby.

Table 8-2. New Melones Reservoir Resource Management Elements

- Recreation
- Vegetation
- Wetlands and riparian vegetation
- Wildlife
- Fisheries
- Paleontological resources
- Cultural resources
- Cave resources
- Grazing
- Fire management
- Public safety
- Mineral resources
- Trespass and unauthorized use
- Hunting and recreational shooting
- Water quality
- Jurisdictional issues and coordination
- Volunteerism and partnerships
- Interpretive program and visitor information

When the RMP was in the final stages of development, federal funding for implementation was severely curtailed. As a result, the Ad Hoc Work Group formed the New Melones Partners, a volunteer committee to carry out many action items in the plan. To kick off the effort, the RMP consultant donated a brochure soliciting volunteers for the New Melones Partners. The Partners, along with the Bureau, then appealed for donated supplies and labor and have subsequently obtained grants and other funding. A subgroup, composed of members of the National Speleological Society, was formed to refine and implement cave exploration and management improvements. Five osprey nest platforms were constructed and installed through volunteer efforts, four of which have been successfully used by the raptors. Committee members created a specific trails master plan for review and approval by the Bureau, and continue to use their professional skills to develop a three-way public-private venture (Bureau of Reclamation, public members, and the marina concession holder) to seek funding for floating restrooms for boaters.

Implementing the action items demonstrates how clearly defined plan objectives and the engagement of a committed stakeholder group can contribute to the long-term success of a potentially contentious watershed management plan.

What Might the Future Hold?

Much of this book has been devoted to methods for projecting and planning for the future. The only true crystal ball suggests that uncertainties are certain, new information will be introduced constantly, policies and politics will shift, and even the hydrologic setting is likely to change. Adaptation and flexibility are a necessary element in water resources plans.

Forecasting is difficult; especially about the future.

– Paraphrased from the late comedian and pianist, Victor Borge

What major event or change might alter how Californians plan for water? Long-term climate change is certainly one scenario. Experts debate the magnitude or rate of change, but most scientists agree that a global average temperature rise of two to five degrees centigrade over the next century is forecast. This could have dramatic effects on the reliability of water supply. Snowpack in the Sierra Nevada would be reduced and occur at elevations up to 1500 feet higher, shifting runoff patterns and producing a much earlier runoff and a much earlier spring and summer carryover of water. Sea level rise could result in levee failures in the Delta, degraded water quality, and reduced outflow. Flood levels could also increase. The results could alter many assumptions about how water is captured and stored and how much is available for consumptive use.

Security issues are another significant risk. Recent events have highlighted how vulnerable major facilities might be to attack or degradation. Damage to or contamination of a few major facilities would lead to significant dislocation of water use.

Shifts in policy direction could modify the way plans are implemented. The laws most likely to be subject to scrutiny are various environmental statutes such as the Endangered Species Act or Clean Water Act (particularly section 404). If the ESA were modified to be more stringent, such as additional listing of aquatic species, or reducing the flexibility provided by habitat conservation planning, then water supply options would be affected. If made less stringent, the ESA would significantly tip the balance between water use and environmental interests discussed at length in this chapter. And changing energy policies could influence how storage reservoirs operate, that in turn could affect water supply and in-stream protection.

The overlapping labyrinth of laws, institutions, and programs in the water arena could buffer any dramatic shift, but flexibility will certainly be needed. Without that true crystal ball, careful planning is a necessity.

Appendices

These appendices include excerpts from key water resources documents. The full text is available from the original agency or organization, or from various web sites.

Excerpts from the Department of Water Resources' Model Urban Water Management Plan (developed in the late 1990s to help water purveyors with their most recent plan submittals in 2000) are presented here. The various water supply and demand calculation worksheets, detailed appendices, and background data are published on the DWR web site (www.water.ca.gov).

Also presented here are excerpts from the Memorandum of Understanding Regarding Urban Water Conservation in California. Signed and agreed to by several hundred major urban water purveyors in the State, this document provides the most up-to-date best management practices for water use efficiency along with a series of methodologies for assessing cost effectiveness and benefits from the measures. Background data, including detailed cost-effectiveness analyses and the latest work on best management practices, are published on the California Urban Water Conservation Council's web site (www.cuww.org).

APPENDIX A

Institutional Framework for Allocating and Managing Water Resources

Appendix 2A to the California Water Plan, Bulletin 160-98
California Department of Water Resources

In California, water use and supplies are controlled and managed under an intricate system of federal and State laws. Common law principles, constitutional provisions, State and federal statutes, court decisions, and contracts or agreements all govern how water is allocated, developed, or used. All of these components constitute the institutional framework for allocation and management of water resources in California.

This appendix presents an overview of California's institutional framework, highlighting some of the more recent changes. Summarized here are major constitutional requirements, statutes, court decisions, and agreements that form the groundwork for many water resource management and planning activities. Changes since the publication of Bulletin 160-93 are covered in the chapter 2 text.

Allocation and Management of California's Water Supplies

The following subsections condense basic water rights laws and doctrines governing allocation and use of California's water supplies.

California Constitution Article X, Section 2

The keystone of California's water law and policy, Article X, Section 2 of the California Constitution, requires that all uses of the State's water be both reasonable and beneficial. It places a significant limitation on water rights by prohibiting the waste, unreasonable use, unreasonable method of use, or unreasonable method of diversion of water.

Riparian and Appropriative Rights

California operates under a dual system of water rights for surface water which recognizes both riparian rights and appropriative rights. Under the riparian doctrine, the owners of land have the right to divert, but not store, a portion of the natural flow of water flowing by their land for reasonable and beneficial use upon their land adjacent to the stream and within its watershed, subject to certain limitations. Generally, all riparian water right holders must reduce their water use in times of water shortages. Under the prior appropriation doctrine, a person may acquire a right to divert, store, and use water regardless of whether the land on which it is used is adjacent to a stream or within its watershed, provided that the water is used for reasonable and beneficial uses and is surplus to water from the same stream used by earlier appropriators. The rule of priority between appropriators is "first in time is first in right."

Water Rights Permits and Licenses

The Water Commission Act, which took effect in 1914 following a referendum, recognized the overriding interest of the people in the waters of the State, but provided that private rights to use water may be acquired in the manner provided by law. The act established a system of State-issued permits and licenses to appropriate water. Amended over the years, it now appears in Division 2 (commencing with Section 1000) of the Water Code. These provisions place responsibility for administering appropriative water rights with SWRCB; however, the permit and license provisions do not apply to pre-1914 appropriative rights (those initiated before the act took effect in 1914). The act also provides procedures for adjudication of water rights, including court references to SWRCB and statutory adjudications of all rights to a stream system.

Groundwater Management

Generally, groundwater is available to any person who owns land overlying the groundwater basin. Groundwater management in California may be accomplished either by a judicial adjudication of the respective rights of overlying users and exporters, or by local management of rights to extract and use groundwater as authorized by statute or agreement. Statutory management may be granted to a public agency that also manages surface water, or to a groundwater management agency created expressly for that purpose by a special district act.

In 1991, the Water Code was amended by AB 255 to allow local water agencies overlying critically overdrafted groundwater

205

basins to develop groundwater management plans. Only a few local agencies adopted plans pursuant to that authorization. In 1992, the Legislature adopted new sections authorizing another form of groundwater management, also available to any local agency that provides water service, if the groundwater was not subject to management under other provisions of law or a court decree. Plans adopted pursuant to the 1992 statute (commonly called AB 3030 plans) may include control of salt water intrusion; identification and protection of wellhead and recharge areas; regulation of the migration of contaminated water; provisions for abandonment and destruction of wells; mitigation of overdraft; replenishment; monitoring; facilitating conjunctive use; identification of well construction policies; and construction of cleanup, recharge, recycling, and extraction projects by the local agency.

Public Trust Doctrine

In the 1980s, the public trust doctrine was used by courts to limit traditional water rights. Under the equal footing doctrine of the U.S. Constitution, each state has title to tidelands and the beds of navigable lakes and streams within its borders. The public trust doctrine–recognized in some form by most states–embodies the principle that the state holds title to such properties within the state in trust for the beneficial use of the public, and that public rights of access to and use of tidelands and navigable waters are inalienable. Traditional public trust rights include navigation, commerce, and fishing. California law has expanded the traditional public trust uses to include protection of fish and wildlife, preserving trust lands in their natural condition for scientific study and scenic enjoyment, and related open-space uses.

In 1983, the California Supreme Court extended the public trust doctrine's limitation on private rights to appropriative water rights. In *National Audubon Society v. Superior Court of Alpine County,* the court held that water right licenses held by the City of Los Angeles to divert water from streams tributary to Mono Lake remain subject to ongoing State supervision under the public trust doctrine. The court held

that public trust uses must be considered and balanced when rights to divert water away from navigable water bodies are considered. The court also held that California's appropriative rights system and the public trust doctrine embody important precepts which "…make the law more responsive to the diverse needs and interests involved in planning and allocation of water resources." Consequently, in issuing or reconsidering any rights to appropriate and divert water, the State must balance public trust needs with the needs for other beneficial uses of water. In 1994, the SWRCB issued a final decision on Mono Lake (Decision 1631) in which it balanced the various uses in determining the appropriate terms and conditions of the water rights permit for the City of Los Angeles. The public trust doctrine will also be applied by the SWRCB in its current consideration of water rights in the Bay-Delta.

Since the 1983 National Audubon decision, the public trust doctrine has been involved in several other cases. In *United States v. State Water Resources Control Board* (commonly referred to as the *Racanelli* Decision and discussed below), the State Court of Appeal reiterated that the public trust doctrine is a significant limitation on water rights. The public trust doctrine was also a basis for the decision in *Environmental Defense Fund v. East Bay Municipal Utility District*. In this case, EDF claimed that EBMUD should not contract with USBR for water diverted from the American River upstream from the Sacramento urban area in a manner that would harm instream uses including recreational, scenic, and fish and wildlife preservation purposes. The Superior Court upheld the validity of EBMUD's contract with USBR, but placed limitations on the timing and amounts of deliveries to EBMUD. As a result of these cases, the SWRCB now routinely implements the public trust doctrine through regulations and through terms and conditions in water rights permits and licenses.

Federal Power Act

The Federal Power Act created a federal licensing system administered by the Federal

Energy Regulatory Commission and required that a license be obtained for nonfederal hydroelectric projects proposing to use navigable waters or federal lands. The act contains a clause modeled after a clause in the Reclamation Act of 1902, which disclaims any intent to affect state water rights law.

In a number of decisions dating back to the 1940s, the U.S. Supreme Court held that provisions of the Reclamation Act and the Federal Power Act preempted inconsistent provisions of law. Decisions under both acts found that these clauses were merely "saving clauses" which required the United States to follow minimal state procedural laws or to pay just compensation where vested nonfederal water rights are taken.

In *California v. United States* (1978), however, the U.S. Supreme Court disavowed dicta in a number of earlier Supreme Court decisions which stated that under the Reclamation Act the United States need not comply with state water law. It held that the Reclamation Act clause requires the USBR to comply with conditions in state water rights permits unless those conditions conflict with "clear Congressional directives." In *California v. FERC* (1990), commonly referred to as the *Rock Creek* Decision, the U.S. Supreme Court rejected California's argument that the Federal Power Act clause required deference to state water law, as the Reclamation Act did. The Supreme Court distinguished between the two acts, finding that the Federal Power Act envisioned a broader and more active oversight role than did the Reclamation law. The Federal District Court case of *Sayles Hydro Association v. Maughan* (1993), reinforced this view by holding that federal law prevents any state regulation of federally licensed power projects other than determining proprietary water rights.

In 1994, the U.S. Supreme Court issued a decision referred to as the *Elkhorn* decision or *Tacoma* decision (*PUD No. 1 of Jefferson County and City of Tacoma v. Washington Department of Ecology*). The Supreme Court held that a state minimum instream flow requirement is a permissible condition of a

Clean Water Act Section 401 certification, in response to a proposal to construct a hydroelectric project on the Dosewallips River. Pursuant to Section 401 of the Clean Water Act, the project proponents were required to obtain state certification for the hydroelectric project. The State of Washington set an instream flow requirement in its certification process to protect the river's designated use as fish habitat. Section 303 of the Clean Water Act requires states to establish water quality standards for intrastate waters, with the standards to include both numeric water quality criteria and designated uses.

Area of Origin Protections

During the years when California's two largest water projects, the CVP and SWP, were being planned and developed, area of origin provisions were added to the water code to protect local Northern California supplies from being depleted as a result of the projects. County of origin statutes reserve water supplies for counties in which the water originates when, in the judgment of the SWRCB, an application for the assignment or release from priority of State water right filings will deprive the county of water necessary for its present and future development. Watershed protection statutes are provisions which require that the construction and operation of elements of the CVP and the SWP not deprive the watershed, or area where water originates (or immediately adjacent areas which can be conveniently supplied with water) of the prior right to water reasonably required to supply the present or future beneficial needs of the watershed area or any of its inhabitants or property owners.

The Delta Protection Act, enacted in 1959 (not to be confused with the Delta Protection Act of 1992, which relates to land use), declares that the maintenance of an adequate water supply in the Delta to maintain and expand agriculture, industry, urban, and recreational development in the Delta area and provide a common source of fresh water for export to areas of water deficiency is necessary for the peace, health, safety, and welfare of the people of the State, and is subject to the County of Origin

and Watershed Protection laws. The act requires the SWP and the CVP to provide salinity control in the Delta and an adequate water supply for water users in the Delta.

In 1984, additional area of origin protections were enacted covering the Sacramento, Mokelumne, Calaveras, and San Joaquin Rivers; the combined Truckee, Carson, and Walker Rivers; and Mono Lake. The protections prohibit the export of groundwater from the combined Sacramento River and Delta Basins, unless the export is in compliance with local groundwater plans.

Environmental Regulatory Statutes and Programs

Endangered Species Act

Under the federal ESA, an endangered species is one that is in danger of extinction in all or a significant part of its range, and a threatened species is one that is likely to become endangered in the near future. The ESA is designed to preserve endangered and threatened species by protecting individuals of the species and their habitat and by implementing measures that promote their recovery. The ESA sets forth a procedure for listing species as threatened or endangered. Final listing decisions are made by USFWS or NMFS.

Once a species is listed, Section 7 of the act requires that federal agencies, in consultation with the USFWS or NMFS, ensure that their actions do not jeopardize the continued existence of the species or habitat critical for the survival of that species. The federal wildlife agencies are required to provide an opinion as to whether the federal action would jeopardize the species. The opinion must include reasonable and prudent alternatives to the action that would avoid jeopardizing the species' existence. Federal actions subject to Section 7 include issuance of federal permits such as the dredge and fill permit required under Section 404 of the federal Clean Water Act, which requires that the project proponent demonstrate that there is no feasible alternative consistent with the project goals that would not affect listed species. Mitigation

of the proposed project is not considered until this hurdle is passed.

State agencies and private parties also are subject to the ESA. Section 9 of the ESA prohibits the "take" of endangered species and threatened species for which protective regulations have been adopted. Take has been broadly defined to include actions that harm or harass listed species or that cause a significant loss of their habitat. State agencies and private parties are generally required to obtain a permit from the USFWS or NMFS under Section 10(a) of the ESA before carrying out activities that may incidentally result in taking listed species. The permit normally contains conditions to avoid taking listed species and to compensate for habitat adversely impacted by the activities.

California Endangered Species Act

The California Endangered Species Act is similar to the federal ESA. Listing decisions are made by the California Fish and Game Commission.

All State lead agencies are required to consult with the Department of Fish and Game about projects that impact State listed species. DFG is required to render an opinion as to whether the proposed project jeopardizes a listed species and to offer alternatives to avoid jeopardy. State agencies must adopt reasonable alternatives unless there are overriding social or economic conditions that make such alternatives infeasible. For projects causing incidental take, DFG is required to specify reasonable and prudent measures to minimize take. Any take that results from activities that are carried out in compliance with these measures is not prohibited.

Many California species are both federally listed and State listed. CESA directs DFG to coordinate with the USFWS and NMFS in the consultation process so that consistent and compatible opinions or findings can be adopted by both federal and State agencies.

Natural Community Conservation Planning

Adopted in 1991, California's Natural Community Conservation Planning Act establishes a program to identify the habitat needs of species before they become listed as threatened or endangered, and to develop appropriate voluntary conservation methods compatible with development and growth. Participants in the program develop plans to protect certain habitat and will ultimately enter into agreements with DFG to ensure that the plans will be carried out. Plans must be created so that they are consistent with endangered species laws.

Dredge and Fill Permits

Section 404 of the federal Clean Water Act regulates the discharge of dredged and fill materials into waters of the United States, including wetlands. The term "discharge of dredged and fill material" has been defined broadly to include the construction of any structure involving rock, soil, or other construction material. No discharge may occur unless a permit is obtained from the USACE. Generally, the project proponent must agree to mitigate or have plans to mitigate environmental impacts caused by the project before a permit is issued. The EPA has the authority to veto permits issued by the Corps for projects that have unacceptable adverse effects on municipal water supplies, fisheries, wildlife, or recreational areas.

Section 404 allows the issuance of a general permit on a state, regional, or nationwide basis for certain categories of activities that will cause only minimal environmental effects. Such activities are permitted without the need of an individual permit application. Installation of a stream gaging station along a river levee is one example of an activity which falls within a nationwide permit.

The USACE also administers a permitting program under Section 10 of the 1899 Rivers and Harbors Act. Section 10 generally requires a permit for obstructions to navigable water. The scope of the permit under Section 10 is narrower than under Section 404 since the term "navigable waters" is more limited than "waters of the United States."

The majority of water development projects must comply with Section 404, Section 10, or both.

Public Interest Terms and Conditions

The Water Code authorizes the SWRCB to impose public interest terms and conditions to conserve the public interest, specifically the consideration of instream beneficial uses, when it issues permits to appropriate water. It also considers environmental impacts of approving water transfers under its jurisdiction. Frequently, it reserves jurisdiction to consider new instream uses and to modify permits accordingly.

Releases of Water for Fish

Fish and Game Code Section 5937 provides protection to fisheries by requiring that the owner of any dam allow sufficient water at all times to pass through the dam to keep in good condition any fisheries that may be planted or exist below the dam. In *California Trout, Inc. v. the State Water Resources Control Board* (1989), the court determined that Fish and Game Code sections 5937 and 5946 required the SWRCB to modify the permits and licenses issued to the City of Los Angeles to appropriate water from the streams feeding Mono Lake to ensure sufficient water flows for downstream fisheries. The SWRCB reconsidered Los Angeles' permits and licenses in light of Fish and Game Code Section 5937 and the public trust doctrine. In 1994, the SWRCB adopted D-1631, which requires Los Angeles to allow sufficient flows from the streams feeding Mono Lake to reach the lake to allow it to rise to the level of 6,391 feet in approximately twenty years.

Streambed Alteration Agreements

Fish and Game Code Sections 1601 and 1603 require that any governmental entity or private party altering a river, stream, lakebed, bottom, or channel enter into an agreement with DFG. When the project may substantially impact an existing fish or wildlife resource, DFG may require that the agreement include provisions designed to protect riparian habitat, fisheries, and wildlife. New water development projects and ongoing maintenance activities are often subject to these sections.

Migratory Bird Treaty Act

This act implements various treaties for the protection of migratory birds and prohibits the "taking" (broadly defined) of birds protected by those treaties without a permit. The Secretary of the Interior determines conditions under which a taking may occur, and criminal penalties are provided for unlawfully taking or transporting protected birds. Liability imposed by this act was one of several factors leading to the decision to close the San Luis Drain and Kesterson Reservoir.

Environmental Review and Mitigation

Another set of environmental statutes compels governmental agencies and private individuals to document and consider the environmental consequences of their actions. They define the procedures through which governmental agencies consider environmental factors in their decision-making process.

National Environmental Policy Act

NEPA directs federal agencies to prepare an environmental impact statement for all major federal actions which may have a significant effect on the human environment. It states that it is the goal of the federal government to use all practicable means, consistent with other considerations of national policy, to protect and enhance the quality of the environment. It is a procedural law requiring all federal agencies to consider the environmental impacts of their proposed actions during the planning and decision-making processes.

California Environmental Quality Act

CEQA, modeled after NEPA, requires California public agency decision-makers to document and consider the environmental impacts of their actions. It requires an agency to identify ways to avoid or reduce environmental damage, and to implement those measures where feasible. CEQA applies to all levels of California government, including the State, counties, cities, and local districts.

CEQA requires that a public agency carrying out a project with significant environmental effects prepare an environmental impact report. An EIR contains a description of the project; a discussion of the project's environmental impacts, mitigation measures, and alternatives; public comments; and the agency's responses to the comments. In other instances, a notice of exemption from the application of CEQA may also be appropriate.

NEPA does not generally require federal agencies to adopt mitigation measures or alternatives provided in the EIS. CEQA imposes substantive duties on all California governmental agencies that approve projects with significant environmental impacts to adopt feasible alternatives or mitigation measures that substantially lessen these impacts, unless there are overriding reasons. When a project is subject to both CEQA and NEPA, both laws encourage the agencies to cooperate in planning the project and to prepare joint environmental documents.

Fish and Wildlife Coordination Act

The Fish and Wildlife Coordination Act expresses congressional policy to protect the quality of the aquatic environment as it affects the conservation, improvement, and enjoyment of fish and wildlife resources. Under this act, any federal agency that proposes to control or modify any body of water, or to issue a permit allowing control or modification of a body of water, must first consult with the USFWS and State wildlife officials. This requires coordination early in the project planning and environmental review processes.

Protection of Wild and Natural Areas

Water use and management are also limited by several statutes designed to set aside resources or areas to preserve their natural conditions. These statutes preclude many activities, including most water development projects, within the areas set aside.

Federal Wild and Scenic Rivers System

In 1968, Congress passed the National Wild and Scenic Rivers Act to preserve, in their freeflowing condition, rivers which possess "outstandingly remarkable scenic, recreational, geologic, fish and wildlife, historic, cultural, or other similar values." The act also states "...that the established national policy of dam and other construction at appropriate sections of rivers of the United States needs to be complemented by a policy that would preserve other selected rivers or sections thereof in their freeflowing condition to protect the water quality of such rivers and to fulfill other vital national conservation purposes."

The act prohibits federal agencies from constructing, authorizing, or funding the construction of water resources projects having a direct and adverse effect on the values for which a river was designated. This restriction also applies to rivers designated for potential addition to the National Wild and Scenic Rivers System. Included in the system are most rivers protected under California's State Wild and Scenic Rivers Act; these rivers were included in the national system upon California's petition on January 19, 1981. The West Walker and East Fork Carson Rivers are not included in the federal system.

California Wild and Scenic Rivers System

In 1972, the Legislature passed the California Wild and Scenic Rivers Act, declaring that specified rivers possess extraordinary scenic, recreational, fishery, or wildlife values, and should be preserved in a freeflowing state for the benefit of the people of California. It declared that such use of the rivers would be the highest and most beneficial use within the meaning of Article X, Section 2 of the California Constitution. The act prohibits construction of any dam, reservoir, diversion, or other water impoundment on a designated river. Diversions needed to supply domestic water to residents of counties through which the river flows may be authorized, if the Secretary for Resources determines that the

diversion will not adversely affect the river's free-flowing character.

The major difference between the national and State acts is that if a river is designated wild and scenic under the State act, FERC can still issue a license to build a dam on that river, thus overriding the State system. (*See* Federal Power Act discussion above.) This difference explains why national wild and scenic designation is often sought.

National Wilderness Act

The Wilderness Act sets up a system to protect federal land designated by Congress as a "wilderness area" and preserve it in its natural condition. Wilderness is defined as undeveloped federal land retaining its primeval character and influence without permanent improvements or human habitation. Commercial enterprise, permanent roads, motor vehicles, aircraft landings, motorized equipment, or construction of structures or installations (such as dams, diversions, conveyance facilities, and gaging stations) are prohibited within designated wilderness areas.

Water Quality Protection

Water quality is an important aspect of water resource management. The SWRCB plays a central role in determining both water rights and regulating water quality. The Department of Health Services has regulatory oversight over drinking water quality, a program administered in coordination with county environmental health agencies. Discussed below are key State and federal laws governing water quality.

Porter-Cologne Water Quality Control Act

This act is California's comprehensive water quality control law and is a complete regulatory program designed to protect water quality and beneficial uses of the State's water. The act requires the adoption of water quality control plans by the State's nine RWQCBs for areas within their regions. These plans are subject to the approval of the SWRCB, and ultimately the federal EPA. The plans are to be reviewed and updated.

The primary method of implementing the plans is to require each discharger of waste that could impact the waters of the State to meet formal waste discharge requirements. Anyone discharging waste or proposing to discharge waste into the State's waters must file a "report of waste discharge" with the regional water quality control board within whose jurisdiction the discharge lies. Dischargers are subject to a wide variety of administrative, civil, and criminal actions for failing to file a report. After the report is filed, the regional board may issue waste discharge requirements that set conditions on the discharge. The waste discharge requirements must be consistent with the water quality control plan for the body of water and protect the beneficial uses of the receiving waters. The regional boards also implement Section 402 of the federal Clean Water Act, which allows the State to issue a single discharge permit for the purposes of both State and federal law.

Clean Water Act-National Pollutant Discharge Elimination System

Section 402 of the Clean Water Act established a permit system known as the National Pollutant Discharge Elimination System to regulate point sources of discharges in navigable waters of the United States. The EPA was given the authority to implement the NPDES, although the act also authorizes states to implement the act in lieu of the EPA, provided the state has sufficient authority.

In 1972, the Legislature amended the Porter-Cologne Act to give California the authority and ability to operate the NPDES permits program. Before a permit may be issued, Section 401 of the Clean Water Act requires that the regional water quality control board certify that the discharge will comply with applicable water quality standards. After making the certification, the regional board may issue the permit, satisfying both State and federal law. In 1987, Section 402 was amended to require the regulation of storm water runoff under the NPDES.

Safe Drinking Water Act

The SDWA, enacted in 1974 and significantly amended in 1986 and 1996, directed the EPA to set national standards for drinking water quality. It required the EPA to set maximum contaminant levels for a wide variety of constituents. Local water suppliers are required to monitor their water supplies to assure that regulatory standards are not exceeded.

The 1986 amendments set a timetable for the EPA to establish standards for specific contaminants and increased the range of contaminants local water suppliers were required to monitor to include contaminants that did not yet have an MCL established. The amendments included a wellhead protection program, a grant program for designating sole-source aquifers for special protection, and grant programs and technical and financial assistance to small systems and states.

The 1996 amendments added a provision requiring states to create their own revolving funds in order to be eligible to receive federal matching funds for loans and grants to public water systems. More details of the 1996 amendments are described in chapter 2.

California Safe Drinking Water Act

In 1976, California enacted its own Safe Drinking Water Act, requiring the Department of Health Services to regulate drinking water, including: setting and enforcing federal and State drinking water standards; administering water quality testing programs; and administering permits for public water system operations. The federal Safe Drinking Water Act allows the State to enforce its own standards in lieu of the federal standards so long as they are at least as protective as the federal standards. Significant amendments to the California act in 1989 incorporated the new federal safe drinking water act requirements into California law, gave DHS discretion to set more stringent MCLs, and recommended public health levels for contaminants. DHS was authorized to consider the technical and economic feasibility of reducing contaminants in setting MCLs. The standards established by DHS are found in the California Code of Regulations, Title 22.

Historical Background– Bay-Delta Regulatory Actions

The SWRCB issued the first water rights permits to the USBR for operation of the CVP in 1958, and to the Department for operation of the SWP in 1967. In these and all succeeding permits issued for the CVP and SWP, the SWRCB reserved jurisdiction to reformulate or revise terms and conditions relative to salinity control, effect on vested rights, and fish and wildlife protection in the Delta. SWRCB has a dual role of issuing both water rights permits and regulating water quality.

Decision 1485

In 1976, SWRCB initiated proceedings leading to the adoption of D-1485 in 1978. D-1485 set forth conditions–including water quality standards, export limitations, and minimum flow rates for SWP and CVP operations in the Delta and superseded all previous water rights decisions for the SWP and CVP operations in the Delta. Among beneficial uses to be protected by the decision were: municipal and industrial water supply, agriculture, and fish and wildlife.

In formulating D-1485, the SWRCB asserted that Delta water quality should be at least as good as it would have been if the SWP and CVP had not been constructed. In other words, both the SWP and the CVP were to be operated to meet "without project" conditions. D-1485 standards included different levels of protection to reflect variations in hydrologic conditions during different types of water years.

To help implement these water quality standards, D-1485 mandated an extensive monitoring program. It also called for special studies to provide critical data about major concerns in the Delta and Suisun Marsh for which information was insufficient. D-1485 included water quality standards for Suisun Marsh, as the Delta, requiring the Department and USBR to develop a plan for the marsh that would ensure meeting long-term standards.

Recognizing that the complexities of project operations and water quality conditions would change over time, the SWRCB also specified that the Delta water right hearings would be reopened within ten years of the date of adoption of D-1485, depending upon changing conditions in the BayDelta region and the availability of new evidence on beneficial uses of water.

Racanelli Decision

Lawsuits by various interests challenged D-1485 and the decision was overturned by the trial court in 1984. Unlike its predecessor, D-1379, whose standards had been judicially stayed, D1485 remained in effect. In 1986, the appellate court in the *Racanelli* Decision (named after Judge Racanelli who wrote the opinion) broadly interpreted the SWRCB's authority and obligation to establish water quality objectives, and its authority to set water rights permit terms and conditions that provide reasonable protection of beneficial uses of Delta water.

The court stated that SWRCB needed to separate its water quality planning and water rights functions. SWRCB needs to maintain a "global perspective" in identifying beneficial uses to be protected (not limited to water rights) and in allocating responsibility for implementing water quality objectives (not just to the SWP and CVP, nor only through the SWRCB's own water rights processes). The court recognized the SWRCB's authority to look to all water rights holders to implement water quality standards and advised SWRCB to consider the effects of all Delta and upstream water users in setting and implementing water quality standards in the Delta, as well as those of the SWP and the CVP.

SWRCB Bay-Delta Proceedings

Hearings to adopt a water quality control plan and water rights decision for the Bay-Delta estuary began in July 1987. Their purpose was to develop a Bay-Delta water quality control plan and to consider public interest issues related to Delta water rights, including implementation of water quality objectives. During the first phase of the proceedings, testimony was heard on issues pertaining to the reasonable and beneficial uses of the estuary's water. The second phase of the Bay-Delta hearings was to come up with a water quality control plan. SWRCB adopted a final plan in May 1991. The federal EPA rejected this plan in September 1991, setting the stage for preparation of federal water quality standards for the Bay-Delta.

With the adoption of the water quality control plan, the SWRCB began the EIR scoping phase and held several workshops during 1991 to receive testimony regarding planning activities, facilities development, negotiated settlements, and flow objectives.

Concurrently, under the broad authority of the ESA, the federal regulatory process was proceeding toward development of Delta standards and upstream measures applicable to the CVP and SWP for the protection of the threatened winter-run chinook salmon. In February 1993, the NMFS issued a long-term biological opinion governing operations of the CVP and SWP with Delta environmental regulations that, in certain months, were more restrictive than SWRCB's proposed measures. In March 1993, the USFWS listed the Delta smelt as a threatened species and shortly thereafter indicated that further restrictions of CVP and SWP operations would be required. In December 1993, EPA announced its proposed standards for the estuary in place of the SWRCB water quality standards that EPA had rejected in 1991. In addition, USFWS proposed to list the Sacramento splittail as a threatened species, and NMFS announced its decision to change the status of winter-run salmon from threatened to endangered.

The impending regulatory gridlock lead to the negotiation and signing of the June 1994 Framework Agreement for the Bay-Delta estuary. The Framework Agreement and subsequent Bay-Delta activities are described in Chapter 2.

To mitigate fish losses at Delta export facilities, the Department and USBR have entered into agreements with DFG. As part of the environmental review process for installing four additional pumps at SWP's Banks Pumping Plant in the Delta in 1992, DFG and the Department negotiated an agreement to preserve fish potentially affected by the operation of the pumps. This agreement, signed by the two departments in 1986, identifies the steps needed to offset adverse impacts of the Banks Pumping Plant on fisheries. It sets up a procedure to calculate direct fishery losses annually and requires the Department to pay for mitigation projects that would offset the losses. Losses of striped bass, chinook salmon, and steelhead are to be mitigated first. Mitigation of other species is to follow as impacts are identified and appropriate mitigation measures found. In recognition of the fact that direct losses today would probably be greater if fish populations had not been depleted by past operations, the Department also provided $15 million for a program to increase the probability of quickly demonstrated results. In 1996, the Department and DFG agreed to extend the period for expending the remainder of the $15 million to the year 2001.

Following negotiation of the agreement for Banks Pumping Plant, DFG negotiated a similar agreement with USBR for its CVP Tracy Pumping Plant.

Surface Water Management

The following sections are brief descriptions of major statutes affecting surface water management in California.

CVPIA

The Central Valley Project Improvement Act (Title 34 of PL 102-575) made significant changes to the CVP's legislative authorization, amending the project's purposes to place fish and wildlife mitigation and restoration on a par with water supply, and to place fish and wildlife enhancement on a par with power generation. Major provisions of the act are summarized below.

The act prohibits execution of new CVP water supply contracts for purposes other than fish and wildlife (with a few limited exceptions) until all environmental restoration actions specified in the act have been completed. Existing long-term water supply contracts are to be renewed for a 25-year term, with the possibility of subsequent 25-year renewals thereafter. Only interim contract renewals are allowed until the programmatic EIS required by the act is completed. Renewed contracts are to incorporate CVPIA's new requirements, such as restoration fund payments.

The act allows transfers of project water to users outside of the CVP service area, under numerous specified conditions. The conditions include a right of first refusal to a proposed transfer by existing CVP water users (under the same terms and conditions specified in the proposed transfer), and a requirement that proposed transfers of more than 20 percent of a contracting agency's project water supply be subject to review and approval by the contracting agency.

The act requires DOI to develop water conservation criteria, and to review conservation plans submitted by contracting agencies pursuant to Reclamation Reform Act requirements for conformance to the CVPIA criteria. Tiered pricing is to be included in CVP water supply contracts when they are renewed. Project water supply and repayment contractors' surface water delivery systems are to be equipped with water measurement devices.

The act directs DOI to develop a program, by October 1995, to make all reasonable efforts to double, by 2002, natural production (based on 1967-91 fishery population levels) of specified anadromous fish in the Central Valley, and to implement that program. (A portion of the San Joaquin River is exempted from this provision.) The act dedicates 800 taf/yr of CVP yield to fish and wildlife purposes, and authorizes DOI to acquire supplemental water for meeting the fish doubling goal. The act further requires that DOI provide an annual Trinity River instream flow of at least 340 taf through 1996, via releases from Lewiston Dam, with subsequent instream flow requirements to be determined by a USFWS instream flow study.

The act requires DOI to provide, from CVP supplies, firm water supplies (i.e., deliver water corresponding to existing non-firm supplies such as agricultural drainage) to specified federal, State, and private wildlife refuges in the Sacramento and San Joaquin Valleys. DOI is to acquire, from willing sellers, an additional increment of water supply for the wildlife areas, corresponding to their full habitat development needs. All of the supplemental water needs are to be met by 2002.

The act requires DOI to implement numerous specified environmental restoration actions, such as constructing a temperature control device at Shasta Dam, remedying fish passage problems at Red Bluff Diversion Dam, replenishing spawning gravel, and assisting in screening non-federal diversions. Costs of some of these restoration actions are allocated in part to the State of California. DOI is required to enter into a cost-sharing agreement with California for the environmental restoration actions whose costs are allocated in part to California.

The act requires DOI to prepare specified reports and studies, to implement a Central Valley fish and wildlife monitoring program, and to develop ecosystem and water operations models. Examples of reports to be prepared include a least-cost plan to replace the 800 taf/yr of project yield dedicated to environmental purposes, and an evaluation of water supply and development requirements for 120,000 acres of wetlands identified in a Central Valley Habitat Joint Venture report. DOI is also directed to prepare, by October 1995, a programmatic EIS analyzing impacts of CVPIA implementation.

The act authorizes DOI to carry out a land retirement program, and specifies categories of land that may be acquired. San Joaquin Valley drainage-impaired lands are among the authorized categories.

The act establishes a CVPIA restoration fund within the federal treasury, and directs DOI to collect mitigation and restoration payments from project water and power users. DOI is authorized to use appropriations from the fund to carry out the environmental restoration measures required by the act. Payments are capped at $6/af for agricultural water contractors and $12/af (1992 dollars) for municipal and industrial water contractors, but the caps are subject to adjustment for inflation. (An additional restoration payment is assessed against contractors in the Friant Division, in lieu of requiring Friant Dam releases for instream flows in the San Joaquin River between Gravelly Ford and the Mendota Pool.)

Regional and Local Water Agency Formation

In general, there are two methods in California for forming special districts which develop, control, or distribute water: enactment of a general act under which the districts may be formed as set forth in the act, and enactment of a special act creating the district and prescribing its powers. There are more than 40 different statutes under which local agencies may be so organized. In addition, there are a number of special act districts, such as the Metropolitan Water District of Southern California. The Department's Bulletin 155-94, General Comparison of Water District Acts (March 1994), presents a comparison of various water district acts in California.

In addition to public agencies, there are other entities that may provide water supply. Mutual water companies, for example, are private corporations that perform water supply and distribution functions similar to public water districts. Investor-owned utilities may also be involved in water supply activities, sometimes as an adjunct of hydroelectric power development.

Water Use Efficiency

Article X, Section 2 of the California Constitution prohibits the waste, unreasonable use, unreasonable method of use, or unreasonable method of diversion of water. It also declares that the conservation and use of water "shall be exercised with a view to the reasonable and beneficial use thereof in the public interest and for the public welfare." Although provisions and requirements of the Constitution are self executing, the Constitution states that the Legislature may enact statutes to advance its policy. Water Code Section 275 directs the Department and SWRCB to "take all appropriate proceedings or actions before executive, legislative, or judicial agencies to prevent waste or unreasonable use of water." SWRCB's Water Right Decision 1600, directing the Imperial Irrigation District to adopt a water conservation plan, is an example of an action brought under Article X, Section 2. SWRCB's authority to order preparation of such a plan was upheld in 1990 by the courts in *Imperial*

Irrigation District v. State Water Resources Control Board.

Urban Water Management Planning Act

Since 1983, this act has required urban water suppliers that serve more than 3,000 customers or more than 3,000 af/yr to prepare and adopt urban water conservation plans. The act authorizes the supplier to implement the water conservation program. The plans must contain several specified elements, including estimates of water use, identification of existing conservation measures, identification of alternative conservation measures, a schedule of implementation of actions proposed by the plan, and identification of the frequency and magnitude of water shortages. In 1991, the act was amended in response to the drought to require water suppliers to estimate water supplies available at the end of one, two, and three years, and to develop contingency plans for severe shortages. The act also requires water suppliers to review and update their plans at least once every five years.

Water Conservation in Landscaping Act

The Water Conservation in Landscaping Act required the Department, with the assistance of an advisory task force, to adopt a model water-efficient landscape ordinance. The model ordinance was adopted in August 1992, and has been codified in Title 23 of the California Code of Regulations. It establishes methods of conserving water through water budgeting plans, plant use, efficient irrigation, and auditing.

Cities and counties were required to review the model ordinance and adopt a water-efficient landscape ordinance by January 1, 1993, if they had not done so already. Alternatively, cities and counties could make a finding that such an ordinance is unnecessary due to climatic, geological, or topographic conditions, or water availability. If a city or county failed to adopt a water efficient landscape ordinance or make findings by January 31, 1993, the model ordinance became effective in that jurisdiction.

Agricultural Water Management Planning Act

Under this act, agricultural water suppliers supplying more than 50 taf of water annually were required to submit a report to the Department indicating whether a significant opportunity exists to conserve water or reduce the quantity of highly saline or toxic drainage water through improved irrigation water management. The act provided that agricultural water suppliers who indicated that they had an opportunity to conserve water or reduce the quantity of highly saline or toxic water should prepare a water management plan and submit it to the Department. The Department was required to review the plans and submit a report to the Legislature by January 1993.

Agricultural Water Suppliers Efficient Management Practices Act

The Agricultural Water Suppliers Efficient Management Practices Act, adopted in 1990, required that the Department establish an advisory committee to review efficient agricultural water management practices. Under the act, the Department was required to offer assistance to agricultural water suppliers seeking to improve the efficiency of their water management practices. The committee developed a Memorandum of Understanding to imple-

ment the practices, and to establish an Agricultural Water Management Council. The advisory committee adopted the MOU in October 1996. The MOU was declared in effect in May 1997 after 15 agricultural water suppliers, representing 2 million irrigated acres, had signed. The Council was established and held its first meeting in July 1997.

Agricultural Water Conservation and Management Act of 1992

This act gives any public agency that supplies water for agricultural use authority to institute water conservation or efficient management programs. The programs can include irrigation management services, providing information about crop water use, providing irrigation consulting services, improving the supplier's delivery system, providing technical and financial assistance to farmers, encouraging conservation through pricing of water, and monitoring.

Water Recycling Act of 1991

This act describes the environmental benefits and public safety of using recycled water as a reliable and cost-effective method of helping to meet California's water supply needs. It sets a statewide goal to recycle 700 taf/yr by the year 2000 and 1 maf/yr by 2010.

APPENDIX B

Model Urban Water Management Plan–
City of New Albion, 2000

This appendix presents a model Urban Water Management Plan, developed by the California Department of Water Resources in 2000, that water suppliers may find useful when developing their plans. It is, of course, a hypothetical community.

List of Tables

City of New Albion 2000 Urban Water Management Plan

CONTACT SHEET

Date plan submitted to the Department of Water Resources: 12/10/00

Name of person preparing this plan: Mary McKinney, Mayor

Phone: (XOX) 777-7777
Fax: (XOX) 777-1111
E-mail address: Mayor@NewAlbion.city.gov

The Water supplier is a: Municipality
The Water supplier is a: Retailer

Utility services provided by the water supplier include: Water, Recycled Water

Is This Agency a Bureau of Reclamation Contractor? Yes

Is This Agency a State Water Project Contractor? No

Public Participation Law

10642. Each urban water supplier shall encourage the active involvement of diverse social, cultural, and economic elements of the population within the service area prior to and during the preparation of the plan. Prior to adopting a plan, the urban water supplier shall make the plan available for public inspection and shall hold a public hearing thereon. Prior to the hearing, notice of the time and place of hearing shall be published.... After the hearing, the plan shall be adopted as prepared or as modified after the hearing.

Public Participation

The City of New Albion has actively encouraged community participation in its urban water management planning efforts since the first plan was developed in 1985. Public meetings were held on the 1985, 1990, 1995 and 2000 plans.

For this update to the Urban Water Management Plan, a series of public meetings was held. These included (1) a scoping session, (2) "open house" discussions on water conservation opportunities for specific customer sectors (for example, an ultra-low flush toilet replacement for tourist-serving businesses), and (3) meetings on water recycling opportunities (to gain public support, determine potential customers, and design marketing and funding approaches). Formal public sessions were held for review and comment on the draft plan before the City Council's approval. Public interest groups that participated in the development of the plan are listed in Appendix A.

A special effort was made to include grassroots community and public interest organizations (such as neighborhood associations, church and service groups), the Chamber of Commerce, League of Women Voters, Citizens for Lagoon Wildlife Refuge, local environmental groups, and landscape and growers' associations. Notices of public meetings were included as inserts in City water bills and were posted on the City's homepage on the Internet. Legal public notices for each meeting were published in the local newspapers, posted at City facilities and high usage commercial establishments such as grocery stores, and were distributed through the public schools. Copies of the draft plan were available at City offices, schools and libraries.

Plan Adoption

The City of New Albion prepared this update of its Urban Water Management Plan during summer 2000. The updated plan was adopted by City Council in December 2000 and submitted to the California Department of Water Resources within 30 days of Council approval. Attached to the cover letter addressed to the Department of Water Resources and as Appendix B are copies of the signed Resolution of Plan Adoption. This plan includes all information necessary to meet the requirements of California Water Code Division 6, Part 2.6 (Urban Water Management Planning).

Agency Coordination Law

10620(d)(2). Each urban water supplier shall coordinate the preparation of its plan with other appropriate agencies in the area, including other water suppliers that share a common source, water management agencies, and relevant public agencies, to the extent practicable.

Coordination Within the City

City water department staff met and coordinated the development of this plan with the Mayor's Office, City health, planning, fire, building, police, and emergency services offices.

On May 1 each year, the Water Department notifies the Planning Commission about the outlook on the water supplies for the City for the next 12 months. In 1991, the Planning Commission adopted guidelines, which require that adequate water supply and wastewater treatment capacities be available before new development can be approved. In the event of a declared water shortage, the City has adopted a policy to establish a moratorium on new water service permits. *See* Appendix C.

The New Albion Water and Planning Departments completed a study in December 1997 which examined and forecasted reliable water supplies and demands for the city to 2040. Data from this study were utilized in this document. New Albion County Water Authority (NACWA), the County, California State University (CSU)

New Albion, and various local groups developed a digitized map of the County, which will include all water agency service area boundaries, the potable, recycled, and waste water distribution systems, and other water system features.

Interagency Coordination

The City of New Albion is a member agency of the NACWA. All water sources for the City of New Albion are shared in common with other urban and agricultural interests in the area. The City therefore coordinated the development of this plan with the following agencies:

- NACWA (acts as a wholesaler) and its member agencies
- Drake Reservoir Joint Powers Authority and its members
- Watermaster for the Edisto Groundwater Basin Management District and parties to the adjudication
- New Albion County Regional Sanitation District (NACRSD)
- Other local public agencies, including County health, planning, fire, and building departments; Office of Emergency Services; New Albion School District; New Albion Community College and CSU New Albion and the Santa Veronica Mountains Resource Conservation District.

Table 1 summarizes the efforts New Albion has taken to include various agencies and citizens in its planning process.

TABLE 1
Coordination and Public Involvement

| Entities | COORDINATION AND PUBLIC INVOLVEMENT ACTIONS | | | | | |
	Helped write the plan	Was contacted for assistance	Was sent a copy of the draft	Commented on the draft	Attended public meetings	Was sent a notice of intention to adopt
Wholesaler		X	X	X	X	X
Retailers						
Wastewater Agency		X	X	X	X	X
Special Interest Groups		X	X	X	X	X
Citizen Groups		X	X	X	X	X
General Public			X	X	X	X
Public Library						X
Other		X	X	X	X	X

Supplier Service Area

Law

10631 A plan shall be adopted in accordance with this chapter and shall do all of the following:

10631(a) Describe the service area of the supplier, including current and projected population, climate, and other demographic factors affecting the supplier's water management planning. The projected population estimates shall be based upon data from the state, regional, or local service agency population projections within the service area of the urban water supplier and shall be in five-year increments to 20 years or as far as data is available.

Climate

New Albion has a Mediterranean coastal climate. Summers are mild and dry, and winters are cool, with an annual average of 16 inches of precipitation. The region is subject to wide variations in annual precipitation, and also experiences periodic wildland fires in the native chaparral and oak lands. Summer fog helps reduce summer irrigation requirements.

Deviation from the average annual precipitation was experienced in 1998 due to the El Nino conditions for the western United States. Total rainfall for that year was 37.5 inches.

Other Demographic Factors

The City of New Albion is located on the western slope of the Santa Veronica Mountains in New Albion County. It occupies an area of about 14.4 square miles (9,200 acres). Incorporation of the City occurred in 1926, and water service is provided to all residential, commercial, industrial, and agricultural customers, and for environmental and fire protection uses.

The Santa Veronica Mission was founded in 1793. The first commercial activity in the area was cattle grazing, but due to the temperate climate, vineyards and orchards soon followed. The community (incorporated 1926) soon became the economic center of the region. In the early days, groundwater was the major water supply, since there were few year-round springs,

creeks, or rivers. Enough naturally occurring recharge meant the groundwater was sufficient to meet the needs of the area.

Beginning in the 1920s, New Albion (along with most of California) experienced an economic boom, and there were large increases in the residential (both single family and multi-family), commercial, and industrial sectors. During the 1940s and 1950s, the following features were constructed: (1) a military base on the outskirts of the city limits to the west, (2) a State highway, (3) a commercial airport, and (4) CSU New Albion. In the late 1950s, the city remodeled portions of the downtown area (adding shops and hotels) to attract tourists.

As the population increased in the City and region, the demand for water also increased. Groundwater levels dropped, some saline water started to intrude into the Edisto aquifer, and it became evident that groundwater was insufficient to meet growing

needs. Additional water supply became necessary, and the NACWA was established in 1946 to coordinate acquisition of water for the County. Drake Reservoir was built nearby on the Santa Veronica River and delivery systems were installed. The Edisto Basin was adjudicated in 1955 to prevent further declines in groundwater levels and to reduce the saline intrusion threat. In 1977 the Southwest Aqueduct was built to convey imported water.

Between 1920 and 1970, population increases for New Albion were quite steady. Population during the 1970s remained relatively constant due to relocation of two businesses out of the area. However, the City began to experience rapid growth again during the 1980s when the population nearly doubled. Significant increases in both tourist and part-year (winter season) resident populations also occurred.

Table 2 shows the population total for the City from 2000, with projections to 2020.

TABLE 2
Population Projections

	2000	2005	2010	2015	2020
Service Area Populations	51,155	55,600	60,440	65,700	71,420

Past Drought, Water Demand, and Conservation Information

The local region experienced a prolonged drought from 1987 through 1992. The City met its customers' needs through careful conjunctive management of groundwater and local reservoir supplies, and by investing in water conservation and water recycling. Community involvement made it possible to have voluntary rationing during 1987–89. By 1990, however, because of worsening local conditions, and reduced imported water supplies due to drought conditions in Northern California, the City established a mandatory 25% rationing program.

Since 1995, new water demand has slowed to a growth rate of about 1–2% per year (Table 5), due in part to effects of the drought and in part to a general slow-down

in the region's economy. From 1996 to 2000, the population increased by 4,000 full year residents, to a current population of 51,155 and new water demand has kept pace with the growth. The City continues to have a modest but growing industrial sector. The commercial sector is increasing more rapidly due to increased tourism. The agricultural economy is based on vineyards, citrus, avocados, strawberries, other truck crops, and floriculture.

The citizens of New Albion have a high commitment to quality of life and environmental issues and are active participants in resource and planning discussions held by City staff and the City Council. Water conservation is one of several high priority policies actively implemented in the City, and programs such as residential water audits, ultra-low flush toilet replacements, and landscape water audits are well accepted. A community-based urban stream and wetland restoration project was established and is maintained with widespread community support, and there are over 120 miles of bike lanes and trails in the County.

A 1978 City ordinance requires greenbelts in new developments. A General Plan was developed in 1989, and updated in 1997, with active community input and support, specifically addressing the land use planning relationships among growth, water, transportation, air quality, and other resources.

As a result of several severe wildland fires in the late 1980s, a countywide firescaping policy was incorporated into the efficient landscape policy and all replacement construction must meet current building code requirements. The City adopted a residential fire sprinkler ordinance in 1995. The City has applied for a grant to conduct a demonstration project to retrofit fire sprinklers in selected "older" non-current code residential structures, since most fires occur in these structures.

A countywide recycling policy was adopted in 1990, as part of an effort towards local sustainability. The policy addresses both solid waste and water, and directs public agencies to use recycled materials in their own operations (such as paper, compost, and crushed toilets for roadbed materials).

Water Sources (Supply)

Law

10631 A plan shall be adopted in accordance with this chapter and shall do all of the following:

10631(b) Identify and quantify, to the extent practicable, the existing and planned sources of water available to the supplier over the same five-year increments [to 20 years or as far as data is available.]

Water Supply Sources

The City of New Albion fortunately has a variety of water sources, including: groundwater, local surface, imported, and recycled. The City has potential additional supplies from additional imported water,

ocean water desalination, and short- and long-term water transfers.

Groundwater

The City obtains about 2,200 acre-feet per year (AFY) from four wells, from an average depth of 125 feet (Table 3). The Edisto Groundwater Basin was adjudicated in 1955; the City of New Albion is a party to the adjudication. There has been some saline intrusion into the Basin, and the water is a little high in several metals, but water quality is within standards set for acceptable drinking water by the federal government and the California Department of Health Services. If the City does not extract 2,200 AFY, the Watermaster allows "banking" credit up to 1,000 acre-feet cumulative for future additional pumping.

During a declared water shortage, under the terms of the Edisto Basin Decree, the Watermaster may allow the City to extract up to 2,600 AFY for a maximum of two years. The additional water pumped must be returned within five years by reduced future pumping or by recharge. Two years of groundwater extraction at this higher level would reduce allowed extraction in the third year to below the normal year 2,200 AF level. The City manages its water supply so that the additional groundwater pumping is reserved for years when the other water supplies are in shortfall, keeping groundwater as a local reserve.

The Watermaster, New Albion County Water District (NACWD), NACRSD, and the City are conducting a feasibility study on potential conjunctive use using recycled water from the proposed tertiary wastewater treatment plant. The study is examining feasibility to construct and operate a groundwater recharge facility in or near the Santa Veronica River channel, upstream from the City's well field. State and local health officials are supportive in concept. Based on the amount of tertiary recycled water which may become available, and on the geology of the basin, the study indicates that tertiary wastewater recharge could increase the City's groundwater supply by 90 acre-feet per year in 2005, by 180 acre-feet per year by 2010, by 270 acre-feet by 2015 and by 360 acre-feet per year by

TABLE 3
Current and Projected Water Supplies

Water Supply Sources	2000	2005	2010	2015	2020
Purchased from USBR					
Purchased from DWR					
Purchased from wholesaler (Imported Water from NACWA)	4,000	4,000	4,000	4,000	4,000
City produced groundwater	2,200	2,200	2,200	2,200	2,200
City produced surface water	15,000	15,000	15,000	15,000	15,000
Transfers					
Exchanges in					
Recycled Water	910	1,005	1,180	1,350	1,520
Recycled Water used for groundwater recharge (adds to gw supply)	0	90	180	270	360
Other					
TOTAL	22,110	22,295	22,560	22,820	23,080

Unit of Measure: Acre-feet/Year

© Recycled water supply figures are prepared in Table 15 in the Water Recycling Section of this plan.

2020 (Table 3). The City may choose to "bank" this water against future surface and/or imported water shortages.

Local Surface Water from Drake Reservoir (Santa Veronica River watershed)

Drake Reservoir is located on the Santa Veronica River about 25 miles northeast of the City. It is operated for both flood control and water supply purposes; recreational uses include camping, fishing, and boating. It is operated by the Drake Joint Powers Authority, which consists of the City, NACWA, and three irrigation districts. The watershed consists primarily of rangeland with some forested areas. The watershed is protected and managed with limited public access, so the water quality remains good.

The Santa Veronica River is a typical coastal stream; the watershed experiences wide fluctuations in runoff from year to year. Although Drake Reservoir carry-over storage smoothes out some of this fluctuation, this supply is not as reliable as the City once thought, particularly during consecutive year shortages. Drake Reservoir's useable capacity is 140,000 acre-feet, designed for a four-year supply, with an average ("firm") yield of 35,000 AFY. According to the City's contract, the City is entitled to 15,000 AFY. In a normal water year, the City depends on Drake Reservoir supply for over 65% of its total water supply.

When Drake Reservoir storage exceeds 100,000 acre-feet, the City's annual supply is 15,000 acre-feet. In any year when storage is between 80,000 and 100,000 acre-feet, the annual yield is reduced to 80% of average (the City's share is 12,000 acre-feet). If storage is between 60,000 and 80,000 acre-feet, the annual yield is reduced to 60% of average (the City's share is 9,000 acre-feet). At storage levels less than 60,000 acre-feet, the annual yield is only 40% of average (the City's share is 6,000 acre-feet). Under a declared water shortage, all members receive equal percentage reductions. Table 4 uses these reduced yields to analyze supply reliability.

In 1993, the Santa Veronica River watershed received above normal precipitation, ending the 1987–1992 drought. 2000 was

again above average. Currently, the Reservoir has about 120,000 acre-feet of storage, sufficient for full deliveries for 2001. However, should precipitation be below average, the City would only receive 12,000 acre-feet in 2002.

Imported Water through the New Albion County Water Authority (NACWA)

NACWA was formed in 1946 to acquire and manage countywide water supplies. The seven members are the City of New Albion, four other small cities, an irrigation district, and a mutual water company; four of these depend on NACWA for their water supplies. NACWA receives 25% of Drake Reservoir's annual yield, and has contractual rights to 15,000 AFY of imported water. Imported water is conveyed through the Southwest Aqueduct, which was completed in 1977. The City has a contractual agreement with NACWA for 4,000 AFY of imported water.

NACWA members proposed and ratified a mutual aid agreement in 1992. This agreement addresses the allocation of water during water supply shortages caused by severe water shortages or disasters. Because NACWA members have differing sources of water, if NACWA's Board of Directors declare a water shortage, NACWA members have agreed that they may not get equal percentage reductions in imported water, to avoid major health and/or economic disruptions for any member agency. NACWA is investigating feasibility of additional imported water supplies through long-term water transfers and constructing an additional pipeline to help "earthquake proof" the distribution system. It is also investigating possible conjunctive use and banking programs with its members, whereby urban and permanent crop agricultural water demand could be met in water short years by groundwater supplies. *See* the Water Shortage Contingency Plan section of this plan for additional actions to be taken during a water shortage.

Before 1992, the three NACWA members with local water supplies were physically unable to provide emergency water to the other NACWA agencies. Because of this, a NACWA-wide emergency conveyance

system was completed in 1994. It allows for transfer of water supplies among all NACWA members, and consists of 40 miles of new pipeline, additional valves and interties, standby diesel generators and pumps to reverse flows in pipelines, should it ever become necessary. Generators were sized to start pumps, as well as run them.

Recycled Water

The New Albion County Regional Sanitation District (NACRSD) built a regional wastewater treatment plant (RTP) in 1962, and upgraded it in 1990 to produce disinfected Secondary 2.2 treatment level wastewater. (Wastewater treatment levels and suitable uses of recycled water are defined by the California Department of Health Services under California Administrative Code, Title 22, Division 4.)

The City currently purchases and sells 910 AFY of this disinfected Secondary 2.2 water as recycled water for appropriate uses by customers and for use by the City itself. The recycled water quality is excellent. Use of recycled water has gained wide support in the community, and there are agricultural, commercial landscapes, and industrial customers who would like to convert some or most of their water use to recycled water.

The NACWA, NACRSD, Edisto Basin Watermaster, the City and others have coordinated planning to expand the reclamation capacity and upgrade treatment levels at the RTP. Recognizing that this is an expensive proposition, an extensive market survey was conducted. It appears that tertiary level treatment is technically, financially, and politically feasible, so NACRSD will likely upgrade to tertiary level treatment. By 2020, the City expects to purchase up to 1,520 AFY for sale to a mix of users, including agricultural, parks and schools, and several commercial and industrial users (Table 3).

Reliability Planning

Law

10631 A plan shall be adopted in accordance with this chapter and shall do all of the following:

10631(c) Describe the reliability of the water supply and vulnerability to seasonal or climatic shortage, to the extent practicable.

10631(c) For any water source that may not be available at a consistent level of use, given specific legal, environmental, water quality, or climatic factors, describe plans to replace that source with alternative sources or water demand management measures, to the extent practicable.

10631(c) Provide data for each of the following: (1) An average water year, (2) A single dry water year, (3) Multiple dry water years.

10632 The plan shall provide an urban water shortage contingency analysis which includes each of the following elements which are within the authority of the urban water supplier:

10632(b) An estimate of the minimum water supply available during each of the next three-water years based on the driest three-year historic sequence for the agency's water supply.

Reliability

The costs of demand management or supply augmentation options to reduce the frequency and severity of shortages are now high enough that city planners must look more carefully at the costs of unreliability to make the best possible estimate of the net benefit of taking specific actions, hence the term "reliability planning." Reliability is a measure of a water service system's expected success in managing water shortages.

To plan for long-term water supply reliability, planners examine an increasingly wide array of supply augmentation and demand reduction options to determine the best courses of action for meeting water service needs. Such options are generally evaluated using the water service reliability planning approach.

In addition to climate, other factors that can cause water supply shortages are earthquakes, chemical spills, and energy outages at treatment and pumping facilities. City Planners include the probability of catastrophic outages when using the reliability planning approach.

Reliability planning requires information about: (1) the expected frequency and severity of shortages; (2) how additional water management measures are likely to affect the frequency and severity of shortages; (3) how available contingency measures can reduce the impact of shortages when they occur.

The City of New Albion adopted a system-wide annualized demand reduction target of no more than 25 percent. It is believed that anything over a 25% reduction would cause an economic hardship within the city. The 25 percent criterion is an overall use reduction target which will result in an estimated 31% reduction to residential users, 25% reduction to commercial and institutional users, and 10% reduction to most industrial users.

The City used the Department of Water Resources' Bulletin 160-98 the California Water Plan Update, chapters 7, 8 and 9, Options for Meeting Future Water Needs, in the development of the reliability comparison section.

Frequency and Magnitude of Supply Deficiencies

The City experienced a severe drought during 1976–77; a County-wide ordinance was adopted in 1976 to suspend all residential and commercial landscape watering for the duration of the water shortage. During 1987–89, the community was better prepared to handle drought impacts, due to: (1) the adoption by the City Council of a "No-Waste" Ordinance in 1983 (see Appendix C); (2) successful voluntary rationing on the part of the community; and (3) effective water conservation programs, including: free showerheads and toilet leak detection dye tablets for all residential customers, an

educational water conservation program with the local schools, and residential water audits. Approximately a 15% reduction in water demand was achieved.

However, due to the continuing local drought, and concurrent reductions in imported water, in 1990 the City established a mandatory rationing program (see Appendix C). The rationing program established water allotments based on customer type and use history, a conservation-oriented rate structure, and defined shortage stages and triggering levels. A 20% reduction was necessary, and the community achieved sustained reductions of 31%.

The current and future supply projections through 2020 are shown in Table 3. The future supply projections assume normal inflows to Drake Reservoir and average annual recharge to the Edisto Aquifer.

Plans to Assure a Reliable Water Supply

The future supply projections assume normal inflows to Drake Reservoir and average annual recharge to the Edisto Aquifer. Recycled water is a very reliable water source, because it is consistently available. The likeliest interruption would be as a result of loss of power or facility failure at the RTP. Potable water can still be provided to all recycled water users through a backup system.

Reliability Comparison

Table 4 details estimated water supply projections associated with several water supply reliability scenarios. For further information on the data, *see* Three-year Minimum Supply and Water Shortage Contingency Plan sections.

TABLE 4
Supply Reliability

Average/Normal Water Year 2000 (Volume)	Single Dry Water Year (Volume)	MULTIPLE DRY WATER YEARS		
		Year 1 (Volume) 2001	Year 2 (Volume) 2002	Year 3 (Volume) 2003
22,110	17,110 (23%)	22,110 (0%)	18,710 (15%)	18,710 (15%)

Unit of Measure: Acre-feet/Year

Three Year Minimum Water Supply

Based on experiences during the recent drought, the community recognizes that it is better to enter into a water shortage alert early, at a minimal level, to establish necessary rationing programs and policies, to gain public support and participation, and to reduce the likelihood of more severe shortage levels later. As the community continues to become more water efficient, it may become more difficult for customers to reduce their water use during water shortages (this is called "demand hardening"). Staff does not believe that City customers are yet approaching demand hardening, because there are still large potential water efficiency improvements in residential plumbing fixtures, appliances, and landscapes, and in the commercial, industrial, and institutional sectors. However, improved water use efficiency does mean that water supply reserves must be larger and that water shortage responses must be made early to prevent severe economic and environmental impacts.

In April each year, the City forecasts three-year minimum water supply availability for each of its sources of water, and projects its total water supply for the current and three subsequent years. Based on the water shortage stages and triggers a water shortage condition may be declared. The driest three-year historic sequence for the City's water supplies was from 1990 to 1992. Because shortages can have serious economic and environmental impacts, the City will make every effort to limit water shortages to no more than 25%. Refer to Appendix D table G5 for costs associated with reduced water supply.

Transfer or Exchange Opportunities

Law

10631 A plan shall be adopted in accordance with this chapter and shall do all of the following:

10631(d) Describe the opportunities for exchanges or transfers of water on a short-term or long-term basis.

Water Transfers

The City is exploring dry year water transfer options with agricultural districts locally and statewide and individual growers. It is estimated that up to 1,000 acre-feet could be purchased by the City as emergency water supply. Since the Edisto Basin is adjudicated, groundwater pumping is regulated, and growers would have to fallow lands in order to make water available for transfer. This has economic consequences on individual growers, the County, and the region.

In conjunction with NACWA, the City is discussing long-term transfers with other agencies in other parts of the State. NACWA is also conducting preliminary discussion with the adjacent county, where there is adequate groundwater for temporary water supply transfers during shortages.

Water Use Provisions

Law

10631 A plan shall be adopted in accordance with this chapter and shall do all of the following:

10631(e)(1) Quantify, to the extent records are available, past and current water use, over the same five-year increments described in subdivision (a), and projected water use, identifying the uses among water use sectors including, but not necessarily limited to, all of the following uses: (A) Single-family residential; (B) Multi-family; (C) Commercial; (D) Industrial; (E) Institutional and governmental; (F) Landscape; (G) Sales to other agencies; (H) Saline water intrusion barriers, groundwater recharge, or conjunctive use, or any combination thereof; and (I) Agricultural.

(2) The water use projections shall be in the same 5-year increments to 20 years or as far as data is available.

Past, Current and Projected Water Use

Since 1990, new connections are being added at a rate about 2% per year, but because of new plumbing efficiency standards, landscape guidelines, and other conservation programs, water demand is only increasing at a rate of about 1% per year. Unaccounted water losses average about 5% of total production. Table 5 illustrates Past, Current, and Projected Water Use 1990–2020 in acre-feet per year, and Table 6 illustrates Past, Current, and Projected Water Use 1990–2020 in number of customers per year.

TABLE 5
Past, Current, and Projected Water Use

Water Use Sectors	1990	1995	2000	2005	2010	2015	2020
Single-family residential	6,608	6,409	6,217	6,555	6,912	7,288	7,684
Multi-family residential	4,050	3,928	3,811	4,018	3,897	3,780	3,667
Commercial	1,759	1,774	1,788	1,802	1,817	1,832	1,847
Industrial	1,235	1,248	1,261	1,274	1,287	1,300	1,313
Institutional and governmental	1,100	1,122	1,144	1,167	1,191	1,214	1,239
Sales to other agencies	863	865	867	869	871	873	875
Saline barriers							
Groundwater recharge (recycled water)							
Conjunctive use			0	100	200	300	400
Agriculture*	5,000	5,000	5,000	5,000	5,000	4,900	4,800
Unaccounted-for system losses	1,020	1,045	1,060	1,110	1,119	1,133	1,146
TOTAL	21,635	21,391	21,148	21,896	22,294	22,260	22,971

Unit of Measure: Acre-feet/Year   * Agricultural water does not include water that is privately pumped.

TABLE 6
Number of Connections by Customer Type

Water Use Sectors	1990	1995	2000	2005	2010	2015	2020
Single-family residential	9,040	9,617	10,231	11,121	12,089	13,140	14,284
Multi-family residential	6,985	7,092	7,200	7,826	8,507	9,247	10,051
Commercial	132	144	156	167	174	186	197
Industrial	36	42	47	53	60	67	71
Institutional and governmental	69	75	81	88	93	99	105
Landscape/recreation	35	38	41	44	46	49	52
Agricultural	25	22	22	22	22	22	20
Other (Recycle water)	0						
TOTAL	16,322	17,030	17,778	19,321	20,990	22,810	24,780

Under rationing, it became apparent that the City needed to improve information about its customers. Previously, the City identified and billed customers on the basis of street address and the meter size. The City was unable to easily distinguish an industrial customer (using water for food processing, for example), from a large landscape customer, from a hotel, from a hospital (with emergency water priority requirements to meet health and safety), nor from a large multi-family complex. Obviously, each would have different needs and different appropriate rationing allocations. Therefore, the City redesigned its water billing system, used student interns to verify customers' categories, and now has classified the accounts by use class and can identify each customer by sector and usage category.

Residential Sector

In the City of New Albion, single family residential customers average 3.1 persons per connection. Multi-family residential customers average 2.7 persons per housing unit, and average 10 units per multi-family complex. Total system per capita water use (excluding agricultural water use) averages 170 gallons per capita per day. Water efficiency improvements appear to be reducing per capita water use, which will prevent a return to pre-drought levels.

A Demand Offset program was established in 1992, where new development pays additional fees to help offset their water demand by increasing the water use efficiencies of existing customers. This program has provided funding to support water use surveys for residential and public facilities,

and ultra-low flush toilet replacement programs. Single and multi-family residential connections are projected to increase at about 2% per year over the next 20 years, but the efficiency improvements will significantly help offset the water demand of new customers.

Commercial Sector

The City has a complex mix of commercial customers, ranging from markets, restaurants, antique stores, insurance offices, beauty shops, and gas stations to multistory office buildings, outlet and regional shopping centers, and high-volume restaurants and other facilities serving the visitor population. The sector is growing at about 2% per year, driven particularly by the need for services by the increasing permanent population. Businesses for the growing tourist industry are also contributing. This trend is expected to continue through 2020.

Industrial Sector

The City has a small industrial sector, primarily centered on food production (wineries, canning and bottling) and light manufacturing. The industrial sector has not grown much in the last decade but has been growing at an increasing rate recently. It is expected to increase at about 3% in the next ten years due to relocation of two metal fabrication factories and associated facilities.

Institutional/Governmental Sector

The City has a stable institutional/governmental sector, primarily local government, schools, visitor serving public facilities, and

a public hospital. This sector will keep pace with the growth of the city.

Landscape/Recreational Sector

Landscape and Recreational customer demand is expected to increase approximately 2% per year for the next 20 years, due to continued growth in visitor-serving facilities, proposed golf courses and a waterslide amusement park. Increased efficiency and landscape conversions at existing parks, golf courses, and cemeteries should help offset new demand resulting from projected increases in this sector.

Agricultural Sector

Agricultural water demand is projected to remain constant for the next ten years, and then probably gradually decrease over the next twenty to thirty years. Agricultural land use within the City of New Albion is protected by City ordinance. The City's General Plan reflects local citizen interest in open space, quality of life, environmental values, and the long-term maintenance of a diverse economic base. Even so, it is projected that more agricultural land will eventually be converted to urban uses.

The City's 20 agricultural accounts irrigate about 2,000 acres: 1,300 acres of orchards/vineyards (avocados, lemons, and grapes); 400 acres of annual crops (strawberries, vegetables, and seed flowers); and 300 acres of flower/nurseries. Agriculture irrigates with 4,250 AFY from the City's potable water, 750 AFY of disinfected Secondary 2.2 wastewater from NACRSD's RTP, and 800 AFY privately pumped from the adjudicated groundwater basin.

Because of the high cost of water for agricultural uses, all City agricultural customers base their irrigation applications on estimates of daily crop evapotranspiration. A response to the last drought was agricultural customers' installation of efficient irrigation systems such as micro-spray in orchards and subsurface drip systems in the row crops. The City, NACWA, and other water suppliers cooperate with the local University of California's Cooperative Extension program, and contribute funds to support the county-wide Mobile Lab for agricultural and large landscape irrigation evaluations, and make California Irrigation Management Information System (CIMIS) weather data available on a daily basis. Because water for agricultural use is so expensive in New Albion, irrigation is highly efficient.

Supply and Demand Comparison Provisions

Law

10635(a) Every urban water supplier shall include, as part of its urban water management plan, an assessment of the reliability of its water service to its customers during normal, dry, and multiple dry water years. This water supply and demand assessment shall compare the total water supply sources available to the water supplier with the total projected water use over the next 20 years, in five-year increments, for a normal water year, a single dry water year, and multiple dry water years. The water service reliability assessment shall be based upon the information compiled pursuant to Section 10631, including available data from the state, regional, or local agency population projections within the service area of the urban water supplier.

Supply and Demand Comparison

Table 7 compares current, and projected water supply and demand. It indicates that in average precipitation years, the City of New Albion has sufficient water to meet its customers' needs, through 2020. This is based on continued commitment to conservation programs, additional recycled water becoming available when the RTP produces tertiary water and additional conjunctive use of groundwater.

TABLE 7
Projected Supply and Demand Comparison

	2000	2005	2010	2015	2020
Supply Total	22,110	22,295	22,560	22,820	23,080
Demand Total	21,194	21,901	22,303	22,629	22,979
Difference	916	394	257	191	101

Unit of Measure: Acre-feet/Year

In any one dry year, the City will need to carefully manage its water supply. In the second consecutive dry year, the City will probably need to enter into a Stage I water shortage response. In the third consecutive dry year, or in the event of a major system failure, the City may continue a Stage I water shortage response or move into a Stage II water shortage reponse. *See* the Water Shortage Contingency Plan and Three-year Minimum Water Supply sections and Table 8 for more detailed information.

Table 8 presents a supply and demand comparison where demand does not fluctuate in conjunction with a change in supply. This analysis demonstrates that if supply were to be reduced from a water supply shortage, the existing supply is not sufficient to meet demands.

Table 8A, 8B, & 8C will detail how supply options and demand options can alter the outcome of a water shortage.

TABLE 8
Single Dry Year and Multiple Dry Water Years

	Current Supply Water Year (Volume)	Single Dry Water Year (Volume)	MULTIPLE DRY WATER YEARS		
			Year 1 (Volume)	Year 2 (Volume)	Year 3 (Volume)
Supply totals	22,110	17,110	22,110	18,710	18,710
Percent shortage		23%	0%	15%	15%
Demand totals	21,194	21,194	21,335	21,476	21,618
Difference	916	(4,084)	775	(2,766)	(2,908)

Unit of Measure: Acre-feet/Year

Table 8A modifies the comparison by increasing the supply available for use with the inclusion of groundwater banking in previous years where demands did not equal the available supply. Demand remains the same as in Table 8. This analysis demonstrates that changes in supply are not sufficient to meet the demand in a water shortage.

TABLE 8A
Reliability and Comparison with Supply Options

	Current Supply Water Year (Volume)	Single Dry Water Year (Volume)	MULTIPLE DRY WATER YEARS		
			Year 1 (Volume)	Year 2 (Volume)	Year 3 (Volume)
Supply totals	22,110	17,610	17,610	18,910	18,910
Percent shortage	21,194	21,194	21,194	21,476	21,618
Difference	916	(3,584)	(3,584)	(2,566)	(2,708)

Unit of Measure: Acre-feet/Year

Table 8B modifies the comparison by implementing demand management measures and other consumption reductions methods. This comparison holds supply at the same level as Table 8. This analysis demonstrates that the use of conservation measures is not sufficient to completely meet the demand during a water shortage.

TABLE 8B
Reliability and Comparison
with Demand Options

| | Current Supply Water Year (Volume) | Single Dry Water Year (Volume) | MULTIPLE DRY WATER YEARS | | |
			Year 1 (Volume)	Year 2 (Volume)	Year 3 (Volume)
Supply totals	22,110	17,110	22,110	18,710	18,710
Demand totals	21,194	19,074	19,074	18,015	18,015
Difference	916	(1,964)	3,036	695	695

Unit of Measure: Acre-feet/Year

Table 8C modifies the comparison by increasing supply and modifying water user habits through conservation measures. It demonstrates that most circumstances of shortage can be planned for. However, effort should be devoted towards securing additional supplies during a catastrophic supply reduction. The City is looking at recycled water to increase the supply during a catastrophic reduction. This can be done through direct reuse and/or groundwater recharge.

TABLE 8C
Reliability and Comparison with
Supply and Demand Options

| | Current Supply Water Year (Volume) | Single Dry Water Year (Volume) | MULTIPLE DRY WATER YEARS | | |
			Year 1 (Volume)	Year 2 (Volume)	Year 3 (Volume)
Supply totals	22,110	17,610	22,410	18,910	18,910
Demand totals	21,194	19,074	19,074	18,015	18,015
Difference	916	(1,964)	3,336	895	895

Unit of Measure: Acre-feet/Year

Active water efficiency improvements and additional water supply will be necessary to meet the City's projected water demand. The City will continue to examine supply enhancement options, including additional water recycling, groundwater recharge and conjunctive use, water transfers, desalination and additional imported water supplies. Other water management options, including dredging Drake Reservoir and raising Drake Dam, will also be considered. *See* the Water Shortage Contingency Plan section for further information.

Water Demand Management Measures

Law

10631(f) Provide a description of the supplier's water demand management measures. This description shall include all of the following:

(1) A description of each water demand management measure that is currently being implemented, or scheduled for implementation, including the steps necessary to implement any proposed measures, including, but not limited to, all of the following:

The City of New Albion is committed to implementing water conservation and water recycling programs. This Section discusses water conservation.

As mentioned in the cover letter to this Plan, the City of New Albion is not a signatory to the Memorandum of Understanding regarding Urban Water Conservation in California (MOU) and is therefore not a member of the California Urban Water Conservation Council (CUWCC)). The City will vote on the issue of becoming a member of the CUWCC and a signatory to the MOU in 2001. The following are just some of the benefits of being a member of the CUWWC: conferences, BMP workshops, free publications, research regarding water management practices, leadership on water legislation and networking with other agencies and interest groups.

For the purpose of responding to the Urban Water Management Planning Act the City will address the 16 Demand Management Measures. Descriptions of the City's water conservation programs are below. The City has, in good faith, tried to address and comply with all of the BMP targets listed in the CUWCC MOU where applicable.

DMM 1–Interior and Exterior Water Audits for Single Family and Multi-Family Customers

IMPLEMENTATION DESCRIPTION: Since 1995, in cooperation with NACWA, NACRSD, and the local energy utilities, the City has offered free residential water use surveys to single-family and multi-family customers (refer to table 6). The City has specifically focused on the top 20% of water users in each sector, but has also continued to offer surveys to any customer who so requests. It is the City's goal to complete surveys for 15% of the single family and 15% of the multi-family connections over the next ten years.

The City's computer services department developed an inquiry program to sort billing records by water use within sectors, so that letters offering the free surveys can be mailed to the highest water users. If a customer does not participate and remains on the highest water use list the subsequent year, the customer receives up to three additional letters offering a water use survey, with hose shut-off nozzles offered as a further incentive to participate.

The City recruits and trains young adults through a City Job Training Program to conduct the water use surveys. The training program is conducted and certified through the local community college, so survey team members can become eligible for permanent employment opportunities in the water and energy conservation field. Part of the landscape training is conducted by local master gardeners, who helped develop the curriculum on landscape efficiency improvements and are knowledgeable about the plants that are commonly grown in the area.

Single family surveys take about two hours and are conducted by two-member teams. During the interior portion of the survey, the team: measures flow rates of existing plumbing fixtures and tests for toilet leakage with dye tablets; offers and installs showerheads and faucet aerators (if necessary); provides materials on the City's ultra-low flush toilet replacement programs (rebates are offered, or toilets are made available–see DMM 16); straps the hot water tank (if necessary) for earthquake safety and disaster water supply, adjusts the hot water temperature and installs an insulation blanket for energy efficiency; provides other energy efficiency materials (such as energy saving florescent lights); and checks smoke detectors.

The team then conducts the landscape survey. The team: shows the customer the

location of the water meter and how to read it: measures the landscaped areas, tests the sprinkler system for irrigation efficiency, and distribution uniformity; teaches the customer how to set the irrigation controller; develops a three-season irrigation schedule (based on soil type, evapotranspiration, and irrigation system), recommends sprinkler system repairs or improvements and provides brochures on water efficient landscaping, design, and plants. Multi-family surveys are similar, but require coordination with owners/ managers, tenants, and landscaping services.

Institutional and governmental customers have also been offered water use surveys. All City-owned facilities including the City Hall, Hospitals, libraries, fire stations, the City's corporation yard facilities, and public restrooms have been surveyed and retrofitted. Due to lack of in-house expertise, and legal concerns about potential liability, the City hired a consultant to perform the hospital and large institutional customer audits. (*See* DMM 9.)

IMPLEMENTATION SCHEDULE
and CONSERVATION SAVINGS:

TABLE 9
DMM 1 Implementation Schedule and Water Savings

Year	Surveys Completed Single Family [1]	Surveys Completed Multi-Family [2]	Annual Water Savings (AF)	Cumulative Water Savings (AF)
1995	144	106	Y, YYY	Y, YYY
1996	144	106	Y, YYY	Y, YYY
1997	144	106	Y, YYY	YY, YYY
1998	144	106	Y, YYY	YY, YYY
1999	144	106	Y, YYY	YY, YYY
2000	144e	106e	Y, YYY	YY, YYY
2001	144e	106e	Y, YYY	YY, YYY
2002	144e	106e	Y, YYY	YY, YYY
2003	144e	106e	Y, YYY	YYY, YYY
2004	144e	106e	Y, YYY	YYY, YYY
2005	144e	106e	Y, YYY	YYY, YYY

e = estimate   1 = 15% of (9,617 single family connections/10 years) = 144
2 = 15% of (7,092 multi-family connections/10 years) = 106

METHODS TO EVALUATE EFFECTIVENESS: For each dwelling unit the survey team completes a customer data form (including number of people per household, number of bathrooms, age of appliances, and lot and landscaped area square footage). This data is used to analyze the customer's water use, and to refine the program.

Beginning in spring of 2000, City staffs now review the surveyed customers' water use records, and compare historic with current use for one year after the survey. If the reduction in water use is not in line with DMM water savings estimates, staff will flag the customer's account and offer a follow up survey.

BUDGET: Proposed annual budget: $XXX,XXX, includes Job Training Program

staff, brochures, and purchase of showerheads, aerators, dye tablets, and other miscellaneous materials (this budget item does not reflect the costs associated with ultralow flush toilets–see DMM 16).

DMM 2–Plumbing Retrofit

IMPLEMENTATION DESCRIPTION: Through NACWA, the City participates in the distribution of showerheads, aerators, and toilet tank leak detection tablets at the County fair and during Water Awareness Month. At these events the City also emphasizes water use surveys and ultra-low flush toilet replacement programs (refer to DMM 1 and 16). The City has targeted 10% of the approximate 9,300 (465) pre-1992 single family homes and 7,000 (350) multi-family homes every two years. In order to reach the targeted 10% every two years the City will need to distribute excess devices due to the probability of distribution to people outside the targeted group.

IMPLEMENTATION SCHEDULE: The City will continue to implement this DMM at a targeted rate of 10% of pre-1992 single and

multi-family customers every two years. However, actions required by this DMM are included as part of DMM 1 and

DMM 16, which City staffs believe is a more efficient approach to implementing DMM 2. The table below lists all the water savings devices distributed for both DMM 1 and 2.

TABLE 10
DMM 2 Implementation Schedule and Water Savings

	SHOWERHEADS		AERATORS		LEAK DETECTION TABLETS	
Year	Single Family	Multi-Family	Single Family	Multi-Family	Single Family	Multi-Family
1995	600	355	600	355	600	355
1996	600	355	600	355	600	355
1997	600	355	600	355	600	355
1998	600	355	600	355	600	355
1999	600	355	600	355	600	355
2000	600e	355e	600e	355e	600e	355e
2001	600e	355e	600e	355e	600e	355e
2002	600e	355e	600e	355e	600e	355e
2003	600e	355e	600e	355e	600e	355e
2004	600e	355e	600e	355e	600e	355e
2005	600e	355e	600e	355e	600ee	355e

e = estimate

CONSERVATION SAVINGS:

TABLE 11
DMM 2 Water Savings

Year	Annual Water Savings	Cumulative Water Savings
1995	Y, YYY	Y, YYY
1996	Y, YYY	Y, YYY
1997	Y, YYY	YY, YYY
1998	Y, YYY	YY, YYY
1999	Y, YYY	YY, YYY
2000	Y, YYY	YY, YYY
2001	Y, YYYe	YYY, YYYe
2002	Y, YYYe	YYY, YYYe
2003	Y, YYYe	YYY, YYYe
2004	Y, YYYe	YYY, YYYe
2005	Y, YYYe	YYY, YYYe

e = estimate

METHODS TO EVALUATE EFFECTIVENESS: Refer to DMM 1 and 16.

BUDGET: Proposed annual budget (*see* DMM 1).

DMM 3–Distribution System Water Audits, Leak Detection and Repair

IMPLEMENTATION DESCRIPTION: The City has conducted water audits and leak detection and repair since 1991, as described in its 1990 Urban Water Management Plan. City staffs are trained at AWWA-DWR co-sponsored training programs.

Since the City is located in an earthquake zone, it has permanently incorporated the system water audit and leak detection, and meter calibration (production and customer meters) programs into its utility operations. On average, City water department crews spend about 35 days surveying approximately 70 miles of main and laterals per year. The City also participates in the NACWA-sponsored annual valve exercise program, established in 1991, to

ensure that interconnections with adjacent utilities actually work.

In coordination with the fire department, the water department complied with recent amendments to California Code of Regulations Title 19, Division 1, Chapter 9, pertaining to standardization of fire hydrants and associated fire protection equipment. As a result of several recent major fire-fighting/water shortage disasters in California communities, the City has participated with NACWA and others to acquire standby pumps and generators to assist in water distribution in a disaster. The City meets or exceeds minimum fire flow requirements, in accordance with California Water Works Standards.

IMPLEMENTATION SCHEDULE: The City has permanently incorporated this DMM into its operations and maintenance procedures, and established a three-year rotation schedule. City crews will survey at least 70 miles of main and laterals per year on an on-going basis.

METHODS TO EVALUATE EFFECTIVENESS: The accounting staff annually review the data records to confirm that the unaccounted for water losses stay under 6%.

CONSERVATION SAVINGS: Savings were initially estimated to be about 1300 AFY, but actual results are greater–unaccounted water losses have been reduced from 12% to about 5% per year.

BUDGET: Proposed annual budget: $XXX,XXX (from operations and maintenance budget).

DMM 4–Metering with Commodity Rates

IMPLEMENTATION DESCRIPTION: The City is fully metered for all customer sectors, including separate meters for single-family residential, commercial, large landscapes, and all institutional/governmental facilities. Since 1990, City policy has been to separately meter each dwelling unit in multi-family complexes. There are approximately 1,300 multi-family complexes, with over 7,000 dwelling units in the City. As of June 2000 all multi-family dwelling units are separately metered.

The City has an inclining multi-block rate structure, with a lifeline allotment of 24 billing units per person per year for residential customers (and other customers with permanent residential populations, such as retirement homes). A billing unit is one hundred cubic feet (748 gallons), commonly abbreviated HCF or CCF. For rate information, *see* DMM 11 or Appendix D. Under guidelines developed in 1989, the City has required irrigation meters for all large landscape customers (three or more acres), to separate outside from interior water use, and easily allow recycled water conversions. The metering was done in partnership with the City and the landowners and completed January of 1999. During water shortages, this will help develop equitable rationing allocations for non-residential customers with both interior and landscape uses.

Commercial/industrial/institutional customers are required to have fire sprinkler systems. Since 1991, the City requires residential fire sprinklers in all new single and multi-family construction. Separate meters are required on fire sprinkler systems, with associated monthly service charges. The City has also installed separate meters on all recycled water services.

IMPLEMENTATION SCHEDULE: The City will continue to install and read meters on all new services, and will continue to conduct its meter calibration and replacement program.

METHODS TO EVALUATE EFFECTIVENESS: Periodic review of customer water use, comparing current water use per capita with historic data.

CONSERVATION SAVINGS: Metered accounts may result in a 20% reduction in demand compared to non metered accounts.

BUDGET: Meter installation costs are part of new service connection fees.

DMM 5—Large Landscape Water Audits and Incentives

IMPLEMENTATION DESCRIPTION: Irrigation surveys have been conducted for 80% of the City's large landscape customers (currently defined as three acres or greater). The NACWA-sponsored Mobile Lab team conducts the surveys. During the survey, the team calculates a water budget for the

site–the amount of water necessary for that site based on the size of the landscape and the climate. The water budget is then used as the water allotment for that site, and any water use which exceeds the water budget is billed at a higher rate. City staff review landscape customers' water use monthly. If the water budget is exceeded for three consecutive months, the customer is offered technical assistance. On-site follow-up evaluations are recommended for customers whose annual water use exceeds their water budget.

The City installed a California Irrigation Management Information System (CIMIS) weather station at Westside Park in April 1992. Daily climatological data (temperatures, relative humidity, wind velocity, and precipitation) are made available on a telephone recording for the public and through the City's website. By special arrangement with the Santa Veronica Mountains Resource Conservation District, landscape managers (and agricultural customers) are instructed on the use of these data to develop irrigation schedules.

The City is now completing an inventory of landscaped areas over one acre, based on the County's and the California Department of Water Resources' Geographical Information System (GIS). The City offers Spanish/English language irrigator training classes. The City is considering a financial incentive program to encourage high water users to convert to more water efficient landscapes. Financial incentives may include: irrigation system conversions, automatic controllers, soil moisture sensors, automated CIMIS scheduling, and plants and other landscape materials. The water department continually works with the parks department and the school district to improve water use efficiency at public landscapes and greenbelts. This sometime includes the redesigning of a landscape. All City parks now have automated CIMIS-based controllers with soil moisture sensors.

IMPLEMENTATION SCHEDULE and METHODS TO EVALUATE EFFECTIVENESS: The City plans to complete the few remaining large landscape customers' water use surveys over the next five years. The City will continue to implement this DMM by annual review

of customers' water use, and by offering on-site follow-up evaluations to customers whose total water use exceeds their total annual water budget.

CONSERVATION SAVINGS: Landscapes that are upgraded based on survey recommendations could result in a 15% reduction in water demand.

BUDGET: Proposed annual budget: $XXX,XXX, for contractual support of the Mobile Lab program, and materials.

DMM 6—Landscape Water Conservation Requirements

IMPLEMENTATION DESCRIPTION: In 1992, motivated by the drought, the City established a landscape ordinance. Later, it was amended to include firescaping guidelines and to conform to California Water Code section 65590 et seq. (AB 325), which covers new and existing commercial, industrial, institutional/governmental, and multi-family customers, and includes new single-family homes.

The City continues to work in partnership with the local fire department, local nurseries, landscape designers, contractors and the local floriculture growers to help educate landowners in regards to water efficient landscapes (WEL). In cooperation with the Santa Veronica Mountains Resource Conservation District (RCD), an information pamphlet was developed to explain evapotranspiration and procedures involved in developing irrigation schedules. The City also has a very popular WEL/firescape demonstration garden.

The City has WEL at all median strips. The benefits are as listed: (1) the public can see attractive low-water using landscapes; (2) the City is demonstrating its commitment to improved efficiencies in public water uses, (3) City public works crews have improved safety records, because of reduced exposure to injury while maintaining landscaping in the median strips, and (4) there have been cost savings associated with lower water bills, reduced median strip maintenance, and fewer street and gutter repairs as a result of eliminating runoff.

IMPLEMENTATION SCHEDULE: The City has permanently incorporated this DMM into its ordinances.

METHODS TO EVALUATE EFFECTIVENESS: The City will monitor the cost savings on all city properties, the attendance to the Water Efficient Landscape (WEL) demonstration garden and the number of WEL materials distributed. The RCD will report annually on the landscape water savings associated with this DMM to the City. CONSERVATION SAVINGS: The landscape ordinance may lead to a similar 15% reduction due to landscape surveys and water budget irrigation scheduling.

BUDGET: Proposed annual budget: $XXX,XXX, for materials and contract money with the RCD.

DMM 7–Public Information

IMPLEMENTATION DESCRIPTION: The City promotes water conservation and other resource efficiencies in coordination with NACWA, NACRSD, and the energy utilities. The City distributes public information through bill inserts, brochures, community speakers, paid advertising, and many special events every year. City water bills were redesigned in 1990 to show gallons used per day for the last billing period compared to the same period the previous year (previously, the bill only indicated total billing period usage in billing units (one hundred cubit feet of water, which is 748 gallons).

The City formed a Citizens' Advisory Committee, to assist in developing new ways to communicate with the public and the media about water conservation and other resource issues. Due to high numbers of visitors into the region, it also has become a priority to develop conservation materials focused on the visitors themselves though working with restaurants and hotels. In July of 1998, the City established a World Wide Web Home Page, which includes information on water conservation, recycling, and other resource issues.

IMPLEMENTATION SCHEDULE: The City will continue to provide public information services and materials to remind the public about water and other resource issues.

METHODS TO EVALUATE EFFECTIVENESS: The City will track the commentary regarding the information provided.

CONSERVATION SAVINGS: The City has no method to quantify the savings of this DMM but believes that this program is in the public's interest.

BUDGET: Proposed annual budget: $XXX,XXX, (from public affairs office budget) for staff and materials.

DMM 8–School Education

IMPLEMENTATION DESCRIPTION: The City continues to work with NACWA and the school district to promote water conservation and other resource efficiencies at school facilities and to educate students about these issues. As part of the commercial/industrial/institutional water conservation programs, all public school toilets, urinals, showerheads, and faucet aerators have been replaced with ultra-low flow models, and a study is underway to determine cost-sharing retrofit of school kitchens with water and energy efficient icemakers and dishwashers. The City also co-funded the complete retrofit of school playground irrigation systems.

The City contracts with a consultant (a former teacher) to implement DMM 8. The City provides educational materials for several grade levels, State and County water system maps, posters, workbooks, interactive computer software, videos, tours (for example, Drake Reservoir and the surrounding watershed, water and wastewater treatment facilities), and sponsors teachers' Project Water Education for Teachers (WET) training, science fairs, and water conservation contests.

For Water Awareness Month during May 2000, school water conservation activities consisted of a "fun run," fishing contest at Drake Reservoir, and special classroom activities for all fourth grade classes in the City. The fourth grade activity consists of a home interior and exterior water survey that the students fill out with their parents' assistance. For every completed survey handed in, the students received low flow showerheads and faucet aerators to install at home. Each class with 100% home surveys completed, received a native tree to plant on the school grounds, courtesy of the New Albion Tree Foundation.

NACWA, the City, and the school district cooperatively established a high school water management/ultra-low flush toilet distribution program. Selected students attend a workshop on conservation and leadership. These students became team leaders of an ultra low flush toilet replacement program. The team leaders then recruit other students who encourage parents and neighbors to participate in the program. Toilets are made available at the High School on designated dates, and customers can install them within two weeks or request student assistance for installation. When old toilets are returned to the High School for recycling, new toilet seats are provided. The school receives $15 for each toilet installed. In 1999, these funds were used to purchase new athletic equipment and four new computers for students' use in the library. For more information on this element of this DMM, *see* DMM 16.

IMPLEMENTATION SCHEDULE: The City will continue to implement this DMM at the levels described.

METHODS TO EVALUATE EFFECTIVENESS: The City will continue to survey the institutions and educators on the number of programs, materials and attendance at water conservation activities.

CONSERVATION SAVINGS: The City has no method to quantify the savings of this DMM but believes that this program is in the public's interest.

BUDGET: Proposed annual budget: $XXX,XXX, for consultant and materials (ULF toilets are separately budgeted–*see* DMM 16).

DMM 9–Commercial and Industrial Water Conservation

IMPLEMENTATION DESCRIPTION: For the last several years, the City has provided water use audits to any commercial/industrial/institutional (CII) customer who so requested. The City recently complete a computerized analysis of all CII customers by monthly and annual water usage, to identify the top 10% of the commercial customers and the top 20% of the industrial and institutional customers. The City contacts these customers by letter, and follows up with telephone calls, to offer audits. So far, about 50 customers have been surveyed for water use efficiency. City staff reviews these customers' billing records annually.

In 1996, the City developed a billing insert which includes water survey information and continues to distributed the October 1994 DWR publication Water Efficiency Guide for Business Managers and Facility Engineers. Staff also, completed a program to identify CII customers by Standard Industrial classification (SIC) codes.

Audits are coordinated and cost-shared with NACWA, local energy utilities, the New Albion County Regional Sanitation District, and the Air Quality District, and are conducted by a consulting industrial engineer and engineering student interns from California State University New Albion.

IMPLEMENTATION SCHEDULE and CONSERVATION SAVINGS: The City will continue to implement this DMM at the annual target rate for at least the next five years. Savings evaluations are provided to the City and the customer by the consultant.

the base block, which is the same as the health and safety allotment under rationing. Large landscape and agricultural customers have individualized water budgets, billed at the first block rate. Usage above the water budget is billed at a higher block rate.

Due to adverse financial impacts during rationing, the rate structure was redesigned in 1992. A rate stabilization fund was established to provide a buffer in future shortages. New rates were adopted in 1994, with a 3% annual increase for three years. The City will conduct its next rate study in 2002. Sewer service is provided by the NACRSD, which has a flat rate for all customer types, except industrial customers, which are monitored for water quality, metered, and charged according to quality and volume of discharge.

METHODS TO EVALUATE EFFECTIVENESS: Monitor the number of violators who use water in excess of their established allotment.

CONSERVATION SAVINGS: The incentive of this DMM is to decrease the customers water costs and water use through price incentives as described above.

The expected annual water savings is YYY.

BUDGET: Proposed annual budget: $XXX,XXX for consultant (building department staff costs are separately budgeted).

TABLE 12
DMM 9 Implementation Schedule and Water Savings

Year	Surveys Completed CII	Annual Water Savings	Cumulative Water Savings
1995	0	Y, YYY	Y, YYY
1996	10	Y, YYY	Y, YYY
1997	10	Y, YYY	YY, YYY
1998	10	Y, YYY	YY, YYY
1999	10	Y, YYY	YY, YYY
2000	10	Y, YYY	YY, YYY
2001	10e	Y, YYYe	YYY, YYYe
2002	10e	Y, YYYe	YYY, YYYe
2003	10e	Y, YYYe	YYY, YYYe
2004	10e	Y, YYYe	YYY, YYYe
2005	10e	Y, YYYe	YYY, YYYe

e = estimate

METHODS TO EVALUATE EFFECTIVENESS: The City will continue to implement this DMM by annual review of customers' water use, and by offering on-site follow-up evaluations to customers whose total water use exceeds their total annual water budget.

BUDGET: Proposed annual budget: $XXX,XXX, for consultant and interns.

DMM 10–New Commercial and Industrial Water Use Review

IMPLEMENTATION DESCRIPTION: The City building department coordinates the implementation of this DMM in a committee with NACWA, NACRSD, and others. An industrial engineering consultant reviews the building plans to determine the water use efficiency before a permit is issued to the new customer.

IMPLEMENTATION SCHEDULE: The City will continue to implement this DMM.

METHODS TO EVALUATE EFFECTIVENESS: The consultant reports on all plan improvements and compares it with historical data to determine the increase in water use efficiency.

CONSERVATION SAVINGS: Commercial water reduction achieved from DMMs excluding Ultra Low Flush Toilet Replacement is estimated at 12% to 15% in gallons per employee per day.

BUDGET: Proposed annual budget: $XXX,XXX for consultant (building department staff costs are separately budgeted).

DMM 11–Conservation Pricing, Water Service and Sewer Service

IMPLEMENTATION DESCRIPTION: The City of New Albion has an inclining block rate structure for all customer sectors. Residential customers receive a lifeline allotment as

DMM 12–Landscape Water Conservation for New and Existing Single Family Homes

IMPLEMENTATION DESCRIPTION: As discussed under DMM 6, the City has a landscape ordinance which pertains to new and existing single family homes, and an active landscape conservation program. The City has a WEL/firescape demonstration garden, and works with NACWA and others to promote efficient landscaping practices. The City is also considering a financial incentive program to help homeowners convert to more water efficient landscapes (which may include landscape materials, irrigation conversions, automatic controllers, soil moisture sensors, gray water, etc.).

IMPLEMENTATION SCHEDULE: The City has permanently incorporated this DMM into its ordinances, and will continue to distribute brochures to all new service connections.

METHODS TO EVALUATE EFFECTIVENESS: Refer to DMM 1 and 6.

CONSERVATION SAVINGS: Refer to DMM 1 and 6.

BUDGET: Proposed annual budget: $XXX,XXX, for materials.

DMM 13–Water Waste Prohibition

IMPLEMENTATION DESCRIPTION: The City established a "No-Waste" ordinance in 1983, which is actively enforced. Enforcement includes the "gutter flooder" patrol, to educate customers, and if necessary, issue warnings and citations for violations. During the last drought, the City installed flow restrictors on the meters of five customers for one week. Each customer had incurred three waste-of-water violations. *See* Appendix C for the "No Waste" Ordinance and information on regulations, restrictions and enforcement.

IMPLEMENTATION SCHEDULE: The City has permanently incorporated this DMM into its ordinances.

METHODS TO EVALUATE EFFECTIVENESS: All citations and violations are reported annually. Over the period of this DMM the City has seen a reduction in the number of violations.

CONSERVATION SAVINGS: The City has no method to quantify the savings of this DMM but believes that this program is in the public's interest.

BUDGET: Enforcement costs are a part of the water department's overhead.

DMM 14–Water Conservation Coordinator

IMPLEMENTATION DESCRIPTION: The City designated a full-time water conservation coordinator in 1989. In addition, the City currently has one additional staff person (who works 70% on water conservation and 30% on curbside recycling), and part time staff who coordinates the landscape programs. The City also employs student interns from New Albion Community College and Cal State University New Albion. Also, the City contracts with consultants to implement a number of DMMs.

IMPLEMENTATION SCHEDULE: The City will continue to implement this DMM.

METHODS TO EVALUATE EFFECTIVENESS: The City will continue to survey the institutions and educators on the number of programs, materials and attendance at water conservation activities.

CONSERVATION SAVINGS: The City has no method to quantify the savings of this DMM but believes that this program is in the public's interest.

BUDGET: New Albion takes pride in setting new standards for the Water Conservation Coordinator. Proposed annual budget: $300,000 for water conservation staff costs. In addition the lead conservation coordinator receives a new Range Rover with free parking, downtown Victorian home, an unlimited City credit card, monthly hair cut with pedicure and manicure, an office with a window with a view, personal secretary, weekly therapeutic massage, a three day work week with no paperwork, private workout room with full bath, 3 months of vacation time per year and weekly lunch with the City's Mayor.

DMM 15–Financial Incentives

IMPLEMENTATION DESCRIPTION: The City and other local government agencies cost-share commercial and industrial audit costs, and may establish a loan program so that commercial/industrial/institutional customers more fully implement audit recommendations (*see* DMM 9). The City is also considering establishing incentive programs to encourage customers to convert to more water efficient landscapes (*see* DMMs 5 and 12).

The City has a very active water-recycling program, which includes a low interest loan program and other financial incentives to help appropriate customers convert from potable to recycled water. *See* the Recycled Water Section of this plan for further information.

IMPLEMENTATION SCHEDULE: The City anticipates establishing financial incentive programs for this DMM (and water recycling) during 2001–2002.

METHODS TO EVALUATE EFFECTIVENESS: Actual water use will be monitored and compared with the estimated water savings proposed in the project loan/grant applications.

CONSERVATION SAVINGS: Water conservation savings will need to be quantified on a project by project basis. This DMM will not be implemented until 2001. The City projects water savings in excess of YYYY based on the success of the City's other implemented DMMs.

BUDGET: Proposed annual budget: $XXX,XXX, for materials. An auxiliary budget request will be submitted if the City Council approves the financial incentives program.

DMM 16–Ultra-low Flush Toilet Replacement

IMPLEMENTATION DESCRIPTION: The City established a high visibility ultra-low flush toilet replacement program in 1990. Initially, City Council members' homes and City Hall were converted to ultra-low flush models, followed by student and faculty toilets (and later urinals) at New Albion High School. Initially, rebates up to $100 per toilet were offered. All public facilities in the City now have ULF toilets, urinals, showerheads, and self-closing faucets. Funding for replacement programs has come in part from the Demand Offset Program, where new development provides funds to improve the water use efficiency of existing customers. Currently, since ultra-low flush toilets have become more widely available, the City offers rebates up to $75 per toilet.

The City also helped establish the County-wide recycling policy, which directs that recycled toilets (and other locally generated waste materials such as sludge from the NACRSD treatment plant) should be used by government in its own operations. As a result, recycled toilets are used as crushed aggregate road base in both the County and City.

In coordination with NACWA and NACRSD, the City continues to offer rebates to customers, has established a direct installation program, and has provided toilets and urinals for installation at public facilities including schools, libraries, and fire department facilities. DMM 16 is also implemented in coordination with DMM 1,

DMM 2, and DMM 8. The City considers its ULFT program to be exemplary, because nearly 40% of the non-conserving toilets in the City have now been replaced with ultra-low flush models.

IMPLEMENTATION SCHEDULE: The City will continue to implement this DMM until the City's goal is met: at least 80% of all non-conserving and low-flush model toilets in the City will be replaced with ultra-low flush models.

TABLE 13
ULFT Retrofit Program

Year	No. of ULFT Retrofits
1995	#,###
1996	#,###e
1997	#,###e
1998	#,###e
1999	#,###e
2000	#,###e
2001	#,###e
2002	#,###e
2003	#,###e
2004	#,###e
2005	#,###e

e = estimate

METHODS TO EVALUATE EFFECTIVENESS: The City will calculate annual ULFT replacement program water savings to confirm the savings are within 10% of calculated retrofit-on-resale water savings, using the CUWCC MOU Exhibit 6 methodology and water savings estimates. Exhibit 6 has become an industry standard for evaluation of ULFT replacement programs.

CONSERVATION SAVINGS: Projected total annual water savings from toilet retrofits at full implementation are YYYY per year.

BUDGET: Proposed annual budget: $XXX,XXX, for materials, rebates, and administrative costs.

Agricultural Water Conservation Programs

Since the City has 20 agricultural water accounts, it participates in several countywide agricultural water conservation programs. As discussed earlier, the City makes CIMIS information available on a daily basis, contributes funding to a Mobile Lab program and the Cooperative Extension Service, and has developed water budgets and tiered pricing for each agricultural customer.

The City will consider becoming a signatory to the Memorandum of Understanding Regarding Efficient Water Management Practices by Agricultural Water Suppliers in California. The Ag. Council has a goal to advance efficient water management through voluntarily planning, implementing, and evaluating irrigation practices.

Water Shortage Contingency Plan for Catastrophic Water Supply Interruption

Law

10632 The plan shall provide an urban water shortage contingency analysis which includes each of the following elements which are within the authority of the urban water supplier:

10632(c) Actions to be undertaken by the urban water supplier to prepare for, and implement during, a catastrophic interruption of water supplies including, but not limited to, a regional power outage, an earthquake, or other disaster.

Water Shortage Emergency Response

In 1991, in accordance with the requirements of Assembly Bill 11X, the City water, fire, and emergency services departments developed a comprehensive water shortage contingency plan, which was incorporated into the City's Emergency Response Plan in early 1992. The City's plan is consistent with provisions in the County's Emergency Response Plan. Both plans contain procedures for the distribution of potable water in a disaster; these procedures are consistent with guidelines prepared by the California State Office of Emergency Services.

The County plan recommended the following: (1) the purchase of water purification equipment; (2) purchase of standby generators and auxiliary pumps; and (3) construction of emergency water conveyance and supply storage facilities. Because of this, a NACWA-wide emergency conveyance system was completed in 1994. As of June 1995, all of the crucial items have been acquired and/or constructed. Opera-

tion testing and maintenance are performed monthly on these items.

In addition, specific water-critical customers (such as hospitals, nursing facilities, schools, and a few individual customers with medical conditions dependent on continuous water availability) have been identified. Likely potable water distribution sites have been identified. Standby procurement documents have been developed for emergency bulk purchase of bottled water; standby arrangements have also been made with several local trucking firms to provide tankers to distribute potable water (certified by the California Department of Health Services for safe transportation of potable water). All existing water supply storage, treatment, and distribution, and wastewater treatment facilities are now inspected monthly.

Be assured that the City recognizes the importance of the DMMs in reducing water demand and would continue to implement the programs. Also, the City would increase media attention to the water supply situation during a shortage and would step up public water education programs, encourage property owners to apply for a landscape and interior water use survey and continue to advertise the importance of customers to install ULF plumbing fixtures.

During declared shortages, or when a shortage declaration appears imminent, the Public Works Director, who serves as chair, activates a City water shortage response team. The team includes: water, fire, planning, health, emergency services, public affairs, parks and recreation, and the Mayor's Office. The team played a major role in the preparation of this 2000-updated Urban Water Management Plan. During a declared water shortage, the City will accept applications for new building permits but will not issue permits until the shortage declaration is rescinded. An appeal process was established after several protests were brought to the City Council during 1991.

Supplemental Water Supplies

To offset future potential water shortages due to drought or disaster, the City is considering the following supplemental water supplies.

Desalination

NACWA has commissioned a study on whether to construct a seawater desalination plant. The City is participating in the discussion and analysis to determine if desalination would be cost-effective for drought water shortage mitigation and/or as an emergency water supply. Preliminary analysis indicates that since desalination remains both expensive and energy intensive, it would probably be cost effective only if the City's other water supplies were greatly reduced or not available at all. Desalinated water would probably only be made available to meet health and safety needs (one would probably not use desalination to wash a car, for instance).

Challenges include that the current water distribution system is not designed for potable water to be input at ocean level, and therefore desalination water would have to be pumped up into the service area. There are a number of potential desalination plant sites, including the proposed tertiary treatment plant site adjacent to the RTP. In the event of a major disaster, electric service could be disrupted, so desalinated water might have to be produced and distributed using diesel power. Achieving all

necessary permits, arranging funding and actual construction could be time consuming and would probably take years. Feasibility study results are expected by early 2001.

Water Transfers

See the Transfer or Exchange Opportunities section.

Long-Term Additional Water Supply Options

To meet future long-term water demand beyond 2020, the City is participating in two water supply proposals. NACWA is negotiating for additional imported water, via a proposed additional imported water aqueduct or pipeline. Although very expensive, this will help "disaster proof" the imported water system, and may also increase water supply availability.

Drake Reservoir is being evaluated for two storage enhancement options: the first, to raise Drake Dam, could increase the storage capacity from 140,000 acre-feet to 170,000 acre-feet. The second, dredging Drake, is also being evaluated. Both appear to be very expensive.

The following table summarizes the actions the water agency will take during a water supply catastrophe.

Water Shortage Contingency Ordinance/Resolution

Law

10632 The plan shall provide an urban water shortage contingency analysis which includes each of the following elements which are within the authority of the urban water supplier:

10632(h) A draft water shortage contingency resolution or ordinance.

City of New Albion Water Shortage Response

As mentioned earlier, the City adopted a "No-Waste" Ordinance in 1983, and based on rationing experience, the City has developed a Resolution to Declare a Water Shortage Emergency. The City adopted a policy in 1991 to implement a Moratorium on New Connections during declared water shortages (see Appendix C).

Stages of Action

Law

10632 The plan shall provide an urban water shortage contingency analysis which includes each of the following elements which are within the authority of the urban water supplier:

10632(a) Stages of action to be undertaken by the urban water supplier in response to water supply shortages, including up to a 50 percent reduction in water supply and an outline of specific water supply conditions which are applicable to each stage.

Rationing Stages and Reduction Goals

The City has developed a four stage rationing plan (see Table 15) to invoke during declared water shortages. The rationing plan includes voluntary and mandatory rationing, depending on the causes, severity, and anticipated duration of the water supply shortage.

TABLE 14
Preparation Actions for a Catastrophe

Examples of Actions	Check If Discussed
Determine what constitutes a proclamation of a water shortage.	X
Stretch existing water storage.	X
Obtain additional water supplies.	X
Develop alternative water supplies.	X
Determine where the funding will come from.	X
Contact and coordinate with other agencies.	X
Create an Emergency Response Team/Coordinator.	X
Create a catastrophe preparedness plan.	X
Put employees/ contractors on-call.	X
Develop methods to communicate with the public.	X
Develop methods to prepare for water quality interruptions.	X

TABLE 15
Water Rationing Stages and Reduction Goals

Shortage Condition	Stage	Customer Reduction Goal	Type of Rationing Program
Up to 15%	I	15%	Voluntary
15% – 25%	II	25%	Mandatory
25% – 35%	III	35%	Mandatory
35% – 50%	IV	50% or >	Mandatory

Priority by Use

Priorities for use of available potable water during shortages were based on input from the City Emergency Response Team, citizen groups, and legal requirements set forth in the California Water Code, Sections 350–358. Water allocations are established for all customers according to the following ranking system:

- Minimum health and safety allocations for interior residential needs (includes single-family, multi-family, hospitals and convalescent facilities, retirement and mobile home communities, and student housing, and fire fighting and public safety)

- Commercial, industrial, institutional/governmental operations (where water is used for manufacturing and for minimum health and safety allocations for employees and visitors), to maintain jobs and economic base of the community (not for landscape uses)

- Permanent agriculture (orchards, vineyards, and other commercial agriculture which would require at least five years to return to production).

- Annual agriculture (floriculture, strawberries, other truck crops)

- Existing landscaping

- New customers, proposed projects without permits when shortage declared.

Note: It is not expected that any potable water supply reductions would result in recycled water shortages. However, this may change in the future, as more customers use recycled water and if the proposed groundwater recharge project is built.

Health and Safety Requirements

Based on commonly accepted estimates of interior residential water use in the United States, Table 16 indicates per capita health and safety water requirements. In Stage I

TABLE 16
Per Capita Safety Health and Safety
Water Quantity Calculations

	Non-Conserving Fixtures		Habit Changes [1]		Conserving Fixtures [2]	
Toilets	5 flushes x 5.5 gpf	27.5	3 flushes x 5.5 gpf	16.5	5 flushes x 1.6 gpf	8.0191
Shower	5 min x 4.0 gpm	20.0	4 min x 3.0 gpm	12.0	5 min x 2.0	10.0
Washer	12.5 gpcd	12.5	11.5 gpcd	11.5	11.5 gpcd	11.5
Kitchen	4 gpcd	4.0	4 gpcd	4.0	4 gpcd	4.0
Other	4 gpcd	4.0	4 gpcd	4.0	4 gpcd	4.0
HCF per capita per year		-68.0		-48.0		-37.5
		-33.0		-23.0		-18.0

1. Reduced shower use results from shorter and reduced flow. Reduced washer use results from fuller loads.
2. Fixtures include ULF 1.6 gpf toilets, 2.0 gpm showerheads and efficient clothes washers.

shortages, customers may adjust either interior or outdoor water use (or both), in order to meet the voluntary water reduction goal.

However, under Stage II, Stage III and Stage IV mandatory rationing programs, the City has established a health and safety allotment of 68 gpcd (which translates to 33 HCF per person per year), because that amount of water is sufficient for essential interior water with no habit or plumbing fixture changes. If customers wish to change water use habits or plumbing fixtures, 68 gpcd is sufficient to provide for limited non-essential (i.e., outdoor) uses.

Stage IV mandatory rationing, which is likely to be declared only as the result of a prolonged water shortage or as a result of a disaster, would require that customers make changes in their interior water use habits (for instance, not flushing toilets unless "necessary" or taking less frequent showers).

Water Shortage Stages and Triggering Mechanisms

As the water purveyor, the City of New Albion must provide the minimum health and safety water needs of the community at all times. The water shortage response is designed to provide a minimum of 50% of normal supply during a severe or extended water shortage. The rationing program triggering levels shown below were established to ensure that this goal is met.

Rationing stages may be triggered by a shortage in one water source or a combination of sources. Although an actual shortage may occur at any time during the year, a shortage (if one occurs) is usually forecasted by the Water Department on or about April 1 each year. If it appears that it may be a dry year, the City contacts its agricultural customers in March, so that they can minimize potential financial impacts.

The City's potable water sources are groundwater, local surface, and imported. Rationing stages may be triggered by a supply shortage or by contamination in one source or a combination of sources. Because shortages overlap Stages, triggers automatically implement the more restrictive Stage. Specific criteria for triggering the City's rationing stages are shown in Table 17.

TABLE 17
Water Shortage Stages and Triggering Mechanisms

	WATER CONDITION			
	Stage I Up to 15% Reduction	Stage II 15–25% Reduction	Stage III 25–35% Reduction	Stage IV 35–50% > Reduction
Current Supply	Total supply is 85–90% of "normal." And Below "normal" year is declared	Total supply is 75–85% of "normal." Or Below "normal" year is declared	Total supply is 65–75% of "normal." Or Fourth consecutive below "normal" year is declared.	Total supply is less than 65–75% of "normal." Or Fifth consecutive below "normal" year is declared.
	Or	Or	Or	Or
Future Supply	Projected supply insufficient to provide 80% of "normal" deliveries for the next two years.	Projected supply insufficient to provide 75% of "normal" deliveries for the next two years.	Projected supply insufficient to provide 65% of "normal" deliveries for the next two years.	Projected supply insufficient to provide 50% of "normal" deliveries for the next two years.
	Or	Or	Or	Or
Groundwater	No excess groundwater pumping undertaken.	First year of excess groundwater pumping taken, must be "replaced" within four years.	Second year of excess groundwater pumping taken, must be "replaced" within four years.	No excess groundwater pumping undertaken.
	Or	Or	Or	Or
Water Quality	Contamination of 10% of water supply (exceeds primary drinking water standards)	Contamination of 20% of water supply (exceeds primary drinking water standards)	Contamination of 30% of water supply (exceeds primary drinking water standards)	Reduced groundwater pumping due to replenishment of previously pumped groundwater.
				Or
Disaster Loss				Disaster Loss

Water Allotment Methods

The City has established the following allocation method for each customer type. *See* Appendix C for sample water shortage rationing allocation method.

- Single Family Hybrid of Per-capita and Percentage Reduction
- Multifamily Hybrid of Per-capita and Percentage Reduction
- Commercial Percentage Reduction
- Industrial Percentage Reduction
- Gvt/Institutional Percentage Reduction
- Agricultural-Permanent Percentage Reduction–vary by efficiency
- Agricultural-Annual Percentage Reduction–vary by efficiency
- Recreational Percentage Reduction–vary by efficiency
- New Customers per-capita (no allocation for new landscaping during a declared water shortage.)

Based on current and projected customer demand, Appendix C indicates the water allocated to each customer type by priority and rationing stage during a declared water shortage.

Individual customer allotments are based on a five-year period. This gives the City a more accurate view of the usual water needs of each customer and provides additional flexibility in determining allotments and reviewing appeals. However, no allotment may be greater than the amount used in the most recent year of the five-year base period.

The Water Department Manager shall classify each customer and calculate each customer's allotment according to the Sample Water Rationing Allocation Method. The allotment shall reflect seasonal patterns. Each customer shall be notified of their classification and allotment by mail before the effective date of the Water Shortage Emergency. New customers will be notified at the time the application for service is made. In a disaster, prior notice of allotment may not be possible; notice will be provided by other means. Any customer may appeal the Water Department Manager's classification on the basis of use or the allotment on the basis of incorrect calculation.

Prohibitions, Consumption Reduction Methods and Penalties

Law

10632 The plan shall provide an urban water shortage contingency analysis which includes each of the following elements which are within the authority of the urban water supplier:

10632(d) Additional, mandatory prohibitions against specific water use practices during water shortages, including, but not limited to, prohibiting the use of potable water for street cleaning.

10632(e) Consumption reduction methods in the most restrictive stages. Each urban water supplier may use any type of consumption reduction methods in its water shortage contingency analysis that would reduce water use, are appropriate for its area, and have the ability to achieve a water use reduction consistent with up to a 50 percent reduction in water supply.

10632(f) Penalties or charges for excessive use, where applicable.

Mandatory Prohibitions on Water Wasting

The New Albion "No Waste" Ordinance (*see* Appendix C) includes prohibitions on various wasteful water uses such as lawn watering during mid-day hours, washing sidewalks and driveways with potable water, and allowing plumbing leaks to go uncorrected more than 24 hours after customer notification.

TABLE 18
Examples of Consumption Reduction Methods

	Stage When Method Takes Effect
Demand reduction program	All stages
Reduce pressure in water lines	
Flow restriction	IV
Restrict building permits	II, III, IV
Restrict for only priority uses	
Use prohibitions	All stages
Water shortage pricing	All stages
Per capita allotment by customer type	IV
Plumbing fixture replacement	
Voluntary rationing	I
Mandatory rationing	II, III, IV
Incentives to reduce consumption	
Education Program	All stages
Percentage reduction by customer type	II, III, IV
Other	
Other	

See Appendix C, the "No Waste" Ordinance and Moratorium on New Connections–which details the reduction methods, regarding Table 18.

Excessive Use Penalties

Any customer violating the regulations and restrictions on water use set forth in the "No Waste" Ordinance shall receive a written warning for the first such violation. Upon a second violation, the customer shall receive a written warning and the district may cause a flow-restrictor to be installed in the service. If a flow-restrictor is placed, the violator shall pay the cost of the installation and removal. Any willful violation occurring subsequent to the issuance of the second written warning shall constitute a misdemeanor and may be referred to the Albion County District Attorney's office for prosecution pursuant. If water service is disconnected, it shall be restored only upon payment of the turn-on charge fixed by the Board of Directors.

Revenue and Expenditure Impacts and Measures to Overcome Impacts

Law

10632 The plan shall provide an urban water shortage contingency analysis which includes each of the following elements which are within the authority of the urban water supplier:

10632(g) An analysis of the impacts of each of the actions and conditions described in subdivisions (a) to (f), inclusive, on the revenues and expenditures of the urban water supplier....

10632(g) [An analysis of the impacts of each of the] proposed measures to overcome those [revenue and expenditure] impacts, such as the development of reserves and rate adjustments.

All surplus revenues that the City collects are currently used to fund the Rate Stabilization Fund, conservation, recycling, and other capital improvements. The City estimated projected ranges of water sales by shortage stage to best understand the impact each level of shortage will have on projected revenues and expenditures by each shortage stage.

This analysis is undertaken first with no additional water purchases and no rate increases and then with a 25% rate increase at Stage II; 50% at Stage III, and a 100% increase at Stage IV. To cover increased expenses and decreased sales, rate increases would need to be "severe."

See Appendix D for the City's efforts to establish an Emergency Fund and a Rate Stabilization Fund.

Reduction Measuring Mechanism

Law

10632 The plan shall provide an urban water shortage contingency analysis which includes each of the following elements which are within the authority of the urban water supplier:

10632(i) A mechanism for determining actual reductions in water use pursuant to the urban water shortage contingency analysis.

Mechanism to Determine Reductions in Water Use

Under normal water supply conditions, potable water production figures are recorded daily. Totals are reported weekly to the Water Treatment Facility Supervisor. Totals are reported monthly to the Water Department Manager and incorporated into the water supply report.

During a Stage I or Stage II water shortage, daily production figures are reported to the Supervisor. The Supervisor compares the weekly production to the target weekly production to verify that the reduction goal is being met. Weekly reports are forwarded to the Water Department Manager and the Water Shortage Response Team. Monthly reports are sent to the City Council. If reduction goals are not met, the Manager will notify the City Council so that corrective action can be taken.

During a Stage III or Stage IV water shortage, the procedure listed above will be followed, with the addition of a daily production report to the Manager.

During emergency shortages, production figures are reported to the Supervisor hourly and to the Manager and the Water Shortage Response Team daily. Daily reports will also be provided to the City Council and the New Albion County Office of Emergency Services.

APPENDIX C

Senate Bill 221
Senate Bill 610

Senate Bill No. 221

CHAPTER 642

An act to amend Section 11010 of the Business and Professions Code, and to amend Section 65867.5 of, and to add Sections 66455.3 and 66473.7 to, the Government Code, relating to land use.

[Approved by Governor October 9, 2001.
Filed with Secretary of State October 9, 2001.]

LEGISLATIVE COUNSEL'S DIGEST

SB 221, Kuehl. Land use: water supplies

(1) Under the Subdivision Map Act, a legislative body of a city or county is required to deny approval of a tentative map, or a parcel map for which a tentative map is not required, if it makes any of a number of specified findings. Under the Planning and Zoning Law, a city, county, or city and county may not approve a development agreement unless the legislative body finds that the agreement is consistent with the general plan and any applicable specific plan.

This bill would prohibit approval of a tentative map, or a parcel map for which a tentative map was not required, or a development agreement for a subdivision of property of more than 500 dwelling units, except as specified, including the design of the subdivision or the type of improvement, unless the legislative body of a city

or county or the designated advisory agency provides written verification from the applicable public water system that a sufficient water supply is available or, in addition, a specified finding is made by the local agency that sufficient water supplies are, or will be, available prior to completion of the project.

By increasing the duties of local legislative bodies and local planning agencies and commissions, the bill would impose a state-mandated local program.

(2) Existing law requires any person who intends to offer subdivided lands within California for sale or lease to file with the Department of Real Estate an application for a public report consisting of a notice of intention and a completed questionnaire that includes, among other things, a true statement of the provisions, if any, that have been made for public utilities in the proposed subdivision, including water, electricity, gas, telephone, and sewerage facilities.

This bill would provide that for proposed subdivisions subject to specified requirements of the Subdivision Map Act, the true statement of the provisions that have been made for water is satisfied by submitting a copy of the written verification of the availability of a sufficient water supply, obtained pursuant to specified requirements as described in (1) above.

(3) The California Constitution requires the state to reimburse local agencies and school districts for certain costs mandated by the state. Statutory provisions establish procedures for making that reimbursement.

This bill would provide that no reimbursement is required by this act for a specified reason. The people of the State of California do enact as follows:

SECTION 1. Section 11010 of the Business and Professions Code is amended to read:

11010. (a) Except as otherwise provided pursuant to subdivision (c) or elsewhere in this chapter, any person who intends to offer subdivided lands within this state for sale or lease shall file with the Department of Real Estate an application for a public report consisting of a notice of intention and a completed questionnaire on a form prepared by the department.

(b) The notice of intention shall contain the following information about the subdivided lands and the proposed offering:

(1) The name and address of the owner.

(2) The name and address of the subdivider.

(3) The legal description and area of lands.

(4) A true statement of the condition of the title to the land, particularly including all encumbrances thereon.

237

(5) A true statement of the terms and conditions on which it is intended to dispose of the land, together with copies of any contracts intended to be used.

(6) A true statement of the provisions, if any, that have been made for public utilities in the proposed subdivision, including water, electricity, gas, telephone, and sewerage facilities. For subdivided lands that were subject to the imposition of a condition pursuant to subdivision (b) of Section 66473.7 of the Government Code, the true statement of the provisions made for water shall be satisfied by submitting a copy of the written verification of the available water supply obtained pursuant to Section 66473.7 of the Government Code.

(7) A true statement of the use or uses for which the proposed subdivision will be offered.

(8) A true statement of the provisions, if any, limiting the use or occupancy of the parcels in the subdivision.

(9) A true statement of the amount of indebtedness that is a lien upon the subdivision or any part thereof, and that was incurred to pay for the construction of any onsite or offsite improvement, or any community or recreational facility.

(10) A true statement or reasonable estimate, if applicable, of the amount of any indebtedness which has been or is proposed to be incurred by an existing or proposed special district, entity, taxing area, assessment district, or community facilities district within the boundaries of which, the subdivision, or any part thereof, is located, and that is to pay for the construction or installation of any improvement or to furnish community or recreational facilities to that subdivision, and which amounts are to be obtained by ad valorem tax or assessment, or by a special assessment or tax upon the subdivision, or any part thereof.

(11) (A) As to each school district serving the subdivision, a statement from the appropriate district that indicates the location of each high school, junior high school, and elementary school serving the subdivision, or documentation that a statement to that effect has been requested from the appropriate school district.

(B) In the event that, as of the date the notice of intention and application for issuance of a public report are otherwise deemed to be qualitatively and substantially complete pursuant to Section 11010.2, the statement described in subparagraph (A) has not been provided by any school district serving the subdivision, the person who filed the notice of intention and application for issuance of a public report immediately shall provide the department with the name, address, and telephone number of that district.

(12) The location of all existing airports, and of all proposed airports shown on the general plan of any city or county, located within two statute miles of the subdivision.

(13) A true statement, if applicable, referencing any soils or geologic report or soils and geologic reports that have been prepared specifically for the subdivision.

(14) A true statement of whether or not fill is used, or is proposed to be used in the subdivision and a statement giving the name and the location of the public agency where information concerning soil conditions in the subdivision is available.

(15) Any other information that the owner, his or her agent, or the subdivider may desire to present.

(c) The commissioner may, by regulation, or on the basis of the particular circumstances of a proposed offering, waive the requirement of the submission of a completed questionnaire if the commissioner determines that prospective purchasers or lessees of the subdivision interests to be offered will be adequately protected through the issuance of a public report based solely upon information contained in the notice of intention.

SEC. 2.   Section 65867.5 of the Government Code is amended to read:

65867.5   (a)   A development agreement is a legislative act that shall be approved by ordinance and is subject to referendum.

(b)   A development agreement shall not be approved unless the legislative body finds that the provisions of the agreement are consistent with the general plan and any applicable specific plan.

(c)   A development agreement that includes a subdivision, as defined in Section 66473.7, shall not be approved unless the agreement provides that any tentative map prepared for the subdivision will comply with the provisions of Section 66473.7.

SEC. 3.   Section 66455.3 is added to the Government Code, to read:

66455.3.   Not later than five days after a city or county has determined that a tentative map application for a proposed subdivision, as defined in Section 66473.7, is complete pursuant to Section 65943, the local agency shall send a copy of the application to any water supplier that is, or may become, a public water system, as defined in Section 10912 of the Water Code, that may supply water for the subdivision.

SEC. 4.   Section 66473.7 is added to the Government Code, to read:

66473.7. (a) For the purposes of this section, the following definitions apply:

(1) "Subdivision" means a proposed residential development of more than 500 dwelling units, except that for a public water system that has fewer than 5,000 service connections, "subdivision" means any proposed residential development that would account for an increase of 10 percent or more in the number of the public water system's existing service connections.

(2) "Sufficient water supply" means the total water supplies available during normal, single-dry, and multiple-dry years within a 20-year projection that will meet the projected demand associated with the proposed subdivision, in addition to existing and planned future uses, including, but not limited to, agricultural and industrial uses. In determining "sufficient water supply," all of the following factors shall be considered:

(A) The availability of water supplies over a historical record of at least 20 years.

(B) The applicability of an urban water shortage contingency analysis prepared pursuant to Section 10632 of the Water Code that includes actions to be undertaken by the public water system in response to water supply shortages.

(C) The reduction in water supply allocated to a specific water use sector pursuant to a resolution or ordinance adopted, or a contract entered into, by the public water system, as long as that resolution, ordinance, or contract does not conflict with Section 354 of the Water Code.

(D) The amount of water that the water supplier can reasonably rely on receiving from other water supply projects, such as conjunctive use, reclaimed water, water conservation, and water transfer, including programs identified under federal, state, and local water initiatives such as CALFED and Colorado River tentative agreements, to the extent that these water supplies meet the criteria of subdivision (d).

(3) "Public water system" means the water supplier that is, or may become as a result of servicing the subdivision included in a tentative map pursuant to subdivision (b), a public water system, as defined in Section 10912 of the Water Code, that may supply water for a subdivision.

(b) (1) The legislative body of a city or county or the advisory agency, to the extent that it is authorized by local ordinance to approve, conditionally approve, or disapprove the tentative map, shall include as a condition in any tentative map that includes a subdivision a requirement that a sufficient water supply shall be available. Proof of the availability of a sufficient water supply shall be requested by the subdivision applicant or local agency, at the discretion of the local agency, and shall be based on written verification from the applicable public water system within 90 days of a request.

(2) If the public water system fails to deliver the written verification as required by this section, the local agency or any other interested party may seek a writ of mandamus to compel the public water system to comply.

(3) If the written verification provided by the applicable public water system indicates that the public water system is unable to provide a sufficient water supply that will meet the projected demand associated with the proposed subdivision, then the local agency may make a finding, after consideration of the written verification by the applicable public water system, that additional water supplies not accounted for by the public water system are, or will be, available prior to completion of the subdivision that will satisfy the requirements of this section. This finding shall be made on the record and supported by substantial evidence.

(4) If the written verification is not provided by the public water system, notwithstanding the local agency or other interested party securing a writ of mandamus to compel compliance with this section, then the local agency may make a finding that sufficient water supplies are, or will be, available prior to completion of the subdivision that will satisfy the requirements of this section. This finding shall be made on the record and supported by substantial evidence.

(c) The applicable public water system's written verification of its ability or inability to provide a sufficient water supply that will meet the projected demand associated with the proposed subdivision as required by subdivision (b) shall be supported by substantial evidence. The substantial evidence may include, but is not limited to, any of the following:

(1) The public water system's most recently adopted urban water management plan adopted pursuant to Part 2.6 (commencing with Section 10610) of Division 6 of the Water Code.

(2) A water supply assessment that was completed pursuant to Part 2.10 (commencing with Section 10910) of Division 6 of the Water Code.

(3) Other information relating to the sufficiency of the water supply that contains analytical information that is substantially similar to the assessment required by Section 10635 of the Water Code.

(d) When the written verification pursuant to subdivision (b) relies on projected water supplies that are not currently available to the public water system, to provide a sufficient water supply to the subdivision, the written verification as to those projected water supplies shall be based on all of the following elements, to the extent each is applicable:

(1) Written contracts or other proof of valid rights to the identified water supply that identify the terms and conditions under which the water will be available to serve the proposed subdivision.

(2) Copies of a capital outlay program for financing the delivery of a sufficient water supply that has been adopted by the applicable governing body.

(3) Securing of applicable federal, state, and local permits for construction of necessary infrastructure associated with supplying a sufficient water supply.

(4) Any necessary regulatory approvals that are required in order to be able to convey or deliver a sufficient water supply to the subdivision.

(e) If there is no public water system, the local agency shall make a written finding of sufficient water supply based on the evidentiary requirements of subdivisions (c) and (d) and identify the mechanism for providing water to the subdivision.

(f) In making any findings or determinations under this section, a local agency, or designated advisory agency, may work in conjunction with the project applicant and the public water system to secure water supplies sufficient to satisfy the demands of the proposed subdivision. If the local agency secures water supplies pursuant to this subdivision, which supplies are acceptable to and approved by the governing body of the public water system as suitable for delivery to customers, it shall work in conjunction with the public water system to implement a plan to deliver that water supply to satisfy the long-term demands of the proposed subdivision.

(g) The written verification prepared under this section shall also include a description, to the extent that data is reasonably available based on published records maintained by federal and state agencies, and public records of local agencies, of the reasonably foreseeable impacts of the proposed subdivision on the availability of water resources for agricultural and industrial uses within the public water system's service area that are not currently receiving water from the public water system but are utilizing the same sources of water. To the extent that those reasonably foreseeable impacts have previously been evaluated in a document prepared pursuant to the California Environmental Quality Act (Division 13 (commencing with Section 21000) of the Public Resources Code) or the National Environmental Policy Act (Public Law 91-190) for the proposed subdivision, the public water system may utilize that information in preparing the written verification.

(h) Where a water supply for a proposed subdivision includes groundwater, the public water system serving the proposed subdivision shall evaluate, based on substantial evidence, the extent to which it or the landowner has the right to extract the additional groundwater needed to supply the proposed subdivision. Nothing in this subdivision is intended to modify state law with regard to groundwater rights.

(i) This section shall not apply to any residential project proposed for a site that is within an urbanized area and has been previously developed for urban uses, or where the immediate contiguous properties surrounding the residential project site are, or previously have been, developed for urban uses, or housing projects that are exclusively for very low and low-income households.

(j) The determinations made pursuant to this section shall be consistent with the obligation of a public water system to grant a priority for the provision of available and future water resources or services to proposed housing developments that help meet the city's or county's share of the regional housing needs for lower income households, pursuant to Section 65589.7.

(k) The County of San Diego shall be deemed to comply with this section if the Office of Planning and Research determines that all of the following conditions have been met:

(1) A regional growth management strategy that provides for a comprehensive regional strategy and a coordinated economic development and growth management program has been developed pursuant to Proposition C as approved by the voters of the County of San Diego in November 1988, which required the development of a regional growth management plan and directed the establishment of a regional planning and growth management review board.

(2) Each public water system, as defined in Section 10912 of the Water Code, within the County of San Diego has adopted an urban water management plan pursuant to Part 2.6 (commencing with Section 10610) of the Water Code.

(3) The approval or conditional approval of tentative maps for subdivisions, as defined in this section, by the County of San Diego and the cities within the county requires written communications to be made by the public water system to the city or county, in a format and with content that is substantially similar to the requirements contained in this section, with regard to the availability of a sufficient water supply, or the reliance on projected water supplies to provide a sufficient water supply, for a proposed subdivision.

(l) Nothing in this section shall preclude the legislative body of a city or county, or the designated advisory agency, at the request of the applicant, from making the determinations required in this section earlier than required pursuant to subdivision (a).

(m) Nothing in this section shall be construed to create a right or entitlement to water service or any specific level of water service.

(n) Nothing in this section is intended to change existing law concerning a public water system's obligation to provide water service to its existing customers or to any potential future customers.

(o) Any action challenging the sufficiency of the public water system's written verification of a sufficient water supply shall be governed by Section 66499.37.

SEC. 5. No reimbursement is required by this act pursuant to Section 6 of Article XIII B of the California Constitution because a local agency or school district has the authority to levy service charges, fees, or assessments sufficient to pay for the program or level of service mandated by this act, within the meaning of Section 17556 of the Government Code.

Senate Bill No. 610

CHAPTER 643

An act to amend Section 21151.9 of the Public Resources Code, and to amend Sections 10631, 10656, 10910, 10911, 10912, and 10915 of, to repeal Section 10913 of, and to add and repeal Section 10657 of, the Water Code, relating to water.

[Approved by Governor October 9, 2001. Filed with Secretary of State October 9, 2001.]

LEGISLATIVE COUNSEL'S DIGEST

SB 610, Costa. Water supply planning

(1) Existing law requires every urban water supplier to identify, as part of its urban water management plan, the existing and planned sources of water available to the supplier over a prescribed 5-year period. Existing law prohibits an urban water supplier that fails to prepare or submit its urban water management plan to the Department of Water Resources from receiving drought assistance from the state until the plan is submitted.

This bill would require additional information to be included as part of an urban water management plan if groundwater is identified as a source of water available to the supplier. The bill would require an urban water supplier to include in the plan a description of all water supply projects and programs that may be undertaken to meet total projected water use. The bill would prohibit an urban water supplier that fails to prepare or submit the plan to the department from receiving funding made available from specified bond acts until the plan is submitted. The bill, until January 1, 2006, would require the department to take into consideration whether the urban water supplier has submitted an updated plan, as specified, in determining eligibility for funds made available pursuant to any program administered by the department.

(2) Existing law, under certain circumstances, requires a city or county that determines an environmental impact report is required in connection with a project, as defined, to request each public water system that may supply water for the project to assess, among other things, whether its total projected water supplies will meet the projected water demand associated with the proposed project. Existing law requires the public water system to submit the assessment to the city or county not later than 30 days from the date on which the request was received and, in the absence of the submittal of an assessment, provides that it shall be assumed that the public water system has no information to submit. Existing law makes legislative findings and declarations concerning "Proposition C," a measure approved by the voters of San Diego County relating to regional growth management, and provides that the procedures established by a specified review board established in connection with that measure are deemed to comply with the requirements described above relating to water supply planning by a city or county.

This bill would revise those provisions. The bill, instead, would require a city or county that determines a project is subject to the California Environmental Quality Act to identify any public water system that may supply water for the project and to request those public water systems to prepare a specified water supply assessment, except as otherwise specified. The bill would require the assessment to include, among other information, an identification of existing water supply entitlements, water rights, or water service contracts relevant to the identified water supply for the proposed project and water received in prior years pursuant to those entitlements, rights, and contracts. The bill would require the city or county, if it is not able to identify any public water system that may supply water for the project, to prepare the water supply assessment after a prescribed consultation. The bill would revise the definition of "project," for the purposes of these provisions, and make related changes.

The bill would prescribe a timeframe within which a public water system is required to submit the assessment to the city or county and would authorize the city or county to seek a writ of mandamus to compel the public water system to comply with requirements relating to the submission of the assessment.

The bill would require the public water system, or the city or county, as applicable, if that entity concludes that water supplies are, or will be, insufficient, to submit the plans for acquiring additional water supplies. The bill would require the city or county to include the water supply assessment and certain other information in any environmental document prepared for the project pursuant to the act. By establishing duties for counties and cities, the bill would impose a state-mandated local program.

The bill would provide that the County of San Diego is deemed to comply with these water supply planning requirements if the Office of Planning and Research determines that certain requirements have been met in connection with the implementation of "Proposition C."

(3) The bill would incorporate additional changes in Section 10631 of the Water Code proposed by AB 901, to be operative only if this bill and AB 901 are enacted and become effective on or before January 1, 2002, each bill amends Section 10631 of the Water Code, and this bill is enacted last.

(4) The California Constitution requires the state to reimburse local agencies and school districts for certain costs mandated by the state. Statutory provisions establish procedures for making that reimbursement.

This bill would provide that no reimbursement is required by this act for a specified reason.

The people of the State of California do enact as follows:

SECTION 1. (a) The Legislature finds and declares all of the following:

(1) The length and severity of droughts in California cannot be predicted with any accuracy.

(2) There are various factors that affect the ability to ensure that adequate

water supplies are available to meet all of California's water demands, now and in the future.

(3) Because of these factors, it is not possible to guarantee a permanent water supply for all water users in California in the amounts requested.

(4) Therefore, it is critical that California's water agencies carefully assess the reliability of their water supply and delivery systems.

(5) Furthermore, California's overall water delivery system has become less reliable over the last 20 years because demand for water has continued to grow while new supplies have not been developed in amounts sufficient to meet the increased demand.

(6) There are a variety of measures for developing new water supplies including water reclamation, water conservation, conjunctive use, water transfers, seawater desalination, and surface water and groundwater storage.

(7) With increasing frequency, California's water agencies are required to impose water rationing on their residential and business customers during this state's frequent and severe periods of drought.

(8) The identification and development of water supplies needed during multiple-year droughts is vital to California's business climate, as well as to the health of the agricultural industry, environment, rural communities, and residents who continue to face the possibility of severe water cutbacks during water shortage periods.

(9) A recent study indicates that the water supply and land use planning linkage, established by Part 2.10 (commencing with Section 10910) of Division 6 of the Water Code, has not been implemented in a manner that ensures the appropriate level of communication between water agencies and planning agencies, and this act is intended to remedy that deficiency in communication.

(b) It is the intent of the Legislature to strengthen the process pursuant to which local agencies determine the adequacy of existing and planned future water supplies to meet existing and planned future demands on those water supplies.

SEC. 2. Section 21151.9 of the Public Resources Code is amended to read:

21151.9 Whenever a city or county determines that a project, as defined in Section 10912 of the Water Code, is subject to this division, it shall comply with Part 2.10 (commencing with Section 10910) of Division 6 of the Water Code.

SEC. 3. Section 10631 of the Water Code is amended to read:

10631. A plan shall be adopted in accordance with this chapter and shall do all of the following:

(a) Describe the service area of the supplier, including current and projected population, climate, and other demographic factors affecting the supplier's water management planning. The projected population estimates shall be based upon data from the state, regional, or local service agency population projections within the service area of the urban water supplier and shall be in five-year increments to 20 years or as far as data is available.

(b) Identify and quantify, to the extent practicable, the existing and planned sources of water available to the supplier over the same five-year increments as described in subdivision (a). If groundwater is identified as an existing or planned source of water available to the supplier, all of the following information shall be included in the plan:

(1) A copy of any groundwater management plan adopted by the urban water supplier, including plans adopted pursuant to Part 2.75 (commencing with Section 10750), or any other specific authorization for groundwater management.

(2) A description of any groundwater basin or basins from which the urban water supplier pumps groundwater. For those basins for which a court or the board has adjudicated the rights to pump groundwater, a copy of the order or decree adopted by the court or the board and a description of the amount of groundwater the urban water supplier has the legal right to pump under the order or decree. For basins that have not been adjudicated, information as to whether the department has identified the basin or basins as overdrafted or has projected that the basin will become overdrafted if present management conditions continue, in the most current official departmental bulletin that characterizes the condition of the groundwater basin, and a detailed description of the efforts being undertaken by the urban water supplier to eliminate the long-term overdraft condition.

(3) A detailed description and analysis of the amount and location of groundwater pumped by the urban water supplier for the past five years. The description and analysis shall be based on information that is reasonably available, including, but not limited to, historic use records.

(4) A detailed description and analysis of the location, amount, and sufficiency of groundwater that is projected to be pumped by the urban water supplier. The description and analysis shall be based on information that is reasonably available, including, but not limited to, historic use records.

(c) Describe the reliability of the water supply and vulnerability to seasonal or climatic shortage, to the extent practicable, and provide data for each of the following:

(1) An average water year.

(2) A single dry water year.

(3) Multiple dry water years.

For any water source that may not be available at a consistent level of use, given specific legal, environmental, water quality, or climatic factors, describe plans to replace that source with alternative sources or water demand management measures, to the extent practicable.

(d) Describe the opportunities for exchanges or transfers of water on a short-term or long-term basis.

(e) (1) Quantify, to the extent records are available, past and current water use, over the same five-year increments described in subdivision (a), and projected water use, identifying the uses among water use sectors, including, but not necessarily limited to, all of the following uses:

(A) Single-family residential.

(B) Multifamily.

(C) Commercial.

(D) Industrial.

(E) Institutional and governmental.

(F) Landscape.

(G) Sales to other agencies.

(H) Saline water intrusion barriers, groundwater recharge, or conjunctive use, or any combination thereof.

(I) Agricultural.

(2) The water use projections shall be in the same five-year increments as described in subdivision (a).

(f) Provide a description of the supplier's water demand management measures. This description shall include all of the following:

(1) A description of each water demand management measure that is currently being implemented, or scheduled for implementation, including the steps necessary to implement any proposed measures, including, but not limited to, all of the following:

(A) Water survey programs for single-family residential and multifamily residential customers.

(B) Residential plumbing retrofit.

(C) System water audits, leak detection, and repair.

(D) Metering with commodity rates for all new connections and retrofit of existing connections.

(E) Large landscape conservation programs and incentives.

(F) High-efficiency washing machine rebate programs.

(G) Public information programs.

(H) School education programs.

(I) Conservation programs for commercial, industrial, and institutional accounts.

(J) Wholesale agency programs.

(K) Conservation pricing.

(L) Water conservation coordinator.

(M) Water waste prohibition.

(N) Residential ultra-low-flush toilet replacement programs.

(2) A schedule of implementation for all water demand management measures proposed or described in the plan.

(3) A description of the methods, if any, that the supplier will use to evaluate the effectiveness of water demand management measures implemented or described under the plan.

(4) An estimate, if available, of existing conservation savings on water use within the supplier's service area, and the effect of such savings on the supplier's ability to further reduce demand.

(g) An evaluation of each water demand management measure listed in paragraph (1) of subdivision (f) that is not currently being implemented or scheduled for implementation. In the course of the evaluation, first consideration shall be given to water demand management measures, or combination of measures, that offer lower incremental costs than expanded or additional water supplies. This evaluation shall do all of the following:

(1) Take into account economic and noneconomic factors, including environmental, social, health, customer impact, and technological factors.

(2) Include a cost-benefit analysis, identifying total benefits and total costs.

(3) Include a description of funding available to implement any planned water supply project that would provide water at a higher unit cost.

(4) Include a description of the water supplier's legal authority to implement the measure and efforts to work with other relevant agencies to ensure the implementation of the measure and to share the cost of implementation.

(h) Include a description of all water supply projects and water supply programs that may be undertaken by the urban water supplier to meet the total projected water use as established pursuant to subdivision (a) of Section 10635. The urban water supplier shall include a detailed description of expected future projects and programs, other than the demand management programs identified pursuant to paragraph (1) of subdivision (f), that the urban water supplier may implement to increase the amount of the water supply available to the urban water supplier in average, single dry, and multiple dry water years. The description shall identify specific projects and include a description of the increase in water supply that is expected to be available from each project. The description shall include an estimate with regard to the implementation timeline for each project or program.

(i) Urban water suppliers that are members of the California Urban Water Conservation Council and submit annual reports to that council in accordance with the "Memorandum of Understanding Regarding Urban Water Conservation in California," dated September 1991, may submit the annual reports identifying water demand management measures currently being implemented, or scheduled for implementation, to satisfy the requirements of subdivisions (f) and (g).

SEC. 3.5. Section 10631 of the Water Code is amended to read:

10631. A plan shall be adopted in accordance with this chapter and shall do all of the following:

(a) Describe the service area of the supplier, including current and projected population, climate, and other demographic factors affecting the supplier's water management planning. The projected population estimates shall be based upon data from the state, regional, or local service agency population projections within the service area of the urban water supplier and shall be in five-year increments to 20 years or as far as data is available.

(b) Identify and quantify, to the extent practicable, the existing and planned sources of water available to the supplier over the same five-year increments as described in subdivision (a). If groundwater is identified as an existing or planned source of water available to the supplier, all of the following information shall be included in the plan:

(1) A copy of any groundwater management plan adopted by the urban water supplier, including plans adopted pursuant to Part 2.75 (commencing with Section 10750), or any other specific authorization for groundwater management.

(2) A description of any groundwater basin or basins from which the urban water supplier pumps groundwater. For those basins for which a court or the board has adjudicated the rights to pump groundwater, a copy of the order or decree adopted by the court or the board and a description of the amount of groundwater the urban water supplier has the legal right to pump under the order or decree. For basins that have not been adjudicated, information as to whether the department has identified the basin or basins as overdrafted or has projected that the basin will become overdrafted if present management conditions continue, in the most current official departmental bulletin that characterizes the condition of the groundwater basin, and a detailed description of the efforts being undertaken by the urban water supplier to eliminate the long-term overdraft condition.

(3) A detailed description and analysis of the location, amount, and sufficiency of groundwater pumped by the urban water supplier for the past five years. The description and analysis shall be based on information that is reasonably available, including, but not limited to, historic use records.

(4) A detailed description and analysis of the amount and location of groundwater that is projected to be pumped by the urban water supplier. The description

and analysis shall be based on information that is reasonably available, including, but not limited to, historic use records.

(c) Describe the reliability of the water supply and vulnerability to seasonal or climatic shortage, to the extent practicable, and provide data for each of the following:

(1) An average water year.

(2) A single dry water year.

(3) Multiple dry water years.

For any water source that may not be available at a consistent level of use, given specific legal, environmental, water quality, or climatic factors, describe plans to supplement or replace that source with alternative sources or water demand management measures, to the extent practicable.

(d) Describe the opportunities for exchanges or transfers of water on a short-term or long-term basis.

(e) (1) Quantify, to the extent records are available, past and current water use, over the same five-year increments described in subdivision (a), and projected water use, identifying the uses among water use sectors, including, but not necessarily limited to, all of the following uses:

(A) Single-family residential.

(B) Multifamily.

(C) Commercial.

(D) Industrial.

(E) Institutional and governmental.

(F) Landscape.

(G) Sales to other agencies.

(H) Saline water intrusion barriers, groundwater recharge, or conjunctive use, or any combination thereof.

(I) Agricultural.

(2) The water use projections shall be in the same five-year increments as described in subdivision (a).

(f) Provide a description of the supplier's water demand management measures. This description shall include all of the following:

(1) A description of each water demand management measure that is currently being implemented, or scheduled for implementation, including the steps necessary to implement any proposed measures, including, but not limited to, all of the following:

(A) Water survey programs for single-family residential and multifamily residential customers.

(B) Residential plumbing retrofit.

(C) System water audits, leak detection, and repair.

(D) Metering with commodity rates for all new connections and retrofit of existing connections.

(E) Large landscape conservation programs and incentives.

(F) High-efficiency washing machine rebate programs.

(G) Public information programs.

(H) School education programs.

(I) Conservation programs for commercial, industrial, and institutional accounts.

(J) Wholesale agency programs.

(K) Conservation pricing.

(L) Water conservation coordinator.

(M) Water waste prohibition.

(N) Residential ultra-low-flush toilet replacement programs.

(2) A schedule of implementation for all water demand management measures proposed or described in the plan.

(3) A description of the methods, if any, that the supplier will use to evaluate the effectiveness of water demand management measures implemented or described under the plan.

(4) An estimate, if available, of existing conservation savings on water use within the supplier's service area, and the effect of the savings on the supplier's ability to further reduce demand.

(g) An evaluation of each water demand management measure listed in paragraph

(1) of subdivision (f) that is not currently being implemented or scheduled for implementation. In the course of the evaluation, first consideration shall be given to water demand management measures, or combination of measures, that offer lower incremental costs than expanded or additional water supplies. This evaluation shall do all of the following:

(1) Take into account economic and noneconomic factors, including environmental, social, health, customer impact, and technological factors.

(2) Include a cost-benefit analysis, identifying total benefits and total costs.

(3) Include a description of funding available to implement any planned water supply project that would provide water at a higher unit cost.

(4) Include a description of the water supplier's legal authority to implement the measure and efforts to work with other relevant agencies to ensure the implementation of the measure and to share the cost of implementation.

(h) Include a description of all water supply projects and water supply programs that may be undertaken by the urban water supplier to meet the total projected water use as established pursuant to subdivision (a) of Section 10635. The urban water supplier shall include a detailed description of expected future projects and programs, other than the demand management programs identified pursuant to paragraph (1) of subdivision (f), that the urban water supplier may implement to increase the amount of the water supply available to the urban water supplier in average, single dry, and multiple dry water years. The description shall identify specific projects and include a description of the increase in water supply that is expected to be available from each project. The description shall include an estimate with regard to the implementation timeline for each project or program.

(i) Urban water suppliers that are members of the California Urban Water Conservation Council and submit annual reports to that council in accordance with the "Memorandum of Understanding Regarding Urban Water Conservation in California," dated September 1991, may submit the annual reports identifying water demand management measures currently being implemented, or scheduled for implementation, to satisfy the requirements of subdivisions (f) and (g).

SEC. 4. Section 10656 of the Water Code is amended to read:

10656. An urban water supplier that does not prepare, adopt, and submit its urban water management plan to the department in accordance with this part, is ineligible to receive funding pursuant to Division 24 (commencing with Section 78500) or Division 26 (commencing with Section 79000), or receive drought assistance from the state until the urban water management plan is submitted pursuant to this article.

SEC. 4.3. Section 10657 is added to the Water Code, to read:

10657. (a) The department shall take into consideration whether the urban water supplier has submitted an updated urban water management plan that is consistent with Section 10631, as amended by the act that adds this section, in determining whether the urban water supplier is eligible for funds made available pursuant to any program administered by the department.

(b) This section shall remain in effect only until January 1, 2006, and as of that date is repealed, unless a later enacted statute, that is enacted before January 1, 2006, deletes or extends that date.

SEC. 4.5. Section 10910 of the Water Code is amended to read:

10910. (a) Any city or county that determines that a project, as defined in Section 10912, is subject to the California Environmental Quality Act (Division 13 (commencing with Section 21000) of the Public Resources Code) under Section 21080 of the Public Resources Code shall comply with this part.

(b) The city or county, at the time that it determines whether an environmental impact report, a negative declaration, or a mitigated negative declaration is required for any project subject to the California Environmental Quality Act pursuant to Section 21080.1 of the Public Resources Code, shall identify any water system that is, or may become as a result of supplying water to the project identified pursuant to this subdivision, a public water system, as defined in Section 10912, that may supply water for the project. If the city or county is not able to identify any public water system that may supply water for the project, the city or county shall prepare the water assessment required by this part after consulting with any entity serving domestic water supplies whose service area includes the project site, the local agency formation commission, and any public water system adjacent to the project site.

(c) (1) The city or county, at the time it makes the determination required under Section 21080.1 of the Public Resources Code, shall request each public water system identified pursuant to subdivision (b) to determine whether the projected water demand associated with a proposed project was included as part of the most recently adopted urban water management plan adopted pursuant to Part 2.6 (commencing with Section 10610).

(2) If the projected water demand associated with the proposed project was accounted for in the most recently adopted urban water management plan, the public water system may incorporate the requested information from the urban water management plan in preparing the elements of the assessment required to comply with subdivisions (d), (e), (f), and (g).

(3) If the projected water demand associated with the proposed project was not accounted for in the most recently adopted urban water management plan, or the public water system has no urban water management plan, the water supply assessment for the project shall include a discussion with regard to whether the public water system's total projected water supplies available during normal, single dry, and multiple dry water years during a

20-year projection will meet the projected water demand associated with the proposed project, in addition to the public water system's existing and planned future uses, including agricultural and manufacturing uses.

(4) If the city or county is required to comply with this part pursuant to subdivision (b), the water supply assessment for the project shall include a discussion with regard to whether the total projected water supplies, determined to be available by the city or county for the project during normal, single dry, and multiple dry water years during a 20-year projection, will meet the projected water demand associated with the proposed project, in addition to existing and planned future uses, including agricultural and manufacturing uses.

(d) (1) The assessment required by this section shall include an identification of any existing water supply entitlements, water rights, or water service contracts relevant to the identified water supply for the proposed project, and a description of the quantities of water received in prior years by the public water system, or the city or county if either is required to comply with this part pursuant to subdivision (b), under the existing water supply entitlements, water rights, or water service contracts.

(2) An identification of existing water supply entitlements, water rights, or water service contracts held by the public water system, or the city or county if either is required to comply with this part pursuant to subdivision (b), shall be demonstrated by providing information related to all of the following:

(A) Written contracts or other proof of entitlement to an identified water supply.

(B) Copies of a capital outlay program for financing the delivery of a water supply that has been adopted by the public water system.

(C) Federal, state, and local permits for construction of necessary infrastructure associated with delivering the water supply.

(D) Any necessary regulatory approvals that are required in order to be able to convey or deliver the water supply.

(e) If no water has been received in prior years by the public water system, or the city or county if either is required to comply with this part pursuant to subdivision (b), under the existing water supply entitlements, water rights, or water service contracts, the public water system, or the city or county if either is required to comply with this part pursuant to subdivision (b), shall also include in its water supply assessment pursuant to subdivision (c), an identification of the other public water systems or water service contractholders that receive a water supply or have existing water supply entitlements, water rights, or water service contracts, to the same source of water as the public water system, or the city or county if either is required to comply with this part pursuant to subdivision (b), has identified as a source of water supply within its water supply assessments.

(f) If a water supply for a proposed project includes groundwater, the following additional information shall be included in the water supply assessment:

(1) A review of any information contained in the urban water management plan relevant to the identified water supply for the proposed project.

(2) A description of any groundwater basin or basins from which the proposed project will be supplied. For those basins for which a court or the board has adjudicated the rights to pump groundwater, a copy of the order or decree adopted by the court or the board and a description of the amount of groundwater the public water system, or the city or county if either is required to comply with this part pursuant to subdivision (b), has the legal right to pump under the order or decree. For basins that have not been adjudicated, information as to whether the department has identified the basin or basins as overdrafted or has projected that the basin will become overdrafted if present management conditions continue, in the most current bulletin of the department that characterizes the condition

of the groundwater basin, and a detailed description by the public water system, or the city or county if either is required to comply with this part pursuant to subdivision (b), of the efforts being undertaken in the basin or basins to eliminate the long-term overdraft condition.

(3) A detailed description and analysis of the amount and location of groundwater pumped by the public water system, or the city or county if either is required to comply with this part pursuant to subdivision (b), for the past five years from any groundwater basin from which the proposed project will be supplied. The description and analysis shall be based on information that is reasonably available, including, but not limited to, historic use records.

(4) A detailed description and analysis of the amount and location of groundwater that is projected to be pumped by the public water system, or the city or county if either is required to comply with this part pursuant to subdivision (b), from any basin from which the proposed project will be supplied. The description and analysis shall be based on information that is reasonably available, including, but not limited to, historic use records.

(5) An analysis of the sufficiency of the groundwater from the basin or basins from which the proposed project will be supplied to meet the projected water demand associated with the proposed project. A water supply assessment shall not be required to include the information required by this paragraph if the public water system determines, as part of the review required by paragraph (1), that the sufficiency of groundwater necessary to meet the initial and projected water demand associated with the project was addressed in the description and analysis required by paragraph (4) of subdivision (b) of Section 10631.

(g) (1) Subject to paragraph (2), the governing body of each public water system shall submit the assessment to the city or county not later than 90 days from the date on which the request was received.

The governing body of each public water system, or the city or county if either is required to comply with this act pursuant to subdivision (b), shall approve the assessment prepared pursuant to this section at a regular or special meeting.

(2) Prior to the expiration of the 90-day period, if the public water system intends to request an extension of time to prepare and adopt the assessment, the public water system shall meet with the city or county to request an extension of time, which shall not exceed 30 days, to prepare and adopt the assessment.

(3) If the public water system fails to request an extension of time, or fails to submit the assessment notwithstanding the extension of time granted pursuant to paragraph (2), the city or county may seek a writ of mandamus to compel the governing body of the public water system to comply with the requirements of this part relating to the submission of the water supply assessment.

(h) Notwithstanding any other provision of this part, if a project has been the subject of a water supply assessment that complies with the requirements of this part, no additional water supply assessment shall be required for subsequent projects that were part of a larger project for which a water supply assessment was completed and that has complied with the requirements of this part and for which the public water system, or the city or county if either is required to comply with this part pursuant to subdivision (b), has concluded that its water supplies are sufficient to meet the projected water demand associated with the proposed project, in addition to the existing and planned future uses, including, but not limited to, agricultural and industrial uses, unless one or more of the following changes occurs:

(1) Changes in the project that result in a substantial increase in water demand for the project.

(2) Changes in the circumstances or conditions substantially affecting the ability of the public water system, or the city

or county if either is required to comply with this part pursuant to subdivision (b), to provide a sufficient supply of water for the project.

(3) Significant new information becomes available which was not known and could not have been known at the time when the assessment was prepared.

SEC. 5. Section 10911 of the Water Code is amended to read:

10911. (a) If, as a result of its assessment, the public water system concludes that its water supplies are, or will be, insufficient, the public water system shall provide to the city or county its plans for acquiring additional water supplies, setting forth the measures that are being undertaken to acquire and develop those water supplies. If the city or county, if either is required to comply with this part pursuant to subdivision (b), concludes as a result of its assessment, that water supplies are, or will be, insufficient, the city or county shall include in its water supply assessment its plans for acquiring additional water supplies, setting forth the measures that are being undertaken to acquire and develop those water supplies. Those plans may include, but are not limited to, information concerning all of the following:

(1) The estimated total costs, and the proposed method of financing the costs, associated with acquiring the additional water supplies.

(2) All federal, state, and local permits, approvals, or entitlements that are anticipated to be required in order to acquire and develop the additional water supplies.

(3) Based on the considerations set forth in paragraphs (1) and (2), the estimated timeframes within which the public water system, or the city or county if either is required to comply with this part pursuant to subdivision (b), expects to be able to acquire additional water supplies.

(b) The city or county shall include the water supply assessment provided pursuant to Section 10910, and any information provided pursuant to subdivision (a), in any environmental document prepared

for the project pursuant to Division 13 (commencing with Section 21000) of the Public Resources Code.

(c) The city or county may include in any environmental document an evaluation of any information included in that environmental document provided pursuant to subdivision (b). The city or county shall determine, based on the entire record, whether projected water supplies will be sufficient to satisfy the demands of the project, in addition to existing and planned future uses. If the city or county determines that water supplies will not be sufficient, the city or county shall include that determination in its findings for the project.

SEC. 6. Section 10912 of the Water Code is amended to read:

10912. For the purposes of this part, the following terms have the following meanings:

(a) "Project" means any of the following:

(1) A proposed residential development of more than 500 dwelling units.

(2) A proposed shopping center or business establishment employing more than 1,000 persons or having more than 500,000 square feet of floor space.

(3) A proposed commercial office building employing more than 1,000 persons or having more than 250,000 square feet of floor space.

(4) A proposed hotel or motel, or both, having more than 500 rooms.

(5) A proposed industrial, manufacturing, or processing plant, or industrial park planned to house more than 1,000 persons, occupying more than 40 acres of land, or having more than 650,000 square feet of floor area.

(6) A mixed-use project that includes one or more of the projects specified in this subdivision.

(7) A project that would demand an amount of water equivalent to, or greater than, the amount of water required by a 500 dwelling unit project.

(b) If a public water system has fewer than 5,000 service connections, then "project" means any proposed residential, business, commercial, hotel or motel, or industrial development that would account for an increase of 10 percent or more in the number of the public water system's existing service connections, or a mixed-use project that would demand an amount of water equivalent to, or greater than, the amount of water required by residential development that would represent an increase of 10 percent or more in the number of the public water system's existing service connections.

(c) "Public water system" means a system for the provision of piped water to the public for human consumption that has 3000 or more service connections. A public water system includes all of the following:

(1) Any collection, treatment, storage, and distribution facility under control of the operator of the system which is used primarily in connection with the system.

(2) Any collection or pretreatment storage facility not under the control of the operator that is used primarily in connection with the system.

(3) Any person who treats water on behalf of one or more public water systems for the purpose of rendering it safe for human consumption.

SEC. 7. Section 10913 of the Water Code is repealed.

SEC. 8. Section 10915 of the Water Code is amended to read:

10915. The County of San Diego is deemed to comply with this part if the Office of Planning and Research determines that all of the following conditions have been met:

(a) Proposition C, as approved by the voters of the County of San Diego in November 1988, requires the development of a regional growth management plan and directs the establishment of a regional planning and growth management review board.

(b) The County of San Diego and the cities in the county, by agreement, designate the San Diego Association of Governments as that review board.

(c) A regional growth management strategy that provides for a comprehensive regional strategy and a coordinated economic development and growth management program has been developed pursuant to Proposition C.

(d) The regional growth management strategy includes a water element to coordinate planning for water that is consistent with the requirements of this part.

(e) The San Diego County Water Authority, by agreement with the San Diego Association of Governments in its capacity as the review board, uses the association's most recent regional growth forecasts for planning purposes and to implement the water element of the strategy.

(f) The procedures established by the review board for the development and approval of the regional growth management strategy, including the water element and any certification process established to ensure that a project is consistent with that element, comply with the requirements of this part.

(g) The environmental documents for a project located in the County of San Diego include information that accomplishes the same purposes as a water supply assessment that is prepared pursuant to Section 10910. SEC. 9. Section 3.5 of this bill incorporates amendments to Section 10631 of the Water Code proposed by both this bill and AB 901. It shall only become operative if (1) both bills are enacted and become effective on or before January 1, 2002, (2) each bill amends Section 10631 of the Water Code, and (3) this bill is enacted after AB 901, in which case Section 3 of this bill shall not become operative.

SEC. 10. No reimbursement is required by this act pursuant to Section 6 of Article XIII B of the California Constitution because a local agency or school district has the authority to levy service charges, fees, or assessments sufficient to pay for the program or level of service mandated by this act, within the meaning of Section 17556 of the Government Code.

APPENDIX D

Memorandum of Understanding Regarding Urban Water Conservation in California

As amended December 11, 2002

This appendix contains the main body of the Memorandum of Understanding Regarding Urban Water Conservation in California, as well as Exhibit 1, which demonstrates how Best Management Practices should be addressed. Since the Memorandum is updated periodically, please check the California Urban Water Conservation Council web site (www.CUWCC.org/Memorandum) for the most current and complete version.

Table of Contents

Memorandum of Understanding Regarding Urban Water Conservation in California

This Memorandum of Understanding Regarding Urban Water Conservation in California ("MOU") is made and entered into on the dates set forth below among the undersigned parties ("signatories"). The signatories represent urban water suppliers, public advocacy organizations and other interested groups as defined in Section 1 of this MOU.

AMENDED

September, 1991
February 10, 1993
March 9, 1994
September 30, 1997
April 8, 1998
December 9, 1998 (By-Laws only)
September 16, 1999
September 21, 2000
March 14, 2001
December 11, 2002
March 10, 2004

RECITALS

A. The signatories to this MOU recognize that California's economy, quality of life and environment depend in large part upon the water resources of the State. The signatories also recognize the need to provide reliable urban water supplies and to protect the environment. Increasing demands for urban, agricultural and environmental water uses

249

call for conservation and the elimination of waste as important elements in the overall management of water resources. Many organizations and groups in California have an interest in urban water conservation, and this MOU is intended to gain much needed consensus on a complex issue.

B. The urban water conservation practices included in this MOU (referred to as "Best Management Practices" or "BMPs") are intended to reduce long-term urban demands from what they would have been without implementation of these practices and are in addition to programs which may be instituted during occasional water supply shortages.

C. The combination of BMPs and urban growth, unless properly accounted for in water management planning, could make reductions in urban demands during short-term emergencies such as droughts or earthquakes more difficult to achieve. However, notwithstanding such difficulties, the signatory water suppliers will carry out the urban water conservation BMP process as described in this MOU.

D. The signatories recognize that means other than urban water conservation may be needed to provide long-term reliability for urban water suppliers and long-term protection of the environment. However, the signatories may have differing views on what additional measures might be appropriate to provide for these needs. Accordingly, this MOU is not intended to address these issues.

E. A major benefit of this MOU is to conserve water which could be used for the protection of streams, wetlands and estuaries and/or urban water supply reliability. This MOU leaves to other forums the issue of how conserved water will be used.

F. It is the intent of this MOU that individual signatory water suppliers (1) develop comprehensive conservation BMP programs using sound economic criteria and (2) consider water conservation on an equal basis with other water management options.

G. It is recognized that present urban water use throughout the State varies according to many factors including, but not limited to, climate, types of housing and landscaping, amounts and kinds of commercial, industrial and recreational development, and the ex-

tent to which conservation measures have already been implemented. It is further recognized that many of the BMPs identified in Exhibit 1 to this MOU have already been implemented in some areas and that even with broader employment of BMPs, future urban water use will continue to vary from area to area. Therefore, this MOU is not intended to establish uniform per capita water use allotments throughout the urban areas of the State. This MOU is also not intended to limit the amount or types of conservation a water supplier can pursue or to limit a water supplier's more rapid implementation of BMPs.

H. It is recognized that projections of future water demand should include estimates of anticipated demand reductions due to changes in the real price of water.

TERMS

Section 1. Definitions

For purposes of this MOU, the following definitions apply:

1.1 **Best Management Practices.** A Best Management Practice ("BMP") means a policy, program, practice, rule, regulation or ordinance or the use of devices, equipment or facilities which meets either of the following criteria:

(a) An established and generally accepted practice among water suppliers that results in more efficient use or conservation of water;

(b) A practice for which sufficient data are available from existing water conservation projects to indicate that significant conservation or conservation related benefits can be achieved; that the practice is technically and economically reasonable and not environmentally or socially unacceptable; and that the practice is not otherwise unreasonable for most water suppliers to carry out.

Although the term "Best Management Practices" has been used in various statutes and regulations, the definitions and interpretations of that term in those statutes and regulations do not apply to this MOU. The term "Best Management Practices" or "BMPs" has an independent and special meaning in this MOU and is to be applied for purposes of this MOU only as defined above.

1.2 **Implementation.** "Implementation" means achieving and maintaining the staffing, funding, and in general, the priority levels necessary to achieve the level of activity called for in the descriptions of the various BMPs and to satisfy the commitment by the signatories to use good faith efforts to optimize savings from implementing BMPs as described in Section 4.4 of this MOU. Section B of Exhibit 1 to this MOU establishes the schedule for initial implementation of BMPs.

1.3 **Signatory Groups.** For purposes of this MOU, signatories will be divided into three groups as follows:

(a) Group 1 will consist of water suppliers. A "water supplier" is defined as any entity, including a city, which delivers or supplies water for urban use at the wholesale or retail level.

(b) Group 2 will consist of public advocacy organizations. A "public advocacy organization" is defined as a non profit organization:

(i) whose primary function is not the representation of trade, industrial, or utility entities, and

(ii) whose prime mission is the protection of the environment or who has a clear interest in advancing the BMP process.

(c) Group 3 will consist of other interested groups. "Other interested groups" is defined as any other group which does not fall into one of the two groups above.

1.4 **California Urban Water Conservation Council.** The California Urban Water Conservation Council or "Council" will have responsibility for monitoring the implementation of this MOU and will be comprised of signatories to this MOU grouped according to the definitions in Section 1.3 above. The duties of the Council are set forth in Section 6 and in Exhibit 2 to this MOU.

Section 2. Purposes

2.1 This MOU has two primary purposes:

(1) to expedite implementation of reasonable water conservation measures in urban areas; and

(2) pursuant to Section 5 of this MOU, to establish assumptions for use in calculating estimates of reliable future water

conservation savings resulting from proven and reasonable conservation measures. Estimates of reliable savings are the water conservation savings which can be achieved with a high degree of confidence in a given service area. The signatories have agreed upon the initial assumptions to be used in calculating estimates of reliable savings. These assumptions are included in Exhibit 1 to this MOU. It is probable that average savings achieved by water suppliers will exceed the estimates of reliable savings.

Section 3. Limits to Applicability of MOU

3.1 **Relationship Between Water Suppliers.** No rights, obligations or authorities between wholesale suppliers, retail agencies, cities or other water suppliers are created or expanded by this MOU. Moreover, wholesale water suppliers are not obligated to implement BMPs at the retail customer level except within their own retail service area, if any.

3.2 **Agriculture.** This MOU is intended to apply only to the delivery of water for domestic, municipal and industrial uses. This MOU is not intended to apply directly or indirectly to the use of water for irrigated agriculture.

3.3 **Reclamation.** The signatory water suppliers support the reclamation and reuse of wastewater wherever technically and economically reasonable and not environmentally or socially unacceptable, and agree to prepare feasibility studies on water reclamation for their respective service areas. However, this MOU does not apply to that aspect of water management, except where the use of reclaimed water may otherwise qualify as a BMP as defined above.

3.4 **Land Use Planning.** This MOU does not deal with the question of growth management. However, each signatory water supplier will inform all relevant land planning agencies at least annually of the impacts that planning decisions involving projected growth would have upon the reliability of its water supplies for the water supplier's service area and other areas being considered for annexation.

3.5 **Use of Conserved Water.** A major benefit of this MOU is to conserve water which could be used for the protection of streams, wetlands and estuaries and/or urban water supply reliability. This MOU leaves to other forums the issue of how conserved water will be used.

Section 4. Implementation of Best Management Practices

4.1 **The Best Management Practices List, Schedule of Implementation and Assumptions.** Exhibit 1 to this MOU contains:

(a) In Section A: A list identifying those practices which the signatories believe presently meet the definition of a BMP as set forth in Section 1.1 of this MOU.

(b) In Section B: A schedule for implementing the BMPs to be followed by signatory water suppliers unless exempted under Section 4.5 of this MOU or an alternative schedule is prepared pursuant to Section 4.6 of this MOU.

(c) In Section C: Coverage requirements for implementing BMPs. Coverage requirements are the expected level of implementation necessary to achieve full implementation of BMPs. Coverage requirements may be expressed either in terms of activity levels by water suppliers or as water savings achieved.

(d) In Section D: Reporting Requirements for Documenting BMP Implementation. These requirements vary by BMP, are considered the minimum record keeping and reporting requirements for water suppliers to document BMP implementation levels, and will provide the basic data used evaluate BMP implementation progress by water suppliers.

(e) In Section E: Criteria to determine BMP implementation status of water suppliers. These criteria will be used to evaluate BMP implementation progress. Evaluation criteria vary by BMP, and are derived from the implementation guidelines and schedules presented in Sections A, B, and C.

(f) In Section F: Assumptions for use in developing estimates of reliable savings from the implementation of BMPs. Estimates of reliable savings are the water conservation savings which can be achieved with a high degree of confidence in a given service area. The estimate of reliable savings for each BMP depends upon the nature of the BMP and upon the amount of data available to evaluate potential savings. For some BMPs (e.g., public information) estimates of reliable savings may never be generated. For others, additional data may lead to significant changes in the estimate of reliable savings. It is probable that average savings achieved by water suppliers will exceed the estimates of reliable savings.

(g) In Section G: A list of "Potential Best Management Practices" ("PBMPs"). PBMPs are possible conservation practices which have not been promoted to the BMP list.

4.2 **Initial BMPs, PBMPs, Schedules, and Estimates of Reliable Savings.** The initial position of conservation practices on the BMP and PBMP lists, the initial schedule of implementation and study for the BMP list, the initial schedule of study for the PBMP list, and the initial estimates of reliable savings represent compromises by the signatories to move the process forward both for purposes of the present Bay/Delta proceedings as defined in Section 5 and to promote water conservation generally. The signatories agree that as more and better data are collected in the future, the lists, the schedules, and the estimates of reliable savings will be refined and revised based upon the most objective criteria available. However, the signatories agree that the measures included as initial BMPs in Section A of Exhibit 1 are economically justified on a statewide basis.

4.3 **Future Revision of BMPs, PBMPs, Schedules, and Estimates of Reliable Savings.** After the beginning of the initial term of the MOU as provided in Section 7.1, the California Urban Water Conservation Council ("Council") will, pursuant to Section 6 of this MOU and Exhibit 2, alter the composition of the BMP and PBMP lists, redefine individual BMPs, alter the schedules of implementation, and update the assumptions of reliable savings as more data becomes available. This dynamic BMP assessment process includes the following specific commitments:

(a) The assumptions of reliable savings will be updated at least every 3 years.

(b) The economic reasonableness of a BMP or PBMP will be assessed by the Council using the economic principles in Sections 3 and 4 of Exhibit 3.

(c) A BMP will be removed from the BMP list if, after review of data developed during implementation, the Council determines that the BMP cannot be made economically reasonable or determines that the BMP otherwise fails to conform to the definition of BMPs in Section 1.1.

(c) A PBMP will be moved to the BMP list and assigned a schedule of implementation if, after review of data developed during research, and/or demonstration projects, the Council determines that the PBMP is economically reasonable and otherwise conforms to the definition of BMPs in Section 1.1.

[Note: In 1997, the Council substantially revised the BMP list, definitions, and schedules contained in Exhibit 1. These revisions were adopted by the Council September 30, 1997.].

4.4 **Good Faith Effort.** While specific BMPs and results may differ because of varying local conditions among the areas served by the signatory water suppliers, a good faith effort to implement BMPs will be required of all signatory water suppliers. The following are included within the meaning of "good faith effort to implement BMPs":

(a) The proactive use by a signatory water supplier of legal authorities and administrative prerogatives available to the water supplier as necessary and reasonable for the implementation of BMPs.

(b) Where implementation of a particular BMP is not within the legal authority of a signatory water supplier, encouraging timely implementation of the BMP by other entities that have the legal authority to carry out the BMP within that water supplier's service area pursuant to existing legal authority. This encouragement may include, but is not limited to, financial incentives as appropriate.

(c) Cooperating with and encouraging cooperation between other water suppliers and other relevant entities whenever possible and within existing legal authority to promote the implementation of BMPS.

(d) Optimizing savings from implementing BMPs.

(e) For each signatory water supplier and all signatory public advocacy organizations, encouraging the removal of institu-tional barriers to the implementation of BMPs within that water supplier's service area. Examples of good faith efforts to remove institutional barriers include formal presentations and/or written requests to entities requesting approval of, or amendment to, local ordinances, administrative policies or legislation which will promote BMP implementation.

4.5 **Exemptions.** A signatory water supplier will be exempt from the implementation of specific BMPs for as long as the supplier substantiates each reporting period that based upon then prevailing local conditions, one or more of the following findings applies:

(a) A full cost-benefit analysis, performed in accordance with the principles set forth in Exhibit 3, demonstrates that either the program (i) would not be cost-effective overall when total program benefits and costs are considered; OR (ii) would not be cost-effective to the individual water supplier even after the water supplier has made a good faith effort to share costs with other program beneficiaries.

(b) Adequate funds are not and cannot reasonably be made available from sources accessible to the water supplier including funds from other entities. However, this exemption cannot be used if a new, less cost-effective water management option would be implemented instead of the BMP for which the water supplier is seeking this exemption.

(c) Implementation of the BMP is (i) not within the legal authority of the water supplier; and (ii) the water supplier has made a good faith effort to work with other entities that have the legal authority to carry out the BMP; and (iii) the water supplier has made a good faith effort to work with other relevant entities to encourage the removal of institutional barriers to the implementation of BMPs within its service area.

Signatory water suppliers shall submit exemptions to the Council within two months following the start of the reporting period for which the exemptions are being claimed.

4.6 **Schedule of Implementation.** The schedule of implementation for BMPs is set forth in Section B of Exhibit 1 to this MOU. However, it is recognized by the signatories that deviations from this schedule by water sup-pliers may be necessary. Therefore, a water supplier may modify, to the minimum extent necessary, the schedule for implementation of BMPs if the water supplier substantiates one or more of the following findings:

(a) That after a good faith effort to implement the BMP within the time prescribed, implementation is not feasible pursuant to the schedule. However, implementation of this BMP is still required as soon as feasible within the initial term of this MOU as defined in Section 7.1.

(b) That implementation of one or more BMPs prior to other BMPs will have a more positive effect on conservation or water supplies than will adherence to the schedule.

(c) That implementation of one or more Potential BMPs or other conservation measures prior to one or more BMPs will have a more positive effect on conservation or water supplies than will adherence to the schedule.

Section 5.   Bay/Delta Proceedings

[Note: The following section was adopted with the initial MOU and has been retained in subsequent revisions. The "present proceedings" refers to the State Water Resources Control Board water rights process then underway to implement new Bay-Delta flow and export standards. As of the date this note was adopted (April 8, 1998), proceedings to implement updated standards are still underway. Therefore, the joint recommendations of the signatories to the SWRCB contained in this letter continue to apply.]

5.1 **Use of MOU for Bay/Delta Proceedings.** The BMPs, the estimates of reliable savings and the processes established by this MOU are agreed to by the signatories for purposes of the present proceedings on the San Francisco Bay/Sacramento-San Joaquin Delta Estuary ("Bay/Delta") and in order to move the water conservation process forward. "Present Bay/Delta proceedings" is intended to mean those Bay/Delta proceedings presently underway and those conducted until a final water rights decision is reached by the State Water Resources Control Board ("State Board"). The willingness of the signatories to enter into this MOU for purposes of the present Bay/ Delta proceedings in no way limits the signatories' ability to propose different conservation practices, different estimates of savings, or different processes in a forum other than the present Bay/Delta proceedings, or for non-urban water suppliers or for other water management issues. By signing this MOU, public advocacy organization signatories are not agreeing to use the initial assumptions of reliable conservation savings in proceedings other than the present Bay/Delta proceedings. The signatories may present other assumptions of reliable conservation savings for non-signatory water suppliers in the present Bay/Delta proceedings, provided that such assumptions could not have adverse impacts upon the water supplies of any signatory water supplier. Furthermore, the signatories retain the right to advocate any particular level of protection for the Bay/Delta Estuary, including levels of freshwater flows, and do not necessarily agree on population projections for California. This MOU is not intended to address any authority or obligation of the State Board to establish freshwater flow protections or set water quality objectives for the Estuary, or to address any authority of the Environmental Protection Agency.

5.2 **Recommendations for Bay/Delta Proceedings.** The signatories will make the following recommendations to the State Board in conjunction with the present Bay/Delta proceedings and to the EPA to the extent the EPA concerns itself with the proceedings:

(a) That for purposes of the present Bay/Delta proceedings, implementation of the BMP process set forth in this MOU represents a sufficient long-term water conservation program by the signatory water suppliers, recognizing that additional programs may be required during occasional water supply shortages;

(b) That for purposes of the present Bay/Delta proceedings only, the State Board and EPA should base their estimates of future urban water conservation savings on the implementation of all of the BMPs included in Section A of Exhibit 1 to this MOU for the entire service area of the signatory water suppliers and only on those BMPs, except for (I) the conservation potential for water supplied by urban agencies for agricultural purposes, or (ii) in cases where higher levels of conservation have been mandated.

(c) That for the purposes of the present Bay/Delta proceedings, the State Board and EPA should make their estimates of future urban water conservation savings by employing the reliable savings assumptions associated with those BMPs set forth in Section C of Exhibit 1 to this MOU;

(d) That the State Board should include a policy statement in the water rights phase of the Bay/Delta proceedings supporting the BMP process described in this MOU and that the BMP process should be considered in any documents prepared by the State Board pursuant to the California Environmental Quality Act as part of the present Bay/Delta proceedings.

5.3 **Letter to State Board.** Within 30 days of signing this MOU, each signatory will jointly or individually convey the principles set forth in Sections 5.1 and 5.2 above by sending a letter to the State Board, copied to the EPA, in the form attached to this MOU as Exhibit 4.

5.4 **Withdrawal from MOU.** If during the present Bay/Delta proceedings, the State Board or EPA uses future urban water conservation savings that are inconsistent with the use of BMPs as provided in this MOU, any signatory shall have the right to withdraw from the MOU by providing written notice to the Council as described in Section 7.4(a)(I) below.

Section 6. California Urban Water Conservation Coucil

6.1 **Organization.** The California Urban Water Conservation Council ("Council") will be comprised of all signatories to this MOU grouped according to the definition in Section 1. The signatories agree to the necessary organization and duties of the Council as specified in Exhibit 2 to this MOU. Within 30 days of the effective date of this MOU, the Council will hold its first meeting.

6.2 **BMP Implementation Reports.** The signatory water suppliers will submit standardized reports every other year to the Council providing sufficient information to inform the Council on the progress being made towards implementing the BMP process. The Council will make annual reports to the State Board. An outline for the Council's annual report to the State Board is attached as Exhibit 5 to this MOU.

Section 7. General Provisions

7.1 **Initial Term of MOU.** The initial term of this MOU shall be for a period of 10 years. This initial term shall commence on September 1, 1991.

7.2 **Signatories.** Signatories shall consist of three groups: water suppliers, public advocacy organizations and other interested groups, arranged according to the definition in Section 1.3. Such arrangement will be made by a Council membership committee comprised of three representatives from the water suppliers' group and three representatives from the public advocacy organizations' group.

7.3 **Renewal of MOU.** The MOU shall be automatically renewed after the initial term of 10 years on an annual basis as to all signatories unless a signatory withdraws as described below in Section 7.4.

7.4 **Withdrawal from MOU.** Signatories to the MOU may withdraw from the MOU in three separate ways as described in sections (a), (b) and 8 below.

(a) Withdrawal prior to expiration of initial term. Before the expiration of the initial term of 10 years, a signatory may withdraw by providing written notice to the Council declaring its intent to withdraw. This written notice must include a substantiated finding that one of the two provisions (i) or (ii) below applies:

(i) During the present Bay/Delta proceedings, the State Board or EPA used future urban water conservation savings that are inconsistent with the use of BMPs as provided in this MOU; OR

(ii) After a period of 5 years from the commencement of the initial term of the MOU:

(1) Specific signatory water suppliers representing more than 10 percent of the population included within the combined service areas of the signatory water suppliers have failed to act in good faith pursuant to Section 4.4 of the MOU; and

(2) The signatory wishing to withdraw has attached findings to its past two annual reports to the Council beginning no earlier than the fourth annual report identifying these same signatory water suppliers

and giving evidence based upon the information required to be submitted in the annual reports to the Council to support the allegations of failure to act in good faith; and

(3) The State Board has failed to require conservation efforts by the specific water suppliers adequate to satisfy the requirements of this MOU, and

(4) Discussions between the signatory wishing to withdraw and the specific signatories named have failed to satisfy the objections of the signatory wishing to withdraw.

After a signatory declares an intent to withdraw under Section 7.4(a), the MOU shall remain in effect as to that signatory for 180 days.

(b) Withdrawal after expiration of initial term. After the initial term of 10 years, any signatory may declare its intent to withdraw from the MOU unconditionally by providing written notice to the Council. After a signatory has declared its intent to withdraw as provided in this section, the MOU will remain in effect as to that signatory for 180 days.

(c) Immediate withdrawal. Any signatory who does not sign a modification to the MOU requiring a 2/3 vote as described in Exhibit 2 of this MOU may withdraw from the MOU by providing written notice to the Council. The withdrawing signatory's duties under this MOU will be terminated effective immediately upon providing such written notice.

If a signatory withdraws from the MOU under any of the above methods, the MOU shall remain in effect as to all other signatories.

7.5 **Additional Parties.** Additional parties may sign the MOU after September 1, 1991 by providing written notice to and upon approval by the Council. Additional parties will be assigned by the Council to one of the three signatory groups defined in Section 1.3 before entry into the Council. All additional signatory water suppliers shall be subject to the schedule of implementation provided in Exhibit 1.

7.6 **Legal Authority.** Nothing in this MOU is intended to give any signatory, agency, entity or organization expansion of any existing authority. No organization formed pursuant to this MOU has authority beyond that specified in this MOU.

7.7 **Non-Contractual Agreement.** This MOU is intended to embody general principles agreed upon between and among the signatories and is not intended to create contractual relationships, rights, obligations, duties or remedies in a court of law between or among the signatories.

7.8 **Modifications.** The signatories agree that this writing constitutes the entire understanding between and among the signatories. The general manager, chief executive officer or executive director of each signatory or their designee shall have the authority to vote on any modifications to this MOU and its exhibits. Any modifications to the MOU itself and to its exhibits shall be made by the Council as described in Exhibit 2.

Exhibit 1   BMP Definitions, Schedules and Requirements

This Exhibit contains Best Management Practices (BMPs) that signatory water suppliers commit to implementing. Suppliers' water needs estimates will be adjusted to reflect estimates of reliable savings from this category of BMPs. For some BMPs, no estimate of savings is made.

It is recognized by all parties that a single implementation method for a BMP would not be appropriate for all water suppliers. In fact, it is likely that as the process moves forward, water suppliers will find new implementation methods even more effective than those described. Any implementation method used should be at least as effective as the methods described below.

Best Management Practices will be implemented by signatory water suppliers according to the schedule set forth in Section B of each BMP's definition. These schedules set forth the latest dates by which implementation of BMPs will be underway. It is recognized that some signatories are already implementing some BMPs, and that these schedules do not prohibit signatories from implementing BMPs sooner than required.

"Implementation" means achieving and maintaining the staffing, funding, and in general, the priority levels necessary to achieve the level of activity called for in Section A of each BMP's definition, and to satisfy the commitment by the signatories to use good faith efforts to optimize savings from implementing BMPs as described in Section 4.4 of the MOU. BMPs will be implemented at a level of effort projected to achieve at least the coverages specified in Section C of each BMP's definition, and in accordance with each BMP's implementation schedule.

Section D of each BMP definition contains the minimum record keeping and reporting requirements for agencies to document BMP implementation levels and efforts, and will be used to guide Council development of BMP implementation report forms and database. The evaluation criteria presented in Section E of each BMP definition shall be used to evaluate compliance with the implementation definitions, schedules, and coverage requirements specified in Sections A, B, and C of each BMP definition.

Section F of each BMP definition contains the assumptions of reliable savings to be used in accordance with Sections 5.1 and 5.2 of the MOU.

1.   Water Survey Programs for Single-Family Residential and Multi-Family Residential Customers

A.   Implementation

Implementation shall consist of at least the following actions:

a)   Develop and implement a strategy targeting and marketing water use surveys to single-family residential and multi-family residential customers.

b)   Directly contact via letter or telephone not less than 20% of single-family residential customers and 20% of multi-family residential customers each reporting period.

c)   Surveys shall include indoor and outdoor components, and at minimum shall have the following elements:

Indoor

i)   Check for leaks, including toilets, faucets, and meter check

ii)   Check showerhead flow rates, aerator flow rates, and offer to replace or recommend replacement, as necessary

iii)   Check toilet flow rates and offer to install or recommend installation of displacement device or direct customer to

ULFT replacement program, as necessary; replace leaking toilet flapper, as necessary

Outdoor

iv) Check irrigation system and timers

v) Review or develop customer irrigation schedule

Recommended but not required

vi) Measure currently landscaped area

vii) Measure total irrigable area

d) Provide customer with evaluation results and water saving recommendations; leave information packet with customer.

e) Track surveys offered, surveys completed, survey results, and survey costs.

B. Implementation Schedule

a) Agencies signing the MOU prior to December 31, 1997, implementation shall commence no later than July 1, 1998.

b) Agencies signing the MOU or becoming subject to the MOU after December 31, 1997, implementation shall commence no later than July 1 of the year following the year the agency signed or became subject to the MOU.

c) Agencies shall develop and implement a strategy targeting and marketing water use surveys to single-family residential and multi-family residential customers by the end of the first reporting period following the date implementation was to commence.

d) The coverage requirement for this BMP, as specified in Section C of this Exhibit, shall be realized within 10 years of the date implementation was to commence.

C. Coverage Requirements

a) Not less than 15% of single-family residential accounts to receive water use surveys within 10 years of the date implementation was to commence. For the purposes of calculating coverage, 15% of single-family residential accounts means the number of accounts equal to 15% of single-family accounts in 1997 or the year the agency signed the MOU, whichever is later.

b) Not less than 15% of multi-family residential units to receive water use surveys within 10 years of the date implementation was to commence. For the purposes of cal-

culating coverage, 15% of multi-family residential units means the number of units equal to 15% of multi-family units in 1997 or the year the agency signed the MOU, whichever is later.

D. Requirements for Documenting BMP Implementation

a) Number of single-family residential accounts in service area.

b) Number of multi-family residential accounts in service area.

c) Number of single-family residential surveys offered during reporting period.

d) Number of single-family residential surveys completed during reporting period.

e) Number of multi-family residential surveys offered during reporting period.

f) Number of multi-family residential surveys completed during reporting period.

E. Criteria to Determine BMP Implementation Status

a) Agency has developed and implemented a strategy targeting and marketing water use surveys to single-family residential and multi-family residential customers by the end of the first reporting period following the date implementation was to commence.

b) Agency has directly contacted not less than 20% of single-family residential accounts and 20% of multi-family residential units during period being reported.

c) Agency is on schedule to complete surveys for 15% of single-family residential accounts and 15% of multi-family units within 10 years of the date implementation was to commence. Agencies will receive credit against the coverage requirement for previously completed residential water use surveys according to the following schedule:[1]

---

1. In its study "What is the Reliable Yield from Residential Home Water Survey Programs: The Experience of LADWP" (AWWA Conf. Proceedings, 1995), A & N Technical Services, Inc., found that the average level of savings from home water surveys decreased over time, reaching about 50% of initial yield by the fourth year following the survey, on average. The above decay schedule used for crediting past surveys utilizes these findings to recognize and account for the limited persistence of water savings over time from home water use surveys.

	% Credit
Before 1990	0.0%
1990	12.5%
1991	25.0%
1992	37.5%
1993	50.0%
1994	62.5%
1995	75.0%
1996	87.5%
1997	100.0%

d) Agencies will be considered on track if the percent of single-family accounts and the percent of multi-family accounts receiving water use surveys equals or exceeds the following: 1.5% by end of first reporting period following date implementation to commence; 3.6% by end of second reporting period; 6.3% by end of third reporting period; 9.6% by end of fourth reporting period; and 13.5% by end of fifth reporting period.

E. Water Savings Assumptions

	Pre-1980 Construction	Post-1980 Construction
Low-flow showerhead retrofit	7.2 gcd	2.9 gcd
Toilet retrofit (five year life)	1.3 gcd	0.0 gcd
Leak repair	0.5 gcd	0.5 gcd
Landscape survey (outdoor use reduction)	10%	10%

2. Residential Plumbing Retrofit

A. Implementation

Implementation shall consist of at least the following actions:

a) Identify single-family and multi-family residences constructed prior to 1992. Develop a targeting and marketing strategy to distribute or directly install high-quality, low-flow showerheads (rated 2.5 gpm or less), toilet displacement devices (as needed), toilet flappers (as needed) and faucet aerators (rated 2.2 gpm or less) as practical to residences requiring them.

b) Maintain distribution and/or direct installation programs so that devices are distributed to not less than 10% of single-family connections and multi-family units each reporting period, or require through enforceable ordinance the replacement of high-flow showerheads and other water using fixtures with their low-flow counterparts, until it can be demonstrated in accordance with Section E of this Exhibit that 75% of single-family residences and 75% of multi-family units are fitted with high-quality, low-flow showerheads.

e) Track the type and number of retrofits completed, devices distributed, and program costs.

B. Implementation Schedule

a) Agencies signing the MOU prior to December 31, 1997, implementation shall commence no later than July 1, 1998.

b) Agencies signing the MOU or becoming subject to the MOU after December 31, 1997, implementation shall commence no later than July 1 of the year following the year the agency signed or became subject to the MOU.

c) Agencies shall develop and implement a strategy targeting the distribution and/or installation of high-quality, low-flow plumbing devices to single-family residential and multi-family residential customers by the end of the first reporting period following the date implementation was to commence.

d) An agency may elect to discontinue its device distribution programs without filing a formal budget or cost-effectiveness exemption when it can demonstrate that 75% of its single-family residences and 75% of its multi-family units constructed prior to 1992 are fitted with high-quality, low-flow showerheads.

C. Coverage Requirements

a) Plumbing device distribution and installation programs to be maintained at a level sufficient to distribute high-quality, low-flow showerheads to not less than 10% of single-family residences and 10% of multi-family units constructed prior to 1992 each reporting period; or the enactment of an enforceable ordinance requiring the replacement of high-flow showerheads and other water use fixtures with their low-flow counterparts.

b) Plumbing device distribution and installation programs to be operated until it can be demonstrated in accordance with Section E of this Exhibit that 75% of single-family residences and 75% of multi-family units are fitted with high-quality, low-flow showerheads.

D. Requirements for Documenting BMP Implementation

a) The target population of pre-1992 single-family residences and multi-family units to be provided showerheads and other water saving devices.

b) The number of showerhead retrofit kits distributed during previous reporting period.

c) The number of device retrofits completed during the previous reporting period.

d) The estimated percentage of pre-1992 single-family residences and multi-family units in service area fitted with low-flow showerheads.

E. Criteria to Determine BMP Implementation Status

a) Agency has developed and implemented a strategy targeting and marketing water use surveys to single-family residential and multi-family residential customers by the end of the first reporting period following the date implementation was to commence.

b) Agency has tracked the type and number of retrofits completed, devices distributed, and program costs.

c) Agency EITHER

i) has distributed or directly installed high-quality, low-flow showerheads and other low-flow plumbing devices to not less than 10% of single-family residences and 10% of multi-family units constructed prior to 1992 during the reporting period; and/or has enacted an ordinance requiring the replacement of high-flow shower-heads and other water use fixtures with their low-flow counterparts.

OR

ii) can demonstrate through customer surveys with 95% statistical confidence and a ±10% error that 75% of single-family residences and 75% of multi-family units constructed prior to 1992 are fitted with low-flow showerheads.

F. Water Savings Assumptions

• Pre-1980 Post-1980

• Construction Construction

• Low-flow showerhead retrofit 7.2 gcd 2.9 gcd

• Toilet retrofit (five year life) 1.3 gcd 0.0 gcd

3   System Water Audits, Leak Detection and Repair

A. Implementation

Implementation shall consist of at least the following actions:

a) Annually complete a prescreening system audit to determine the need for a fullscale system audit. The prescreening system audit shall calculated as follows:

i) Determine metered sales;

ii) Determine other system verifiable uses;

iii) Determine total supply into the system;

iv) Divide metered sales plus other verifiable uses by total supply into the system. If this quantity is less than 0.9, a fullscale system audit is indicated.

b) When indicated, agencies shall complete water audits of their distribution systems using methodology consistent with that described in AWWA's Water Audit and Leak Detection Guidebook.

c) Agencies shall advise customers whenever it appears possible that leaks exist on the customer's side of the meter; perform distribution system leak detection when warranted and cost-effective; and repair leaks when found.

B. Implementation Schedule

a) Agencies signing the MOU prior to December 31, 1997, implementation shall commence no later than July 1, 1998.

b) Agencies signing the MOU or becoming subject to the MOU after December 31, 1997, implementation shall commence no later than July 1 of the year following the year the agency signed or became subject to the MOU.

C. Coverage Requirements

a) Agency shall maintain an active distribution system auditing program.

b) Agency shall repair identified leaks whenever cost-effective.

D. Requirements for Documenting BMP Implementation

a) Prescreening audit results and supporting documentation;

b) Maintain in-house records of audit results or the completed AWWA Audit Worksheets for each completed audit period.

E. Criteria to Determine BMP Implementation Status

a) Agency has annually completed a pre-screening distribution system audit.

b) Agency has conducted a full system audit consistent with methods described by AWWA's Manual of Water Supply Practices, Water Audits and Leak Detection whenever indicated by a pre-screening audit.

F. Water Savings Assumptions

Unaccounted water losses assumed to be no more than 10% of total water into the water supplier's system.

4   Metering with Commodity Rates for All New Connections and Retrofit of Existing Connections

A. Implementation

Implementation shall consist of at least the following actions:

a) Requiring meters for all new connections and billing by volume of use.

b) Establishing a program for retrofitting existing unmetered connections and billing by volume of use.

c) Identifying intra- and inter-agency disincentives or barriers to retrofitting mixed use commercial accounts with dedicated landscape meters, and conducting a feasibility study to assess the merits of a program to provide incentives to switch mixed use accounts to dedicated landscape meters.

B. Implementation Schedule

a) Agencies signing the MOU prior to December 31, 1997, implementation shall commence no later than July 1, 1999.

b) Agencies signing the MOU or becoming subject to the MOU after December 31, 1997, implementation shall commence no later than July 1 of the second year following the year the agency signed or became subject to the MOU.

c) A plan to retrofit and bill by volume of use existing unmetered connections to be completed by end of the first reporting period following the date implementation was to commence.

d) A feasibility study examining incentive programs to move landscape water uses on mixed-use meters to dedicated landscape meters to be completed by end of the first reporting period following the date implementation was to commence.

C. Coverage Requirements

100% of existing unmetered accounts to be metered and billed by volume of use within 10 years of date implementation was to commence.

D. Requirements for Documenting BMP Implementation

a) Confirmation that all new connections are metered and are being billed by volume of use.

b) Number of unmetered accounts in the service area. For the purposes of evaluation, this shall be defined as the baseline meter retrofit target, and shall be used to calculate the agency's minimum annual retrofit requirement.

c) Number of unmetered connections retrofitted during the reporting period.

d) Number of CII accounts with mixed-use meters.

e) Number of CII accounts with mixed-use meters retrofitted with dedicated irrigation meters during reporting period.

E. Criteria to Determine BMP Implementation Status

a) Agency with existing unmetered connections has completed a meter retrofit plan by end of first reporting period following the date implementation was to commence.

b) Agency has completed a feasibility study examining incentive programs to move landscape water uses on mixed-use meters to dedicated landscape meters by end of first reporting period following the date implementation was to commence.

c) Agency with existing unmetered connections is on track to meter these connections within 10 years of the date implementation was to commence. An agency will be considered on track if the percent of unmetered accounts retrofitted with meters equals or exceeds the following: 10% by end of first reporting period following date implementation to commence; 24% by end of

second reporting period; 42% by end of third reporting period; 64% by end of fourth reporting period; and 90% by end of fifth reporting period.

F. Water Savings Assumptions

Assume meter retrofits will result in a 20% reduction in demand by retrofitted accounts.

5   Large Landscape Conservation Programs and Incentives

A. Implementation

Implementation shall consist of at least the following actions:

Customer Support, Education and Assistance

a) Agencies shall provide non-residential customers with support and incentives to improve their landscape water use efficiency. This support shall include, but not be limited to, the following:

Accounts with Dedicated Irrigation Meters

a) Identify accounts with dedicated irrigation meters and assign ETo-based water use budgets equal to no more than 100% of reference evapotranspiration per square foot of landscape area in accordance with the schedule given in Section B of this Exhibit.

b) Provide notices each billing cycle to accounts with water use budgets showing the relationship between the budget and actual consumption in accordance with the schedule given in Section B of this Exhibit; agencies may choose not to notify customers whose use is less than their water use budget.

Commercial/Industrial/Institutional Accounts with Mixed-Use Meters or Not Metered

a) Develop and implement a strategy targeting and marketing large landscape water use surveys to commercial/industrial/institutional (CII) accounts with mixed-use meters. Each reporting period, directly contact via letter or telephone not less than 20% of CII accounts with mixed-use meters and offer water use surveys. (Note: CII surveys that include both indoor and outdoor components can be credited against coverage requirements for both BMP 5 and BMP 9.)

b) Unmetered service areas will actively market landscape surveys to existing accounts with large landscapes, or accounts with landscapes which have been determined by the purveyor not to be water efficient.

c) Offer the following measures when cost-effective:

i) Landscape water use analysis/surveys

ii) Voluntary water use budgets

iii) Installation of dedicated landscape meters

iv) Training (multi-lingual where appropriate) in landscape maintenance, irrigation system maintenance, and irrigation system design.

v) Financial incentives to improve irrigation system efficiency such as loans, rebates, and grants for the purchase and/or installation of water efficient irrigation systems.

vi) Follow-up water use analyses/surveys consisting of a letter, phone call, or site visit where appropriate.

d) Survey elements will include: measurement of landscape area; measurement of total irrigable area; irrigation system check, and distribution uniformity analysis; review or develop irrigation schedules, as appropriate; provision of a customer survey report and information packet.

e) Track survey offers, acceptance, findings, devices installed, savings potential, and survey cost.

New or Change of Service Accounts

Provide information on climate-appropriate landscape design, efficient irrigation equipment/management to new customers and change-of-service customer accounts.

Recommended

a) Install climate appropriate water efficient landscaping at water agency facilities, and dual metering where appropriate.

b) Provide customer notices prior to the start of the irrigation season alerting them to check their irrigation systems and make repairs as necessary. Provide customer notices at the end of the irrigation season advising them to adjust their irrigation system timers and irrigation schedules.

B. Implementation Schedule

a) Agencies signing the MOU prior to December 31, 1997, implementation shall commence no later than July 1, 1999.

b) Agencies signing the MOU or becoming subject to the MOU after December 31, 1997, implementation shall commence no later than July 1 of the second year following the year the agency signed or became subject to the MOU.

c) Develop ETo-based water use budgets for all accounts with dedicated irrigation meters by the end of the second reporting period from the date implementation was to commence.

d) Develop and implement a plan to target and market landscape water use surveys to CII accounts with mixed-use meters by the end of the first reporting period from the date implementation was to commence.

e) Develop and implement a customer incentive program by the end of the first reporting period from the date implementation was to commence.

C. Coverage Requirements

a) ETo-based water use budgets developed for 90% of CII accounts with dedicated irrigation meters by the end of the second reporting period from the date implementation was to commence.

b Not less than 20% of CII accounts with mixed-use meters contacted and offered landscape water use surveys each reporting period.

c) Irrigation water use surveys completed for not less than 15% of CII accounts with mixed-use meters within 10 years of the date implementation was to commence. (Note: CII surveys that include both indoor and outdoor components can be credited against coverage requirements for both BMP 5 and BMP 9.) For the purposes of calculating coverage, 15% of CII accounts means the number of accounts equal to 15% of CII accounts with mixed-use meters in 1997 or the year the agency signed the MOU, whichever is later.

D. Requirements for Documenting BMP Implementation

Dedicated Landscape Irrigation Accounts

Agencies shall preserve water use records and budgets for customers with dedicated landscape irrigation accounts for a period of not less than two reporting periods. This information may be used by the Council to verify the agency's reporting on this BMP.

a) Number of dedicated irrigation meter accounts.

b) Number of dedicated irrigation meter accounts with water budgets.

c) Aggregate water use for dedicated landscape accounts with budgets.

d) Aggregate budgeted water use for dedicated landscape accounts with budgets.

Mixed Use Accounts

a) Number of mixed use accounts.

b) Number, type, and dollar value of incentives, rebates, and no, or low interest loans offered to, and received by, customers.

c) Number of surveys offered.

d) Number of surveys accepted.

e) Estimated annual water savings by customers receiving surveys and implementing recommendations.

E. Criteria to Determine BMP Implementation Status

a) Agency has developed water use budgets for 90% of accounts with dedicated irrigation meters by end of second reporting period from date implementation was to commence.

b) Agency has implemented irrigation water use survey program for CII accounts with mixed-use meters, and directly contacts and offers surveys to not less than 20% of accounts each reporting period. (A program to retrofit mixed-use accounts with dedicated landscape meters and assigning water use budgets, or a program giving mixed-use accounts ETo-based budgets for irrigation uses satisfies this criterion.)

c) Agency is on track to provide water use surveys to not less than 15% of CII accounts with mixed-use meters within 10 years of the date implementation was to commence. Agency may credit 100% of the number of landscape water use surveys for CII accounts with mixed-use meters completed prior to July 1, 1996, that have received a follow-up inspection against the coverage requirement; and 50% of surveys that have not received follow-up inspections. Agency may credit 100% of the number of landscape water use surveys completed for CII accounts with mixed-use meters after July 1, 1996 against the coverage requirement. (A program to retrofit mixed-use accounts with dedicated landscape accounts, or a program giving mixed-use accounts

ETo-based budgets for irrigation uses satisfy this criterion.)

d) An agency will be considered on track if the percent of CII accounts with mixed-use meters receiving a landscape water use survey equals or exceeds the following: 1.5% by end of first reporting period following date implementation to commence; 3.6% by end of second reporting period; 6.3% by end of third reporting period; 9.6% by end of fourth reporting period; and 13.5% by end of fifth reporting period. (A program to retrofit mixed-use accounts with dedicated landscape accounts, or a program giving mixed-use accounts ETo-based budgets for irrigation uses satisfy this criterion.)

e) Agency has implemented and is maintaining customer incentive program(s) for irrigation equipment retrofits.

F. Water Savings Assumptions

Assume landscape surveys will result in a 15% reduction in demand for landscape uses by surveyed accounts.

6 High-Efficiency Washing Machine Rebate Programs
(This version expires June 30, 2004)

A. Implementation

Implementation shall consist of at least the following actions:

Council Actions and Responsibilities

a) Within 6 months from the adoption of this BMP, the Council will develop interim estimates of reliable water savings attributable to the use of high-efficiency washing machines based on the results of the THELMA Study and other available data. Water purveyors may defer implementing this BMP until the Council has adopted these interim estimates. [NOTE: INTERIM ESTIMATE OF RELIABLE WATER SAVINGS ADOPTED BY COUNCIL PLENARY APRIL 8, 1998, SEE SECTION F.]

b) Within two years from the adoption of this BMP, the Council will complete studies quantifying reliable savings attributable to the use of high-efficiency washing machines.

c) At the end of two years following the adoption of this BMP, the Council will appoint a committee to evaluate the effectiveness of triggering high-efficiency washing machine financial incentive programs operated by MOU signatories with pro-

grams operated by energy service providers. This committee will consist of 2 group 1 representatives, 2 group 2 representatives, and the Council Administrator or Executive Director or his/her designee. This BMP will be modified by the appointed committee to require agencies to implement financial incentive programs for high-efficiency washing machines whenever cost-effective and regardless of the absence of a program operated by an energy service provider if the committee concludes from available evidence the following:

i) the Council has verified that significant water savings are available from high-efficiency washing machines;

ii) there is widespread product availability; and

iii) financial incentive programs offered by energy service providers in California have either not materialized, been largely discontinued or significantly scaled back.

Water Purveyor Responsibilities

a) In conjunction with the Council, support local, state, and federal legislation to improve efficiency standards for washing machines.

b) If an energy service provider or waste water utility within the service territory is offering a financial incentive for the purchase of high-efficiency washing machines, then the water agency shall also offer a cost-effective financial incentive based on the marginal benefits of the water savings. Incentive levels shall be calculated by using methods found in A Guide to Customer Incentives for Water Conservation prepared by Barakat and Chamberlain for the CUWA, CUWCC, and US EPA, February 1994. A water purveyor is not required to implement a financial incentive program if the maximum cost-effective rebate is less than $50.

B. Implementation Schedule

a) Agencies signing the MOU prior to December 31, 1997, implementation shall commence no later than July 1, 1999.

b) Agencies signing the MOU or becoming subject to the MOU after December 31, 1997, implementation shall commence no later than July 1 of the second year following the year the agency signed or became subject to the MOU.

C. Coverage Requirements

Cost-effective customer incentive for the purchase of high-efficiency washing machine offered if incentives are being offered by local energy service providers or waste water utility.

D. Requirements for Documenting BMP Implementation

a) Customer incentives to purchase high-efficiency washing machines being offered by local energy service providers, if any.

b) Customer incentives to purchase high-efficiency washing machines being offered by agency, if any.

E. Criteria to Determine BMP Implementation Status

a) Agency has determined if energy service providers or waste water utilities operating within service territory offer financial incentives for the purchase of high- efficiency washing machines.

b) If energy service provider or waste water utility operating within agency's service territory is offering financial incentives, agency has calculated cost-effective customer incentive using methods found in A Guide to Customer Incentives for Water Conservation prepared by Barakat and Chamberlain for the CUWA, CUWCC, and US EPA, February 1994, and is offering this incentive to customers in service territory.

F. Water Savings Assumptions

The interim estimate of reliable annual water savings per replacement of a low-efficiency washing machine with a high-efficiency washing machine is 5,100 gallons, which is the mean yearly water savings derived from THELMA study data on water savings and washing machine load frequencies. Signatory water suppliers may use an estimate of annual water savings exceeding 5,100 gallons at their discretion, and may also select a lower estimate, so long as it is not below 4,600 gallons per year per retrofit, and there is a data supported reason for adopting an estimate lower than 5,100 gallons.

7 Public Information Programs

A. Implementation

Implementation shall consist of at least the following actions:

a) Implement a public information program to promote water conservation and water conservation related benefits.

b) Program should include, but is not limited to, providing speakers to employees, community groups and the media; using paid and public service advertising; using bill inserts; providing information on customers' bills showing use in gallons per day for the last billing period compared to the same period the year before; providing public information to promote water conservation practices; and coordinating with other government agencies, industry groups, public interest groups, and the media.

B. Implementation Schedule

a) Agencies signing the MOU prior to December 31, 1997, implementation shall commence no later than July 1, 1998.

b) Agencies signing the MOU or becoming subject to the MOU after December 31, 1997, implementation shall commence no later than July 1 of the first year following the year the agency signed or became subject to the MOU.

C. Coverage Requirements

Agencies shall maintain an active public information program to promote and educate customers about water conservation.

D. Requirements for Documenting BMP Implementation

a) Number of public speaking events relating to conservation during reporting period.

b) Number of media events relating to conservation during reporting period.

c) Number of paid or public service announcements relating to conservation produced or sponsored during reporting period.

d) Types of information relating to conservation provided to customers.

e) Annual budget for public information programs directly related to conservation.

E. Criteria to Determine BMP Implementation Status

Agency has implemented and is maintaining a public information program consistent with BMP 7's definition.

F. Water Savings Assumptions

Not quantified.

8 School Education Programs

A. Implementation

Implementation shall consist of at least the following actions:

a) Implement a school education program to promote water conservation and water conservation related benefits.

b) Programs shall include working with school districts and private schools in the water suppliers' service area to provide instructional assistance, educational materials, and classroom presentations that identify urban, agricultural, and environmental issues and conditions in the local watershed. Education materials shall meet the state education framework requirements, and grade appropriate materials shall be distributed to grade levels K-3, 4-6, 7-8, and high school.

B. Implementation Schedule

a) Agencies signing the MOU prior to December 31, 1997, implementation shall commence no later than July 1, 1998.

b) Agencies signing the MOU or becoming subject to the MOU after December 31, 1997, implementation shall commence no later than July 1 of the first year following the year the agency signed or became subject to the MOU.

C. Coverage Requirements

Agencies shall maintain an active school education program to educate students in the agency's service areas about water conservation and efficient water uses.

D. Requirements for Documenting BMP Implementation

a) Number of school presentations made during reporting period.

b) Number and type of curriculum materials developed and/or provided by water supplier, including confirmation that curriculum materials meet state education framework requirements and are grade-level appropriate.

c) Number of students reached.

d) Number of in-service presentations or teacher's workshops conducted during reporting period.

e) Annual budget for school education programs related to conservation.

E. Criteria to Determine BMP Implementation Status

Agency has implemented and is maintaining a school education program consistent with BMP 8's definition.

F. Water Savings Assumptions

Not quantified.

9 Conservation Programs for Commercial, Industrial, and Institutional (CII) Accounts

A. Implementation

Implementation shall consist of at least the following actions:

BOTH (a) AND (b)

(a) CII Accounts

Identify and rank commercial, industrial, and institutional (CII) accounts (or customers if the agency chooses to aggregate accounts) according to water use. For purposes of this BMP, CII accounts are defined as follows:

Commercial Accounts: any water use that provides or distributes a product or service, such as hotels, restaurants, office buildings, commercial businesses or other places of commerce. These do not include multi-family residences, agricultural users, or customers that fall within the industrial or institutional classifications.

Industrial Accounts: any water users that are primarily manufacturers or processors of materials as defined by the Standard Industrial Classifications (SIC) Code numbers 2000 through 3999.

Institutional Accounts: any water-using establishment dedicated to public service. This includes schools, courts, churches, hospitals, and government facilities. All facilities serving these functions are to be considered institutions regardless of ownership.

(b) 3-Year Interim CII ULFT Program

Implementation shall consist of at least the following actions:

i) A program to accelerate replacement of existing high-water-using toilets with ultra-low- flush (1.6 gallons or less) toilets in commercial, industrial, and institutional facilities.

ii) Programs shall be at least as effective as facilitating toilet replacements over a

3-year implementation period, commencing July 1, 2001, sufficient to produce cumulative water savings over 10 years equal to 3% of Total Water Savings Potential, as defined by Exhibit 8 of this MOU.

iii) Annual reporting to the Council of all available information described in Section D, subsection (b) of this BMP. The Council shall develop and provide agencies with a concise reporting form by March 31, 2001.

iv) By July 1, 2004, a committee selected by the Steering Committee shall complete for submittal to the Steering Committee a written evaluation of the interim program, including an assessment of program designs, obstacles to implementation, program costs, estimated water savings, and cost-effectiveness. By August 2004, the Steering Committee will reconvene to review the evaluation and recommend to the Plenary the next course of action on BMP 9 targets for CII toilet replacement programs.

AND EITHER (c) OR (d)

(c) CII Water-Use Survey and Customer Incentives Program

Implement a CII Water-Use Survey and Customer Incentives Program. Develop a customer targeting and marketing strategy to provide water use surveys and customer incentives to CII accounts such that 10% of each CII sector's accounts are surveyed within 10 years of the date implementation is to commence. Directly contact (via letter, telephone, or personal visit) and offer water use surveys and customer incentives to at least 10% of each CII sector on a repeating basis. Water use surveys must include a site visit, an evaluation of all water-using apparatus and processes, and a customer report identifying recommended efficiency measures, their expected payback period and available agency incentives. Within one year of a completed survey, follow-up via phone or site visit with customer regarding facility water use and water saving improvements. Track customer contacts, accounts (or customers) receiving surveys, follow-ups, and measures implemented. The method for crediting water use surveys completed prior to the revision of this BMP is described in Section E.

(d) CII Conservation Performance Targets

Achieve a water use reduction in the CII sectors equaling or exceeding the CII Conservation Performance Target. Implement programs to achieve annual water use savings by CII accounts by an amount equal to 10% of the baseline use of CII accounts in the agency's service area over a ten-year period. The target amount of annual water use reduction in CII accounts is a static value calculated from the baseline amount of annual use. Baseline use is defined as the use by CII accounts in 1997. Water purveyors may justify to the Council the use of an alternative baseline year.

B. Implementation Schedule

(a) For agencies signing the MOU prior to December 31, 1997, implementation other than CII ULFTs shall commence no later than July 1, 1999. Implementation of Section A (b)–CII ULFTs–shall commence July 1, 2001.

(b) For agencies signing the MOU or becoming subject to the MOU after December 31, 1997, implementation other than the 3-Year Interim CII ULFT Program shall commence no later than July 1 of the second year following the year the agency signed or became subject to the MOU. Implementation of Section A (b)–CII ULFTs–shall commence July 1, 2001. Agencies signing the MOU or becoming subject to the MOU after July 1, 2001 shall not be subject to the Coverage Requirements set forth in Section C, subsection (a)–3-Year Interim CII ULFT Program.

(c) The coverage requirement for this BMP, as specified in Section C of this Exhibit, with the exception of CII ULFTs, shall be realized within 10 years of the date implementation was to commence.

C. Coverage Requirements

(a) 3-Year CII ULFT Program

CII ULFT program water savings equal to 3% of Total Water Savings Potential, as defined by Exhibit 8 of this MOU, by July 1, 2004.

EITHER

(b) CII Water Use Survey and Customer Incentives Program

10% of each of the CII sector's accounts to accept a water use survey within

10 years of the date implementation is to commence. For the purposes of calculating coverage, 10% of CII accounts means the number of accounts equal to 10% of CII accounts in 1997 or the year the agency signed the MOU, whichever is later.

OR

(c) CII Conservation Performance Targets

Reduce annual water use by CII accounts by an amount equal to 10% of the annual baseline water use within 10 years of the date implementation is to commence, including savings resulting from implementation of section A (b) -- CII ULFTs.

D. Requirements for Documenting BMP Implementation

(a) CII Accounts

The number of accounts (or customers) and amount of water use within each of the CII sectors.

(b) 3-Year Interim CII ULFT Replacement Program

(1) Customer participant information, including retail water utility account ID's, primary contact information, facility address, facility type, number of toilets being replaced, number of toilets in facility (if available), primary reasons for toilet replacement and program participation (if available).

(2) Number of CII ULFTs replaced or distributed by CII sub sector by year.

(3) Total program cost by year, including administration and overhead, labor (staff salaries and benefits), marketing, outside services, incentives, and implementation (agency installation, rebate, permitting and remedial costs), and any required evaluation and reporting by the Council. Costs for program development and program operation shall be reported separately.

(4) Total program budget by year.

(5) Program funding sources by year, including intra-agency funding mechanisms, inter-agency cost-sharing, and state/federal financial assistance sources.

(6) Description of program design and implementation, such as types of incentives, marketing, advertising methods and levels, customer targeting methods, customer contact methods, use of outside services (e.g.,

consultants or community-based organizations), and participant tracking and follow up.

(7) Description of program acceptance or resistance by customers, any obstacles to implementation, and other issues affecting program implementation or effectiveness.

(8) General assessment of program effectiveness.

AND EITHER (c) OR (d)

(c) CII Water Use Survey and Customer Incentives Program

1) The number of CII accounts (or customers) offered water use surveys during the reporting period.

2) The number of new water use surveys completed during the reporting period.

3) The number of follow-ups completed during the reporting period.

4) The type and number of water saving recommendations implemented.

5) Agency's program budget and actual program expenditures.

(d) CII Conservation Performance Target

The estimated reduction in annual water use for all CII accounts due to agency programs, interventions, and actions. Agencies must document how savings were realized and the method and calculations for estimating savings, including the savings resulting from agency-assisted CII ULFTs replacements under section A (b).

E. Criteria to Determine BMP Implementation Status

(a) CII Accounts

Agency has identified and ranked by water use its CII accounts.

(b) CII ULFTs

Agency is on schedule to meet the coverage requirement for section A (b) within 3 years of the start of implementation. An agency will be considered on track if by the end of the first year of implementation the 10-year cumulative water savings equals or exceeds 0.5% of Total Savings Potential; by the end of the second year of implementation the 10-year cumulative water savings equals 1.5% of Total Savings Potential; and by the end of the third year of implemen-

tation the 10-year cumulative water savings equals or exceeds 3.0% of Total Savings Potential.

During the 3-year interim implementation period, cumulative savings from CII ULFT replacement programs occurring prior to January 1, 2001, may not be applied towards the interim coverage requirement. However, cumulative savings from all previous agency CII ULFT replacement programs may be applied toward any long-term CII ULFT coverage requirement.

AND EITHER (c) OR (d) OR (e)

(c) CII Water Use Survey and Customer Incentives Program

1) Agency has developed and implemented a strategy targeting and marketing water use surveys to CII accounts (or customers) by the end of the first reporting period following the date implementation is to commence.

2) Agency is on schedule to complete surveys for 10% of commercial accounts, 10% of industrial accounts, and 10% of institutional accounts within 10 years of the date implementation is to commence. Agencies may credit 50% of the number of surveys completed prior to July 1, 1996 that have not received follow-up verification of implementation, and 100% of the number of surveys completed prior to July 1, 1996 that have received a follow-up survey. Agencies may credit 100% of the number of surveys completed after July 1, 1996 against the coverage requirement.

3) Agencies will be considered on track if the percent of CII accounts receiving a water use survey, in aggregate, equals or exceeds the following: 0.5% of the total number of surveys required by end of first reporting period following date implementation is to commence; 2.4% by end of second reporting period; 4.2% by end of third reporting period; 6.4% by end of fourth reporting period; and 9.0% by end of fifth reporting period.

(d) CII Conservation Performance Targets

1) Agency is on schedule to reduce water use by CII accounts by an amount equal to 10% of baseline use (as defined in Section A) for CII accounts within

10 years of the date implementation is to commence.

2) Agencies will be considered on track if estimated savings as a percent of baseline water use equals or exceeds the following: 0.5% by end of first reporting period following date implementation is to commence; 2.4% by end of second reporting period; 4.2% by end of third reporting period; 6.4% by end of fourth reporting period; and 9.0% by end of fifth reporting period.

3) Credited water savings must be realized through agency actions performed to increase water use efficiency within the CII sector. Agencies may credit 100% of estimated annual savings of interventions since 1991 that have been site verified, and 25% of estimated annual savings of interventions that have not been site verified.

4) Agencies may claim the estimated savings for regulations, ordinances, or laws intended to increase water use efficiency by the CII sector, subject to the review and approval of the savings estimates by the Council. To avoid double counting, agencies justifying savings on the basis of rate structure changes may not claim savings from any other actions undertaken by CII customers, third parties, or the agency.

(e) Combined Targets

Agencies may choose different tracks for different CII sectors, and will be considered in compliance with this BMP if they are on track to meet each applicable coverage requirement for each sector. In addition, agencies may implement both tracks for a given CII sector, and will be considered in compliance with this BMP if the percent of surveys completed and the percent of water savings realized, when added together, equals or exceeds the applicable compliance requirement. For example, at the end of the second reporting cycle an agency would be considered on track to meet the coverage requirement if the percent of surveys completed and the percent of water savings achieved, when added together, equaled or exceeded 2.4%. Agencies may combine tracks only if they make a convincing demonstration that savings attributable to counted surveys are not also included in their estimate of water savings for meeting the water savings performance track.

F. Water Savings Assumptions

Commercial water reduction results from Best Management Practices such as Interior and Landscape Water Surveys, Plumbing Codes, and Other Factors (Includes savings accounted for in other BMPs.) Estimated reduction in gallons per employee per day in year 2000 use occurring over the period 1980–2000: 12%.

Industrial water reduction results from Best Management Practices, Waste Discharge Fee, New Technology, Water Surveys, Plumbing Codes and Other Factors (Includes savings accounted for in other BMPs.) Estimated reduction in gallons per employee per day in year 2000 use occurring over the period 1980–2000: 15%.

10 Wholesale Agency Assistance Programs

(Version adopted March 10, 2004 and effective July 1, 2004)

A. Implementation

Implementation shall consist of at least the following actions:

Financial Support

1) Wholesale water suppliers will provide financial incentives, or equivalent resources, as appropriate, beneficial, and mutually agreeable to their retail water agency customers to advance water conservation efforts and effectiveness.

2) All BMPs implemented by retail water agency customers which can be shown to be cost-effective in terms of avoided cost of water from the wholesaler's perspective, using Council cost-effectiveness analysis procedures, will be supported.

Technical Support

Wholesale water agencies shall provide conservation-related technical support and information to all retail agencies for whom they serve as a wholesale supplier. At a minimum this requires:

3) Conducting or funding workshops addressing the following topics:

    a) Council procedures for calculating program savings, costs and cost-effectiveness.

    b) Retail agencies' BMP implementation reporting requirements.

    c) The technical, programmatic, strategic or other pertinent issues and developments associated with water conservation activities in each of the following areas: ULFT replacement; residential retrofits; commercial, industrial and institutional surveys; residential and large turf irrigation; and conservation-related rates and pricing.

4) Having the necessary staff or equivalent resources available to respond to retail agencies' technical and programmatic questions involving the Council's BMPs and their associated reporting requirements.

Program Management

Wholesale and retail agencies will retain maximum local flexibility in designing and implementing locally cost-effective BMP conservation programs. Cooperatively designed regional programs are encouraged.

5) When mutually agreeable and beneficial, the wholesaler may operate all or any part of the conservation-related activities which a given retail supplier is obligated to implement under the BMP's cost-effectiveness test. The inability or unwillingness of the wholesaler to perform this function, however, in no way relieves or reduces the retailer's obligation to fully satisfy the requirements of all BMPs which are judged cost-effective from the retailer's perspective.

Water Shortage Allocations

6) Wholesale agencies shall work in cooperation with their customers to identify and remove potential disincentives to long-term conservation created by water shortage allocation policies; and to identify opportunities to encourage and reward cost-effective investments in long-term conservation shown to advance regional water supply reliability and sufficiency.

B. Implementation Schedule

1) Agencies signing the MOU prior to December 31, 1997, implementation shall commence no later than July 1, 1999.

2) Agencies signing the MOU or becoming subject to the MOU after December 31, 1997, implementation shall commence no later than July 1 of the second year following the year the agency signed or became subject to the MOU.

C. Coverage Requirements

1) Cost-effectiveness assessments completed for each BMP the wholesale agency is potentially obligated to support. The methodology used will conform to Council standards and procedures, and the information reported will be sufficient to permit independent verification of the cost-effectiveness calculations and of any exemptions claimed on cost-effectiveness grounds. . Any subset of the BMPs being directly implemented by a wholesale agency will be reported.

All other BMPs supportable by the retailers located in a wholesaler's service area will be considered for financial and technical support, and will be dependent on agreement between the wholesaler and its retailers.

2) Agency avoided cost per acre-foot of new water supplies. The methodology used will conform to Council standards and procedures, and the information reported will be sufficient to permit independent verification of the avoided cost calculations.

3) The total monetary amount of financial support, incentives, staff support and equivalent resources provided to retail members to assist, or to otherwise support, the implementation of BMPs.

4) The total amount of verified water savings achieved by each wholesaler-assisted BMP.

5) At each reporting cycle, wholesale agencies shall provide a written offer of support to each of their retailers, and request a response from each retailer. Verification of such offers and responses shall be submitted to the Council at each regular reporting cycle via the "notes" section in the BMP reporting database.

It is recognized that wholesale agencies have limited control over retail agencies that they serve, and must act in cooperation with those retail agencies on implementation of BMPs. Thus, wholesale agencies cannot be held responsible for levels of implementation by individual retailers in their wholesale service areas.

6) Wholesale agencies will receive full credit and acknowledgement for previous BMP implementation.

D. Requirements for Documenting BMP Implementation

1) The total monetary amount of financial incentives and equivalent resources provided to retail members to assist, or to otherwise support, the implementation of BMPs, subtotaled by BMP.

2) The total amount of verified water savings achieved by each wholesaler-assisted BMP.

E. Criteria to Determine BMP Implementation Status

1) Timely and complete reporting of all information as provided for above under "Reporting and Record Keeping Requirements."

2) Offering workshops covering all topics listed above under "Technical Support."

3) Timely reconciliation of wholesaler and retailer BMP reports as provided for above under "BMP Reporting."

F. Water Savings Assumptions

Not quantified. Wholesalers shall use the Council's Cost and Savings Document to assess the total amount of water savings achieved by each wholesaler-supported BMP.

11 Conservation Pricing

A. Implementation

Implementation methods shall be at least as effective as eliminating non-conserving pricing and adopting conserving pricing. For signatories supplying both water and sewer service, this BMP applies to pricing of both water and sewer service. Signatories that supply water but not sewer service shall make good faith efforts to work with sewer agencies so that those sewer agencies adopt conservation pricing for sewer service.

a) Non-conserving pricing provides no incentives to customers to reduce use. Such pricing is characterized by one or more of the following components: rates in which the unit price decreases as the quantity used increases (declining block rates);rates that involve charging customers a fixed amount per billing cycle regardless of the quantity used; pricing in which the typical bill is determined by high fixed charges and low commodity charges.

b) Conservation pricing provides incentives to customers to reduce average or

peak use, or both. Such pricing includes: rates designed to recover the cost of providing service; and billing for water and sewer service based on metered water use. Conservation pricing is also characterized by one or more of the following components: rates in which the unit rate is constant regardless of the quantity used (uniform rates) or increases as the quantity used increases (increasing block rates); seasonal rates or excess-use surcharges to reduce peak demands during summer months; rates based upon the longrun marginal cost or the cost of adding the next unit of capacity to the system.

c) Adoption of lifeline rates for low income customers will neither qualify nor disqualify a rate structure as meeting the requirements of this BMP.

CUWCC Rate Impact Study

Within one year of the adoption of this BMP revision, the Council shall undertake a study to determine the relative effect of conservation rate structure influence on landscape and indoor water use. The study shall develop sample areas that incorporate varying rate structure environments (e.g., low, uniform commodity rates,; high uniform commodity rates; increasing block rates, etc.). As practical, the study shall utilize direct metering of customer end uses, and shall control for weather, climate, land use patterns, income, and other factors affecting water use patterns. If the study shows significant potential savings, as determined by a balanced committee of voting Council representatives, a revised pricing BMP containing numeric targets or other appropriate standards shall be developed for a Council vote.

B. Implementation Schedule

a) Agencies signing the MOU prior to December 31, 1997, implementation shall commence no later than July 1, 1998.

b) Agencies signing the MOU or becoming subject to the MOU after December 31, 1997, implementation shall commence no later than July 1 of the first year following the year the agency signed or became subject to the MOU.

C. Coverage Requirements

Agency shall maintain rate structure consistent with BMP 11's definition of conservation pricing.

D. Requirements for Documenting BMP Implementation

a) Report annual revenue requirement by customer class for the reporting period.

b) Report annual revenue derived from commodity charges by customer class for the reporting period.

c) Report rate structure by customer class for water service and sewer service if provided.

E. Criteria to Determine BMP Implementation Status

Agency rate design shall be consistent with the BMP 11's definition of conservation pricing.

F. Water Savings Assumptions

Not quantified.

12   Conservation Coordinator

A. Implementation

Implementation shall consist of at least the following actions:

a) Designation of a water conservation coordinator and support staff (if necessary), whose duties shall include the following:

i) Coordination and oversight of conservation programs and BMP implementation;

ii) Preparation and submittal of the Council BMP Implementation Report;

iii) Communication and promotion of water conservation issues to agency senior management; coordination of agency conservation programs with operations and planning staff; preparation of annual conservation budget; participation in the Council, including regular attendance at Council meetings; and preparation of the conservation elements of the agency's Urban Water Management Plan.

b) Agencies jointly operating regional conservation programs are not expected to staff duplicative and redundant conservation coordinator positions.

B. Implementation Schedule

a) Agencies signing the MOU prior to December 31, 1997, implementation shall commence no later than July 1, 1998.

b) Agencies signing the MOU or becoming subject to the MOU after December 31, 1997, implementation shall commence no later than July 1 of the first year following the year the agency signed or became subject to the MOU.

C. Coverage Requirements

Agency shall staff and maintain the position of conservation coordinator and provide support staff as necessary.

D. Requirements for Documenting BMP Implementation

a) Conservation Coordinator name, staff position, and years on job.

b) Date Conservation Coordinator position created by agency.

c) Number of Conservation Coordinator staff.

d) Duties of Conservation Coordinator and staff.

E. Criteria to Determine BMP Implementation Status

a) Creating and staffing a Conservation Coordinator position within the agency organization.

b) Providing the Conservation Coordinator with the necessary resources to implement cost-effective BMPs and prepare and submit Council BMP Implementation Reports.

F. Water Savings Assumptions

Not quantified.

13   Water Waste Prohibition

A. Implementation

Implementation methods shall be enacting and enforcing measures prohibiting gutter flooding, single pass cooling systems in new connections, non-recirculating systems in all new conveyer car wash and commercial laundry systems, and non-recycling decorative water fountains.

Signatories shall also support efforts to develop state law regarding exchange-type water softeners that would: (1) allow the sale of only more efficient, demand-initiated regenerating (DIR) models; (2) develop minimum appliance efficiency standards that (a) increase the regeneration efficiency standard to at least 3,350 grains of hardness removed per pound of common salt used; and (b) implement an identified maximum number of

gallons discharged per gallon of soft water produced; (3) allow local agencies, including municipalities and special districts, to set more stringent standards and/or to ban on-site regeneration of water softeners if it is demonstrated and found by the agency governing board that there is an adverse effect on the re-claimed water or groundwater supply.

Signatories shall also include water softener checks in home water audit programs and include information about DIR and exchange-type water softeners in their educational efforts to encourage replacement of less efficient timer models.

B. Implementation Schedule

a) Agencies signing the MOU prior to December 31, 1997, implementation shall commence no later than July 1, 1998.

b) Agencies signing the MOU or becoming subject to the MOU after December 31, 1997, implementation shall commence no later than July 1 of the first year following the year the agency signed or became subject to the MOU.

C. Coverage Requirements

Agency shall adopt water waste prohibitions consistent with the provisions for this BMP specified in Section A of this Exhibit.

D. Requirements for Documenting BMP Implementation

Description of water waste prohibition ordinances enacted in service area.

E. Criteria to Determine BMP Implementation Status

Agency's water waste prohibition ordinances meet the requirements of the BMP definition.

F. Water Savings Assumptions

Not quantified.

14   Residential ULFT Replacement Programs

A. Implementation

Implementation shall consist of at least the following actions:

a) Implementation of programs for replacing existing high-water-using toilets with ultra-low- flush (1.6 gallons or less) toilets in single-family and multi-family residences.

b) Programs shall be at least as effective as requiring toilet replacement at time

of resale; program effectiveness shall be determined using the methodology for calculating water savings in Exhibit 6 of this MOU.

After extensive review, on July 30 1992, the Council adopted Exhibit 6, "ASSUMPTIONS AND METHODOLOGY FOR DETERMINING ESTIMATES OF RELIABLE WATER SAVINGS FROM THE INSTALLATION OF ULF TOILETS." Exhibit 6 provides a methodology for calculating the level of effort required to satisfy BMP 14.

B. Implementation Schedule

a) Agencies signing the MOU prior to December 31, 1997, implementation shall commence no later than July 1, 1998.

b) Agencies signing the MOU or becoming subject to the MOU after December 31, 1997, implementation shall commence no later than July 1 of the first year following the year the agency signed or became subject to the MOU.

c) The coverage requirement for this BMP, as specified in Section C of this Exhibit, shall be realized within 10 years of the date implementation was to commence.

C. Coverage Requirements

Water savings from residential ULFT replacement programs to equal or exceed water savings achievable through an ordinance requiring the replacement highwater-using toilets with ultra-low-flow toilets upon resale, and taking effect on the date implementation of this BMP was to commence and lasting ten years.

D. Requirements for Documenting BMP Implementation

a) The number of single-family residences and multi-family units in service area constructed prior to 1992.

b) The average number of toilets per single-family residence; the average number of toilets per multi-family unit.

c) The average persons per household for single-family residences; the average persons per household for multi-family residences.

d) The housing resale rate for single-family residences in service area; the housing resale rate for multi-family residences in service area.

e) The number of ULFT installations credited to the agency's replacement program, by year.

f) Description of ULFT replacement program

g) Estimated cost per ULFT replacement.

h) Estimated water savings per ULFT replacement

E. Criteria to Determine BMP Implementation Status

Calculated ULFT replacement program water savings at the end of each reporting period are within 10% of calculated retrofit-on-resale water savings, using Exhibit 6 methodology and water savings estimates.

F. Water Savings Assumptions

See Exhibit 6.

Potential Best Management Practices

This section contains Potential Best Management Practices (PBMPs) that will be studied. Where appropriate, demonstration projects will be carried out to determine if the practices meet the criteria to be designated as BMPs. Within one year of the initial signing of this MOU, the Council will develop and adopt a schedule for studies of these PBMPs.

1. Rate Structure and other Economic Incentives and Disincentives to Encourage Water Conservation.

This is the top priority PBMP to be studied. Such studies should include seasonal rates; increasing block rates; connection fee discounts; grant or loan programs to help finance conservation projects; financial incentives to change landscapes; variable hookup fees tied to landscaping; and interruptible water service to large industrial, commercial or public customers. Studies on this PBMP will be initiated within 12 months from the initial signing of the MOU. At least one of these studies will include a pilot project on incentives to encourage landscape water conservation.

2. Efficiency Standards for Water Using Appliances and Irrigation Devices

3. Replacement of Existing Water Using Appliances (Except Toilets and Showerheads Whose Replacements are Incorporated as Best Management Practices) and Irrigation Devices.

4. Retrofit of Existing Car Washes.

5. Graywater Use

6. Distribution System Pressure Regulation.

7. Water Supplier Billing Records Broken Down by Customer Class

8. Swimming Pool and Spa Conservation including Covers to Reduce Evaporation

9. Restrictions or Prohibitions on Devices that use Evaporation to Cool Exterior Spaces.

10. Point of Use Water Heaters, Recirculating Hot Water Systems and Hot Water Pipe Insulation.

11. Efficiency Standards for New Industrial and Commercial Processes.

Flow Charts Illustrating the NEPA and CEQA Environmental Review Process

CEQA Process
Flow Chart

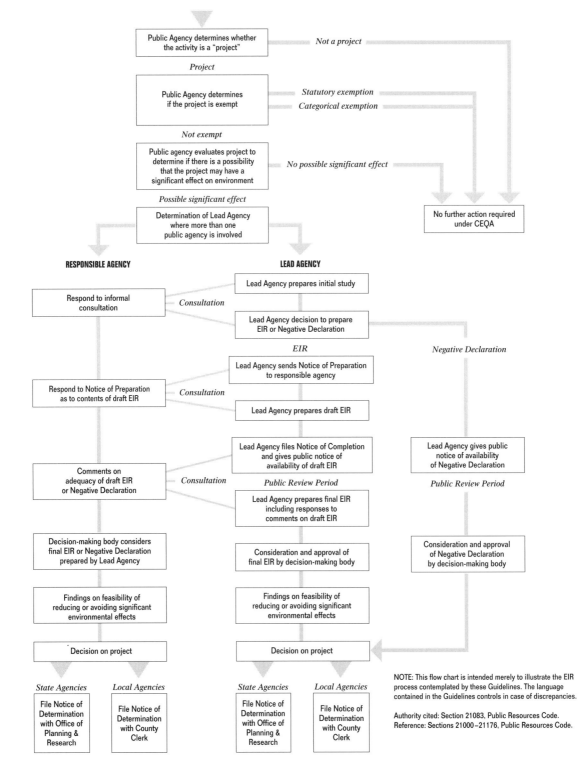

Public Agency determines whether the activity is a "project"

Not a project

Project

Public Agency determines if the project is exempt

Statutory exemption

Categorical exemption

Not exempt

Public agency evaluates project to determine if there is a possibility that the project may have a significant effect on environment

No possible significant effect

Possible significant effect

Determination of Lead Agency where more than one public agency is involved

No further action required under CEQA

RESPONSIBLE AGENCY

LEAD AGENCY

Respond to informal consultation

Consultation

Lead Agency prepares initial study

Lead Agency decision to prepare EIR or Negative Declaration

EIR

Negative Declaration

Respond to Notice of Preparation as to contents of draft EIR

Consultation

Lead Agency sends Notice of Preparation to responsible agency

Lead Agency prepares draft EIR

Comments on adequacy of draft EIR or Negative Declaration

Consultation

Lead Agency files Notice of Completion and gives public notice of availability of draft EIR

Public Review Period

Lead Agency prepares final EIR including responses to comments on draft EIR

Lead Agency gives public notice of availability of Negative Declaration

Public Review Period

Decision-making body considers final EIR or Negative Declaration prepared by Lead Agency

Consideration and approval of final EIR by decision-making body

Consideration and approval of Negative Declaration by decision-making body

Findings on feasibility of reducing or avoiding significant environmental effects

Findings on feasibility of reducing or avoiding significant environmental effects

Decision on project

Decision on project

State Agencies

File Notice of Determination with Office of Planning & Research

Local Agencies

File Notice of Determination with County Clerk

State Agencies

File Notice of Determination with Office of Planning & Research

Local Agencies

File Notice of Determination with County Clerk

NOTE: This flow chart is intended merely to illustrate the EIR process contemplated by these Guidelines. The language contained in the Guidelines controls in case of discrepancies.

Authority cited: Section 21083, Public Resources Code.
Reference: Sections 21000–21176, Public Resources Code.

NEPA Environmental Review Process: An Overview

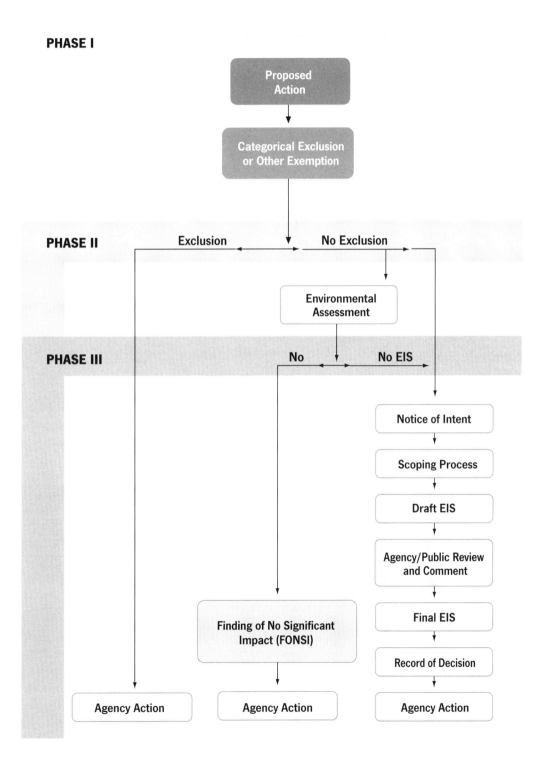

Water Quality Vulnerability Zone Development– San Francisco PUC Technical Memorandum

San Francisco Water Department
San Francisco Watershed
Management Plans

Technical Memorandum No. 2
Prepared for EDAW, Inc.

July 1996

MONTGOMERY WATSON
TECHNICAL MEMORANDUM NO. 2

TO: Ed Stewart, SFWD
Dave Blau, EDAW
Tina Stott, EDAW

DATE: Updated July 22, 1996
March 25,1994

PREPARED
BY: Karen Johnson
Carol Ruth James

CLIENT: EDAW, Inc.

REVIEWED
BY: San Francisco
Water Department

FILE: Watershed Planning
Committee and Technical
Advisory Committee
637.0040

SUBJECT: Water Quality Vulnerability
Zone Development

Introduction

Technical Memorandum No. 2 summarizes the development process for the water quality vulnerability zone maps. This memorandum is divided into two sections:

- A section which describes the natural watershed characteristics which influence each water quality parameter group of concern, and

- A section which discusses the method used for compositing the natural watershed characteristics into water quality parameter vulnerability zone maps.

In order to develop a tool for determining watershed lands vulnerable to current and future activities within the San Francisco Water Department's Peninsula and Alameda watersheds, five water quality parameter groups were selected for the evaluation. These water quality parameter groups were selected based on current and potential water quality regulations, industry-wide water quality issues, and the current activities within each watershed. The five groups include: particulates, synthetic organic compounds (SOCs) and pesticides, microorganisms, trihalomethane (THM) precursors of concern, and nutrients (nitrogen and phosphorus).

For each of these five water quality parameter groups, appropriate watershed characteristics were evaluated regarding their potential influence on the concentrations of these parameter groups in the watershed

waterbodies. The two influences are the transport of the parameter group and the parameter group as a "contaminant" source. The watershed characteristics evaluated include: soils, slope, vegetation, proximity to water bodies, and wildlife concentrations (including cattle). The relative importance of each of these characteristics for each water quality parameter group is summarized.

The goal of this evaluation is to develop a composite vulnerability zone map of the water quality parameter groups for each watershed. These vulnerability zone maps identify those areas in the watershed which are considered high, medium, and low vulnerability zones with regards to their potential for increasing the concentration of a particular water quality parameter group in the receiving waterbodies. When considering new or reconsidering existing activities in the watershed, the high vulnerability zones, in particular, should be managed to avoid any potential for water quality degradation.

In order to develop the water quality vulnerability zone maps, GIS data for each characteristic were evaluated and ranked as high, medium, and low and plotted on a separate GIS data-interpreted layer. These layers were then combined and an overall high, medium, and low vulnerability zone map was developed for each water quality parameter group. A discussion of the development of these layers for each water quality parameter group is provided in the "Water Quality Parameter Groups" section.

Activities within the waterbodies were not analyzed in this study but should be considered in the overall management of the watershed. For example, birds which use the waterbodies, particularly waterfowl, defecate directly into the waterbodies and, therefore, may have a direct impact on water quality.

Conclusions

Composite water quality vulnerability zones were developed for the five water quality parameter groups–particulates, SOCs and pesticides, microorganisms, THM precursors of concern (surrogate for all disinfection by-product precursors), and nutrients. These vulnerability zones were defined based on four physical characteristics of each watershed–soils, slope, vegetation, and proximity to water. Through this analysis it was determined that inadequate data exists regarding wildlife movement within the watershed, and the proximity to water characteristic includes a broad enough boundary around all water bodies (reservoirs and streams, including intermittent streams) such that a separate wildlife concentration area need not be defined at this time. However, as additional wildlife information becomes available in the future, a wildlife vulnerability zone should be developed. Another finding is that the available data for both THM precursors of concern (i.e., organic carbon) and nutrients are limited to the extent that the vulnerability zones for these two water quality groups are identical. In order to better define these two water quality zones, monitoring for total organic carbon, nitrogen, and phosphorus would need to be militated.

Ultimately the water quality vulnerability zones were composited based upon the approach summarized below.

- The high vulnerability areas defined for the "proximity to water" layer take precedence and, therefore, are defined as high vulnerability zones on all water quality composite maps.

- For other areas to be defined as a "high," slope must be high and either soils or vegetation must be high.

- For areas to be defined as a "low," two of either slope, soils, or vegetation must be low.

- All other areas not already defined based on the three points above are defined as medium.

Verification of this approach was achieved by using evaluation tools from both the agricultural (Universal Soil Loss Equation) and forestry (Erosion Hazard Rating) industries. The agricultural tool was the most compatible because of its emphasis on soils (such as clays) which can be more easily transported through water and cause treatment related water quality problems. Both evaluation tools placed importance on slope and its potential for impacting water quality. As a result of the verification step, the water quality vulnerability zones have been finalized and are now being used in the development and analysis of the watershed management plan alternatives.

In final, it will be important for a watershed/reservoir monitoring program to be developed and initiated as soon as is possible. A water quality baseline is important to establish in the near term for two reasons. First, an assessment can be made regarding the water quality of the sources as they enter the SFWD-owned portion of the watersheds–particularly the Alameda Watershed. Two-thirds of the Alameda Watershed are owned by other parties and, therefore, SFWD cannot directly control the water qualities influenced by these properties.

Second, once a watershed management plan is established, monitoring will be a tool for evaluating the plan. Having a baseline of data and a monitoring program which is established for this assessment will be important. Current monitoring programs do not address this need.

Water Quality Parameter Groups–Impacts of Natural Watershed Characteristics

Participate Vulnerability Zone

The impact of each of the following watershed characteristics on paniculate vulnerability was defined by the tendency of the characteristic to influence particle transport.

- **Soils**–high, medium, and low classifications for soils were defined based on the inverse of the dry density of each soil type. Dry density refers to the mass (weight) of a unit volume of dry soil. Dry density was chosen over both bulk (includes solids and pores) and particle density (includes solids) because of its universal use and availability. In addition, it was assumed that the highest increase of particulates into the waterbodies due solely to the soil-type occurs with the first major storm event when the dry density is more apt to represent the soils. In general, clays which have a low dry density are classified as high, loams which have a medium dry density are classified as medium, and sands/gravels which have a high dry density are classified as low.

- **Slope**–high, medium, and low classifications for the slope ranges were defined based on the US Forest Service classifications for debris slumping or increased particle transport. These slope ranges are different than those used for sediment yield analyses (debris avalanche). In sediment yield analyses the evaluation is focused on mass loadings of sediment.

high	greater than 30%
medium	15 to 30%
low	0 to 15%

- **Vegetation**–high, medium, and low classifications for vegetation were determined based on the ability of the different vegetation communities to provide a protective layer (intercept the kinetic energy) between rainfall and soil and to a lesser degree, stabilize the soils with the presence of leaf debris and roots. Given this line of reasoning, forested areas were considered the most protective (low), woodlands, scrubs and chaparral medium (medium), and grasses the least protective (high).

- **Proximity to Water**–the "proximity to water" boundary was established based on three sources of information–other watershed investigations, rainfall intensity, and time of concentration.

Watershed Investigations–most current "proximity to water" information pertaining to watershed studies identifies buffer zones for development purposes as a filter barrier for protecting water quality. Information pertaining to watershed studies documented in the AWWA Effective Watershed Management manual and a study conducted in

Taiwan which, in part, addressed this issue, were used. A range of 50 to 300 feet was ascertained as the distance required to adequately impede the movement of particulates, nutrients, and pesticides into the watershed waterbodies. This range of distances would also be adequate for the control of microorganisms–impeding their movement into the water bodies. These distances, of course, are greatly impacted by type of vegetation, slope, and soil types. However, these physical watershed characteristics are addressed in this analysis.

Reduction of the 300-foot distance is possible if establishing buffer zones as a control mechanism for land development is the goal of a particular study. However, in the San Francisco study, because protection of water quality is the predominant goal, the use of the 300-foot distance as the baseline proximity boundary is both defensible and considered prudent.

Rainfall Intensity–given that the intensity of rainfall plays an important role in the movement of particulates, the intensity of rainfall was determined for each of the five reservoirs. The rainfall intensity for each reservoir provides a basis for developing a relationship between the five reservoirs regarding the "proximity to water" boundary distance. Based on the average 24-hour maximum rainfall for various periods reported for each reservoir, the following rainfall intensities were defined. These intensities suggest that San Antonio Reservoir would likely have the shortest proximity to water boundary and Pilarcitos Reservoir the longest.

Rainfall Intensity (inches/24-hour period
Reservoir average maximum)

San Antonio	1.67
Calaveras	1.81
Crystal Springs	2.57
San Andreas	3.16
Pilarcitos	3.71

Time of Concentration–Time of concentration is a technically accurate approach for comparing the relative differences in precipitation and, also, the relative differences in land surface characteristics. Because the movement of particulates is due to overland runoff, the proximity to water classification is actually a function of the overland flow characteristics–characteristics of the land and rainfall event. The most important land surface characteristics are slope, soil type, soil moisture, and roughness of the land. The most important rainfall characteristics are intensity and duration of the rainfall event. Time of concentration incorporates these characteristics to varying degrees. A detailed discussion of this analysis can be found in the Appendix. Below is a summary of the time of concentrations and the corresponding proximity to water boundaries defined for each reservoir. As suggested by the rainfall intensity data and confirmed by the time of concentration analysis, the San Antonio Reservoir has the shortest and Pilarcitos Reservoir the longest proximity to water boundaries.

Duration (Tc) of 1.3"/hr storm
Proximity to Water

Reservoir	minutes	feet
San Antonio	11.5	300
Calaveras	12	380
Crystal Springs	18	600
San Andreas	20	900
Pilarcitos	25	1,300

Given this information, the following classifications were defined for the proximity to water vulnerability zones.

high	0 to 1,300 feet from the high water line of the reservoir (maximum value varies depending upon the reservoir, see above) 0 to 1,300 feet from the centerline of stream (maximum value varies depending upon in which precipitation isoline a particular tributary is located)
medium	a medium classification was not defined for this characteristic because it was not deemed defensible
low	areas outside the 300 to 1,300-foot proximity and within 2,000 feet of SFWD owned lands

• Wildlife Concentration Areas–those areas which are identified as having high wildlife concentrations were intended to be targeted as high vulnerability zones because of the disturbance caused to the soils which may increase particle transport. In part, these areas are included in the proximity to water layer because mammals must travel to and from the reservoirs for water. Data were insufficient to allow any further classifications to be made outside the proximity to water layer.

SOCs and Pesticides Vulnerability Zone

The impact of each of the following watershed characteristics on SOC and pesticide vulnerability was defined by the tendency of the characteristic to influence SOC and pesticide transport into the waterbodies as a result of an activity within the watershed. SOCs and pesticides from an activity are assumed to either be present in an aqueous form or adsorbed onto the soil. SOC and pesticide transport, therefore, occurs through either aqueous or particle transport.

• Soils–based on the transport mechanisms mentioned above, the impact of soils on SOC and pesticide transport is influenced by the soil's permeability and adsorptive capacity. If a soil has a low permeability then ponding may occur which means aqueous transport is a viable transport mechanism. If a soil has a high adsorption capacity then particle transport becomes the important transport mechanism.

Adsorption capacity refers to the ability of a particular soil to adsorb a chemical. The cation exchange capacity of each soil was used as an indicator of adsorption capacity.

In general, soils with low permeability have high adsorption capacity. For example, clays tend to have low permeability and high adsorption capacity, loams medium, and sands/gravel have high permeability and low adsorption capacity. This relationship suggests parallel relationships between the soils' high, medium and low classifications for both of these characteristics. Therefore, clays would have a high classification, loams a medium classification and sands/gravel a low classification.

The one exception to this interpretation of the impact of soils on SOCs and pesticides is the consideration pertaining to groundwater. In general, those soils with high permeability would have a high vulnerability because they would allow the SOCs and pesticides to penetrate down to the groundwater aquifer. This is an opposite interpretation of permeability and its impact on surface water. This concern regarding groundwater, however, is included in the definition of the proximity to water layer.

- **Slope**–because both the aqueous and particle transport mechanisms are important for SOC and pesticide transport, slopes which enhance runoff versus particle transport were used as the **criteria for** establishing the high, medium, and low classifications.

Storm water management design criteria were used to define the ranges summarized below.

high	greater than 30%
medium	10 to 30%
low	0 to 10%

- **Vegetation**–high, medium, and low classifications for vegetation were determined based on the ability of the different vegetation communities to provide a protective layer between rainfall and soil–soils which may contain adsorbed SOCs/pesticides thus reducing particle transport. Given this line of reasoning, forested areas were considered the most protective (low), woodlands, scrubs and chaparral medium (medium), and grasses the least protective (high).

- **Proximity to Water**–the justification for selecting the proximity classification below is summarized under the Paniculate Vulnerability Zone section. In addition, a high classification was established for the Sunol Valley aquifer. The ease of transport of SOCs and pesticides through alluvial deposits into the upper aquifer, which is considered "under the influence of surface water," and the potential impact of SOCs and pesticides on downstream users were influential in this decision.

high	0 to 1,300 feet from the high water line of the reservoir (maximum value varies depending upon the reservoir, see above)
	0 to 1,300 feet from the centerline of stream (maximum value varies depending upon in which precipitation isoline a particular tributary is located)

Sunol Valley–alluvial valley defined as the 360-foot contour, where alluvial soils are present

medium	a medium classification was not defined for this characteristic because it was not deemed defensible

low	areas outside the 300 to 1,300-foot proximity and within 2,000 feet of SFWD owned lands

- **Wildlife Concentration Areas**–those areas which are identified as having high wildlife concentrations were intended to be targeted for consideration in developing the overall SOC/pesticide vulnerability zones. The disturbance caused to soils–which may contain adsorbed SOCs/pesticides–is the key issue and their ultimate transport into the waterbodies. In part, these areas are included in the proximity to water layer because mammals must travel to the reservoirs for water. Data were insufficient to allow any further classifications to be made outside the proximity to water layer.

Microorganisms Vulnerability Zone

The impact of each of the following watershed characteristics on microorganism vulnerability was defined by the tendency of the characteristic to increase microbiological survival and ultimate transport into the waterbodies within each watershed. The microorganisms of concern include total coliforms, Giardia, and Cryptosporidium. Because of the difficulty in treating Cryptosporidium, when compared to total coliforms and Giardia, emphasis was placed on this microbe when the vulnerability zones were defined for each watershed characteristic below.

- **Soils**–when considering microorganism survival in a non-waterbody environment, moisture content, nutrients (carbon, nitrogen and phosphorus), and pH were considered important environmental conditions. Of these three, moisture content is considered the most important for Cryptosporidium survival (Cryptosporidium is known to survive in moist environments for up to six months without entering a waterbody). Therefore, moisture content defined by available water capacity or water-holding capacity was used as the soil characteristic of interest. Available water capacity or water-holding capacity is defined by the U.S. Natural Resources Conservation Service (NRCS). In general, clay has a high moisture content, loam a medium content, and sand/gravel a low moisture content.

- **Slope**–the two transport mechanisms being considered for this project include aqueous and particle transport. Microorganisms are assumed to fall into the particle transport category. Therefore, the high, medium, and low classifications for the microorganism slope ranges were defined based on increased particle transport.

high	greater than 30%
medium	10 to 30%
low	0 to 15%

- **Vegetation**–high, medium, and low classifications for vegetation were determined based on the ability of the different vegetation communities to provide a protective layer from sunshine, thereby providing for higher moisture conditions to exist which will allow Cryptosporidium to survive longer. Given this line of reasoning, forested areas were considered the most protective (high), woodlands, scrubs and chaparral medium (medium), and grasses the least protective (low) from the sun.

- **Proximity to Water**–the justification for selecting the proximity classification below is summarized under the Paniculate Vulnerability Zone section.

high	0 to 1,300 feet from the high water line of the reservoir (maximum value varies depending upon the reservoir, see above)
	0 to 1,300 feet from the centerline of stream (maximum value varies depending upon in which precipitation isoline a particular tributary is located)
medium	a medium classification was not defined for this characteristic because it was not deemed defensible
low	areas outside the 300 to 1,300-foot proximity and within 2,000 feet of SFWD owned lands

- **Wildlife Concentration Areas**–those areas which are identified as having high wildlife concentrations and which are near the waterbodies will be targeted for consideration in developing the overall microorganism vulnerability zones. It is these areas where high concentrations of mammals, such as cattle and deer, may pass to drink water. It is assumed that these areas are where higher concentrations of waste products can be found which, in turn, reflects the potential for a higher source area for microorganisms. These areas are included in the proximity to water layers.

THM Precursor Vulnerability Zone

The impact of each of the watershed characteristics on THM precursor vulnerability was defined by the tendency of the characteristic to influence THM precursor loading and transport into the waterbodies within each watershed. THM precursors refers to the natural organic carbon which exists in each watershed in the form of decayed vegetation, bark, and animal carcasses as well as animal wastes. THM precursor is the terminology used here to represent the precursor for disinfection by-products (DBFs) in general.

These THM precursors can occur in one of several forms: decaying, decayed, and layered within the soil, decayed and adsorbed onto soil, and/or decayed and existing in water. The dissolved organic carbon concentrations in sheet flows are reduced when the water comes in contact with adsorptive clays, thus reducing the concentration in runoff but increasing the carbon content in clay soils. Therefore, from a land management water quality perspective, particle transport is the mechanism of concern for moving THM precursors into the waterbodies.

- **Soils**—as described above, particle transport mechanisms are of interest. The natural organic content, defined by the natural fertility of soils, was determined based on information provided in soil survey manuals. Given that data pertaining to the organic carbon content of soils in the watersheds are either non-existent or very limited, natural fertility was used as opposed to organic carbon. In general, clay has a high natural fertility, loam a medium natural fertility, and sand/gravel a low natural fertility.

- **Slope**—for this analysis, THM precursors are assumed to fall into the particle transport category. Therefore, the slope ranges were defined based on increased particle transport.

high	greater than 30%
medium	15 to 30%
low	0 to 15%

- **Vegetation**—vegetation was considered from two different perspectives—its contribution to the organic carbon content through litter decomposition, and its protective capabilities regarding rainfall and erosion. With respect to its organic carbon content, information pertaining to the organic carbon content and ease of decay of the vegetation communities is non-existent. Data, limited as it is, is only available for specific vegetation species and, therefore, could not be incorporated into this analysis. Therefore, the vegetation communities were evaluated according to their ability to protect the ground from intense rainfalls, which in turn decreases the transport of THM precursor material. Following this line of reasoning, forested areas were considered the most protective (low), woodlands, scrubs and chaparral medium (medium), and grasses the least protective (high).

- **Proximity to Water**—the justification for selecting the proximity classification below is summarized under the Particulate Vulnerability Zone section.

high	0 to 1,300 feet from the high water line of the reservoir (maximum value varies depending upon the reservoir, see above)
	0 to 1,300 feet from the centerline of stream (maximum value varies depending upon in which precipitation isoline a particular tributary is located)
medium	a medium classification was not defined for this characteristic because it was not deemed defensible
low	areas outside the 300 to 1,300-foot proximity and within 2,000 feet of SFWD owned lands

- **Wildlife Concentration Areas**—those areas which are identified as having high wildlife concentrations were intended to be targeted for consideration in developing the overall THM Precursor vulnerability zones. The disturbance caused to soils—which contain organic carbon—is the key issue and their ultimate transport into the waterbodies. In part, these areas are included in the proximity to water layer because mammals must travel to the reservoirs for water. Data were insufficient to allow any further classifications to be made outside the proximity to water layer.

Nutrient Vulnerability Zone

The impact of each of the watershed characteristics on nutrient vulnerability was defined by the tendency of the characteristic to influence nutrient loading in the watershed and readily transport nutrients into the waterbodies. Nutrients refer to the nitrogen and phosphorus which exists in each watershed. Nutrient sources include vegetation, soils, and animal wastes. The nutrients associated with vegetation matter can only enter the waterbodies if the vegetation releases it during the decaying process. Nutrients, therefore, are associated with decaying vegetation matter and animal wastes, adsorbed onto soils, or leached through runoff. Given these various forms, the nutrients adsorbed onto soils are probably the most abundant which suggests that panicle transport is the predominant mechanism for moving them into the waterbodies.

- **Soils**—the nutrient loading for each soil, defined by the natural fertility of each soil, was determined based on information in the soil survey manuals. Given that data pertaining to the nitrogen and phosphorus content of soils in the watersheds is either non-existent or very limited, natural fertility was used as opposed to nutrient loading. In general, clay has a high natural fertility, loam a medium natural fertility, and sand/gravel a low natural fertility.

- **Slope**—since nutrients are present in both dissolved and particulate forms it was conservatively assumed that slopes which increase runoff will determine the high, medium, and low slope classifications.

high	greater than 30%
medium	10 to 30%
low	0 to 10%

- **Vegetation**—vegetation was considered from two different perspectives—its contribution to the nutrient loading and its protective capabilities regarding rainfall. With respect to its nutrient loading, specific information pertaining to the nutrient loading to soils through litter decomposition or to runoff by leaching versus the cycling of nutrients through vegetation is not available in a format required for this project. Data, limited as it is, is only available for certain specific vegetation species—not communities—

and, therefore, could not be incorporated into this analysis. Instead the vegetation communities were evaluated according to their ability to protect the ground from intense rainfalls, which in turn decreases the transport of nutrients. Following this line of reasoning, forested areas were considered the most protective (low), woodlands, scrubs and chaparral medium (medium), and grasses the least protective (high).

- **Proximity to Water**—the justification for selecting the proximity classification below is summarized under the Particulate Vulnerability Zone section.

high	0 to 1,300 feet from the high water line of the reservoir (maximum value varies depending upon the reservoir, see above)
	0 to 1,300 feet from the centerline of stream (maximum value varies depending upon in which precipitation isoline a particular tributary is located)
medium	a medium classification was not defined for this characteristic because it was not deemed defensible
low	areas outside the 300 to 1,300-foot proximity and within 2,000 feet of SFWD owned lands

- **Wildlife Concentration Areas**—those areas which are identified as having high wildlife concentrations and which are near the waterbodies were targeted for consideration in developing the overall nutrient vulnerability zones. It is these areas where high concentrations of mammals, such as cattle and deer, may pass to drink water. It is assumed that these areas are where higher concentrations of waste products can be found which, in turn, reflects the potential for a higher source area for nutrients, particularly nitrogen. In part, these areas are included in the proximity to water layer

because mammals must travel to the reservoirs for water. Data were insufficient to allow any further classifications to be made outside the proximity to water.

Watershed Characteristics Compositing Method—Rationale and Verification

Table 1 is a summary of the relationships between the five watershed characteristics and the five water quality parameter groups. The rationale for combining the information from each of these five watershed characteristics is discussed below. Five water quality vulnerability zone maps and a composite map are the result of this combination of information, however, the THM Precursor and Nutrient Loading maps are identical due to the lack of pertinent data at this time.

In order to develop a rationale for the compositing approach, the roles of the five watershed characteristics were defined as summarized below:

Soils:
Source/Influence/Transport

Vegetation:
Transport/Source

Slope:
Transport

Proximity to Water:
Transport

Wildlife Concentrations:
Influence/Source

"Source" is defined as the watershed characteristic which is an originator of the water quality parameter group being considered (e.g., wildlife concentrations are a source of microorganisms). Source, used here, does not include watershed land uses and activities (such as roads) which are sources of a parameter. "Influence" indicates the watershed

characteristic which enhances the survival or movement into the waterbodies of the water quality parameter group. "Transport" indicates the watershed characteristic which increases the movement of the water quality parameter group into the waterbodies.

Of these three roles, transport is the most important followed by source and then by influence. In support of this concept is the following rationale: a water quality parameter of concern will never be an issue if it does not reach a waterbody. As a corollary, a water quality parameter which is perceived as a non-issue may become a concern because it reaches the waterbodies. Given the relative importance between the three roles, the following rationale was developed for the composite vulnerability zone maps.

Rationale

Numerical weighting factors were avoided as a tool to be used in the composite approach because of the subjective nature associated with the assignment of the numerical values. It was determined that numerical weighting factors could become a source of criticism and ongoing discussion. Instead, identification of the relative importance of the specific watershed characteristics was used. Also, the high, medium, and low classifications given to the watershed characteristics were used.

Because of its importance to the control (reduction) of the concentration of water quality parameters entering the water bodies, the high vulnerability areas defined for the proximity to water layer will take precedence and, therefore, will be defined as high vulnerability zones on all the composite maps. Since the wildlife concentration area is included in the proximity to water layer, it will not be considered as a separate layer in the composite.

TABLE 1
Relationship Between Watershed Characteristics and Water Quality Vulnerability Zone Development

Water Quality Parameter Groups	WATERSHED CHARACTERISTICS				
	Soils	Vegetation	Slope	Proximity to Water	Wildlife Concentration (includes cattle)
Particulates	Dry Density	Protective Layer	Particulate Transport	Rainfall Intensity	Included in Proximity to Water
SOCs	Adsorption Capacity	Protective Layer	Increased Runoff	Rainfall Intensity plus Alluvial Valley	Included in Proximity to Water
Microorganisms	Moisture Content	Protective Layer	Particulate Transport	Rainfall Intensity	Included in Proximity to Water
THM Precursors	Natural Fertility	Protective Layer	Increased Runoff	Rainfall Intensity	Included in Proximity to Water
Nutrient Loading	Natural Fertility	Protective Layer	Increased Runoff	Rainfall Intensity	Included in Proximity to Water

The remaining three watershed characteristics are soils, vegetation, and slope. For an area to be defined as a "high," slope must be high and either soils or vegetation must be high. For an area to be defined as a "low," two of the three remaining watershed characteristics must be low. All other areas will be defined as medium. In theory this concept makes sense and avoids the pitfalls which may arise out of using numerical weighting factors–the exact values of which can always be disputed.

Verification

In order to verify this rationale for developing the water quality vulnerability zones, two empirically based evaluation techniques were used. One technique, the Universal Soil Loss Equation (USLE), is a common tool used by the agricultural industry. The second technique, the Erosion Hazard Rating (EHR) System, is a common tool used by the forestry industry. As yet a technique has not been developed for the water quality industry, therefore, both of these techniques were used. While both techniques take into account erosion potential, the agricultural industry technique more closely relates to water quality concerns because it places a higher weighting on the soil types (clays, loams) which are more easily transported and ultimately can become a water quality/treatment problem. The forestry industry technique, on the other hand, places emphasis on soils (sand, gravel) which may erode more easily, but tend to settle out more easily once they enter a water body and ultimately do not necessarily present water quality/treatment problems. Both techniques consider slope to be an important characteristic. However, the ULSE is oriented toward slopes in the ranges considered herein (0 to 30 percent) while the EHR System is oriented toward even higher slopes (40 to 80 percent) which are important for major movements of sediment. Given these points, the agricultural technique was used as the main verification tool with the forestry technique being used as a further verification check.

Universal Soil Loss Equation. The USLE is typically presented as:

$$A = RKLSCP,$$

where:

A is the estimated soil loss,

R is the erosivity of the rainfall,

K is the soil credibility,

L is a slope length factor,

S is the slope steepness factor,

C is a cover management factor, and

P is a supporting practices factor.

In order to develop a general weighting approach for all five watersheds the following factors are assumed equal or constant between the five reservoirs: R, L, and P factors. The formula is then simplified and is comprised of a relationship between soil loss and the three characteristics of slope, soil type, and vegetation. These characteristics correspond to the three highlighted above: soil, slope, and vegetation.

Relative soil loss = K S C

Given this relationship, for verification purposes, the three composite vulnerability classifications (high, medium, and low) developed from these three watershed characteristics must be evaluated according to accepted values for the three watershed characteristics used in the USLE.

Wischmeier, *et al.,* in the *Journal of Soil and Water Conservation,* 1971, developed a nomograph relating USLE K factor to soil type. For sandy soils (low vulnerability), this gives a K ranging between 0.10 and 0.25. For loamy soils (medium vulnerability), the nomograph gives a K value between 0.25 and 0.40. For clay soils (high vulnerability), a K value between 0.40 and 0.60 is indicated. Average range values were selected for the K factor corresponding to each of the soil types as follows:

Average Soil Type	Vulnerability	K Factor
Sandy soils	Low	0.175
Loamy soils	Medium	0.325
Clay soils	High	0.500

Slope steepness factor, or S, is related to slope by the following equation:

$$S = 65.4s^2 + 4.56s + .065$$

where:

s is the SINE of the slope angle

The ranges of the slopes identified for particulate transport are as follows: low vulnerability–0 to 15 percent, medium vulnerability–15 to 30 percent, and high vulnerability–greater than 30 percent. Average range values were selected for each of the slope ranges and the S factors calculated as follows:

Slope %	Vulnerability	S Factor
7.5	Low	1,230
22.5	Medium	11,100
40	High	36,500

The cover management factor, or C, provides a measure of the extent to which vegetation intercepts and breaks the kinetic energy of the raindrops thus reducing its erosivity, and the extent to which the movement of water along the ground is impeded by ground cover (leaf litter). The vegetation classifications used in the vulnerability zone development correspond roughly to the following values provided by Wischmeier.

General Vegetation Communities

	Veg. Type	Vulnerability	C Factor
Forests	Trees, no brush	75% cover 80% grnd cover	Low 0.013
Woodlands Scrubs	Brush or bushes,	50% cover 20% grnd cover	Medium 0.16
Grasses	Grasses, no canopy	20% soil contact	High 0.20

Now that values for K, S, and C have been defined, the USLE calculations can be made for the combinations of high, medium, and low classifications corresponding to the soils, vegetation, and slope combinations defined by the composite rationale defined above. Table 2 contains a summary of the 27 possible combinations, the corresponding USLE calculated values, and the composite ratings based on the rationale defined previously.

The combinations in Table 2 are ranked according to their corresponding USLE values. With the exception of a few combinations, the USLE factors verify the compositing rationale defined previously. Given the importance of slope in the composite rationale and verified by the USLE, for compositing purposes the three asterisked ratings are changed as indicated in Table 2.

Surface Soil Erosion Hazard Rating

As further verification and a check on the USLE comparison, the California Department of Forestry EHR System was also applied. The Forestry method states that the erosion hazard rating is the sum of a soil factor, a slope factor, a protective cover factor, and a precipitation intensity factor.

Surface Soil Erosion Hazard Rating =
Soil + Slope + Vegetation + Rainfall

Average values for each factor within each of the five watersheds were determined and input to this formula and the results compared to the composite rationale ratings in Table 2. Although this technique does not address drinking water quality concerns as closely as the agricultural technique of USLE, the results of the analysis do support the verification of the composite rationale. In addition, they also support the emphasis placed on slope and, therefore, the changes highlighted in Table 2 which were based on slope.

Table 2
Verification of Composite Rationale by USLE Calculation

Composite Combinations of Watershed Characteristics			Calculated USLE Factor USLE = K S C	Composite Rationale Rating [1]
Soils	Vegetation	Slope		
High	High	High	3,647	High
High	Medium	High	2,553	High
Medium	High	High	2,370	High
Medium	Medium	High	1,659	Medium*– High[2]
Low	High	High	1,276	High
High	High	Medium	1,112	Medium
Low	Medium	High	893	Medium
High	Medium	Medium	778	Medium
High	Low	High	729	High
Medium	High	Medium	723	Medium
Medium	Medium	Medium	506	Medium
Medium	Low	High	474	Medium
Low	High	Medium	389	Medium
Low	Medium	Medium	272	Medium
Low	Low	High	255	Low*–Medium
High	Low	Medium	222	Medium
Medium	Low	Medium	145	Medium
High	High	Low	123	Medium
High	Medium	Low	86	Medium
Medium	High	Low	80	Medium
Low	Low	Medium	78	Low*–Medium
Medium	Medium	Low	56	Medium
Low	High	Low	43	Low
Low	Medium	Low	30	Low
High	Low	Low	25	Low
Medium	Low	Low	16	Low
Low	Low	Low	9	Low

1. Composite rationale defined previously in Watershed Characteristics Compositing Method section.

2. Asterisked composite rationale ratings indicate they were modified based on the verification evaluation.

Appendix

Proximity to Water Verification

The classification of watershed lands in terms of how close they are to a water body is based upon the typical distance over which particulates might move. Because the movement of particulates is due to overland runoff, the proximity to water classification is actually a function of the overland flow characteristics of the land surface.

Overland flow may be estimated using a number of different techniques, from a simple rational method approach to sophisticated deterministic rainfall runoff models. In any of these techniques, the important factors driving the overland flow are the characteristics of the land surface and the characteristics of the rainfall event. The most important land surface characteristics are slope, soil type, soil moisture, and roughness of the land. The most important rainfall characteristics are intensity and duration of the rainfall event.

If all of the watershed lands had the same surface characteristics, the overland flow, and hence the movement of particulates, would simply be a function of the intensity of the rainfall and duration of the rainfall event. And, if we assume that a certain rainfall intensity is necessary in order to move particulates, the amount of material moved into the water body is directly related to how long that intensity lasts. For example, if one rainfall event lasts twice as long as another, then material may travel from twice as far away, and thus twice as much material may enter the water body.

A minimum distance of 300 feet from the high water line has been established as defining the limit of the high proximity to water vulnerability zone for the San Antonio Reservoir. Comparable proximity distances were established for the other watersheds, based upon the differences in their relative average 24-hour maximum precipitation as compared to the San Antonio Reservoir.

A more technically accurate approach is to compare the relative differences in precipitation and, also, the relative differences in land surface characteristics. In order to accomplish this comparison, the time of concentration was calculated for each reservoir. The time of concentration (Tc) of a basin is used in this analysis as a measure of how long rainfall must continue until all of a designated area within a basin is contributing runoff. The formula for Tc used in this analysis is defined below. This Tc formula is one of the first, and most widely used, relationships proposed for use with ungauged watersheds, developed by C.E. Ramser (1927).

$$Tc = [2.2 \; n \; (Lo) / (So)^{.5}]^{.467}$$

where:

n is the Manning's roughness coefficient

Lo is the overland distance from the point of farthest contribution in meters So is the average slope

The equation can then be rearranged and solved for Lo as follows.

$$Lo = 10 \; [Log(Tc)/.467 -$$

$$Log \; (2.2 \; n / (S0)^{\wedge} 0.5)]$$

The estimated values used for Manning's roughness and slope for each of the watersheds are summarized below. Manning's roughness was varied based upon the identification of the predominant vegetation community (area-wise) which represents each of the five reservoirs. The corresponding values for Manning's roughness were obtained from *Hydrologic Modeling of Small Watersheds* by Haan, Johnson and Brakensier, ASAE, 1982.

Manning's Average Slope

Reservoir	Roughness	%
Pilarcitos	0.6	30
San Andreas	0.5	25
Crystal Springs	0.55	20
Calaveras	0.45	30
San Antonio	0.45	25

If we equate the Lo with our proximity to water characteristic on San Antonio Reservoir (Lo = 300 feet), the equation yields a Tc of 11.5 minutes. Precipitation records from the short interval precipitation station nearest San Antonio Reservoir show that the 2-year return interval, 11.5-minute storm has an intensity of 1.3 inches per hour.

Based on an analysis of precipitation records from all over California, James Goodridge (Bulletin No. 195, "Rainfall Analysis for Drainage Design," DWR, 1976) found a strong relationship between the intensity of heavy rainfall, the duration of rainfall, and the mean annual precipitation. By applying this relationship, it is possible to determine the duration of 1.3 inch per hour rainfall on the other watershed areas, corresponding to the two-year return period event at San Antonio Reservoir. A two-year return period was used because it is a common base frequency used for defining precipitation or rainfall events in watersheds.

Based upon the available rainfall records from stations near each reservoir, and modified to reflect reservoir area conditions, as needed, the corresponding rainfall durations, or Tc, having approximately a 1.3 inch per hour intensity, are defined for each reservoir as summarized below.

Duration of 1.3"/Hr. Storm

Reservoir	(minutes)
San Antonio	11.5
Calaveras	12
Crystal Springs	18
San Andreas	20
Pilarcitos	25

In turn, using these durations in the time of concentration formula as Tc and the Manning's Roughness coefficients (n) and average slopes (So) defined above for each reservoir, the overland flow distances (Lo), or proximity to water, corresponding to 300 feet at San Antonio Reservoir would be as defined below.

Proximity to Water

Reservoir	(feet)
San Antonio	300
Calaveras	380
Crystal Springs	600
San Andreas	900
Pilarcitos	1,300

Examples of Materials Used In Stakeholder Collaboratives

This appendix presents material designed to compliment and augment chapter 8, regarding the use of collaborative approaches in water resources planning and policy. The first two items are examples of ground rules, charters, and protocols that were developed to organize and guide collaborative water resources efforts.

The Santa Margarita Groundwater Management Advisory Committee represents a simple set of ground rules devised to guide a small citizen's committee exploring local groundwater options. These rules were discussed and adopted by the group at its initial meeting.

The Development of a Fisheries and Aquatic Habitat Management and Restoration Plan for the Lower American River for the Lower American River is a more elaborate charter. It not only spells out the basic rules of engagement and group structure, but also the time schedule, work tasks, and how to address those outside the immediate process. Guides of this type can help fashion a set of ground rules or charter appropriate to any water-related process.

Table A-1 identifies and explains key local, state, and federal laws governing public involvement, public disclosure, and public protocols for meetings in California.

Ground Rules for the Santa Margarita Groundwater Advisory Committee

June 2000
Representation and Participation

1. Members of the Santa Margarita Groundwater Advisory Committee (Committee) have been selected based on their expertise and their ability to represent the views of their agency and interest group(s) within the community and to take part in the process and work collaboratively with other Committee members, facilitators and County Staff.

2. The integrity and values of each member will be respected by other members. The motivations and intentions of members will not be criticized and there will be no personal attacks. Delay will not be employed as a tactic to avoid an undesired result. One speaker talks at a time; the facilitator will lead the discussion.

3. Every member is responsible for communicating his/her position on issues under consideration. Voicing these interests is essential to enable meaningful dialogue and full consideration of issues by the Committee.

4. If a member cannot make a scheduled meeting, that person can designate an alternate to attend and represent him or her.

Information Sharing and Issues under Discussion

1. To encourage brainstorming and creative thinking, members agree to examine multiple options for issues under discussion by the Committee.

2. As part of this process of developing multiple options, members are encouraged to put forward tentative proposals for consideration, which may later be withdrawn.

3. Members are asked to provide pertinent information or recommended technical experts for items under discussion. Members have an obligation to share specific information in the form of reports, memos and studies which may affect the deliberations of the members.

Reaching Agreement

1. The goal of this process is to have Committee members make decisions by consensus. In this context, consensus is defined as when the parties are in full agreement, and when not in full agreement, are in substantial agreement, with no member willing to stand in the way of a decision or an agreement. Straw votes may be taken from time to time to gauge the level of agreement on specific issues.

If after a comprehensive discussion, full or substantial agreement is not reached, then a straw vote of Committee members can be taken with majority rule. Primary and secondary positions will be recorded and documented in the minutes and the meeting will proceed.

2. As Committee members discuss and make decisions, the facilitators and/or staff will draft language that reflects the emerging consensus. Draft statements will be circulated to all members for review and agreement.

Media Contact and Interested Parties

1. If approached by the media, members of the Committee and their alternates will be careful to present only their own views and not those of other members. Members are encouraged to suggest that media representatives contact other members who may have different points of view.

2. While the Committee is studying, discussing or evaluating issues, members will not initiate media contact or make public statements except as mutually agreed. No statements prejudging outcomes will be made. Such statements can hamper creative discussion and the group's ability to modify draft proposals.

3. Interested parties are welcome to attend Committee meetings. Members of the community will be provided with opportunities to speak and address the Committee. The facilitator or Committee chair may limit time.

Timetable and Work Products

1. The Committee is committed to participating for up to six facilitated sessions and possible sub-group meetings as needed through February, 2001. Meetings will be held approximately once per month.

2. The facilitators will prepare meeting agendas and written information, as well as summary meeting notes based on discussions and results of Committee meetings.

Development of a Fisheries and Aquatic Habitat Management and Restoration Plan for the Lower American River— Consensus-Building Guidelines
Approved by FISH Group 3/23/00

For any consensus-building process to go smoothly, it is helpful for those involved to agree at the outset on the purpose of the process and on the procedures by which the group will govern its deliberations and decision making.

Purpose and Anticipated Work Products of the Consensus-Building Process

The purpose of this consensus-building process is two-fold:

(1) to involve all primary stakeholders in a collective effort, led by an independent third party and supported by a widely-respected technical consultant, to develop an initial fisheries and aquatic habitat management and restoration plan for the Lower American River; and

(2) to provide strategic advice to proponents of LAR fisheries and aquatic habitat management and restoration projects who seek "early start" status for their projects. Work products include a baseline report summarizing current data on the health of the river, a bibliography on the fisheries and aquatic habitat of the LAR, the initial plan, and the first annual State-of-the-River Report. Further details on each of these assignments are provided in the "Charge" document.

Structure of the Consensus-Building Process

FISH Group. This consensus-building process will primarily take place within the FISH Group, in consultation with the constituencies represented by FISH Group members. The FISH Group will have facilitation support from the California Center for Public Dispute Resolution, technical support from Surface Water Resources, Inc., and project management and administrative support from the Sacramento City-County Office of Metropolitan Water Planning.

Technical Subcommittee. The FISH Group will establish a small technical subcommittee to assist the technical consultant on an as-needed basis in translating FISH Group guidance into draft deliverables for review by the full FISH Group. The Technical Subcommittee will be small, but can be augmented on an issue-specific basis with individuals bringing critical expertise not otherwise available on the Subcommittee.

Members of the Technical Subcommittee need not be members of the FISH Group.

Interested Parties/Related Initiatives. While all FISH Group members are expected to keep their respective constituencies apprised of progress and to bring their constituents' views into FISH Group discussions, there will be a periodic need for more in-depth consultations with several ongoing initiatives to ensure that the resulting plan and projects have broad-based support. These initiatives include:

1. The LAR Task Force and its Bank Protection and Floodway Management Work Groups (which anticipate using this plan as the aquatic habitat element of the overall Lower American River Corridor Management Plan, or "RCMP");[1]

2. The Sacramento Area Flood Control Agency (SAFCA) and its Board of Directors;

3. State and federal resource agencies' senior management teams;

4. CALFED Bay-Delta Program (which is providing financial support for the development of the RCMP because this project embodies CALFED's intent to translate its Environmental Restoration Program Plan into tangible results);

5. The Water Forum (which anticipates using this plan for the Habitat Management Program for the Lower American River as required by the Water Forum Agreement, consistent with the mitigation described and certified in the Water Forum Agreement Environmental Impact Report and associated Mitigation, Monitoring, and Reporting Plan, Or "MMRP");

6. The County Department of Regional Parks, Recreation, and Open Space (which

---

1. To assist with coordination across LAR Task Force work groups: 1) the work groups have some overlap in membership; 2) the work group leaders will meet monthly; 3) agendas for upcoming meetings of the Bank Protection and Floodway Management Work Groups will be provided at FISH Group meetings if available (and vice versa); and 4) FISH Group members are welcome to observe at meetings of these other work groups and of the LAR Task Force, and members of those entities may observe FISH Group meetings.

may want to build upon this planning effort in its next update of the American River Parkway Plan), and its American River Parkway Advisory Committee.

Staff anticipate providing briefings at strategic points on an as-needed basis to other interested parties as well, including elected officials, the Environmental Council of Sacramento, civic associations, and the Sacramento River Watershed Program.

Staff will also provide periodic summary progress reports to interested parties in the form of a memo, newsletter, or article for inclusion in others' newsletters and websites. Newsletters that might be effective vehicles for such outreach include the California Flyfishers Unlimited's newsletter, "On the Fly" and River City Paddlers' newsletter, "River City Reflections." At a minimum, such updates will be posted on the website of the Sacramento City-County Office of Metropolitan Water Planning. There are likely to be two to four such progress reports over the next year to apprise interested parties of milestones such as project launch, completion of draft goals and objectives, completion of list of projects to be considered, availability of State-of-the-River Report, availability of the review draft of the initial fisheries and aquatic habitat management and restoration plan, and availability of the final version of the initial plan.

Additional ways in which FISH Group members can make effective linkages with related initiatives include: (a) the FISH Group's own members, many of whom are involved in related initiatives; (b) guest speakers; (c) field trips; and (d) inclusion of related reports in the bibliography to be provided by the technical consultant.

The Public-at-Large. The FISH Group recognizes that this planning effort will result in recommendations involving the public interest, public policy, and investments of public dollars. To ensure accountability to the public over and above the measures indicated above, this planning effort will include the following measures for keeping the public informed of progress and of opportunities for providing input:

The open invitation to any interested parties to observe FISH Group meetings.[2]

Press releases and media briefings at the strategic milestones in the process. Staff will also be available to assist FG members in obtaining press coverage for substantive achievements on projects that have been endorsed by FG. In such cases, press materials would be expected to include a tagline indicating the FG's endorsement (e.g., "…as endorsed by the Lower American River FISH Group"). All media materials produced on behalf of the FG or carrying the FG tagline require FG review and approval prior to release.

The first annual State-of-the-River Report, to be released in approximately one year.

Fish Group Participation

FISH Group Members. The proposed composition of the FISH Group is available under separate cover. This slate was assembled based on input provided by over 45 diverse stakeholders in interviews conducted by Senior Mediator Marcelle E. DuPraw. (The list of interviewees is attached to the draft convening report.) Organizations included in Ms. DuPraw's recommended slate generally are those suggested by the largest number of interviewees–those named over and over again. Her recommendation reflects the need for balanced representation of all key stakeholders as well as the need to keep the FISH Group to a manageable size. Where there were numerous organizations of a certain type interested in participating (e.g., groups representing canoeists and kayakers), Ms. DuPraw asked them to explore whether they could together identify one person who could appropriately represent that cluster of organizations.

Alternates. Each representative may designate an alternate who will substitute for the representative in the event that he or she cannot attend a session of the FISH Group. However, for continuity, FISH Group members will minimize their use of alter-

2. It is suggested that observers try to accompany a FISH Group member as a guest to ensure that they are provided with some orientation to that day's discussions. For assistance in arranging this, please contact project manager Susan Davidson at (916) 264-1997.

nates to attend meetings, and each time an alternate is required, it should be the same individual. If a primary representative needs to use an alternate for a particular meeting, the primary representative will notify the facilitator in advance.

Individuals who are designated alternates may attend all meetings if they wish and may be placed on the FISH Group membership roster to routinely receive documents distributed to FISH Group members.

Nevertheless, the primary FISH Group representative will be responsible for briefing the alternate on both the substantive issues and procedures of the FISH GROUP. In addition, the primary representative also will be responsible for making sure that the alternate has and understands relevant documents to ensure that he or she can provide informed representation on short notice should the need arise.

If neither the primary representative nor an alternate can attend a meeting, the primary representative should provide comments on the meeting topics to the facilitator verbally or in writing. (However, see also the "Withdrawal" section of this document.)

Additional Parties. Additional representatives may join the FISH Group after its initial formation only with the concurrence of the FISH Group.

Responsibilities of FISH Group Members. Representatives to the FISH Group are expected to consult with their constituents and colleagues and to raise their interests and concerns during the discussions of the FISH Group. Members are also responsible for shaping and endorsing any eventual agreements on behalf of their constituents.

Meetings

Open Meetings. Meetings of the FISH Group will be open to any observers.

Agendas. Agendas for the meetings will be drafted by the facilitator in consultation with FISH Group members and staff. They will be approved or revised at the beginning of each meeting.

Meeting Procedures. Participants in FISH Group meetings will be asked to abide by the following procedures to cultivate a venue for constructive discourse:

- Come with an open mind, and respect for others' interests and differing opinions.
- Treat one another with courtesy.
- Let one person speak at a time.
- Be honest, fair, and as candid as possible.
- Identify those times when you are "taking off your organizational hat" to express an individual opinion.
- Think outside the box and welcome new ideas.
- Respect time constraints–be succinct.

Meeting Summaries. Meeting summaries will be prepared by the project manager, in consultation with the facilitator and technical consultant. Their primary function will be to assist the FISH Group in documenting its progress and agreed-upon action items. The meeting summaries will be brief, summarizing steps taken at the meeting in question toward completing the primary FISH Group deliverables. They will be emailed to FISH Group members for review and comment as soon as possible following each FISH Group meeting. Members will have one calendar week to comment on draft summaries. If changes were requested, the meeting summary will then be revised by the project manager, who will consult with the facilitator and/or technical consultant as necessary. The revised version will be re-emailed to FISH Group members for reference purposes and for use in keeping their constituents informed.

Breaks and Caucuses. When necessary and appropriate, any FISH Group member may request a break in FISH Group deliberations to confer privately with other stakeholders or with the facilitator on time-sensitive matters related to the current deliberations.

Timeline and Level of Effort

It is anticipated that the FISH Group will require approximately one year to develop the initial version of the four work products mentioned above. Due to the nature of the plan, it is likely to benefit from subsequent refinements over a number of years.

The FISH Group generally will meet on the third Thursday of each month from 1:00–4:30 p.m. There may be an occasional exception to this pattern–e.g., to avoid holidays and the occurrence of FISH Group meetings the same week as meetings of the Lower American River Task Force (the FISH Group's parent body). It may be necessary to meet for a full day for particular topics; this will be decided by the FISH Group on a case-by-case basis. A list of proposed meeting dates is available under separate cover.

FISH Group members also can expect to put in several more hours per month reviewing and commenting on documents. In addition, the facilitator and/or technical consultant may request time to consult with individual FISH Group members on selected topics between meetings. Current funding for facilitation and technical support for this effort comes from the Water Forum Agreement, the CALFED Bay-Delta Program, and SAFCA.

Work Plan and Schedule

A combined work plan and schedule is available under separate cover. Most participants communicated significant time constraints during the stakeholder interviews. Consequently, the work plan assumes that the technical consultant (Surface Water Resources, Inc., or "SWRI") will have primary responsibility for drafting text for review and comment by FISH Group members.

The work plan also shows the points throughout the process when SWRI anticipates needing guidance from the FISH Group in the form of both upfront input and feedback on "strawman" documents. Examples occur throughout the process, but include development of goals and objectives, identifying variables to include in the baseline report and documents to include in the bibliography, suggesting projects to be considered for inclusion in the plan, suggesting project selection criteria and approach, and jointly selecting projects to include in the recommended plan.

It is anticipated that FISH Group members may want to review raw data along with

the consultants' analyses, and to sometimes ask colleagues in their respective organizations to review the consultant's work products as well in a form of peer review.

The facilitator will assist SWRI in translating the FISH Group's guidance onto paper. The Sacramento City-County Office of Metropolitan Water Planning, which manages the relevant funds generated by the Water Forum Agreement as well as the CALFED grant, has a fiduciary responsibility to oversee the work of the facilitator and technical consultant on this project.

Decisionmaking

The FISH Group will make decisions by consensus. Consensus will mean that all FISH Group members either fully support or can live with the decision (or overall plan), and believe that their constituents can as well. Consensus does not mean one hundred percent agreement on every issue, but rather support for moving forward with a recommendation taken as a whole. "Straw polls" may be taken on occasion to get a general impression of FISH group members' attitudes about particular topics. Disagreements will be regarded as problems to be solved rather than as battles to be won.

If consensus on a particular aspect of a recommendation is not possible, FISH Group members will describe the areas of agreement and disagreement, the reasons why such differences continue, and how the FISH Group will continue to move forward despite these differences. Inclusion of such a description of remaining areas of disagreement in the plan can be consistent with consensus support for the plan as a whole.

In striving to reach consensus, FISH Group members will consider the interests and concerns of all FISH Group members, regulatory requirements, and other relevant perspectives. They will strive to develop creative proposals and recommendations that address the interests of all stakeholders. FISH Group members will keep in mind various parties' incentives to help develop creative, mutually-acceptable recommendations and strive to enhance those incentives.

Subgroups. Any subgroups established by the FISH Group (e.g, to work out specific issues related to their work products) will develop recommendations or proposals for FISH Group consideration and adoption. Subgroups will not have decision-making authority. Decisions on whether to incorporate the recommendations into FISH Group work products will be made by consensus among the members of the FISH Group.

Agreement. The FISH Group's final agreement on the plan is expected to take the form of a written statement, signed by FISH Group members after they are appropriately authorized by the parties they represent, and included as the foreword to the plan.

Endorsement

The Lower American River Task Force envisions that, once the FISH Group is satisfied with the initial plan, it will be endorsed by all FISH Group members on behalf of their organizations. It will then be submitted to the LAR Task Force for endorsement and incorporation into the over-all River Corridor Management Plan, which the Task Force has recently decided to develop.

The plan developed by the FISH Group will also serve as the Habitat Management Program for the Lower American River as required by the Water Forum Agreement, consistent with the mitigation described and certified in the Water Forum Agreement Environmental Impact Report and associated Mitigation, Monitoring, and Reporting Plan (MMRP).

Both the Water Forum and SAFCA have indicated that they welcome other organizations with related objectives joining with them to ensure that this plan advances others' compatible objectives as well. The Task Force anticipates that the plan will be submitted to other organizations for their use in reviewing, modifying if necessary, and approving the components of the plan for which they are responsible. (For example, the plan may be suitable for incorporation into the next update of the American River Parkway Plan.) The actions and individual projects contemplated by the plan will be subject to further review and final approval by the responsible entities. Each participating organization retains decision-making autonomy.

Early Start Projects

During stakeholder interviews, many interviewees expressed both appreciation for the idea of developing a comprehensive plan based on sound science and concern about spending too much time studying the issues prior to undertaking any restoration projects. Consequently, this planning effort will be available as a "launching pad" for LAR fisheries and/or aquatic habitat management and restoration projects that enjoy overwhelming, broad-based support. FISH Group members will be asked to spend a small portion of selected meetings considering whether to provide a letter of endorsement for selected projects of this kind.

A project proponent who believes his/her project may be appropriate for endorsement by the FISH Group as an "early start project" (ESP) should contact the facilitator to discuss the best way to communicate with the FISH Group about it. If the project as initially presented to the FISH Group is controversial, the proponent can proceed with the project without the FISH Group's endorsement or ask that the project be considered in the normal course of the planning process. Alternatively, if interest is high and time and resources allow, the FISH Group may ask the facilitator to assist interested parties in resolving the associated controversy and then the proponent may re-present his or her proposal to the FISH Group.

Safeguards

Good Faith. All parties agree to act in good faith in all aspects of this consensus-building process, and to communicate their interests in FISH Group meetings. Offers made in frank conversations about creative solutions will not be used against any party in future litigation or public relations. This provision will not restrict the ability of FISH Group members to speak to the press or

pursue legal strategies in the future. Personal attacks and stereotyping will not be acceptable. FISH Group members will refrain from impugning the motivations and intentions of others.

Good faith also requires that parties not make commitments they do not intend to follow through with, and that parties act consistently in the FISH Group and in other forums where the issues under discussion in the FISH Group are also being discussed, including contacts with the press. Good faith also requires that members make a concerted effort to provide information requested by other members, or explain why not.

Withdrawal. Any member may withdraw from the FISH Group at any time. Communication about the reasons for withdrawing would be helpful.

If two or more FISH Group meetings go by without representation from either a primary representative or his/her alternate, that organization will be asked to appoint another representative. An organization also can be asked to appoint another representative if the current representative participates in a way that is inconsistent with the purpose, charge, meeting procedures, or consensus-building guidelines.

Good faith provisions continue to apply to those who withdraw or may be asked to step down.

Press. FISH Group members recognize that the way in which positions are publicly stated may affect the ability of the FISH Group to reach consensus. Therefore, whenever possible, they will refer inquiries from the press regarding the overall progress of the process to the project manager (Susan Davidson) or the facilitator (Merci Du-Praw). They agree not to characterize the positions and views of any other party in public forums or press contacts, and not to attribute comments to other members.

A Brief Summary of Open Meeting Laws
Applicable to California (as of 2002)

Topic	Federal Gov't—Federal Advisory Committee Act	State Government—Bagley-Keene Open Meeting Act	Local Governments—Ralph M. Brown Act
To Whom It Is Applicable	Applies to committees established or utilized by an agency for obtaining advice or recommendations from the committee, as a whole.	Applies to State Boards, Commissions Exceptions: • special meetings • emergency meetings • closed sessions dealing with: personnel matters, licensing of persons, prison terms, parole or release of individuals, conferring honorary degrees, gifts or donations, real property negotiations, proprietary or confidential information, pending litigation	Applies to local government bodies Exceptions: • special meetings • closed sessions dealing with: personnel matters, pending litigation, real estate negotiations, labor negotiations, grand jury testimony, public security, drug law enforcement, hospital peer review and trade secrets, education code exceptions, licensing of applicants
Advisory Committees	Exceptions: • Committees formed by National Academy of Sciences, National Academy of Public Administrations, Central Intelligence Agency, Federal Reserve System, and those not managed or controlled by federal agencies Meetings: • of local, state, federal, and tribal representatives • to obtain advice from individual attendees, to exchange facts or information, to perform operational as opposed to advisory functions, to gather information, conduct research, analyze relevant issues and acts, and draft proposed position papers for deliberation by committee	Applies to any advisory committee or subcommittee that has 3 or more persons if created by formal action of state agency	Applies to citizen groups formed by local body, standing subcommittee of local body that includes quorum of local body, and private organizations that receive public money from local government and includes members appointed by local government
Committee Charters	Committee chartered by responsible federal agency. Charters must be renewed every 2 years or committee will be terminated.	No charter required	No charter required
Committee Membership	Must be balanced in terms of point of view represented and functions to be performed	No requirements	No requirements
Committee Meeting Notices/ Agendas	Meeting notices must be published in Federal Register 15 days prior to meeting. Notice includes time, date, location, purpose, summary of agenda, name and telephone number of the responsible federal official, and a statement whether all or part of the meeting is open to the public or closed.	Meetings noticed to public 10 days before meeting. Notice includes time, date, location, and agenda. Generally item not appearing on agenda may not be discussed or voted on. However, when a member of public raises an issue, the committee may accept testimony and discuss, as long as no action is taken until a subsequent meeting. Notices are to be mailed and provided electronically.	Meetings noticed to public at least 1 week before meeting. Agendas posted at least 72 hours before meeting. Generally, item not appearing on agenda may not be discussed or voted on. However, there can be brief responses or limited comments on such items, as long as no action is taken.
Meeting Minutes and other written materials	Detailed minutes will be kept and must contain: Date and location of meeting, record of attendees, complete and accurate description of matters discussed and conclusions reached, any advice or recommendations to federal agencies. Material provided to committee will be available for public inspection and copying.	Minutes or meeting summaries provided to members will be available for public inspection and copying. Public may be charged for copying.	Minutes or meeting summaries provided to members will be for public inspections and copying. Public may be charged for copying.
Members of General Public	At discretion of agency	Time must be set aside for public comment. Public must be allowed to directly address committee before or during discussion on specific items. Committee may adopt reasonable requirements limiting total amount of time allocated for public comment and for each individual speaker. Members of the public may attend meeting without registering. Any sign in sheet must clearly state that completion of the document is voluntary. A member of the public may be excluded if he or she is clearly disruptive. Members of media not involved in disturbance are permitted to attend meeting.	Time must be set aside for general public comment. Public must be allowed to speak on a specific item on the agenda or other matter germane to the jurisdiction. Committee/council or board may adopt reasonable requirements limiting total amount of time allocated for public comment and for each individual speaker.
Committee Member Compensation	At discretion of agency	At discretion of agency	Not addressed
Designated Agency Officials	Designated federal officials must approve and attend all committee meetings.	Not applicable	Not applicable
Termination of Committee	Committee to be terminated as soon as stated objectives are completed, work is obsolete, or cost of operation is excessive to relation to benefits received.	Not addressed	Not addressed

Source: California Center for Public Dispute Resolution, 2002

Glossary

acre-foot

The volume of water covering one acre of land one foot deep, or 325,851 gallons. On average, an acre-foot can supply one to two households with water for one year.

adjudication

The judicial proceeding in which a priority is assigned to an appropriation (of ground- or surface water) and a decree is issued thus defining the right.

applied water demand

Quantity of water delivered to the intake of a purveyor's water system, or to an end user, directly or by incidental drainage flows.

appropriative rights

The appropriative system of determining who has rights to water. Gives water rights to those who have either used the water first (pre-1914 rights) or to prioritized users based on the appropriation date specified in a state-issued permit or license after 1913.

aquifer

An identified volume of water-bearing materials under the ground surface that can produce groundwater.

artificial storage and recovery

Human addition of water to the groundwater basin through actions such as induced infiltration and spreading basins, or well injection. This water can be recovered (pumped) for use at a later date.

average annual sustainable yield

One of several names for the amount of groundwater that can be withdrawn from an aquifer on a yearly basis over the long term without significant effects (such as land subsidence or seawater intrusion).

beneficial use

Use of an amount of water that is reasonable and appropriate under efficient practices to accomplish, without waste, the purpose for which the diversion is made.

best management practice (BMP)

A policy, program, practice, rule, regulation, or ordinance (or the use of devices, equipment, or facilities) that is a generally accepted practice among water suppliers. The use of a water efficiency BMP results in the conservation of water.

brackish water

A mixture of saltwater and fresh water.

CALFED/Bay-Delta Program

A cooperative State and federal effort established to resolve a series of water and ecosystem management problems in the San Francisco Bay/Sacramento River/San Joaquin River Delta.

California Water Code

The portion of California State statutes addressing water resource law.

charter

A set of operating rules and procedures that, in the context of this book, provides a consistent set of procedures and expectations for collaborative policy groups.

collaborative policy process

A process where a group of stakeholders (interests) work together to resolve particular policy issues–in this book, water-related questions.

conjunctive use

Operation of a groundwater basin in combination with a surface water source and conveyance capability. Typically, water is stored in the basin when surface water is available (wet season or year) and pumped out of the ground during dry seasons or years.

conservation element

One of seven elements of a general plan required under State planning law, addressing natural resources, including water.

daylighting

(of a stream or creek)

Generally implies restoring a watercourse that has been previously confined to a culvert or pipe, and restoring some of the natural bank topography and vegetation to pre-developed conditions.

Delta

The Sacramento River-San Joaquin River Delta.

demand management

Managing demands to result in a savings of overall demands. Demand management can, for example, take the form of pricing water service, reducing unaccounted-for or "lost" water, and water conservation measures.

demineralization

A process designed to treat contaminated water or water with high levels of natural minerals that make it unsuitable for a particular beneficial use. Often applied to groundwater.

desalination

A process designed to treat brackish or sea water to make it useful for potable or non-potable use.

drought

A dry year followed by one or more dry years.

drought contingency plan

Action items to reduce water demands identified for various levels of target droughts.

Drought Water Bank

A water purchasing and allocation program run by the Department of Water Resources (DWR) that allows for the purchase of water from willing sellers and the marketing to buyers under specific critical needs allocation guidelines.

effluent trading

Market-driven transactions in water pollution "credits."

Endangered Species Act

Federal Endangered Species Act (ESA) and State (CESA) statutes designed to protect threatened and endangered plant and animal species and their habitats and enable the species to recover their populations on a sustained basis.

entitlements
(to water)

Used to indicate a quantity of water contractually provided by a water rights holder to a water purchaser under specified terms of a water contract.

environmental water account

Method of accounting for the water and financial assets that can be managed to provide protection for fishery resources beyond legally prescribed flow standards.

environmental water use

Water used for the purposes of sustaining or enhancing environmental resources such as fish habitat.

evapotranspiration

Quantity of water transpired or given off, retained in plant tissues, and evaporated from plant tissues and surrounding soil surfaces.

fallowing

A method of generating urban water by paying farmers to not grow crops. The water not used for irrigation is available for urban or environmental use or stored for future use.

"first flush"

Surface runoff resulting from the first significant rainfall of a season. The first flush usually contains the highest levels of nonpoint sources of pollution.

general plan

Required for all cities and countries, a comprehensive planning document that governs the future growth, development, and conservation of California communities.

gray water

Untreated wastewater that has not been contaminated by toilet discharge, has not been affected by infectious, contaminated, or unhealthy bodily wastes, and does not present a threat of contamination by unhealthful processing, manufacturing, or operating wastes.

ground rules

As related to policy collaboratives, a set of agreed upon procedures for how a group should operate. Ground rules are often used in conjunction with a charter.

groundwater

Waters in groundwater basins (aquifers), underground streams, and the underground flow of a surface stream.

groundwater banking

The practice of storing surface water, through recharge or injection, in groundwater basins in times of surplus for withdrawal in times of shortage. Banking can also involve the use of available surface waters in-lieu of groundwater.

groundwater model

A computerized hydrogeologic model simulating the characteristics of surface water and groundwater conditions and interactions.

groundwater recharge
(or replenishment)

A method of involving pumping or percolating (natural or artificial) precipitation, stormwater runoff or imported water into an aquifer to replenish its supplies.

growth-inducing impact

Defined in the California Environmental Quality Act (CEQA), as any action, policy or program that allows for an increase in population, housing, or job growth whether directly or indirectly.

hydraulic model

A computerized distribution system model simulating the flow and storage of water through constructed features such as pipelines and related facilities.

hydrologic year

See water year.

hydrozone

An area within a landscape that requires a similar amount and timing of water.

indirect potable reuse (IPR)

The use of recycled water for potable uses, such as drinking water. It is "indirect" because the recycled water is blended with groundwater or surface waters and stored, under minimum detention times, in aquifers or surface water reservoirs, before use.

infiltration gallery

A subsurface drain that intercepts infiltrating surface waters (or groundwater flows) in permeable materials and then discharges the captured water (via a sump whose bottom is below the invert of the gallery screen and casing) in a manner that allows the flow to be retrieved.

infiltration or recharge basin

A facility that temporarily impounds runoff or imported surface water supplies and discharges the water through infiltration of the soils below. Purpose is typically to recharge the groundwater basin.

Integrated Resource Plan

A technical policy document combining all aspects of a water supply system to guide future decision-making of a water supplier.

interest-based collaboration

A type of policy process involving multiple stakeholders and interests that seeks to identify key interests and reach agreements among the parties.

LAFCO

Local Agency Formation Commission; a regional government body enabled by State legislation to determine boundaries for cities, counties, and services districts. Every county in California is required to have a LAFCO, typically made up of representatives from the county, municipalities, and at-large members.

maximum day demand

The greatest amount of water delivered over a 24-hour period. For example, the maximum day for a residential system is typically on the first truly hot day in July.

mitigation measure

An action, policy, or program designed to alleviate, reduce, compensate for or lessen an identified effect on the "environment" as defined under the California Environmental Quality Act (CEQA) of the National Environmental Policy Act (NEPA).

net water demand

On a macro level, the amount of water needed in a water service area to meet water requirements. On a micro level, it is the amount of water needed for specific land uses excluding major streets and highways; unit demands or water use factors are usually developed for net or gross water demands.

non-point source pollution

Discharge other than from point sources; erosion of soils and street runoff containing hydrocarbons are examples of non-point sources of pollution.

non-potable supply

Water that is not intended for direct human consumption; can include raw water or recycled water that is not treated for indirect potable reuse purposes.

off-stream storage

Storage of water in a reservoir that is not located on a major river or stream. Involves the conveyance of water into the reservoir for storage.

overdraft

The condition of a groundwater basin where the amount of water withdrawn exceeds the amount of water replenishing the basin over a period of time, leading to one or several basin impacts.

peak hour demand

The greatest amount of water delivered for a one-hour period. For example, the peak hour for a residential system is typically between five and six pm on a summer day.

perennial yield

The amount of groundwater that can be extracted each year for an indefinite period of time without causing significant effects to the basin. It typically cannot exceed the total recharge to that groundwater aquifer or basin on an average, long-term basis.

Porter-Cologne Water Quality Control Act

The umbrella statute in the State of California regulating water quality. Working in concert with the federal Clean Water Act, this law enables the State Water Resources Control Board and Regional Water Quality Control Boards.

potable supply

Drinkable water treated, filtered, or otherwise untreated but of a quality that meets State Health Department drinking water standards.

project EIR

An Environmental Impact Report analyzing the specific effects of a particular project on the environment as per CEQA.

programmatic EIR

An Environmental Impact Report analyzing the generalized effects of a broad-scale planning or policy effort on the environment as per CEQA.

Public Trust Doctrine

Court determination (based on a series of cases) that certain natural resources warrant protection under the broad notion of the "public trust" including some fish and wildlife species and their habitats.

raw water

Refers to water that is not used directly for drinking water purposes based on water quality considerations. Raw water is typically used in reference to water that is not yet treated for drinking water or is used for agriculture.

recycled water

Municipal and/or industrial wastewater that has been treated to a sufficiently high level that it can be reused.

reliability

The degree by which a water system can successfully manage water shortages. Defined by the magnitude and frequency of supply delivery deficiencies in dry years. Supply reliability is a function of hydrology, system storage, and system demands.

return flows

Unconsumed water which returns to its source or other waterbody after its diversion as surface water or its extraction as groundwater.

riparian rights

The riparian system of determining water rights. Gives rights to the owners of the lands adjacent to the bank of a river or any area where water naturally touches land.

safe yield

The maximum quantity of water that can be maintained indefinitely from a groundwater basin or diverted from a stream without adverse effect.

seawater barrier

A physical facility, method of operation, or groundwater injection technique designed to prevent the intrusion of saltwater into a body of fresh water.

seawater intrusion

When a groundwater aquifer becomes contaminated by seawater (typically a part of a coastal basin). The seawater flows into the aquifer along a gradient created by excessive pumping where the groundwater surface falls below sea level.

Section 303(d)

A section of the federal Clean Water Act requiring that polluted water bodies around the U.S. must be designated as "impaired," and requiring watershed-level clean-up plans and programs.

Section 404

A section of the federal Clean Water Act administered by the U.S. Army Corps of Engineers prohibiting public and private entities from dredging or filling "waters of the U.S." (including wetlands) without first obtaining a permit.

service area boundary

A delineated area of land within which a public or private entity (district, agency, private company) serves customers with basic services such as water or wastewater.

Smart Growth

A relatively recent umbrella term describing a philosophy of land use planning and community building that relies on compact and contiguous growth within and around established urban areas. This style of growth tries to avoid low-density, single-use development that has an impact on open land in favor of mixed-use, transit-oriented, and infill development.

specific plan

Under State planning law, specific plans are documents with maps/diagrams detailing the land uses and infrastructure of a designated portion of a community. Once adopted, a specific plan becomes part of the city or county general plan.

sphere of influence

A formally designated boundary of a city or service district/agency within which it has interests and may eventually annex. Sphere-of-influence boundaries must be approved by the local LAFCO.

stakeholder

A person or group with an interest in the outcome of a policy or decision. Stakeholders typically represent different interests in collaborative policy processes and include those with financial "stakes," as well as those with policy or value interests.

Subdivision Map

A diagram recorded typically with the County Assessor's office showing the exact location and boundary of legal parcels of real property. The Subdivision Map Act defines these maps in California, calling land subdivisions of four or less lots a "parcel" map and those of five or more a "subdivision" map.

subsidence

Sinking or downward settling of the ground surface, typically caused by withdrawal of water resulting in the compaction of soils.

Title 34 transfer legislation

The Central Valley Project Improvement Act (Title 34) requirements specific to water transfers.

unaccounted-for water

Difference between production quantities and consumption quantities usually associated with pipeline leaks, non-metered water usage, reservoir evaporation, and meter errors.

unit demands

See water use factors.

urban growth boundary

See urban limit line.

urban limit line

A boundary adopted by local government (or voted by the electorate) that sets the limit of urban growth for a certain length of time or permanently. Not codified in State law, these boundaries are often called urban growth boundaries.

water balance

An accounting of all water inflow to, water outflow from, and changes in water storage within a hydrologic unit over a specified period of time.

water banking

The physical storage, or banking, of water through negotiated agreements for temporary or long-term storage.

water marketing

The process of purchasing or leasing water rights or a contractual right to a supply in order to gain access to a water supply on a temporary or permanent basis.

water master plan

A document providing a plan for the future development or expansion of a potable urban water system, typically focusing on the need for distribution, storage, and treatment facilities.

water transfers

Marketing arrangements that can include the permanent sale or lease of a water right by the water right holder, or the sale or lease of a contractual right to a quantity of water.

water use efficiency

Ratio of the volume of water consumed by a specific beneficial use as compared to the volume of water delivered.

water use factors

Amount of water that a particular land use consumes, on average, on an areal basis for a specific amount of time. For example, a land use may require x acre-feet of water per acre per year, or y gallons per minute per square foot.

Water Year

The state has defined the Water Year from October 1 of the previous year through September 30. For example, the 1986 to 1992 drought actually began in early 1987 and ran through the middle of the 1992 water year. Various agencies use different 12-month periods.

water wheeling

The transfer of water through unused capacity in a water conveyance facility by an entity other than its owner.

Watermaster

A court-appointed person or persons (or agency) given the authority to regulate the quantity of groundwater to be extracted from a designated basin.

watershed

The area from which water drains to a single point. Also called drainage basin.

Wet Year, Above Normal Year, Below Normal Year, Dry Year, Critically Dry Year

Water year types as determined by DWR.

yield

See perennial yield or safe yield.

Abbreviations and Acronyms

ac	acre	CDFG	California Department of Fish and Game	DWSAP	drinking water source assessment and protection
ACOE	U.S. Army Corps of Engineers	CEQA	California Environmental Quality Act	EBMUD	East Bay Municipal Utility District
ACWD	Alameda County Water District	CESA	California Endangered Species Act	EIR	environmental impact report (state)
AEWSD	Arvin-Edison Water Storage District	cfs	cubic feet per second	EIS	environmental impact statement (federal)
af	acre-foot or acre-feet	CPUC	California Public Utilities Commission	ESA	Endangered Species Act
afy	acre-feet per year	CSO	combined (storm and) sewer overflow	ESWTR	Federal Enhanced Surface Water Treatment Rule
ARC/INFO	a geographic information system software program	CUWA	California Urban Water Agencies	EWA	environmental water account
ASR	aquifer storage and recovery	CUWCC	California Urban Water Conservation Council	EWMP	efficient water management practice
AWWA	American Water Works Association	CVP	Central Valley Project	FACA	Federal Advisory Committee Act
AWWARF	American Water Works Association Research Foundation	CVPIA	Central Valley Project Improvement Act	FESA	Federal Endangered Species Act
Bay-Delta	San Francisco Bay-Sacramento River and San Joaquin River Delta	CWA	Federal Clean Water Act	GIS	geographic information system
BAWSCA	Bay Area Water Supply and Conservation Agency	D-1485	Water Rights Decision #1485 from the State Water Resources Control Board	gpcd	gallons per capita per day
BDAC	Bay-Delta Advisory Committee			gpd	gallons per day
		DBCP	dibromochloropropane	gpm	gallons per minute
BMP	best management practice	DBP	disinfection by-product	H$_2$ONet	a commonly used water distribution system computerized model
BVWSD	Buena Vista Water Storage District	DFG	California Department of Fish and Game		
Cal/EPA	California Environmental Protection Agency	DHS	California Department of Health Services	ICR	federal information collection rule
CALFED	cooperative multi-agency (federal and state) program to manage the Delta	DOF	Department of Finance	IID	Imperial Irrigation District
		DPR	California Department of Pesticide Regulation	IPM	integrated pest management
CBDA	California Bay Delta Authority	DWR	California Department of Water Resources	IPR	indirect potable reuse
CCWD	Contra Costa Water District			IRP	integrated resource(s) planning

IWRP	integrated water resource(s) planning	OCWD	Orange County Water District	SWTR	Surface Water Treatment Regulations (federal)
KCWA	Kern County Water Agency	O&M	operations and maintenance	taf	thousand acre-feet
LADWP	Los Angeles Department of Water and Power	POTW	publicly owned treatment works	T&O	taste and odor
LAFCO	Local Agency Formation Commission			TDR	transfer of development rights
LPP	local projects program	ppb	parts per billion	TDS	total dissolved solids
LUD	land use unit (water) demand	ppm	parts per million	THM	trihalomethane
maf	million acre-feet	PVID	Palo Verde Irrigation District	THMFP	trihalomethane formation potential
MCL	maximum contaminant level–enforceable standard	RMP	resource management plan	TMDL	total maximum daily load
MCLG	maximum contaminant level goal–health goal, non-enforceable	RWQCB	California Regional Water Quality Control Board	TOC	total organic carbon
MFR	multi-family residential land use	SCVWD	Santa Clara Valley Water District	TRPA	Tahoe Regional Planning Agency
mgal	million gallons	SDCWA	San Diego County Water Authority	UFW	unaccounted-for water
mgd	millions per day	SDWA	Safe Drinking Water Act (federal)	UGB	urban growth boundary
mg/L	milligrams per liter			ULFT	ultra-low flush toilet
MND	Mitigated Negative Declaration	SFPUC	San Francisco Public Utilities Commission	USB	urban services boundary
M&I	municipal and industrial	SFR	single-family residential land use	USBR	United States Bureau of Reclamation
MOU	memorandum of understanding	SGA	Sacramento Groundwater Authority	USEPA	United States Environmental Protection Agency
MTBE	methyl tertiary butyl ether	SOC	synthetic organic (chemical or) compound	USFWS	United States Fish and Wildlife Service
MWD	Metropolitan Water District of Southern California	SOI	sphere of influence	USLE	universal soil loss equation
N	nitrogen	sq mi	square mile	UWMP	urban water management plan
ND	Negative Declaration	SSO	sanitary sewer overflow	WSS	watershed sanitary survey
NEPA	National Environmental Policy Act	SWA	Sweetwater Authority	WTP	water treatment plant
NMFS	United State National Marine Fisheries Service	SWP	State Water Project	WWTP	wastewater treatment plant
NPDES	National Pollutant Discharge Elimination System	SWPP	source water protection program	WSRA	Wild and Scenic River Act (federal)
NPS	nonpoint source	SWRCB	California State Water Resources Control Board	Zone 7	Alameda County Flood Control and Water Conservation District–Zone 7
NRCS	Natural Resources Conservation Service (formerly Soil Conservation Service)	SWSD	Semitropic Water Storage District		

References

Angers, J. July 2001. "AWWA Small Systems Helpline Specialist," *Opflow*, American Water Works Association.

American Water Works Association. 1999. *Water Audits and Leak Detection* (Manual 36). American Water Works Association.

American Water Works Association. 2001. *Emergency Planning for Water Utility Management*. Manual M19. American Water Works Association.

American Water Works Association Research Foundation. 1999. *Residential End Uses of Water*. American Water Works Association Research Foundation.

American Water Works Association Research Foundation. 2000. *Commercial and Institutional End Uses of Water*. American Water Works Association Research Foundation.

American Water Works Association Research Foundation. 2000. *Long Term Effects of Conservation Rates*. American Water Works Association Research Foundation and American Water Works Association.

Bamezai, A. *et al.* Western Policy Research. March 2001. *Water Efficient Landscape Ordinance (AB 325): A Statewide Implementation Review*. A Report Submitted to the California Urban Water Agencies.

Bass, R.E., A. Herson, and K. Bogdan. 1999. *CEQA Deskbook: A Step-by-Step Guide on How to Comply with the California Environmental Quality Act*. Solano Press Books, Point Arena, California.

Bass, R.E., A. Herson, and K. Bogdan. 2001. *The NEPA Book: A Step-by-Step guide on How to Comply with the National Environmental Policy Act*. Solano Press Books, Point Arena, California.

Bay Area Stormwater Management Agencies Association. January 1997. *Start at the Source*.

Billings, R.B. and C.V. Jones. 1996. *Forecasting Urban Water Demand*. American Water Works Association.

Blomquist, W. 1992. *Dividing the Waters: Governing Groundwater in Southern California*. Center for Self-Governance.

California Department of Health Services. June 2001. *California Health Laws Related to Recycled Water* ("The Purple Book"). Update.

California Department of Water Resources. 2002. *California's Ground Water: Bulletin 118-02*.

California Department of Water Resources. 1998. *California Water Plan, Bulletin 160-98*.

California Department of Water Resources. 2002. *Guidebook for Implementation of Senate Bill 610 and Senate Bill 221 of 2001*.

California Department of Water Resources. 2002. *Sample Urban Water Management Plan* (www.dpla.water.ca.gov/urban...plan/sample/2000-sample-plan).

California Department of Water Resources. 2002. *Water Supply and Water Quality: Groundwater* (www.dpla.water.ca.gov/cgi-bi).

CALFED Bay-Delta Program. August 28, 2000. *Programmatic Record of Decision, Volume 1–Record of Decision and Attachments 1 through 4*.

CALFED Bay-Delta Program. August 2000. *Program Summary*.

CUWCC. July 1997. *Designing, Evaluating, and Implementing Conservation Rate Structures, A Handbook Sponsored by California Urban Water Conservation Council*. California Urban Water Conservation Council.

Carpenter, S.L. and W.J.D. Kennedy. 1988. *Managing Public Disputes: A Practical Guide to Handling Conflict and Reaching Agreements*. Jossey-Bass Inc. Publishers. San Francisco, California.

Connick, S. and J. Innes. 2001. *Outcomes of Collaborative Water Policy Making: Applying Complexity Thinking to Evaluation*. University of California at Berkeley, Institute for Urban and Regional Planning. Working Paper 2001-08.

Cook, G. D. and R. Carlson. 1989. *Reservoir Management for Water Quality and THM Precursor Control.* American Water Works Association Research Foundation.

Curtin, Jr., D.J and Cecily T. Talbert. 2004 edition. *Curtin's California Land Use and Planning Law.* Solano Press Books, Point Arena, California.

Cylinder, R.D. *et al.* 2004. *Wetlands, Streams, and Other Waters: Regulation, Conservation, and Mitigation Planning.* Solano Press Books. Point Arena, California.

Ewing, R. *et al.* 1996. *Best Development Practices.* Planners Press, American Planning Association. Chicago, Illinois.

Faber, S. 1996. *On Borrowed Land: Public Policies for Floodplains.* Lincoln Institute of Land Policy.

Fulton, W. 1999. *Guide to California Planning.* Second edition. Solano Press Books. Point Arena, California.

Garner, E.L. June 2001. *California Water Law and Policy Reporter,* Vol. 11, No 9. June 2001. Argent Communications Group.

Goddard, T. and G. Fiske. 2001. *"Impacts of Municipal Water Shortages."* Report from the City of Santa Cruz Water Department

Gohring, T. April 2002. "Status Report on Preliminary Outcomes–Urban Water Conservation Certification," CALFED-Bay Delta Program.

Hundley, N. 2001. *The Great Thirst: Californians and Water–A History.* Revised edition. University of California Press.

Iacofano, D. 2001. *Meeting of the Minds: A Guide to Successful Meeting Facilitation.* MIG Communication, Inc.

Kahrl, W. 1982. *Water and Power: The Conflict Over Los Angeles' Water Supply in Owens Valley.* University of California Press.

Kaner, S. *et al.* 1996. *Facilitator's Guide to Participatory Decision-Making.* New Society Publishers. Canada.

Kanouse, R. 2001. "Water Supply Planning and Smart Growth," Association of Environmental Professionals, Water Supply and Urban Growth Workshop. Metropolitan Water District Headquarters, Los Angeles.

Leach, W.D. and N.W. Pelkey. November/December 2001. "Making Watershed Partnerships Work: A Review of the Empirical Literature," *Journal of Water Resources Planning and Management.* Vol. 127, No. 6.

Littleworth, A.L. and E.L. Garner. 1995. *California Water.* Solano Press Books, Point Arena, California.

Macler, B.A. and F.W. Pontius. 1997. "Update on the Ground Water Disinfection Rule," *AWWA Journal* 89:17.

Marsh, W.M. 1998. *Landscape Planning Environmental Applications.* Third edition. John Wiley and Sons. New York.

McClurg, S. July/August 2001. "Conjunctive Use: Banking for a Dry Day," *Western Water.* Water Education Foundation.

McClurg, S. 2000. *Water and the Shaping of California.* Water Education Foundation and Heyday Books.

Metropolitan Water District. 1994. *Integrated Resources Plan, Comprehensive Water Resource Management Strategies for Southern California.* MWD.

Metropolitan Water District. March 1996. *Southern California's Integrated Water Resources Plan, Executive Summary.* MWD.

Moore Iacofano Goltsman (MIG), Inc. 2000. *Napa River Watershed Task Force. Phase II: Draft Final Report.* Napa County Board of Supervisors.

Moose, James G. August 2000. "CEQA and Water Supply." Remy, Thomas, Moose and Manley LLP.

Moose, James G. May 2001. "CEQA, Land Use and Water Supply Planning and Groundwater Impact Assessment." Remy, Thomas, Moose and Manley LLP.

Newcom, J. September 2000. "A Briefing on California Water Issues," *California Issues, Water Education Foundation* (www.water-ed.org/california.asp).

Newcom, J. March/April 2001. "Is the California Water Market Open for Business?" *Western Water.* Water Education Foundation.

Placer County Water Agency. March 2001. *Surface Water Supply Update for Western Placer County.* Discussion Paper.

Pekelney, D.M. *et al.* September 1996. *Guidelines to Conduct Cost-Effectiveness Analysis of Best Management Practices for Urban Water Conservation.* Prepared for the California Urban Water Conservation Council.

Pollard, T. October 2001. "Greening the American Dream," *Planning,* Vol. 67, No. 10. American Planning Association.

Prasifka, D. 1988. *Water-Supply Planning, Issues, Concepts and Risks.* Van Nostrand Reinhold Company.

Reisner, M. 1993. *Cadillac Desert.* Revised edition. Penguin Books, New York.

Remy, M.H. *et al.* 1999. *Guide to the California Environmental Quality Act.* Solano Press Books. Point Arena, California.

San Francisco Public Utilities Commission and Bay Area Water Users Association. April 2000. *Water Supply Master Plan.* SFPUC.

Save San Francisco Bay Association. 2000. *Protecting Local Wetlands: A Toolbox for Your Community.* Save San Francisco Bay Association, Oakland, California.

Slater, S. 2002. *California Water Law and Policy: Volume 1 and 2.* Lexis Publishing. San Francisco, California.

State Water Resources Control Board. July 1999. *A Guide to Water Transfers.* Draft. SWRCB.

State Water Resources Control Board. 1993. *California Storm Water Best Management Practices Handbook(s)* (for Municipal, Industrial, and Construction Activities) prepared for the SWRCB Stormwater Quality Task Force.

Strauss, A. February 2001. Director of EPA Region IX Water Division, *Western Water.* Water Education Foundation.

Susskind, L. *et al.* editors. 1999. *The Consensus-Building Handbook.* Sage Publications.

University of California, Davis. 1996. *Report on Water Resources Management at U.C. Davis*

Vista Consulting Group. 1997. *Guidelines for Implementing an Effective Integrated Resource Planning Process.* American Water Works Association Research Foundation and American Water Works Association.

Water Education Foundation. 2000. *Layperson's Guide to California Water.*

Water Education Foundation. 2000. *Layperson's Guide to Water Marketing.*

Water Forum. January 2000. *Water Forum Agreement.*

Index

Integrated Resources Plan (IRP) *(continued)*
    environmental compliance
        considerations, 130–132
    in general, 129–130
    permit requirements, 142–143
    project planning to
        implementation criteria for
            priority recommendations, 141
        environmental compliance/
            permits, 142–143
        financing plan, 141–142
        in general, 140
        phasing and scheduling plan, 141
    Santa Clara Valley Water
        District IRP, 138
    Soquel Creek Water District IRP, 76
    stakeholder involvement, 143–144
    terms
        actions, 132
        goals, 132
        mission statement, 132
        objectives, 132
        problem statement, 132
    why it makes sense, 132
Integrated Storage Investigation (ISI), 52
    See also CALFED/Bay Delta program
Integrated Water Resources Plan
    (IWRP), in general, 129–130
    see also Integrated Resources Plan

interest
    compared to position, 181
    defined, 176
Inyo County, 12
    local groundwater ordinance, 49
IPR. *See* indirect potable reuse
irrigation, 80
ISI. *See* Integrated Storage Investigation
IWRP. *See* Integrated Water
    Resources Plan

K

KCWA. *See* Kern County Water Agency
Kern County
    See also Kern County Water Agency
    local groundwater ordinance, 49
    water banking, 124
Kern County Water Agency (KCWA), 10
    water sale, 123
Kern Delta Water District, 124
    water banking, 124
Kesterson Wildlife Refuge, 154–155
    See also pollution
King's River groundwater
    management plan, 50

L

LAFCO. *See* Local Agency
    Formation Commission
Lake Tahoe, flow management
    and treatment, 162–163
land fallowing, for water
    banking, 123, 124–125
land subsidence, 107

land use. *See also* land use planning
    effect on water quality, 153–157
land use planning
    See also land use unit
        demands; water planning
    compared to water planning, 54f
    development pipeline, 71
    existing land uses, 78–81
    in general, 53
    general plan
        concurrency policies, 57
        conservation element
            requirements, 56–57
        in general, 54
        integrating water analysis, 58–59
        not required to have
            water element, 55–56
        optional water element, 57
        procedural requirements
            for water resources, 55
        substantive requirements
            for water resources, 55–57
    historical background
        for linking water supply
        and land use planning, 66
    integrating water
        planning with, 69–71, 76
    LAFCOs, 62–63, 78
    land use inventory spreadsheet, 88
    local water ordinances, in general, 60
    specific plan
        in general, 57–58
        integrating water analysis, 58–59
    Subdivision Map Act, 59–60
    water demand analysis, 76–77, 92–95
land use unit demands (LUDs)
    application, 87–88
    calculating, 88t, 93f
    in general, 83–85
landscape water conservation
    See also conservation; water use
    in general, 42
    hydrozone grouping, 43n12
    landscape retrofit ordinance, 43–44
    model water-efficient
        landscape ordinance, 42–43
landscaping use, 115. *See also* water use
least Bell's vireo, habitat protection, 149–150
legislation, enabling for water entities, 15–16
livestock grazing, 156, 162
    See also water quality
Local Agency Formation
    Commission (LAFCO)
    boundaries, 78
    discussed, 62–63
    sphere of influence, 78
Long Valley Groundwater
    Management District, 47t, 48f
Los Angeles
    development, 8, 9
    groundwater adjudication, 106
    Mono Lake protections, 12
    Owens Valley water transfers, 8
    plumbing retrofit regulation, 40
    Upper Los Angeles River Area, 47t, 48f

Los Angeles Department of Water and
    Power (LADWP), discussed, 108
Los Angeles Regional Water
    Quality Control Board,
    urban runoff, 171–172
Los Vaqueros Reservoir, 128
    discussed, 82
low impact development (LID), 165
LUDs. *See* land use unit demands
Lux v. Haggin, 7n3

M

Main San Gabriel Basin, 47t, 48f
Making Meetings Work
    (Doyle/Strauss), 175
Managing Public Disputes
    (Carpenter/Kennedy), 175
Map Act. *See* Subdivision Map Act
McGuire Peaks water tank, 162
Meeting of the Minds (Iacofano), 175
Mendocino Community
    Services District, 47t, 48f
    groundwater authority, 48
Merced River groundwater
    management plan, 50
mercury, 157
    See also pollution
methyl tertiary butyl ether (MBTE)
    See also pollution; water quality
    discussed, 33, 156–157
Metropolitan Water District (MWD)
    conjunctive use, 121, 128
    conservation program, 124
    discussed, 9, 10, 39, 108
    IRP, 138–139
    recycled water, 110
    water transfers, 124–125
Migratory Bird Treaty Act, 26t
Milwaukee, water-borne illness, 146–147
mining, 155
    hydraulic mining, 7
mission statement, 132
Mojave River Basin, 47t, 48f
Mojave Water Agency, 123
Mokelumne Aqueduct, 10, 140
Mokelumne River, 10, 15, 108
monitoring, 185
    See also collaborative water planning
Mono County Tri-Valley Ground
    Water Management District, 47t, 48f
Mono Lake, 12
Mono River, 108
Monterey Agreement, 104
Monterey Bay, seawater intrusion, 118
Monterey County Water
    Resources Agency, 118–119
Monterey Peninsula Water
    Management District, 47t, 48f
    groundwater authority, 48
    plumbing retrofit regulation, 40–41
Morro Bay, water use
    off-set ordinance, 61–62
MTBE. *See* methyl tertiary butyl ester
Muir, John, 8

Municipal Water District of Orange
County, landscape retrofit ordinance, 4
MWD. *See* Metropolitan Water District

N

Napa County, erosion, 172
Napa River, as impaired water body, 172
Napa River Watershed
Plan, alternatives, 181, 185
National Environmental Policy
Act (NEPA), 26t, 131, 142, 174
See also California
Environmental Quality Act
National Pollution Discharge
Elimination System (NPDES), 31
See also Clean Water Act
discussed, 27t, 31–32, 147, 173
WDRs, 31–32
National Speleological Society, 199
National Wilderness Act, 27t
Native Americans, 7
Natural Communities
Conservation Planning Act, 26t
ND. *See* negative declaration
negative declaration (ND), 63, 64, 130
See also California
Environmental Quality Act
NEPA. *See* National
Environmental Policy Act
New Melones Lake, 11
New Melones Lake Resource
Management Plan, 148–149
case study, 196–199
New Melones Partners, 199
New Mexico, water budgeting, 62
NOAA Fisheries, 126, 143, 189
North Las Posas Groundwater Project, 138
North Marin Water District
landscape retrofit ordinance, 43–44
plumbing retrofit regulation, 40
NPDES. *See* National Pollution
Discharge Elimination System

O

Oakland, creek protection ordinance, 173
Oceanside, desalination facility, 127
office water use
See also commercial use; water use
water supply assessment, 65
Ojai Groundwater
Management Agency, 47t, 48f
Oliveheim, 128
Orange County, 109
Orange County groundwater
management plan, 50
Orange County Water District, 47t, 48f
groundwater recharge, 109–110
with fees, 46–48
osprey, 199. *See also* wildlife
*Outcomes of Collaborative Water
Policy Making* (Connick/Innes), 186
overdraft. *See* groundwater overdraft
Owens Valley, water transfers, 8, 108
ozone, 147. *See also* water treatment

P

PAC. *See* Public Advisory Committee
Pajaro Valley Groundwater
Management Agency, 47t, 48f, 61
Palo Verde Irrigation District
(PVID), land fallowing, 124–125
Pardee Dam, 10, 15, 140
Permit Handbook (OPR), 142
pesticides/herbicides, 119, 157
See also pollution
Placer County, 187
Placer County Water Agency,
water supply, 89, 150
planning. *See* land use
planning; water planning
plumbing. *See also* plumbing code;
residential development
low-flow fixtures, 39, 40–41
plumbing retrofit regulation, 40–41
water-efficient plumbing, 40–41
plumbing code, upgrades, 97
pollution. *See also specific pollutants*;
total maximum daily load;
water quality; water treatment
arsenic, 155
bromide, 147
chemicals/MTBE, 156–157
contaminant plume, 105, 112, 119
control
effluent trading, 174–175
flow management
and treatment, 162–163
in general, 159
in general/specific plan, 171–173
source reduction, 162
stormwater quality
protection, 165–169
urban design solutions, 163–165
DBP contamination, 119, 154
detention basins, 150
total organic carbon, 150
heavy metals, 157
overdraft affecting, 105, 119
pesticides/herbicides, 119, 157
prioritizing contaminants
and sources, 158
radon, 155
recycled water concerns, 110–111
relation between contaminant
source and water quality, 157t
total organic carbon, 150, 154
turbidity, 154
two-stroke engines, 33
underground fuel tanks, 33
urban pond, 164–165
water supply, 119, 152
Porter-Cologne Water
Quality Control Act, 147
See also water quality
discussed, 27t, 30–31
Powell, John Wesley, 129
precipitation. *See* rainfall and runoff
prioritization criteria, 141
problem statement, 132

Public Advisory Committee (PAC), 76
public health considerations,
water quality, 145
public hearing
See also public involvement
CEQA process, 64, 82
for UWMP, 35
public involvement, 119, 131, 148, 132, 143
discussed, 21
public policy
See collaborative public policy
public trust doctrine, 25t
Puente Basin, 47t, 48f
PVID. *See* Palo Verde
Irrigation District

R

Racanelli decision, 28t
radon, 155
See also radon
rainfall and runoff, 4, 103, 104
See also pollution; water quality;
watershed management
drainage, 45, 170
Village Homes, 170
first flush, 163
flow management
and treatment, 162–163
impervious surface effects, 157
intensity, 155
master planning, 101
San Joaquin Rivers
unimpaired runoff data, 112f
stormwater quality protection,
165–169
curb and swale system, 167, 174p
general/specific plans, 171–173
institutional controls, 169–174
neighborhood-scale
ideas, 167–168f
stream setbacks, 173–174
urban runoff, 171–173
Urban Runoff Diversion System, 163
water quality effects, 145, 154
Rate structures. *See* water rates
Raymond Basin, 47t, 48f
recharge. *See* groundwater recharge
recycled water
See also conservation;
industrial use
in general, 109
gray water, 128
indirect potable reuse, 109–110
public perceptions of, 45
supply reliability, 115
surface water and, 113, 120
third-party impacts, 110–111
Water Recycling Act, 45
Regional Water Quality
Control Board (RWQCB), 30
See also State Water
Resources Control Board
permit requirements, 143, 171–172
"water quality certifications," 32–33

reservoir, 106
 *See also specific reservoir/
 storage facility*; storage
 multipurpose reservoir, 149
 off-stream/expansion, 127–128
 operations and habitat, 149–150
residential development
 See also plumbing; residential
 use; streets and highways
 water supply assessment, 58, 59–60, 65
Residential End Uses of Water (AWWA), 98
residential water use
 See also water use
 conservation, 95–96
 typical single-family
 residential use, 97f
retail water use
 See also water use
 water supply assessment, 65
retention basins, discussed, 163–165
Richard A. Reynolds Groundwater
 Demineralization Facility, 163
riparian corridor
 See also environmental
 uses; riparian rights
 daylighting, 174
 education efforts, 163
 setbacks, 171, 173–174
riparian rights, 7
 See also water rights
Riverside County, 109, 128
 land fallowing, 124–125
runoff. *See* rainfall and runoff
RWQCB. *See* Regional Water
 Quality Control Board

S

Sacramento, 190
Sacramento County, 140, 190
 concurrency policies, 57
Sacramento Groundwater Authority (SGA)
 See also Sacramento Water Forum
 conjunctive use program, 122
 discussed, 49, 50, 190
Sacramento River, 49, 145
 Freeport intake, 140
Sacramento River-San Joaquin Delta (Delta).
 See also CALFED;
 San Francisco Bay/Sacramento
 River-San Joaquin Delta
 discussed, 4, 192
 SWRCB proceedings, 28t
 water contamination, 147
Sacramento Water Forum, 186
 discussed, 12, 45–46, 69–70f
 Agreement, 12, 16, 69
 case study, 187–192
Salinas Valley, seawater intrusion, 118f
San Bernardino Basin, 47t, 48f
San Bernardino County, 109
 groundwater adjudication, 106
San Diego
 plumbing retrofit regulation, 40
 potable reuse project, 110

San Diego County
 local groundwater ordinance, 49
 Sweetwater Authority, 149–150, 163
San Diego County Water
 Authority (SDCWA), 128
 discussed, 108, 173
San Fernando Valley, 8
San Francisco Bay, 145
San Francisco Bay/Sacramento
 River-San Joaquin Delta, 186
 See also CALFED/Bay
 Delta program; Sacramento
 River-San Joaquin Delta
 Water Quality Control Plan, 30–31
San Francisco Public Utilities
 Commission (SFPUC), 108, 159
 Hetch Hetchy system, 2, 8, 10
 IRP, 133
 master plan mission statement, 133
 plumbing retrofit regulation, 40
 relationship with BAWSCA, 133
 watershed management
 process, 160–161, 162
San Joaquin County, local
 groundwater ordinance, 49
San Joaquin River, 197
San Joaquin River groundwater
 management plan, 50
San Joaquin Rivers
 unimpaired runoff data, 112f
San Joaquin Valley, 103, 124
 ag land retirement, 45
 Kesterson Wildlife Refuge, 154–155
 Westlands Water District, 125
San Jose, wastewater recycling, 109
San Luis Obispo, 174
San Vicente Reservoir, 110
Santa Ana Regional Interceptor, 127
Santa Ana River, 109–110, 127
Santa Barbara County
 concurrency policies, 57
 plumbing retrofit regulation, 41
Santa Clara Valley, Watershed
 Management Initiative, 32
Santa Clara Valley Water
 District (SCVWD), 47t, 48f, 108
 discussed, 10
 groundwater recharge with fees, 48
 IRP, 133, 138
Santa Cruz, water shortage assessment
 vs. developing new supply, 139
Santa Cruz County, 76
 concurrency policies, 57
 local water ordinances, 60–61
 riparian education, 163
Santa Fe (NM), water budgeting, 62
Santa Margarita River Watershed, 47t, 48f
Santa Monica, 33
 plumbing retrofit regulation, 40
Santa Paula Basin, 47t, 48f
Santa Ynez River groundwater
 management plan, 50
SB 221, discussed, 29, 35n8, 59–60, 114
SB 610, discussed, 29, 35n8, 65, 113–114
SB 901, discussed, 66

SB 1938, discussed, 50, 51
Scott River Stream System, 47t, 48f
SCVWD. *See* Santa Clara
 Valley Water District
SDCWA. *See* San Diego
 County Water Authority
seawater intrusion, 2–3, 61
 See also groundwater overdraft
 barriers to, 110, 118
 discussed, 105–106, 118–119
 in Salinas Valley, 118f
security issues, 199–200
seismic vulnerability,
 water supply, 117–118
selenium, 155
 See also pollution
Semitropic Water Storage District
 discussed, 138
 water banking, 124, 140
septic system, 156
SGA. *See* Sacramento
 Groundwater Authority
Shasta County, local
 groundwater ordinance, 49
Shasta Dam, 128
Sierra Valley Groundwater
 Management District, 47t, 48f
Six Basins in Santa Ana, 47t, 48f
smart growth, 43, 82
 See also growth
SOI. *See* sphere of influence
Sonoma County, water element, 57
Soquel Creek Water District Integrated
 Resource Plan, discussed, 76
*Southern California Integrated Water
 Resources Plan* (MWD), 138
specific plan
 See also general plan; land use planning
 in general, 57–58
 integrating water
 analysis, 58–59, 171–173
sphere of influence (SOI), 78, 94
 See also Local Agency
 Formation Commission
*Stanislaus Natural Heritage Project
 v. County of Stanislaus*, 67–68
Stanislaus River, 11, 196–199
State Water Plan. *See* California Water Plan
State Water Project (SWP),
 1, 2t, 108, 110, 124, 126, 183
 discussed, 9–10
 relation to CALFED, 51–52, 192
State Water Resources
 Control Board (SWRCB)
 establishment, 30
 Regional Water Quality
 Control Boards, 30, 31
 responsibilities, 31–32, 143, 171, 172
 SF Bay/Delta protection, 28t, 191
 Waste Discharge
 Requirements, 31–32
 water rights, 108
storage. *See also* reservoir;
 water banking/marketing
 artificial storage and recovery, 121

water demand analysis
 land use-based water demands *(continued)*
  land use unit demands, 83–85
  land use unit demands
   application, 87–88
  methodology for distributing
   existing demands, 79f
  phasing demands and
   planning horizons, 92–95
  unaccounted-for water, 85–86
 methods
  coordination with land
   use planning efforts, 76–77
  land use method, 76
  population-based projections, 75
  socioeconomic modeling, 75–76
 unit demands, 83–85, 90–94
 urban demand, typical
  seasonal hydrograph, 96f
"water futures," 13
water management, 12
 See also best management
  practices; water supply evaluation;
  water supply management
 best management practices, 39
 demand management, 94–95
 discussed, 13, 21
 "Efficient Water
  Management Practices," 44
 low impact development, 165
 statues and institutions
  allocating, managing,
  and planning water, 25t–29t
 watershed management, 146
water master plan, 65
 compared to IRP, 130
watermaster, 106
water meter, unused/unread, 84–85
water planning
 See also collaborative water planning;
  land use planning; water demand
  analysis; watershed planning
 compared to land use planning, 54f
 in general, 23–24
 integrating with land use planning, 69–71
 local water ordinances
  comprehensive
   development fee, 60–61
  in general, 60
  water budgeting, 62, 69
  water use off-set, 61–62
 planning horizon, 94
 uncertainty and, 100–101
 with UWMP, 38–39
 water master plan, 65
 watershed planning, 32, 145–146
 water supply and land
  use legislation, 65–67
water purveyor
 See also water agency; water company
 dedication to mandates, 14–15
 "duty to serve," 66
 historical background for
  linking water supply and
  land use planning, 66

water purveyor *(continued)*
 land use planner and, 59
 surface water, primary
  water purveyors, 108
 time horizon, scale, complexity, 17–18
 UWMP requirements, 37
water quality. *See also* desalination/
  demineralization; erosion;
  pollution; water quality
  protection; watershed
 beach closures, 171–172
 brackish water, 118–119, 125
 coliform violations, 147
 disinfectants, 147
 groundwater overdraft
  affecting, 105–106
 impaired water bodies, 27t, 33, 172
 regulation
  Clean Water Act, 31, 32–34
  historic ordinances, 7
  NPDES, 27t, 31–32, 147, 173
  Porter-Cologne Water Quality
   Control Act, 27t, 30–31
 relation to water quantity, 21, 117, 119
 vulnerability zones, 160–161
water quality protection
 drinking water source protection,
  34, 146–147, 150–151
 in general, 145–146
 watershed planning, 145–146
  multiple-goal integration, 148–149
 watershed trends, 147–148
water rates
 conservation-encouraging rates, 95
 effect on demand, 84–85
water rationing, 115–116
 See also drought; water shortage
Water Recycling Act of 1991,
  discussed, 29t, 40, 45
Water ReUse Association, 111
water rights
 groundwater
  adjudication, 106
  overlying right/
   appropriative right, 106
  prescriptive right, 106n1
 historic, 7
 leasing/purchasing, 123
 overdraft affecting, 105
 riparian/appropriative rights, 7, 25t
 surface water, 46
  discussed, 107–108
Water Rights Decision 1485, 28t
water shortage, 13, 103–104
 See also drought, dry year
 assessing risk of vs.
  developing new supply, 139
 water rationing, 115–116
water supply
 See also groundwater;
  water supply evaluation
 comparing supply with
  demand, 113, 115–116
 historical background for linking water
  supply and land use planning, 66

water supply *(continued)*
 IRP strategies for supply
  and demand, 137–140
 potable/non-potable supply, 116
 "reliable water supply," 60
 "sufficient water supply," 60
 water shortage assessment
  vs. developing new supply, 139
water supply evaluation
  See also water management;
  water supply management
 catastrophic event
  contamination, 119
  flooding, 118
  in general, 117
  seawater intrusion, 118–119
  seismic vulnerability, 117–118
  terrorism, 119
  wildfire, 119
 determining
  dry-year and
   seasonal availability, 113–116
  in general, 111
  long-term, average-
   year supplies, 111–113
  potable/non-potable supply, 116
 in general, 103
 groundwater, 104–106, 111–112, 115
 recycled water
  in general, 109
  indirect potable reuse, 109–110
  seawater barrier, 110
  third-party impacts, 110–111
 supply reliability, 114
 supply sources in California, 103–104
 surface water
  dry-year/seasonal availability, 113–116
  facilities, 107
  in general, 106–107, 112
  primary water purveyors, 108
  water rights, 107–108
water supply management
  See also water management
 conjunctive use, 105, 119, 120–121
 desalination, 125–127
 in general, 119–120
 gray water, 128
 off/on-stream storage, 127–128
 water purchases,
  transfers, banking, 122–125
Water-Supply Planning (Prasifka), 95
water transfer. *See* water banking/marketing
water treatment. *See also* pollution
 desalination/demineralization, 127
 DHS requirements, 107
 discussed, 146–147
 disinfection byproducts, 147, 150
  bromide, 147
  chlorine, 147
  ozone, 147
 flow management
  and treatment, 162–163
 groundwater, 107
 permit requirements, 142–143
 recycled water, 109–110

Credits

Illustrations courtesy Kerry Daane Loux

164: Multiple Use Retention Basin; 166: Residential Site Designed for Maximum Permeability; 167: top, Residential Infill Site Showing Low-Impact Stormwater Management Features; bottom, Vegetated Concave Island to Absorb Stormwater in a Small Residential Cul-de-Sac; 168: Neighborhood-Scale Ideas for Stormwater Management; 169: Street and Parking Lot Treatment for Stormwater Management

Photograph courtesy Mary Paasch

10: All-American Canal

Photographs courtesy Karen Johnson / Jeff Loux

4: top, Shasta Lake in drought; bottom, Owens Valley in time of flood; 8: San Francisco's Hetch Hetchy reservoir system; 9: top, Shasta Dam on the Sacramento River; bottom, State Water Project Banks pumping plant; 11: Arcata wetland; 13: top, Los Vaqueros Reservoir; bottom, Modesto; 20: Farmer's road sign; 31: Old mine contamination; 41: Traditional and modern golf courses; 42: Drought-tolerant native grasses and garden; 44: top, CIMIS weather station; middle, Vineyard acreage near Livermore; bottom, Central Valley orchard; 50: Reducing seawater intrusion along Monterey Bay; 52: Delta-Mendota Canal and the California Aqueduct in the San Joaquin Valley; 104: Millerton Reservoir diverting water to the Madera and the Friant-Kern canals; 107: Land subsidence in San Joaquin Valley; 113: Folsom Reservoir during the 1987–1992 drought; 120: Surface water used to recharge groundwater basin; 127: Santa Barbara desalination facility; 129: Fresno water tower; 142: State Water Project's CCWA pipeline; 145: Protecting drinking water; 147: Mt. Tamalpais watershed sign; 150: Old flumes create wetlands; 154: Clay and gravelly soils; 156: Road runoff and livestock waste contamination; 164: Multi-use basin in Visalia; 165: Multi-purpose retention and flood management ponds in an urban environment; 168: Pervious pavement; 169: Naturalized drainage-way in a residential area; 170: Village Homes in Davis; 171: Conventional parking lot and parking lot median; 172: Hillside vineyard; 174: Landscaped swale for stormwater; 187: Sacramento area Water Forum; 189: top, American River; bottom, Planning for growth; 191: Folsom Reservoir on the American River; 192: Groundwater management; 197: Meandering channels in the Sacramento River-San Joaquin River Delta; 198: top, Low reservoir levels; bottom, New Melones Reservoir

Other Guides and References

PLANNING . LAND USE . URBAN AFFAIRS . ENVIRONMENTAL ANALYSIS . REAL ESTATE DEVELOPMENT

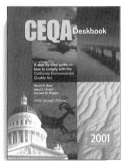

CEQA Deskbook A Step-by-Step Guide on How to Comply with the California Environmental Quality Act

Definitive reference with comprehensive analysis, charts, short articles, graphics, photos, appendices, and index. Recognized by the California AEP with an Award of Excellence. Cited as an Authoritative Source by the California Courts.

Ronald E. Bass, Albert I. Herson, and Kenneth M. Bogdan
1999–2000 (second) edition • Includes 2001 Supplement

Guide to CEQA

Professional, legal guide that offers an in-depth, understandable description of CEQA's requirements for adequate review and preparation of EIRs and other environmental documents. With case law through December 1998 and the complete text of the Statutes and Guidelines. Cited as an Authoritative Source by the California Courts.

Michael H. Remy, Tina A. Thomas, James G. Moose, and Whitman F. Manley • 1999–2000 (tenth) edition

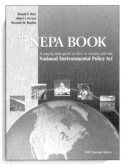

The NEPA Book How to Comply with the National Environmental Policy Act

Practitioner's handbookthat takes you through the critical steps, basic requirements, and most important decision points of the National Environmental Policy Act. With short articles, practice tips, tables, charts, illustrations, and sources of additional information.

Ronald E. Bass, Albert I. Herson, and Kenneth M. Bogdan • 2001 edition

Ballot Box Navigator
A Practical and Tactical Guide to Land Use Initiatives and Referenda in California

This book is the authoritative resource on securing a ballot title, qualifying an initiative or referendum for the ballot, and submitting a measure for an election. With short articles, practice tips, drawings, an index, glossary, and a table of authorities.

Michael Patrick Durkee, Jeffrey A. Walter, David H. Blackwell, and Thomas F. Carey • 2003

California Transportation Law
A Guide to Federal, State, and Regional Requirements

First complete collection of the most important laws and regulations affecting transportation planning in California. Includes ISTEA provisions, Title VI guidelines for mass transit, STIP Guidelines, provisions relating to air quality and equal employment opportunity, civil rights laws, a checklist for mandatory requirements for public outreach, and a subject index and glossary.

Jeremy G. March • 2000 edition

Curtin's California Land Use and Planning Law

Well-known, heavily quoted, definitive summary of California's planning laws that includes expert commentary on the latest statutes and case law. Includes practice tips, figures and tables, suggested reading, a comprehensive table of authorities, and an index.

Daniel J. Curtin, Jr. and Cecily T. Talbert
Revised annually

CALL TOLL-FREE
(800) 931-9373 OR FAX (707) 884-4109

Solano Press Books

Eminent Domain

Explains the processes California public agencies must follow to acquire private property for public purposes through eminent domain. Includes case law, legal references, tips, a table of authorities, sample letters and forms, a glossary, and an index.

Richard G. Rypinski • 2002 (second) edition

Exactions and Impact Fees in California

Designed to help public officials, citizens, attorneys, planners, and developers understand exactions. With tips, case studies, photos, and graphics to illustrate key considerations and legal principles.

William W. Abbott, Peter M. Detwiler, M. Thomas Jacobson, Margaret Sohagi, and Harriet A. Steiner • 2001 (second) edition w/ 2002 Supplement

Guide to California Planning

Describes how planning really works in California, how cities, counties, developers, and citizen groups all interact with each other to shape California communities and the California landscape, for better and for worse. Recipient of the California Chapter APA Award for Planning Education.

William Fulton • 1999 (second) edition

Subdivision Map Act Manual

All-new reference with the latest information and practice tips needed to understand Subdivision Map Act legal provisions, recent court-made law, and the review and approval processes. With the full text of the Map Act, practice tips, a comprehensive table of authorities, and an index.

Daniel J. Curtin, Jr. and Robert E. Merritt • 2003 edition

Redevelopment in California

Definitive guide to both the law and practice of redevelopment in California cities and counties, together with codes, case law, and commentary. Contains short articles, notes, photographs, charts, graphs, and illustrative time schedules.

David F. Beatty et al. • 2004 (third) edition

Telecommunications
The Governmental Role in
Managing the Connected Community

Detailed summary and analysis of federal and state laws governing the location and regulation of physical facilities including cable, telephone, and wireless systems (cellular, paging, and Internet), satellite dishes, and antennas. With practice tips, photos, a glossary, table of authorities, and an index.

Paul Valle-Riestra • 2002

Wetlands, Streams, and Other Waters
Regulation, Conservation, and Mitigation Planning

Practical guide to federal and state wetland identification as well as regulation and permitting processes. Includes detailed information, commentary, and practice tips for those who work with federal and state laws and are engaged in wetland conservation planning. Appendices include relevant federal statutes and regulations, case law summaries, and Section 404 permit application guidelines.

Paul D. Cylinder, Kenneth M. Bogdan, April I. Zohn, and Joel B. Butterworth • 2004 edition